BERLITZ®

DISCOVER
BRITTANY

Edited and Designed by
D & N Publishing,
Lambourn, Berkshire.

Cartography by
Hardlines, Charlbury, Oxfordshire.

Cover photographs: by the author.

Printed by Butler and Tanner Ltd., Frome, Somerset.

Photographic Acknowledgements

All photographs by the author except for those on the following pages: © Berlitz Publishing Co. Ltd: 6, 22, 33, 34, 36, 37, 40, 41 (upper and lower), 49, 50, 51, 52, 58, 74, 77, 138, 155, 177, 191, 247, 302, 304, 306, 307, 313; The Hulton Picture Company: 136.

 The Berlitz tick is used to indicate places or events of particular interest.

Although we have made every effort to ensure the accuracy of all the information in this book, changes occur incessantly. We cannot therefore take responsibility for facts, addresses and circumstances in general that are constantly subject to alteration.

BERLITZ®

DISCOVER
BRITTANY

Michael Marriott

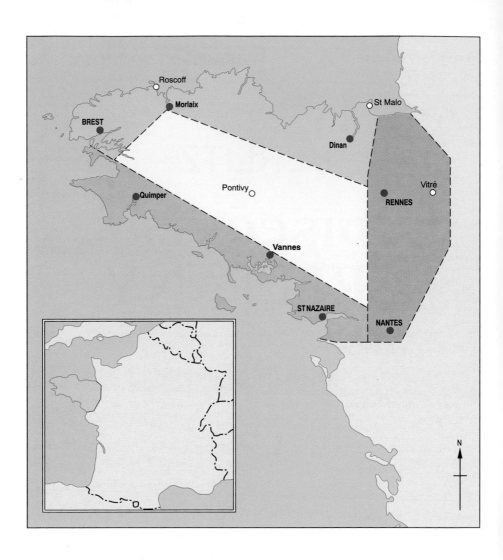

Contents

BRITTANY: FACTS AND FIGURES 7

When To Go 7
Travel Documents 8
Health 9
How To Get There 10
Travel Concession Cards 14
Getting About 14
Driving 17
Accommodation 18
Money 21
Security 21
Gratuities 22
Food 22
Shopping and Services 26
Electrical Appliances 27

BRITTANY: ITS HISTORY AND ITS PEOPLE 29

The French People 29
History 33
Brittany: Land of Legend 38
Religion 40
Politics 42
Economics 44
Geography and Geology 45
Festivals 53
Public Holidays 54
How To Use This Guide 54

ON THE SHORTLIST 56

LEISURE ROUTES AND THEMES 59

IN PRAISE OF BRITTANY 75

DREAM-TIME BRITTANY 81

THE BRETON MARCHES 85

Ille-et-Vilaine 85
Loire-Atlantique 113
A WOMAN OF DESTINY 136

THE ATLANTIC COAST 139

Loire-Atlantique 139
Morbihan 150
Carnac 164
Finistère 174

THE BRITTANY HINTERLAND 199

Finistère 199
Morbihan 212

THE CHANNEL COAST 237

Ille-et-Vilaine 237
A MAN OF LETTERS—
CHATEAUBRIAND 243
Côtes d'Armor 253
A BRETON MAN OF WAR 256
Finistère 290

WHAT TO DO 305

Sport 305
Brittany For Children 311
Wildlife and Nature 313
Château Choice 316
Language Guide 317

USEFUL NUMBERS AND ADDRESSES 324

HOTELS AND RESTAURANTS 327

Index 332

Look Before Leaping to Save Time, Money and Traveller Frustration

Increasingly, English is becoming almost a second language in and around the many resorts of Brittany, and while the best of French cuisine is abundant, so are the fuss-free *crèpes* and *gallettes*, both of which appeal strongly to all tastes. First-time visitors to Brittany can therefore leave all anxieties at home and look forward to a relaxing time in a land of legend and folklore.

When To Go

From June to September, the French Ministry of Tourism assures us France is open! A modest enough claim for a country which has an established winter-sports programme and many areas where leisure may be enjoyed in April, May or even in late October.

The traditional holiday period— June to September—is, however, an ideal time to visit Brittany. The days are long, the nights are short, the sun shines brightest and all the facilities and amenities are open and operating. The French Ministry of Tourism publishes a nationwide list of resorts, both coastal and inland, recommended as long-stay holiday bases—there are some 300 in all, which are called *stations de longue durée*. This list is freely available (it also comes with a map), from most main French tourist offices and includes details of an exceptional variety of diverse holiday activities and facilities where the tariffs are quoted as "advantageous". Among Brittany centres it recommends Dinard, Quiberon and Douarnenez in particular as top coastal bases; just 3 of 21 covering the whole *région*.

Evidence of the more noble France of the past is amply displayed throughout Brittany, as in most other French regions. An example of medieval Vannes.

During the peak month of August though, the whole of the Republic seems *en vacances*, together with vast hordes of foreign visitors. The country can be almost intolerably crowded in places; although this is less true of inland Brittany, for example, than the Riviera or the Atlantic coast between Brest and Bayonne. Given freedom of choice there are better months to visit the north-west corner of France, even though the holiday amenities may not be quite so comprehensive. Early October, along the southern Atlantic coast for instance, is frequently a time of warm golden days that are perfect for country or coastal walks, horse-riding or cycling—exploring a quieter Brittany in uncrowded peace and seclusion. Earlier in the year, in the spring months of April and May, the region is at its most radiant, with the sea cliffs full of colour and the hinterland cloaked in butter-yellow gorse and broom.

The mean annual sunshine average of Brittany is surprisingly high; and is almost the same as the Mediterranean, with a total of 2,000 hours. The mean summer temperature, however, is comfortably moderate at around 18 °C (64 °F) due to the prevalence of sea breezes which do blow fairly steadily and constantly across the whole peninsula. The winters are really quite mild due to the influence of the Gulf Stream, and annual rainfall is fairly high as one would expect in a maritime climate.

Every town, and almost every village, in France provides accommodation for the touring fraternity. The majority are agreeable and efficiently run.

Travel Documents

To visit France you need a valid passport. Keep it as safe as possible and ensure it does not expire while you are

abroad. Campers and caravanners can apply for an International Camping Carnet which is acceptable at all French touring parks and camping grounds and which can be used in lieu of the more valuable passport.

A modest fee is charged for this document, which bears an insurance stamp giving third-party cover in respect of camping equipment. It also entitles the holder to slightly reduced camp fees at some sites.

Drivers must have a full driving licence, third-party insurance indemnity against injury to other persons, a vehicle registration document, and a sticker indicating their country of origin affixed to the rear of their vehicle. A green card is no longer obligatory for EC residents, although it is the document most readily accepted in the case of accident, and it offers cover against damage to another vehicle.

Health

There are few sources of infection to worry about in France; indeed, some would claim that the drinking water, for example, is much better than in other countries. There is a seasonal surfeit of mosquitoes in low-lying areas like the Camargue, or the marshy area of Sologne, but Brittany is not overly plagued by either flying or crawling insects compared to the hotter areas of the south. If you are particularly susceptible to stings or bites though, pack a suitable insect repellent for any high summer visit.

A further cautionary note; never forget that rabies is endemic throughout most of the European mainland. *Never*

A Word of Warning
Unless you have a cast-iron constitution, think carefully about eating shellfish anywhere inland and never drink hotel tap water (one of the most frequent causes of serious stomach upset). Enjoy the Brittany sunshine, but be reasonable about sudden, lengthy exposure, especially on the beach.

go to the assistance of a sick animal, no matter how distressing the case and do not attract the attention of any stray dog, cat or horse when abroad. If you are unfortunate enough to be bitten, seek immediate medical advice, no matter how superficial the wound may appear. The French government is currently investing vast sums in a programme of wildlife vaccination, with tasty baits (often distributed by air-drops) giving the animals immunity for a year or more. According to the medical authorities, France should become virtually rabies-free within about five years. Rabies *is* rare (particularly in Brittany) but it does pay to be aware and circumspect.

Emergency Health Services

Medical expenses in case of injury or illness can be high. Visitors from EC countries should obtain form E111 which entitles the holder to free (or reduced) emergency treatment under an EC reciprocal agreement. The document is permanently valid as long as the holder continues to live in the country where he or she obtained the form and gives detailed information about any procedure taking place abroad in case of emergency. It does not necessarily cover all medical expenses, however, and it never covers the cost of bringing a person back to

9

their own country in the event of serious illness. In France you can expect to be refunded about 75 per cent of the medical fees—if you wish for more comprehensive coverage you should arrange to take out a personal insurance policy.

Embassies and Consulates

If you find yourself in really serious trouble, then contact your embassy or the local consulate:

Australia (embassy and consulate)
4, rue Jean-Rey, 75015 Paris
Tel: 45-75-62-00

Canada (embassy-chancellery)
35, avenue Montaigne,
75008 Paris
Tel: 47-23-01-01

Eire (embassy-chancellery)
12, avenue Foch
75016 Paris
Tel: 45-00-20-87

New Zealand (embassy-chancellery)
7 rue Léonard-de-Vinci
75116 Paris
Tel: 45-00-24-11.

South Africa (embassy)
59, quai d'Orsay
75007 Paris
Tel: 45-55-92-37

United Kingdom (embassy)
35, rue du Faubourg-Saint-Honoré
75383 Paris
Tel: 42-66-91-42

(consulate) 6, rue Lafayette
44000 Nantes
Tel: 40-48-57-47
(consulate) 8, avenue de la
  Libération
35800 Dinard
Tel: 99-46-26-64

USA (embassy-chancellery)
2, avenue Gabriel
75382 Paris
Cedex 08
Tel: 42-96-12-02
(consulate) 2, rue Saint Florentin
75042 Paris
Cedex 01
Tel: 42-96-12-02

How To Get There

By Plane
If coming from Britain, British Airways have daily scheduled flights to Paris from London Heathrow, Birmingham, Manchester, Newcastle, Glasgow, Edinburgh and Belfast. For flight reservations, telephone: 071 795 2525. Try to reserve your seat as far in advance as possible, especially during the high season, bearing in mind that passengers with hand luggage only are generally subjected to shorter check-in times than those with cumbersome excess. Free baggage allowances are: 40kg (88lb) per person in first class, 23kg (50lb) per person paying ordinary fares. There are more airports at Brest, Nantes, Quimper and Rennes, and Air France operate scheduled flights daily to these destination from Heathrow and Gatwick (via Paris). Air France also run flights from regional British

airports, including Birmingham, Manchester and Southampton.

Travellers from other EC countries, North America and Canada can usually arrange to fly direct to Paris from major cities and pick up a connecting flight to Brittany from there. The following operators run scheduled flights to various destinations in Brittany from Paris/Orly West:

Air Inter: for information and reservations telephone Paris (1) 45-46-90-00.

TAT: for information and reservations telephone Paris (1) 42-79-05-05.

Brit Air: for information and reservations telephone Paris (1) 49-75-21-60.

France, almost hexagonal in shape and approximately 950 km (600 miles) wide and 950 km (600 miles) long, is crossed in about one hour by plane—with no delays. These delays afflict charter companies more than scheduled airlines, but it is possible to gain considerable financial concessions if you have no objection to travelling with the former—you simply need to balance your personal priorities.

By Train

The French SNCF (*Société Nationale des Chemins de Fer Français*) is acknowledged as one of the best railways in the world; it is certainly one of the most extensive and innovative. Any SNCF office will provide full information about local and other travel, and where no trains run at all (as in some mountainous areas), there are organized rail–road links with coach or bus companies.

The Brittany peninsula boasts a good railway network, and although the super-speed TGV (*train à grande vitesse*) does not yet serve the whole region, there is a TGV service between Paris and Rennes.

A typical SNCF station, so familiar to backpackers. A top-class service is provided, with extras like local bus connections and cycle hire often available.

Bookings can be made through most travel centres to various towns in Brittany via Paris, while visitors making any stop-over in Paris can call the English-language train information service on (1) 45-82-08-41. The Paris rail terminus is the *gare Montparnasse* to and from all destinations in Brittany. Finally, there is a first-rate Air France—SNCF link service. You fly direct to Paris, then transfer to the train for any of the major Brittany destinations. The fastest train journey time from Paris to Rennes is 3 hours, and to Brest it is 5 hours 40 minutes.

Senior citizens and students can claim an appreciable deduction on travel costs. For details *see* TRAVEL CONCESSION CARDS.

By Coach

The most competitively priced of the transport services, the inter-European coach schedules, have now reached a high level of sophistication, speed, comfort and safety. European coach operators organize services to over 190 destinations, including Saint-Malo and Roscoff. As with rail travel, there are financial concessions for students and senior citizens.

By Car

France is still a wonderful country for leisure motorists, despite the horrendous crush of traffic on major routes on some high days and holidays. There is the prospect of discovering a still largely pastoral country for those prepared to explore minor-road France *en route* to Brittany. Drivers with limited time who want to use the speedy auto route may well opt for the main Paris Brittany road, accessed by the N118 to the west at Boulogne-Billancourt. Follow the signs to Chartres, Le Mans, Laval and Rennes travelling along the A10, A11, and A81. The latter terminates at Rennes. It is *péage* all the way (save for the capital ring road), and this amounts to about half the cost of your fuel. There is also the excellent *national* route from Paris to Rennes, the N12. It is signposted all the way to Rennes and there is no toll charged. It is a somewhat slower journey than by the *péage*, however, as it passes through some built-up areas on the way. The estimated journey times from Paris to Rennes are 3–4 hours if travelling on the *péage* and about one hour longer on the N12. There are no autoroutes in Brittany.

For a more leisurely drive to the Brittany area, there is an alternative route which passes through interesting and even quite dramatic scenery, and which is accessible to those taking the short sea crossing to France from Britain. The coast road either side of Dieppe is inviting—it is pretty around Saint-Valery and Le Tréport and spectacular at Etretat, with its fine cliff walking. West of Caen lie the cluster of World War II invasion beaches, the Cherbourg peninsula which is attractively rugged at the tip, and Mont-Saint-Michel standing as an unmistakable landmark on the Brittany boundary.

Seat belts must be worn in France and young children must be back-seat passengers. A red triangle is compulsory in case of a breakdown or an accident, unless the vehicle is fitted with hazard warning lights. It is probably advisable to have both in a country where driving is inclined to be robust.

A useful feature which adds to both the pleasure and convenience of driving through France. Comprehensive information points like this are commonplace in holiday areas.

Speed limits are: 130 kmph (80 mph); on autoroutes; 110 kmph (68 mph) on dual carriageways; 90 kmph (56 mph) on other roads; and 60 kmph (37 mph) or as directed in built-up areas.

Yellow headlights are not necessary, though adjustment of the dipping system should be made. Ensure that your vehicle is serviced thoroughly before you leave home—the tyres, brakes, clutch and radiator hoses in particular should be checked as they may be affected by the heat. At the peak of summer, it may pay to install a summer-grade thermostat in the radiator.

Motorists from Britain should be careful of driving on the right—it soon becomes second nature, but do pay particular attention to this first thing in the morning. When exiting from a hotel or camping ground it is possible to forget this momentarily, especially if the road is not busy.

Ferry Services

Even the most apprehensive of sea voyagers should not be troubled by crossing from England to France on one of the new generation of super ferries. Meeting the challenge of the charmless Channel, these are bigger and better than ever, and are sophisticated and stable enough to smooth even the choppiest of waters. Both P. & O. and Stena/Sealink now provide blue-riband services on all popular routes. Sailing times are around 75 minutes on the Dover–Calais run, and only 30 minutes on the Dover to Calais Hoverspeed "flight".

It *is* possible to arrive at Dover Eastern Dock, pay, board and be off driving in France within a couple of hours, but you should always book in advance for peak period travel. To book in Britain, the telephone numbers are: P. & O. European Ferries, 0304 214422; Stena/Sealink British Ferries, 0233 47033; and Sally Ferries, 0843 595522. Sally Line operates between Ramsgate and Dunkerque, P.& O. between Portsmouth and Cherbourg or

Plush and Opulent
Genuine shipboard luxury is available too, no matter how busy the P. & O. waterborne giants may be. For a very modest extra charge, passengers have access to a spacious lounge which is opulently furnished and attended by stewards and which has an exclusive bar, complimentary coffee and newspapers, telephone facilities, plus quiet seclusion and unobstructed panoramic views from picture windows. Tickets to the new, much-lauded P. & O. Club Class facility are limited to first-come-first-served, thus space and comfort are guaranteed.

Le Havre, and Stena/Sealink between Southampton and Cherbourg (summer only). Brittany Ferries operate between Portsmouth and Saint-Malo (0705 827701) and Plymouth and Roscoff (0752 221321). Brochures detailing routes, services, timetables and fare structures, can be obtained from:

P. & O. European Ferries, Channel House, Channel View Road, Dover, Kent CT17 9TJ.

Stena/Sealink Holidays, Charter House, Park Street, Ashford, Kent TN24 8EX.

Sally Ferries, Sally Holidays, 81 Piccadilly, London W1V 9HF.

Brittany Ferries, The Brittany Centre, Millbay Docks, Plymouth PL1 3EW.

All the ferry companies offer a range of special inducements for motorists; the more off season you travel and the more unsociable the sailing hours the greater the fare reductions.

Travel Concession Cards

The French have long held in high regard those members of its society at either end of the age range. Students and senior citizens benefit widely as travellers and concessions are now extended to other members of the EC. Students carrying a valid International Student Identity Card are entitled to discounts of up to 50 per cent on train and other travel fares and on museum, theatre and cinema tickets. Young people aged between 12 and 25 years of age inclusive are entitled from 1992 to the *Carrissmo* card. This replaces the *Carte Jeune* and will be transferable, so that only one member of a group travelling together requires a card. It can be purchased for 4 to 8 journeys and reductions will depend on the period when the card is used. The *Carrissmo* card will be available from most railway stations in France.

From May 1992 the *Rail Europ Senior* card will be discontinued, and should be replaced with another scheme for discounted travel for elder citizens. At present the *Rail Europ Senior* card is available from travel agents and French railway offices outside France, who should be also be contacted for information about the replacement card.

All foreign tourists are entitled to a *France Vacances* rail pass and all its advantages.

Getting About

Walking

Perhaps the best and most revealing way of seeing Brittany is on foot: around the Channel coast especially, Brittany is quite compact, with something or somewhere of interest at regular and not too-distant intervals. Ideal are the *Sentiers de Grande Randonnée*—splendid long-distance footpaths which criss-cross the length and breadth of France. In Brittany, the following are favoured pedestrian routes: the GR37/38/39 (mainly inland); the GR34 (south from Mont-Saint-Michel in Normandy, and along the Channel coast); and the GR380 (a circuit trail between Morlaix and the Monts d'Arrée, east of Brest). These major long-distance trails are supplemented

*F*or pedestrian explorers the way-marking of long distance footpaths is generally to a high standard, often colour-coded to assist navigation.

by many local footpaths linking selected towns and villages of scenic interest. Such pedestrian ventures can be greatly rewarding.

For those wishing to stride out with a map and compass, the *Topo-Guides,* produced by the *Fédération Française de la Randonnée Pédestre*, are indispensable companions. These pocket-size booklets describe the routes with

*T*own walking too has become much more pleasurable in recent years, with car-free (or semi-free) centres enabling the visitor to stroll around at ease.

Institut Géographique National (IGN) map reproductions, plus refreshment points and lodging addresses *en route,* local transport information, environmental features and much other useful intelligence.

Bicycles
Cycling as a method of leisure travel involves two quite distinct pursuits— touring, and using pedal-power to get about locally. Touring is very popular with visitors to Brittany, for although there are hill ranges and some up-and-down coastal stretches, the countryside

is really very cyclist-friendly. There is a wind factor (as with any Atlantic peninsula), but in high summer it is usually insignificant.

The best way of arriving in the touring area with your own machine is to travel by air. Bicycles are included as baggage allowance on most scheduled flights, while camping kit in saddlebags or panniers is classified as hand luggage. You may be required to remove the front wheel and pedals, so carry suitable spanners and arrive at the terminal at least an hour earlier than the stipulated time, so as to avoid any hitches. Bicycles are rated as hand baggage on French trains, as they are in Britain, although there is no guarantee that you and your bike will arrive simultaneously. Allow at least two days (sometimes longer) for the bike to catch you up. An alternative for train travellers is to take advantage of the *train-plus-vélo* service operated by the SNCF. Cycles are available for hire on a daily or weekly basis from some 250 railway stations throughout France, and special cycle hire centres are also located in all major holiday towns and recognized outdoor leisure areas.

Travel as light as you can (even if cycle-camping) in the interest of safety, mobility and enjoyment; and don't be too ambitious about daily mileages. Cycling through Brittany should be as serene and deeply pleasurable as the countryside itself. British travellers looking for advice on all aspects of cycle-touring in France should contact the Cyclist Touring Club, a much respected organization which has been looking after riders' interests since 1897. Their address is: *Cyclists Touring Club, Cotterell House, 69 Meadrow, Godalming, Surrey GU7 3HS, UK. Telephone 04868 7217.*

Car Hire

Car hire is possible almost everywhere in France, the best places probably being the major airports and many of the domestic air terminals. Hire is usually on a weekend or weekly basis, and may, or may not, include unlimited mileage. Hiring a car is not cheap, but it does give you valuable independent mobility—a consideration perhaps on any brief visit. Avis have a reservation centre in Boulogne (telephone: 46-09-92-12) where operators are bilingual; for Hertz in Paris telephone 47-74-59-33. The SNCF also runs a car-hire service known as SCETA for rail passengers, who can arrive at around 200 train stations throughout France and find a car ready and waiting. For information on this service, telephone: 05-05-05-11.

On Two Wheels

For those who do not object to the open air—no hardship in summertime Brittany—moped or motor cycle hire is an economical alternative to hiring a car. Most sizeable towns have hire centres, usually run in conjunction with cycle hire. You must be over 21 and have held a full driving licence for more than one year to comply with French law.

Taxis, Buses and Local Trains

Taxi ranks are found in all French towns of reasonable size, certainly at main-line railway stations and often lined up prominently in the town centre. Smaller towns are also efficiently served, and you can usually conjure up a taxi by enquiring at the railway station, the *Syndicat d'Initiative* (tourist information office) the *mairie* (town hall), or the ubiquitous café. These same sources of information are equally reliable about bus services within the *département*. Country bus services do run regularly between strategic towns and villages, but this may not always be immediately apparent to the stranger. The Brittany peninsula also has a very good local train service, serving all major towns and most of the minor ones, save in the extreme north-west of the region.

Driving

French drivers pay no road fund tax but pay extra for their petrol instead, so the car owner pays according to the kilometres covered. Premium petrol is *super*, lower octane is *essence* and lead-free fuel is *sans plomb*. Try to buy fuel from supermarket or hypermarket pumps if you can as it's cheaper, but bear in mind that this service is usually suspended between midday and 2 p.m. (or sometimes 3 p.m).

French drivers seldom cruise, but hustle along on all roads. If you wish to admire a view or whatever, pull up and park, but never do this on a main road as it is illegal. If you enjoy pottering then take to the country routes (not at all difficult in Brittany) where, more often than not (especially outside the peak summer season), you will frequently seem to have the whole of France to yourself. If you dislike legions of TIRs, restrict your transit travel to Saturdays and Sundays when the heavies are virtually silent.

Drive steadily—neither too fast nor too slow—and never make an erratic move if you happen to lose the way. Be extra careful when overtaking, for obvious reasons, and respect the law. There are heavy fines and possible jail sentences for drunken driving, and on-the-spot fines for not wearing seat belts, crossing a double white line, exceeding the speed limit and so on. Such penalties can make a big dent in your holiday budget!

Driving around France is really a delight for the most part. Not long ago the roads were primitive, dangerously cambered, pot-holed, interspersed with crude *pavé* and only sporadically signposted, but within three decades the system has graduated from the worst to the very best. Parking can

*T*he road sign that is often sought by the leisure driver who has time to spare (and to actually enjoy motoring). Use a large-scale touring map to pinpoint these pleasure routes.

sometimes be a problem, but only in major cities and larger town centres. Parking meters and double yellow lines are, as yet, scarcely seen in rural France, and this applies to much of Brittany.

Disabled Visitors

France extends a helping hand where possible to the disabled, for whom using certain forms of transport, negotiating historic public buildings and grounds, or locating suitable accommodation often requires disproportionate effort. Helpful travel hints for the handicapped visitor from Britain are contained within a pamphlet available from the French Tourist Office in London. Hotels with facilities for the disabled are listed regionally, usually available locally through the tourist office or *Syndicat d'Initiative*. For the most comprehensive information on holiday planning and travel abroad, the recognized source in Britain is RADAR (The Royal Association for Disability and Rehabilitation), *25 Mortimer Street, London W1N, UK. Tel: 071 637 5400.*

France now boasts more than 6,000 km (3,700 miles) of autoroute, most of which is toll road (*péage*) except when crossing cities like Lille, and around the Paris *Périphérique*. If you aren't in too much of a hurry, the prettier, less-used *Bison Futé* routes are there for your pleasure and convenience, and are usually signposted simply as *Bis*.

While that erstwhile heart-stopper *priorité à droite* has all but disappeared from the open road with the advent of the international stop sign and the traffic roundabout, it still pays to be wary about traffic entering the mainstream from the right when driving around in cities.

If you are stopped by the police you *must* be able to produce your driving licence, insurance certificate (green card if you have one), and the vehicle registration document.

Accommodation

France provides an extraordinary diversity of traveller accommodation for travellers, from the palatial luxury of the Ritz in Paris and the Negresco in Nice, to the campsite in a natural setting that is no less appealing to the outdoor enthusiast. Between these two extremes, there is a wealth of choice to suit every preference and pocket.

Hotels

In France hotels are graded by the Ministry of Tourism from one star, to four star or luxurious. In Brittany—with a few notable exceptions like Dinard—the average hotel is comfortable and homely rather than sumptuous, and the average two-star room will be reasonably priced. Rates quoted are normally per night for two persons, with Continental breakfast (*café* and *croissants*) usually extra. The rates must, by law, be posted on the door of your room.

Very few single rooms are available, although a third bed for a child will seldom cost more than a third of the room rate, while many hotel chains offer a free extra bed for a child under 12 years of age. Hotels with their own restaurants may expect you to take dinner when staying the night. Room and all meals—full board or *pension*—will usually be offered for a stay of three nights or longer. Half board—

*F*amily-run hotels
throughout Brittany really do
offer all home comforts,
sometimes with just a touch of
luxury. You will almost always
be given value for money at
establishments like this.

demi-pension—comprising bed, breakfast and a main meal, is often available outside the peak holiday period and also increasingly during the high season in recognized resort areas.

There are over 17,000 *hôtels de tourisme* throughout France, and they generally reflect an overall standard which is high for their respective star ratings. In the official *région* of Brittany, there are nearly 300 towns and villages with hotel accommodation listed in the Michelin *Red Guide*, plus a dozen or so more in the annexed territory of Brittany encompassed by the *département* of the Loire Atlantique— now in the *région* of Pays de la Loire.

The lion's share (in excess of 100) is distributed throughout the most westerly Brittany *département*, Finistère.

Brittany is devoted to the traditional idea of good service in comfortable coastal or countryside establishments. Many are family-managed, with the emphasis on highly efficient, low-profile value for money. For this kind of accommodation, coupled with fine quality regional cooking, there are many examples of the famous *logis de France* (there are over 5,000 nationwide, mostly of one- or two-star category). Travellers from Britain who want a free guide and a full list of the addresses of the *logis et auberges de France* should write to:

The French Government Tourist Office, 178 Piccadilly, London W1V OAL, UK. Contact them early in the year and enclose stamps for postage. Advance booking is advisable in July and August almost anywhere in France, while at any of the Brittany seaside resorts it is virtually obligatory.

19

Gîtes de France

There are now more than 20,000 of these reasonably priced self-catering units in France, usually located within or near small country or coastal villages. *Gîtes d'étape* may be small country cottages, village houses, flat extensions or parts of farm outbuildings, while *gîtes ruraux* offer simple accommodation in farms or cottages. Sometimes food supplies are available or cooked meals are served, depending on the locations and the season of the year. There is now also a growing number of "second-generation" *gîtes*, purpose built and often beautifully appointed. These are usually located in areas of dramatic visual impact and their rates reflect their quality and surroundings. For further details send a stamped addressed envelope to *Gîtes de France*, at the address given for the French Government Tourist Office.

An extension of the *gîte* concept is the farmhouse holiday, increasingly attractive to visitors in certain areas of the Republic. The Brittany peninsula is one of the regions most in demand. Visitors live in, taking meals with the resident family. The rates are reasonable and for those parents with perhaps two or three children, who want to sample true country life (and improve their French), the farmhouse holiday is excellent.

Youth Hostels

Auberges de la Jeunesse is a non-profit-making organization founded in 1930 to help young people travel the world, take part in different activities organized in hostels, and meet those from other countries and different backgrounds. The length of stay at French hostels is usually limited to only three or four nights during the peak season. Dormitory sleeping arrangements and communal catering routines are the norm. For full information in Britain about youth hostelling in France, contact: *the YHA, 14 Southampton Street, London WC2E 7H7, UK. Telephone: 071 836 8541.*

Caravanning and Camping

France for the touring fraternity is supreme. The summer climate along with an enormous diversity of terrain, served by the most comprehensive network of touring sites in the world keeps the Republic at number one on the list of countless outdoor enthusiasts of every nationality. Whether you are a caravanner or camper, and whether your preference is for snow-capped mountains, sun-baked beaches, forests, lakes or simply pastoral countryside, there will assuredly be a base of some description for you.

Such havens may range from the simplest of farm pitches, to municipal enclaves, or the most sophisticated leisure parks of outdoor-hotel status, complete with mains electricity and drinking water supply to individual pitches. There are nearly 200 officially registered camping and caravanning sites in Brittany, most of which are located around the coast, although there is a sufficiency inland adjacent to all places of interest. The season is normally from May or June to the end of September, although some sites operate for extended periods, while a few remain open all year round. Probably the most widely used campground guide is the Michelin *Green Guide*, available at most good bookshops.

Money

Currency

The *franc* is the currency of France and is divided into 100 *centimes*. When changing money, do not be afraid to ask the cashier for smaller notes if they might be more useful—200 and 500 *franc* notes are quicker for the teller to dispense, but you may find it hard to change them later.

Banks are open in France from Monday to Friday in major cities and some larger towns and holiday resorts, and often from Tuesday to Saturday in provincial towns. In rural villages they are sometimes only open on market days. There are no standard business hours for banks; 9 a.m. to 12 noon and 2.30–4 p.m. are the best times to try. France has 11 national bank holidays every year, so don't get caught out! Always use a bank to exchange money if you can: although hotels and exchange agencies may be useful in an emergency, their rate will certainly be lower than the official one.

Credit Cards

Out of courtesy, always ask before offering plastic as payment, especially off the beaten tourist track. Increasingly, cards are acceptable in recognized resort areas and this includes most of the Brittany coast and much of the hinterland. Hotels, restaurants, fashionable shops and so on will accept Visa cards, American Express and Diners Club, but may be considerably less enthusiastic about others. Visa cards are the most widely accepted of all cards, with over six million outlets around the world.

Cheques

Traveller's cheques are still the most widely favoured and safest traveller currency; when the cheques are exhausted you know the holiday is over! Rapidly gaining in popularity with travellers within the EC, however, is the Eurocard, issued by banks and used in conjunction with special Eurocheques. With a Eurocard you can withdraw a fixed maximum amount of local currency at any foreign bank and your current account is then debited. Eurocards may become even more attractive than traveller's cheques, particularly since the exact amount of *francs* demanded at the French bank will be delivered.

Security

Everyone is more security-conscious today than it was necessary to be a couple of decades ago, especially when travelling abroad. France is perhaps less plagued by opportunist thieves than most other western European countries, but this should not lead to complacent behaviour on the part of the visitor. France does have its black spots like anywhere esle—the fun-strips of the Riviera and cities like Marseille—but there are very few such areas in Brittany. Nonetheless, if you must take high-value items like jewellery, do not flaunt them. Deposit valuables in hotel safes and never leave anything precious in a hotel room. Thieves can spot a bulging wallet or a quality handbag as swiftly as they can snatch it, so do keep a low profile in places like crowded market places, by dressing down rather than up, and by carrying money in a fully zipped, concealed pouch or pocket. Women who feel that they must carry something in their hand should make it a dreary looking plastic bag—in other words, the message is to appear just a little less affluent than you really are.

Gratuities

You should, however, always tip according to your true worth to gain full Gallic approval from hotel staff, taxi drivers, waiters and (as is always customary in France) cinema and theatre usherettes. Generally, a service charge is included in hotel and restaurant bills (provided it is set down as a *service compris*) and you are under no obligation to pay a *centime* more unless you particularly want to. Small change can be left as a token of appreciation (and this is often the only way of relieving yourself of escalating piles of coins), and a saucer is frequently displayed with pointed prominence on café counters.

In public toilets that are staffed there is a small set fee which, if paid to the exact *centime*, will only raise a reproving glance rather than a farewell smile.

If your hotel or restaurant bill does not display the words *service compris*, you should expect to add around 15 per cent of the total to the amount you pay. If you are in any doubt, or indeed if funds are dwindling, always enquire beforehand about prices. Never be shy, for a certain amount of financial prudence is always appreciated, if not always admired, by the majority of French people.

*T*he fruits of the sea are prolific all around the coast of the peninsula and there is no restaurant that does not offer at least one fish dish.

Food

France is traditionally the gastronomic centre of the western world, although the French are no longer the only nationals who live to eat. In some of the busier cities too, the fast-food habit is on the increase. Nonetheless, in general the choice, preparation and presentation of meals in most French hotels and restaurants is of an enviably high standard. However, don't expect culinary wizardry at every eating place; you won't find it just because you are in France.

Restaurants

Dining out begins at 7.30–8 p.m. (although the majority of French people take their main meal at midday). Restaurants specializing in *déjeuner* (lunch) may put on a restricted menu for *dîner* (dinner), but this is not al-

*A*s with everywhere else throughout France there is every type of eating house ready to give service in most towns, often in delightfully atmospheric settings.

ways the case; look carefully at the menus displayed at restaurant entrances. You may choose an *á la carte* meal, where you select what you fancy, or the fixed-priced dinner, *un menu*. A *menu touristique* indicates a choice of various dishes for each course, served for a fixed price.

Bars

When the sun shines steadily and high in the sky, a priority for the traveller is liquid refreshment.

Happily, in France you will never be far away from one of those ubiquitous little bars. Some are dull, impersonal and staffed by minders all but hostile to casual trade, but most are cosy, atmospheric and welcoming. Many of them serve simple snacks like the *croque monsieur* (toasted cheese sandwich), or *frites,* which hit the spot well, especially when accompanied by a *bière à la pression.*

Eating Out

It pays to shop around when looking for a restaurant. Evening strolling in search of somewhere nice to eat is practised as much by the natives as it is by visitors, and there can be no more pleasant way of honing the appetite than a ramble combined with a casual sightseeing tour of a medieval town in the cool of a summer evening. If there already appears to be a healthy patronage at a potential meal-stop, with cars (especially if they have French number plates) jostling for parking spaces, the place will definitely be worth a visit. If, on the other hand, only the proprietor is visible and there is no alternative, order frugally and stick to simple fare.

If you do find that tell-tale full car park, you will assuredly discover that dining out in a well-run family hotel is one of the great pleasures of being in France. In Brittany you can eat in restaurants noted for their *haute cuisine,* but tucking in with gusto in a cosy bistro alcove, perhaps adjacent to a busy bar, will be equally satisfying. The bistro scene may also reward you with glimpses of everyday French café life, adding richness and variety to your travel.

*T*he pavement cafe is, of course, synonymous with France and the climate, even in the north, is usually benign enough in summer to guarantee full patronage.

Picnics

Many of the French are still *paysans* at heart, never happier than when they are out of doors, so *le pique-nique* is universally popular. Roadside picnic areas abound throughout France, often complete with tables, bench seating and toilet facilities. Enjoy sitting under a shady chestnut tree on the banks of a meandering river with a freshly baked *baguette*, regional cheese, fruit and a bottle of the local *vin rouge*. This is literally "dining out"—the cheapest way of taking lunch anywhere in Europe, and of course one of the most popular among motorists in transit, French and foreign alike.

Village Shops and Open Markets

In almost any market town or village in France, all the ingredients for a bumper picnic lunch can be collected within a hundred metres or so. First to the *boulangerie* for your fresh bread (white, brown or wholemeal nowadays), then to the *épicerie* for cheese,

*T*he Brittany coastal speciality, the quay-side oyster stall. Some of the best shellfish to be found in Europe can be bought—virtually straight from the sea—at such outlets.

the *charcuterie* for *pâté* or a wide choice of cooked meats, often with dishes of prepared salads, and finally to the general grocery store *alimentation,* for wine, soft drinks or bottled water.

Despite fierce competition from supermarkets and hypermarkets on the outskirts of almost every large town, the small shopkeeper retains a great deal of customer loyalty in rural France. For the French, life without the little shops in country towns and in virtually every village would be considered quite intolerable. Outside the big cities, the pace of life remains sanely steady, and it is important to exchange courtesies with, and glean the latest news and views from, the local shopkeeper. This local communication is pleasing to see and experience and also infectious: it soon becomes a habit to say *bonjour* when you enter a shop and *au revoir* when you leave.

The traditional open market, which transforms a small town or village

T he Brittany hinterland provides a wonderous choice of fresh fruit and vegetables, like this display in the covered market of Quimper.

square into an ephemeral bustle of colourful activity once (or more times) a week, is often a treasure-house of local produce, or of specialized items of decorative or practical value. It is fun for browsing and people-watching and perhaps picking up a memento or two, but not really for serious shopping, unless you are fluent in French and know a real bargain when you see one. Exceptions are fresh fruit, preserves, honey, and other products for which the region is renowned.

Sunday morning is the ritual time to visit the *pâtisserie*, and this is almost a religious experience for many French families. The boxed and beribboned examples of the cake-maker's art are very expensive, but most visitors should be tempted at least once during their holiday.

Supermarkets

For all self-catering foreign visitors the *supermarché* is obviously the main food source, if only because of its convenience and because you need to know scarcely a word of French. Supermarket shopping is almost identical the world over, seldom a stimulating experience, but these cathedrals of commerce do form an important, indeed almost vital, part of contemporary, modern living. In France, patronize the supermarket rather than the hypermarket if food is your prime consideration, for the latter does not always dispense top-quality edible produce; and do your shopping at any time other than Friday evening or Saturday if you can. Finally, don't be surprised to find that supermarkets (along with many other establishments) are closed on Mondays.

Food prices are generally comparable to those elsewhere in the EC, although the cost of the whole shopping basket may be a little less if wine and beer are included. This applies to basic foodstuffs only, and not to exotic treats like *pâtisserie* creations.

Shopping and Services

The Paper Shop

The *maison de la presse* is the place for newspapers, magazines, postcards, local maps and guide booklets to surrounding attractions, sometimes available in English language editions. English language newspapers are usually available in larger towns or recognized holiday resorts, coastal or inland, but they will of course cost more than at home, and will often be at least one day out of date. French newspaper shops may also sell photographic film (and be a processing depot), and in some smaller towns the paper shop may stand in for the tourist office or *Syndicat d'Initiative* when the latter is closed, by keeping publicity material on the towns and its environs.

The *Pharmacie*

Although the French now have a funded health service, until quite recently they have had to be heavily self-reliant in remedying ills. For any petty malady, they make not for the local doctor, but for the chemist who is usually highly skilled at diagnosing and dispensing for minor complaints, particularly those apt to affect the holiday visitor, for example, sunburn, diarrhoea, constipation, minor injuries and the like. Every town, even the smallest, boasts a *pharmacie* supplying a wide range of effective panaceas. Opening times vary regionally, but it is common to find dispensaries open until 7.30 p.m. or a little later.

Post and Telephone

In France the post office (*Poste, Téléphone, Télégraphe*) is advertised by the initials *PTT*. Postboxes are yellow, and stamps may be bought not only at post offices but from tobacco shops, kiosks and cafés displaying the *Tabac* sign. Post offices are open from Monday to Friday 8 a.m. to 12 noon, and from 2–7 p.m. Saturday morning

*T*he telephone service
in France nowadays is certainly
no joke; there are even kiosks
for disabled users in some places.
This one is in Dol-de-Bretagne.

opening times are 8 a.m. to 12 noon. A *poste restante* service is available at most main post offices.

Not long ago the telephone service in France was a bit of a joke, but it has now achieved a very high standard of efficiency. Direct-dial telephone boxes (very rarely vandalized) can be found almost anywhere, including the most unlikely rural settings—for example the top of a mountain or beside a secluded lake. Most of these are coin-operated, although card phones are rapidly increasing in number. To call a number outside France, dial 19 (wait for the change of tone), followed by the country code, followed by the area code of the number being called

but *never* the first 0 of an area code number. Finally dial the subscriber's number.

To telephone a Paris number from anywhere in France, prefix the standard eight-digit number with 16 (listen for the change of tone) and then 1 followed by the subscriber's number. Alternatively, to dial a number in France other than Paris, from Paris, dial 16 followed by the eight-digit number. Keep a few coins for calls, because change in an emergency is not always easy to come by, especially 5 *franc* pieces.

The French post office is also a useful information source. Almost all main post offices throughout the Republic operate a Minitel system, covering most service information requirements. Dial for information and the answer comes up on a visual display screen, concerning your required local needs. The traveller needs only a rudimentary knowledge of French to operate this device.

Electrical Appliances

In all areas of Brittany it is possible to obtain good English language radio reception from the BBC in Britain on the long-wave car radios, provided the aerial is efficient. Standard European two-pin electrical plugs are employed for most small appliances, while larger devices are often fitted with three-pin round plugs. Modify any essential appliance accordingly, or take a special plug adaptor—these may be purchased on many ferry boats and aeroplanes nowadays.

A Brief Pointer to the Gallic and Breton World of Jacques and Jeanne

French in the east, Breton in thc west, but uniquely Gallic through-out, this is unmistakably Brittany. This once-remote, desolate spot thrusting almost 250 km (150 miles) into the north Atlantic was first settled by wanderers from that other great continental peninsula, Iberia, when the human race was relatively young. Celtic tribes from central Europe followed, five of which became aggressively dom-inant and thus Armorica (or Bretagne as it later became) stabilized.

The French People

The Frenchman, small of stature, moustached under a black beret, wine glass in one hand and *Gauloise sans fil-tre* in the other is the conceptual archetype gone forever. Nevertheless, there are elements of truth in every well-observed cartoon and the French *do* have certain specific characteristics. While generalizing is largely valueless, it is always fascinating.

T he younger generation are taught not only the basics, but a code of civilized behaviour which, on the whole, produces responsible and socially aware citizens.

Physically the French *are* slightly smaller, lighter of build and with a darker complexion than northern Europeans. They have piercing dark eyes, aquiline noses and employ exag-gerated gestures when conversing: in-herited features and behavioural traits of their Celtic ancestors, an Indo-European race who migrated originally from the East. These, I suppose, might be considered to be their national char-acteristics. Regionally, there are wide ethnic gulfs. The stolid and pragmatic Normandy farmer and the factory worker from Lille are totally different from the mercurial and hedonistic southerner, who basks under the Provençal sun. The Bretons and the Basques of the western seaboard con-sider themselves nationals in their own right, as do the mountain people of the high Auvergne; while the cosmopolitan and urbane Parisian views *all* provincials with tolerant disdain.

Yet there is a curious, powerful bond that welds them irresistibly into a complete and cohesive whole. It was perhaps started by Charlemagne, largely achieved by Napoleon Bonaparte and perpetuated by Charles de Gaulle. The symbol of nationhood—the blue, white and red *Tricolore*—is universally respected, indeed honoured, and flutters above every *mairie*, from the Alps to the Atlantic and from Calais to Cannes.

National pride is instilled early; children quickly learn how privileged they are to have been born French. Those disciplined and well-behaved crocodiles of infants shepherded by dedicated teachers, are being taught according to a national curriculum which places importance not only on the three Rs, but also on decent social behaviour and commendable love of country. Later on, all a schoolchild's energies will be devoted to passing the *baccalauréat*, the passport to university and the *grandes écoles*. Students are politically prickly, hell-raising and ever on the edge of delinquency or revolt, but their early training means that they rarely take out their youthful frustrations through vandalism, and they are almost never overtly hostile to the older generation. Three-quarters of all students reach university standard.

You may encounter awkwardness, rudeness and even verbal aggression on occasion in France (particularly if you are travelling by car), but it will rarely be entirely gratuitous; you may have broken a code of surprising rigid behaviour laid down very early in life, and this will very swiftly bring forth a stream of Gallic invective. In truth, the French *are* very different from the Anglo-Saxons, with distinctly Gallic priorities and aspirations. Those visitors with entrenched prejudices often deride them, but for those for whom the reason to travel is exactly that difference between cultures, the French are a source of endless fascination. They are one of the most complex and colourful races on earth, in turn captivating, infuriating, intelligent and stupid, effusive and sullen, friendly and brusque. They will certainly make their mark on you somehow; no visitor to France can be indifferent to them.

In the final analysis, France is made by its people and frequent visitors will discover that it is one of the most tolerant and liberal of lands. You can do what you like (within lawful reason), wear what you fancy, be as eccentric as you wish, and no one will really give a second glance. There is an atmosphere of freedom for all those who pay their dues promptly, respect the law and do not impinge on the lives of others.

The French at Work and Play

The day of the average French family, whether urban or rural, starts early. The journey to school or workplace is often made in the dark, while most of the important shops, especially the *boulangerie*, are open before it is light. Any impression that life is spent café-lounging during a protracted lunch hour is inaccurate. The French work as hard—and play as hard—as any other race, with an undisputed inventiveness and sense of design. A nation

Le Weekend *is sacrosanct to most French families, nowadays invariably devoted to active, sporting leisure. Love of the outdoors is a natural characteristic.*

that can create high-tech wonders like Concorde and the deadly Exocet missile, as well as low-tech wizardry like the Citroën 2CV, must be peopled by a supermix of artists and artisans.

The French are the fourth-largest producers of motor cars in the world (despite the lamented demise of the 2CV), while their expertise in building nuclear power stations and immense river barrages, along with commercial and domestic building projects on a grand scale, is only surpassed by their flair in agriculture—especially viticulture. France is also the second-largest exporter of agricultural products in the world after the USA. This success is

the result of determined industry and application which places the country firmly in the premier league of the western world. The Gallic life-style has subsequently changed out of all recognition since World War II and new wealth has brought increased leisure opportunities. Superbly appointed sports complexes abound, with athletic tracks, heated swimming pools, football and rugby pitches and top-quality tennis courts (indoors and out), all patronized enthusiastically throughout the whole year. Outside the arenas, joggers and cyclists are mindful of their health as they never once were.

France, though, is still a nation of individualists and despite the bustling achievers, you will still see plenty of recognizable Frenchmen of the old school: *bons viveurs*, who throng the river banks with their fishing rods and ensure the continued existence of countless atmospheric cafés. Their wives, shrewd of intellect and among

F or young and old alike, the great participant sport throughout the Republic is fishing. You'll see anglers casting on nearly every stretch of water.

the best cooks on the planet, are key figures at the ubiquitous market stalls. By contrast, their daughters probably shop at the supermarket, work full- or part-time, look after a home and children, yet still find time for leisure activity in the evenings and most certainly at *le weekend*. As is the case with other European countries, France is peopled by two generations: elders who were born into a world when the motor car was an innovation and when leisure for the masses scarcely existed, and their children and grandchildren who take holidays and technology for granted.

Fortunately, the ways of bygone France are not being allowed to wither

entirely, so old-world habits continue to survive alongside modernity. The French may travel between Paris and Lyon at 270 kmph (170 mph) on their *train à grande vitesse*, but they still have to have their bread baked daily; they drive like Grand Prix racers to the café, yet still spend an inordinate time when they get there over an aperitif; and it is still a truism that no French person will use one word when a thousand will do!

Visitors have been known to level accusations of rudeness, closeness and arrogant self-interest at the inhabitants of the Republic. It must be said that there *is* a national characteristic which reflects an ostensible indifference to the rest of the world, and a Frenchman's consuming interest and concern is for himself and his nearest and dearest. It may make the hackles rise in some, but it is an honest attitude, most noticed by those who make no attempt to learn even the basic courtesies of the language. Learn a smattering of

*F*rench women are as emancipated as any in the world, although they manage to retain a long-envied reputation for efficient home-making and astute husbandry.

French and you are much more likely to enjoy friendly acceptance.

History

Brittany—or Armorica, "land of the sea", as it was called before the Celtic influx of migrants from the British Isles—remained as isolated and mysterious to primitive mainstream Europe as the Iberian peninsula did to the south. While it boasted no natural barrier like the formidable Pyrenees, it was surrounded on three sides by dangerous seas and on the fourth by low-lying boggy terrain. The latter came to be known as the Breton Marches and later became a medieval fortified frontier with Normandy, Maine and Anjou.

Peopled by tribes of Indo-Europeans like the rest of France probably around 1000 BC, individual tribal territories within the peninsula were distinctly defined. The legacy of their existence is perpetuated even today through the names of major Brittany cities: Vannes was the region of the Veneti; Rennes was home of the Redones; and Nante was the territory of the Namnetes.

Apart from the plethora of megaliths for which the region is renowned, (epitomized by the stone legions of Carnac), little is known of Brittany before the Roman era. Shrouded in mystery then, this was to be perpetuated later through Celtic folklore and legendary tales, so that to this day Brittany (like Ireland) is suffused with other-world superstition, overlaid with devout religious belief.

At around 450 AD, the Teutonic Saxons, under the brother chieftains Hengest and Horsa, landed on the Kentish coast of England and, together with the Angles, gradually ousted the native Britons (the Jutes). The Jutes then drifted westwards to Wales and from there, together with Celts from Ireland and lowland Scotland, went to Armorica. Under the weight of its new

Only occasionally remnants of bygone paysan France (like this humble thatched cottage in the Brière marshes) are evident today.

population, Armorica quickly came to be called Bretagne, or "little Britain".

Gallic Resistance
In 55 BC, one year after invading England, Julius Caesar's forces defeated the seafaring Veneti, decimating their fleet of sailing ships in the Bay of Morbihan through wily tactics adopted by the oar-powered Roman galleys. It took four more years to completely subdue the Gallic warrior tribes, despite the sophisticated weaponry and superior military strategy of the disciplined legions. After this four- year struggle though, it was another 400 years before the Romans departed.

The Dark Ages
With the new arrivals, more or less at the beginning of the Dark Ages, came fervent religion which partially replaced pagan belief and practices, and the Celtic language. Britons thus became Bretons and the peninsula became sub-divided once again into warlord territories which were frequently, and often savagely disputed. Proudly independent Breton chieftains defied a succession of Frankish kings, including Clovis in the 5th century and

Charlemagne in the 8th century, who only ever managed to partly subjugate the province. Meanwhile, the more peaceful settlers from the British Isles were creating monastic centres of religion and learning, from which radiated districts of political stability coupled with valuable land-clearance programmes that laid the foundations of a future agrarian society.

Medieval Brittany

From the 9th to the 11th centuries, the Normans thrust westwards into Brittany in repeated invasion sorties, but were largely repulsed by the warlike and determined natives. What the Franks could not achieve by force they attempted through guile, and Nomenoë, a native Breton and count of Rennes, was appointed ruler of the fractious territory in the 9th century. He too rebelled, however, defeating Charles the Bald in 846, forcing him to grant Brittany independence. Another early Breton hero was Alain Barbe-Torte (Twisted Beard), who vanquished the Normans decisively in the 10th century to create, in effect, a self-governing Brittany which was to endure more or less undisturbed for over five centuries.

The counts of Rennes, who ruled during the 10th and 11th centuries, were headed by Geoffrey, who became duke of all Brittany in 992. His grandson, Conan II, placated avaricious nobles about to revolt on one flank, and the future William I (conqueror of Britain in 1066), threatening the other. One of Conan's successors, Alain Fergent, actually defeated William in battle in 1085. In the 12th century the Plantagenet dynasty ruled and Conan

IV, finally usurped by those restless nobles, made an alliance through marriage with the king of England, Henry II, who briefly became overlord of the peninsula.

Henry's son, Geoffrey, Duke of Brittany, was succeeded in turn by his son Arthur who had been nominated by his illustrious uncle, Richard I of England (Richard the Lionheart), as his successor to the throne of England. When Richard was killed at the siege of Chalus in 1199, his brother John became fearful for his crown and—it is claimed—murdered the young Arthur with his own hands at Rouen in 1203. Remembered now only for the sealing of the Magna Carta in 1215, John (the youngest son of Henry II and Eleanor of Aquitaine), was a cruel, cowardly and inept monarch and the assassination of his nephew damned the English king's cause in France. Arthur's sister Alix married one Pierre de Dreux in 1212, who then became Duke of Brittany, thus actually strengthening the French connection and creating another ducal dynasty that was to last until the 16th century.

Anne, Duchess of Brittany, was the last royal ruler of the independent province. A devious intriguer by all accounts, she was the daughter of François II, Duke of Brittany, and was elevated to the title of duchess at the age of 12 on the death of her father in 1488. Only three years later she was forced to marry Charles VIII after Brittany had been invaded by France. Her husband was a feckless young king with delusions of grandeur, who died prematurely as the result of an accident at the château of Amboise. The following year, the newly widowed

35

Divided Dukes

During the Hundred Years War, the Brittany dukes were inevitably divided. Montfort was loyal to the king of England, while Charles, Duke of Blois, rallied behind the king of France. Skirmishing exploded into the War of Succession in 1341, which lasted until 1364, then Jean de Montfort was eventually acclaimed duke of the province. A pyrrhic victory in some respects, for although Charles de Blois was killed, and the great medieval knight (and eventual Constable of France) Bertrand du Guesclin was captured, constant warring between the ducal houses flared periodically for over another century, right up to the rein of Charles VIII of France (1470–98).

*T*he calvary of Saint Thégonnec; doubly fascinating for the historical connection. Protestant Henri IV is said to be the figure tormenting Christ, (on left).

Anne married the successor king, Louis XII, thus preserving to a degree Brittany's autonomy. Before her own death in 1514 at the age of 37, she consented to the marriage of her daughter to the future King François I of France, thus really cementing the bond of reunion between her beloved Brittany and the kingdom of greater France. For this she is fondly remembered, if not revered, by the Breton people and is widely commemorated by enduring memorials scattered throughout the peninsula. From the moment grudging acquiescence was reached between François I and the counts of Brittany at Vannes in 1532, the region remained relatively peaceful, (by medieval standards at least) right up to the French Revolution.

That is to say, while the nobles swore fealty to their king, they were part of a feudal system which demanded more local allegiance, largely because of the difficulties of long-distance communication which were

Religious Persecution

Largely of the Catholic faith, Bretons were also, in the main, loyal to the crown. Subsequently they suffered cruelly during "The Terror" which followed the Revolution. A bitter civil war was conducted against the *Chouannerie*—the *Chouans* as all Royalist Catholics were dubbed—and a programme of brutal repression was instigated by the Convention. This culminated in the deliberate drowning of thousands of prisoners at Nantes and mass executions at Rennes, not only of Bretons, but also of those from the neighbouring Vendée region of Pays de la Loire, to the south. These savage acts of barbarism have not been entirely forgotten or forgiven, even now, in parts of Brittany. There were several subsequent attempts at Royalist revolt during the ensuing years, all of them of course abortive, the last taking place in 1832.

particularly pronounced in remote provinces such as Brittany. In theory, the medieval dukes and counts of France genuflected to the sovereign, but in practice they were virtual kings in their own right, all-powerful and answerable to no one. These omnipotent overlords took centuries to tame, Brittany being the last of the independent duchies to swear genuine loyalty to the French crown in the early years of the 16th century.

Even then, the royal power had to be vigorously exercised for it was periodically resisted. This resistance occurred both in the 17th and 18th centuries, and notably in Brittany which retained its own ducal estates right up to the fall of the Bastille. During the protracted Wars of Religion, Brittany suffered rather less than other regions, although wanton persecution and depredation were suffered acutely in some places. Sufficient in fact, to have the desperate provincial governor appealing to the king for restoration of civil order in the late 16th century. This Henri IV did in 1598, by signing the famous Edict of Nantes, which ensured freedom of religious worship; at least until 1685, when revocation of the Edict was decreed and persecution of

Window in the former cathedral of Saint-Pol-de-Léon, depicting saints and the Stations of the Cross. The building dates back to the Norman Conquest.

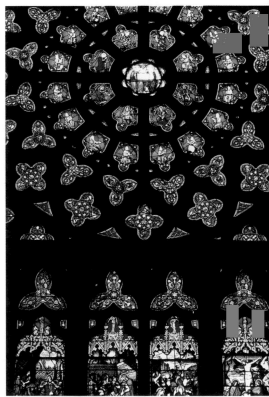

World War I created the Lost Generation of France, bled to the point of exhaustion by staggering battlefield casualties. These are still honoured in almost every town and village in the land.

fortified submarine pens being specific targets of the allied forces. Resistance to the German occupation was strong in Brittany throughout the War, and at the time of the liberation in 1944, most of the peninsula was already in the hands of the French Resistance, although the German naval garrisons held out until May 1945.

Protestant Huguenot worshippers was resumed.

During World War I the Brittany landscape remained untouched, but the human casualties, like every other region of France, were enormous. Then, as now, the French navy was largely manned by Breton sailors and the death-toll was heavy indeed. However, the region did become war-torn (like so many other regions of northern France) during World War II, especially at the Brest, Lorient and Saint-Nazaire naval bases, the heavily

Brittany: Land of Legend

King Arthur or "Artur" (a subject of Bretagne) in France, was said to have ruled over England sometime in the 5th or 6th centuries. A mighty warrior—real or imagined—scholars now generally concede that there *was* a British chieftain who led a great army against Saxon invaders and defeated the enemy several times in battle. Fact or fable, reality and myth thenceforth become inextricably mixed in the swirling mists of centuries-old tales.

Gradually the obscure tribal chieftain was elevated to the rank of monarch and the Arthurian legend was born through the pens of poets and the mouths of story-tellers.

King Arthur and his chivalrous knights like Sir Lancelot became cult heroes of the medieval world; champions of the British, French or Germans, depending on the nationality of the scholars or scribes. Tristan, one of the best known tragic figures of medieval romance, was quite possibly a real contemporary of Arthur and is said to have visited the king's court occasionally. His deeds of derring-do took him far and wide, from Cornwall to Brittany. The nephew of King Mark of Cornwall, Tristan unwittingly drank a love potion intended for the king's bride, Isolde (who also quaffed it accidentally) and the two fell hopelessly and fatally in love. The story, now world-famous through Wagner's opera, contains all the elements of medieval popular fiction, including one interlude where the lovers find themselves in an idyllic sylvan hideaway which might have been in Cornwall, Ireland or France. In any event, it is to Brittany that Tristan flees at one point in the story, from the vengeance of his uncle, to the protection of a stalwart friend, Hoël, Duke of Brittany. Hoël actually existed, and his stronghold, Cornouaille, was created by a bishop from Cornwall, at around the year 495—hence the familiar sounding name of the region now centred on modern Quimper.

This is just one tale amongst a veritable host of dream-time and supernatural stories—sometimes tinged with truth—which pervade the whole

peninsula, especially Finistère; hardly surprising in a land said to contain the Holy Grail itself in the ancient forest of Brocéliande. Here too dwelled Merlin, the Welsh wizard, and advisor to the Jutish king Vortigern at around 450 AD. He is said to have spirited the Stonehenge pillars from Wales to Salisbury Plain and revealed to young Arthur—following the renowned sword-from-the-stone test—(Excalibur) that he was the true king of the Britons.

Despite the cynicism of our age which pervades much of western Europe and certainly most of France, the Breton people—and notably those at the western end of the peninsula—are still steeped in Celtic folklore and are determined to perpetuate their heritage through their language, customs *and* folk-tales. Like all the Celtic races, they are more than ready to temper factual knowledge with the belief that there are more things in heaven and earth than technology and cold logic. There is, for example, still much mystery about the great menhirs of Carnac, as there is about England's Stonehenge. Both are of the same era and both have remained scientific enigmas.

In Brittany, as in Cornwall and Ireland, the local people still claim that there are hobgoblins and mystical fountains, mermaids and spirits, and magicians and wishing wells. This is a faintly glimpsed, timeless other-world of black demons and white, benevolent fairies, which can be traced back through the centuries to pre-Roman Armorica, and the mysterious Argoat, the once deeply forested peninsula interior of Brittany.

Religion

The religion of the French is Roman Catholicism in the main, and although there are still pockets of Protestantism in certain areas, scarcely any of these now exist in Brittany. While the average contemporary French family may be Catholic, they are unlikely to be any more devout than the average Church of England family in Britain or Protestant in the USA. Having said that, although drastically relegated in the second half of the 20th century, religion still plays an important role in the marking of life's milestones, and is of considerably more importance than that in the lives of many Britons. Nationwide, church weddings are still almost obligatory, lavish and often

> **Religious Architecture**
> The legacy of an important religious past is evident in every settlement of the Republic, from the greatest cities to the smallest back-country hamlets. There is a richness and diversity of cathedrals, churches and chapels, now hungrily appreciated by all who are aware that such enduring masterpieces in stone will never be created again. A programme of restoration and preservation is under way to arrest the deterioration of the centuries, while billions of francs are made available through a state-assisted scheme for this urgent task. While these architectural treasures are now comparatively little used for worship, there is a significant increase of return to church pews as the 21st century dawns.

quaintly old-fashioned. But Sunday is also fun day, when leisure is pursued even more fervently than it is on Saturday, and commerce thrives in many towns and villages more than it does on Monday.

Currently, one telling statistic reveals that although eight out of ten French children are still baptized, not more than two out of ten will grow up to be practising Catholics. Of course, strength of faith varies from region to region, and while attendance at mass may be desultory within most *départements* of France, the Church is still respected, and very influential inside the boundaries of Brittany. This staunch allegiance is illustrated by the

*A*ltar screen (retable), in the tiny country church of Commana; many such religious relics are uniquely Breton.

The Breton Coiffe once ubiquitous through all Brittany, now just seen occasionally in the far west and on fête days.

steady—and growing—popularity of those picturesque ceremonies, uniquely peculiar to Brittany, the *pardons.* These impressive religious processions of saintly homage are held annually throughout the peninsula, are attended by great crowds of pilgrims and numbers of curious secular visitors, and, unfortunately are sometimes overblown by commercial influence. Some

Cloister of the Chapelle Saint-Yves, at Tréguier; beautifully proportioned and uncannily peaceful amid the port-town bustle.

of the best of these annual devotions can be seen in country districts of Finistère, where the distinctive traditional costumes and women's *coiffe* head-dresses of ornately worked lace, are worn.

One of the most famous is the Great Pardon of Sainte-Anne-la-Palud (on the southern approach to the Crozon peninsula), held on the 25–26 July. Another is the magnificent 26 July procession of Sainte-Anne-d'Auray, near Carnac and inland from the Gulf of Morbihan—one of several such annual events held here, at the premier pilgrimage centre of Brittany. Genuine holidays (from holy days) start once the religious procession is over, and the events then take on all the characteristics of the high-spirited French *jour de fête*.

No less renowned than the *pardons* are the religious relics of the peninsula, epitomized by a number of very impressive cathedrals (for example, those of Quimper and Nantes), the many churches and chapels with their distinctive belfreys that dot the Brittany countryside, and the famous parish closes. These sanctified areas adjacent to churches display calvary monuments (sometimes of the most intricate carving) and ossuaries (or charnel houses), and are frequently entered via symbolic arch-of-triumph gateways. Most of these calvaries date from the Middle Ages (mainly the 16th century), and while some are simple, others comprise elaborate groups of saints and other religious figures. Of the saints themselves, there are more—far more—in Brittany than anywhere else in France, many of them being known only to a few locals!

Politics

Politically, Brittany has changed quite drastically since the end of World War II. The drift from pastoral to urban life has been considerable in a region that has become quite heavily populated in places. The importance of tourism has ensured a wide programme of restoration and modernization of the infrastructure, which has in turn created problems of ownership of a second home around the coast, coupled with increasing summertime crowding. On the whole, the region has benefited from its new service-industry economy. Sleepy, old-time Brittany has been changed dramatically in the vicinity of great conurbations like Nantes and Brest, and in many country areas by the relentless rescuing and restoration of farmhouse châteaux, villages and even entire town centres. But the restoration work is politically expedient, keeping the majority happy and the municipal coffers healthy.

The experience of Brittany has been the experience of the whole of France, where the much-vaunted "Second Renaissance" has totally transformed the country since World War II, from a predominantly agrarian society to one of high-tech affluence. Four decades have seen changes that are only slightly short of miraculous. During the late 1940s and early 1950s France was in a shambles, and a holiday there was an adventure fraught with hazards and uncertainty. It was a colourful but crumbling country, with governments coming and going almost on a weekly basis, exhausted by two world wars, listless, lacklustre and disillusioned. That France, nostalgically romantic for old-timers perhaps, has now been erased utterly and permanently.

The Republic is now a close-knit and confident land in good heart. The 21 *régions* that comprise metropolitan France have never been so unanimously in accord under the beloved *Tricolore*. Much of this national solidarity has come about with a realization of the value of younger people. Their vitality and determination are seen now to have been the vital ingredients of national success. The new middle class is younger, more ambitious and more ready to indulge in bold merchant-adventuring. The planning and execution of more development projects across France—the road system, the harnessing of nuclear power, the colossal hydroelectric scheme and barraging of major French

---

The Political State of France

Every *préfecture, département*, and government *région*, strives to achieve what the French consider to be really important—personal fulfilment through culture, leisure pursuits, and an educated appreciation of civilized living via cuisine, fashion and animated conversation. During the *ancien régime* all roads led to Paris, but nowadays radiation from the Ile de France national hub is definitely outwards. Parliamentary elections are held every seven years, the President being elected for the same period, and the country is governed by two houses—the National Assembly and the Senate. Despite decentralization, Paris is still the head and the heart of the nation, but the vibrations of its influence now reach the most distant pastoral hamlets where, through the *mairie*, a certain conformity and continuity are ensured.

---

rivers—owe much to this new and youthful driving force.

The threatened "deluge" after General de Gaulle was not that which he had envisaged, but rather it was the surge of the younger, liberated generation. In 1967 the French electorate was the oldest on record; by the next presidential election in 1972 (following serious student unrest), it was the youngest. Successful generals do not necessarily make good politicians!

Perhaps the most significant of the recent drastic political changes in France has been the decentralization of government—a logical, if long overdue process. If each community is dominated by a young, vital electorate who are also diligent, intelligent and reasonably honest, success is almost guaranteed. The proof of that success is plain to see.

The fact that the quiet revolution is working well is quickly apparent to any traveller using the roads, the telephones, the train service, the hotel or campsite network, the supermarkets, or specialized shops or services. And as far as the natural, cultural and historic treasures are concerned, no country has a finer record of presentation or accessibility. This state of affairs owes much to the contented political stability which now (by and large) prevails throughout France. Politics are generally middle-of-the-road socialist, with definite conservative leanings, and this has been confirmed in the polling booths over successive post-War decades. No extreme party, of either the left or right, has made any real headway since the Communist Party came close to power immediately following World War II. Personal advancement is a major—and natural—objective, and the French know that this is only possible through collective effort, in a climate of continued social stability.

Economics

In four decades, France has therefore transformed herself from one of the most backward countries in Western Europe, to one of supermodern and dynamic independence. Much of the catalytic energy for this came from the traumatic experience of World War II. Consciously or otherwise, the country was determined to eradicate that era, and therefore threw itself headlong into the post-War industrial and technical age with a fierce will to work and an innovative Gallic flair. French technological know-how in every field of modern commercial endeavour became much acclaimed, while their award-winning designs were in demand across the world. Cities expanded rapidly through building programmes of massive ambition, incorporating factory and housing complexes which were completed, in many cases, at breakneck speed. The French forged ahead by discovery, development *and* forceful follow-through to market success. This simple, if bold, stratagem paid off handsomely in most cases; particularly in the realm of armaments.

This accelerating pace of change has had other effects. The bland conformity of modern city living, the advance of transatlantic traits, and the increasingly exhausting way of life in built-up areas has led to a revived yearning for country-life simplicity.

Hence the great escape *en masse* of city people at every opportunity, and the institution of *le weekend.* Families will frequently travel up to 150 km (90 miles) from the urban concrete to indulge in increasingly important pastoral interludes.

The countryside they visit, however, has changed immeasurably—largely for economic reasons. Hundreds of thousands of small farms have disappeared nationwide, along with the postage-stamp holdings created through the ancient French laws of inheritance, which divided property equally among children. Now, there are only tens of thousands, and even these are diminishing steadily in an age of agribusiness, conceived and now increasingly practised on a mega-scale.

Happily, the Brittany landscape does not lend itself readily to grand-scale farming, although there is a very productive area—the Golden Belt—roughly between Saint-Malo and the Loire river which is famed for its vegetables, and half the hinterland is devoted to cereal production and dairy herds. Nonetheless, much of the produce is the fruit of small, family-run enterprises, resulting in a variegated, if not cosy, rural scene.

The region has not, of course, escaped the national "economic miracle". As a result of this there are a number of industrial development centres, notably in the ancient area of inland Argoat. Mining projects and granite quarries exist too, but not in abundance, although cities like Rennes, Brest and Nantes have expanded mightily, reflecting the new age of industry and affluence. The Brittany coastline, prime objective of most

T he first stop for most new arrivals, serious about diligent exploration of any given location. Most sizeable towns, and all recognized resorts have very good information centres. This one is at Pont Aven.

holiday visitors, remains relatively green and rural of aspect between the seaside resorts, with small towns and villages that have not spread unduly beyond their pre-War boundaries.

Much of the advance in the quality of Breton life has been gained through tourism, which has exploited the region's natural assets to the full—particularly its naturally beautiful coastline. Extolled with shrewdness to maximum effect, every scenic high spot has its full share of patron throughput and therefore currency. Modern roads, railways, airlines and a wide choice of alternative accommodation

all ensure easy access, and in this way the French have applied their economic talents to the holiday business, again with remarkable success.

Geography and Geology

France, with its triple shoreline totalling nearly 3,000 km (1,900 miles), is geophysically representative of all Europe. It is possible to find scenery and climate closely akin to both northern Norway and southern Spain in certain pockets, while other patches are as gentle as southern England or as harsh as the Russian steppes. Overall, however, France is blessed with a temperate climate, which fluctuates over a surprisingly narrow band. Although contrasting extremes do occur where mountain ranges are of sufficient size, at the other end of the scale one could traverse the northern seaboard, from the Belgian border to the western tip

*T*he Brittany regional logo; the symbolic two seas lapping the green peninsula hinterland, gradually narrowing as it probes the Atlantic.

of the inland areas have been reduced through aeons of time, to form rounded hills and gentle plateaux, punctuated in places by rugged outcrops thrusting above meagre topsoil.

Two main plateaux form the Armorican massif—the Montagnes Noires in the south, the Monts d'Arrée to the north. Today, while the highest points do not exceed 300 m (1,000 ft) or so, the rugged aspect indicates far loftier elevations when the planet was younger. Once almost total forest inland, there are now more pockets of trees to break the sparsely populated heathland, although almost in the nick of time, a tree-planting programme is steadily restoring this dearth. These uplands remained barren moors or *landes* for centuries, and not until the 19th century did really extensive land reclaimation get under way. This successfully converted huge tracts of wilderness heath to lush pastures for sheep and cattle.

of Brittany, then south to La Rochelle without detecting any marked difference in the ambient temperature.

Thus the Brittany climate is benign, maritime and in part as soft as that of Eire, though with a very much higher sunshine average; all of which adds to the appeal for many holidaymakers. The landscape is dominated by granite, the Armorican massif—together with the Ardennes area and the Massif Central further south—being the only parts of France to remain above the waves during the Jurassic period (around 150 million years ago). The Brittany peninsula was created volcanically some 500 million years ago but the once-mighty mountain peaks

Inhospitable Terrain Tamed

The peninsula was a very late developer within the French nation in many respects partially because the terrain was extremely difficult to tame. The coastal country of deep estuaries, offshore reefs and cliff-girt indentations discouraged maritime trade, no less than the barren and inhospitable hinterland. The Breton people themselves—deeply conservative, suspicious and, speaking a distinctly un-French tongue—were not overly or immediately co-operative with their more go-ahead Gallic compatriots. Today, some 60 per cent of Brittany is under cultivation, although only some 25 per cent of the population (approximately 3 million) now live by farming.

*B*rittany's vineyards
are concentrated along the Loire
estuary and are, like most other
regions of France, very
productive.

The coastline is one of the most extensive in all France—well over 1,200 km (750 miles) if all the splintered bays and inlets are included. So extensive is the Brittany shoreline, that no less than seven separate coasts are individually named, as will be revealed later in this section. The variety of coastline ensures that the visitor is never bored with repetitive scenery. There are high cliffs, salt marshes, deep-water estuaries, and some of the best and most expansive sand beaches in the country. The inshore waters which surround the peninsula are among the least polluted in western Europe, despite the oil spills from the *Torrey Canyon* in 1967 and the *Amoco Cadiz* a decade later.

Brittany covers an area of some 46,500 sq km (18,000 sq miles), including the *département* of Loire-Atlantique, some five per cent of the total French land mass. As for inland waters, the peninsula is richly blessed, although not by the wide and handsome watercourses of many other French regions—apart from the Loire estuary. The Vilaine river is one of the most important, rising near Fougères in the north-east, passing through Rennes and spilling into the Atlantic below Redon. Other rivers with attractive reaches are the Rance, which flows through Dinan and into the Dinard/Saint-Malo estuary; the Oust which is very attractive around Josselin; the Blavet which was barraged to form the great inland lake of Guerledan, and which flows through Pontivy and empties into the Lorient estuary; and the tortuous Aulne, which snakes its way between the Noires and Arrée mountains of Finistère. The network of navigable rivers and canals totals over 650 km (400 miles)—the

47

M echanization has encroached on age-old production methods for wine. Mobile bottling plants are now the norm; especially with "young" vintages.

Nantes–Brest canal alone is 359 km (223 miles) long—and provides access to the heart of Brittany by a most restful means; while for anglers, the peninsula's fishing waters if placed end to end, would exceed 9,600 km (6,000 miles)!

Apart from the five *départements* created after the French Revolution, the peninsula is also divided into two historic regions—Upper and Lower Brittany. Haute-Bretagne occupies roughly half of the region; an area stretching from the Normandy boundary to an imaginary line between Paimpol on the northern coast, and the Vilaine estuary below Redon. East of this line the influence is distinctly French, as may be expected from a countryside dominated by Gallic people since the earliest times, and French is the natural language.

Geographically (with impish perversity) Upper Brittany is low lying, while Lower Brittany (Basse Bretagne) contains the lion's share of the peninsula's high country including the two major hill ranges. West of the dividing line the Breton language is spoken along with French; rather as the Welsh tongue survives alongside English in parts of Wales.

Customs and relics of the ancient past are more in evidence too throughout Lower Brittany, and during religious festivals the distinctive traditional costumes are still widely worn. The visitor, however, should not expect the Breton language, customs or costume to be in prolific abundance as the 21st century approaches. Inevitably—again as in Wales—the old way of life has almost evaporated, although there is now a strong move to preserve and revive the Celtic language. Currently, something less than half the contemporary population of Brittany are able to converse in their ancestral tongue, but this does not mean that the people are any less fiercely proud of their Celtic inheritance. There is a vigorous Breton revivalist movement, stimulated through educational channels folk clubs and associations; a reflection of rising regionalism not only, of course, confined to Brittany.

While Upper Brittany is content to be an entity, Lower Brittany is again sub-divided into four ancient regions— Vannetias, Cornouaille, Léon and Tregorrois—although these districts are hardly more acknowledged nowadays than England's Wessex. The five modern *départements* encompassing the whole of the peninsula and covered by this guide, are used below.

*O*ne of the finest medieval towns in northern France; try to set aside at least one full day to see this gem of Ille-et-Vilaine properly.

Ille-et-Vilaine

Occupying the north-eastern corner of the terrain from the bay of Saint-Michel to the rocky headland west of Dinard on the coast, this *département* also encompasses country to the south and west of Rennes (the *préfecture*), covering a total area of 7,000 sq km (2,700 sq miles). Formed from what is largely a geographical depression, there are, however, some gentle hills in the north-east and the west.

The name is derived from the rivers Ille and Vilaine, the latter being a navigable waterway link between Rennes and Redon. There is also the long Rance estuary and another canal connection between Saint-Malo and Rennes. Some of the best agricultural land in Brittany is that around the Bay of Saint-Michel, know as the Dol marshes. The coastline is partially rocky and there are a number of small inland lakes, with a forested area between Rennes and Fougères, and another (the most mystical in Brittany), to the west of Rennes, the remnants of ancient Brocéliande. It is a *département* of diverse scenic interest, pastoral in the main away from large towns, with a host of historic high spots, for examples Vitre; Combourg; Dol; and the premier port of the whole region, Saint-Malo.

Loire-Atlantique

Bureaucrats may decree boundary changes, but for countless Bretons and visitors alike, Brittany, in reality, still stretches south to include the Loire estuary. The decision to cut off the ancient *département* (latterly Loire Inférieure), and cede it to the neighbouring *région* of Pays de la Loire in 1964, was about as popular in northwestern France as the decision to re name part of Yorkshire "Humberside" was in the UK. For Bretons, Loire-Atlantique is still as natural a part of Brittany as it ever was.

Another maritime *département*, this one adjoins the Atlantic, thus enjoying a slightly milder, if more humid, climate than its more northerly neighbour. A land mass created largely out of the Loire river basin, it is one of the

La Baule, known as the "Nice of the North". A Brittany resort on the grandest of scales; from swish apartment balconies like this you can watch France energetically en vacances. Some of the finest beaches in Loire-Atlantique are here.

great flatlands of Brittany, with scarcely an undulation, save for the insignificant low hills along the Loire river bank and another cluster bordering Ille-et-Vilaine.

There is a good deal of marshy landscape, and even peat bogs in places, which are naturally attractive to wildlife. Not least of these is the area north of Saint-Nazaire, known as *le Brière* and which is now a designated nature park.

The *département* covers an area almost identical to that of Ille-et-Vilaine, and the *préfecture* is Nantes, one of the largest and busiest cities in western France. The coastline is celebrated for holiday resorts like La Baule, where the climate is invariably benign and the beaches excellent. High spots are the medieval walled town of Guérande, Châteaubriant castle and Nantes, for its splendid cathedral and castle. Modern history relics are the World War II U-boat pens at Lorient and Saint-Nazaire. There is a scattering of small forest enclosures to the north of here, while the southern terrain of the *département* is traversed by the Nantes–Brest canal.

Morbihan

Covering 7,100 sq km (2,750 sq miles) of southern Brittany, this is landscape with contrast aplenty, from the eastern tail of the Montagnes Noires (the high point of the *département*) to the moors and marshes of the distinctive Landes de Lanvaux, and to the north of

Auray on the banks of a river which is still tidal some 12 km inland. Lots of history here and a good source of ceramic souvenirs. A popular Morbihan base.

Vannes which is the *préfecture*. The Gulf of Morbihan is—as its Celtic name translates—an inland sea, and is dotted with tiny islands, peninsulas and fissured inlets. This area enjoys a high sun average (together with a fairly high annual rainfall though), coupled with extremely mild temperatures. This accounts for much of the semi-tropical vegetation and exotic fruits which thrive. It is an area of some of the major Brittany attractions, including: Carnac; the long finger peninsula of Quiberon; offshore Belle-Ile; and Saint-Anne-d'Auray, where the most impressive of the Breton *pardons* is staged.

Quite large vessels can ascend the Vilaine river (and continue north to the English Channel at Saint-Malo if they so wish), while the river Blavet is canalized throughout its journey through Morbihan, and across quiet heath country between Lorient and Pontivy, where the Nantes–Brest canal is joined. There is a forested, if narrow swathe, adjoining the Landes, and to the north lies **Josselin**; one of the most striking of Brittany's châteaux. It is just one of many in the *département* including those at Rochefort-en-Terre and Vannes, the ancient capital of the peninsula province.

Côtes-d'Armor

This *département* occupies an especially attractive stretch of Channel coastline immediately to the west of Mont-Saint-Michel. It is an area renowned and much visited for its leisure resorts such as Dinard and Paimpol, and for its wealth of safe, sandy beaches like Sables-d'Or-les-Pins. There are fine coastal headlands too, among the most interesting being Cap Fréhel, location of the dramatic Fort-la-Latte, and Trégastel with its famous rose-pink cliffs. Saint-Brieuc is the largest town on the coast and the *département préfecture*, and is located on the huge bay of the same name. This is another rock-girt inlet, dotted with islands like Bréhat (accessible only to pedestrians)

*P*loumanach, adjacent
to the top resort of Côtes
d'Armor, Perros-Guirec. The
roseate rocks and necklace of
sheltered coves are great
attractions.

and the sea-bird sanctuaries of Les
Sept Iles.

Inland, the *département* covers an
area close to 7,250 sq km (2,800 sq
miles), the largest in the Brittany *région*. It is primarily pastoral, the only
sizeable towns being Dinan, Lamballe
and Guingamp. Geologically, Côtes-
d'Amour is a table plateau, the elevation varying between 180–3,300 m
(600–1,000 ft) and partly wooded
mainly towards the western end of the
département. There are three quite

well-defined granite hill ranges and
there is some scenic gorge country in
the south-western corner, also traversed by the Nantes–Brest canal.
Dinan and Lannion are two of the celebrated historic attractions, while
Combourg castle is the imposing birthplace of Brittany's most famous literary son, Châteaubriand.

Finistère

The western extremity of the great
peninsula is the Cornwall of France;
indeed the name of the ancient region,
Cornouaille, is virtually the same. Like
its British counterpart, the coastline is
the major attraction. Finistère covers
an area of 7,000 sq km (2,700 sq
miles), with Quimper as its *préfecture*
and Brest being the great naval base
and one of France's biggest ports.
However, these are the only sizeable
cities and for the rest, Finistère is a
granite bastion thrusting into the
Atlantic, with converging hills splitting
the *département* into three distinct areas.

The many river courses—for example, the Douron, Elorn and Odet—
flow respectively northwards into the
English Channel, westwards into the
Bay of Brest, and south to the Atlantic. Almost the entire coast is interesting, dramatic in places, and occasionally breath-taking in its savage
grandeur. There are some majestic cliff
formations, especially around the Bay
of Douarnenez, and some of the most
picturesque fishing harbours in France.

Inland, Finistère is a world of
windswept heathland with granite outcrops at higher elevations, and interspersed with cereal crops, vegetable
farms, apple orchards and dairy farms

52

in valleys and coastal regions. Even at the lowest landscape levels, there is a fairly constant—and consistent—south-westerly breeze, which frequently rages at storm force during the winter. Yet the climate is very temperate and often quite humid in the summer. There is limited forest terrain, the wooded areas lying mainly within the Armorica National Park, inland of the Crozon peninsula. The main watercourse is the Aulne, some 80 km (50 miles) of which form the Nantes–Brest canal.

Breton Essence

For seekers of traditional Brittany, Finistère is without doubt the richest *département*—particularly away from the mainstream tourist trails—revealing many half-hidden treasures of the past to the energetically curious. It is land of *pardons* and parish closes, calvaries and *coiffes*, the unusual coast of *abers* (estuaries) in the north-west, and the revealing rambling paths which probe the hills west of Huelgoat. Above all perhaps are the intriguing menhirs which abound, adding a fascinating *frisson* of prehistory strangeness, to a land still largely steeped in myth and mystery.

The Brittany Islands

Of the Atlantic islands to the west of France, twelve form an official part of the Brittany *région*. All are accessible to visitors and detailed information is available from:

Association pour la promotion et la protection des Iles du Ponant, BP 122, 56400 Auray. Tel: 97-56-52-57.

The list is as follows: Bréhat; Batz; Ouessant (Ushant); Molène; Sein; Les Glénans; Groix, Houat; Hoedic Belle-Ile; Arz; Ile aux Moines.

Festivals

A selection of principal seasonal religious and secular festivals are listed below. There are also out-of-season ceremonies, some of which are held at around the turn of the year.

Belle-Ile   Breton wrestling contests—third Sunday in July.

Camaret   Sea blessing ceremony—first Sunday in September.

Carantec   Pardon of Notre-Dame-de-Callot—Whit Monday.
Pardon of Saint-Carantec—third Sunday in July.
Blessing of the Sea—first Sunday after 15 August.

Carnac   Festival of the menhirs—third Sunday in August.
Pardon procession—second Sunday in September.

Concarneau   Festival of the Blue Nets—third Sunday in August.

Erquy (near Cap d'Erquy, Saint-Brieuc bay)   Festival of the Sea—first Sunday in August.

Faouët le   Pardon of Sainte-Barbara—last Sunday in June.

Fedrun Isle (in the nature park north of Saint-Nazaire)   Brière festival and barge race—15 August.

Folgoët (north-east of Brest) le   Great Pardon—first (or sometimes second) Sunday in September.

Fouesnant (south-east of Quimper)   Pardon of Sainte-Anne—26 July, or sometimes the following Sunday.

Guingamp   Breton dance festival—mid-August for seven days.

Hennebont   Pardon procession—last Sunday in September.

Josselin   Pardon of Notre-Dame-
du-Roncier—8 September.

Locronan   Petite Troménie
pardon—second Sunday in July.

Lorient   Interceltic festival—first
two weeks in August.

Moncontour (south-east of Saint-
Brieuc)   Pardon of Saint-
Mathurin—Whit Saturday and
Sunday.

Nantes   Carnival—fourth Thursday
and third Sunday before Easter.

Paimpol   Newfoundland and
Iceland festival—fourth Sunday in
July.

Plouguerneau (north of Brest)
Pardon of Saint-Peter and Saint-
Paul—last Sunday in June. Also,
pardon of St-Michel—last Sunday
in September.

Plomodiern (north-west of Quimper)
Menez-Hom folk festival—15th
August.

Pont-Aven   Festival of the Golden
Gorse—first Sunday in August.

Quintin   Pardon of Notre-Dame-de-
Deliverance—second Sunday in
May.

Sainte-Anne-d'Auray   The Great
Pardon—26 July.

Saint-Jean-du-Doigt (north-east of
Morlaix)   Pardon of the Fire—
Last Sunday in June.

Sainte-Anne-la-Palud   Great
Pardon—last Sunday in August
and the following Tuesday.

Vannes   Festival of Arvor—15
August.

Public Holidays

New Year's Day—January 1
Easter Sunday and Monday
Labour Day—May 1
Ascension Day—May 28
Whitsun Sunday and Monday
National Day—July 14
Assumption Day—August 15
All Saints' Day—November 1
Armistice Day—November 11
Christmas Day—December 25
Boxing Day (Alsace and Lorraine
only)—December 26

Official holidays which fall near the beginning or toward the end of any given
week are usually extended to ensure a
long weekend. This is known as *le pont*
(the bridge).

How To Use
This Guide

In the interest of simplicity and di-
rectness of reference, this guide book
is divided into four geographic areas
rather than into political *départements*.
There is a sound practical reason for
this. The reader, who in any case will
choose his or her own destinations
eventually, will be able to assess the
visitor-appeal of the *whole* quarter of
Brittany under review, instead of having to collate a mental list of neighbouring high-spots which may be close
to one another on the ground as it
were, but many pages apart in a guide
restricted to dealing with the *départements* individually.

Thus the first part—Breton
Marches—treats the entire terrain of
Brittany, so-named, from the English
Channel to the Atlantic coast. This

section takes in the two large *départements* of Ille-et-Vilaine and Loire-Atlantique in part with their collective treasures, including a majestic string of castles and châteaux along the north–south route. Additionally, this part embraces all that is most French within the peninsula, as opposed to Breton, so that those who seek French ambience as a holiday essential (characteristically, gastronomically and linguistically) will find it almost undiluted in the eastern sector. Finally, if the weather is doubtful at the northern end, this part also covers the direct route to the south, to the river Loire, the Atlantic coast and possibly a significant climatic improvement.

Families with children, who demand nothing more than a surfeit of sun, sea and sand, will find their fair share of such delights all along the Atlantic coast. Again, this is treated in its entirety in the second section from the Loire estuary to the far western Crozon peninsula, taking in a corner of Loire-Atlantique, Morbihan and Finistère *départements.* Apart from the beaches, all the finest natural features and some quite remarkable historic and prehistoric landmarks are pinpointed along the way.

The third part covers the green and largely pastoral hinterland, where those who are imaginatively stirred by Celtic tales of half-truth and legend can still stand in certain mystical spots, where spine-tingling vibrations of long-distant past may yet be felt. More pragmatically, this is the Brittany beloved by the walker, the cyclist, the inland waterway explorer, and the horse-rider—in short, the active pursuit enthusiast. From Huelgoat and Menez-Hom in the west, to the fairy-tale forest of Paimpont in the east, this is the Brittany of quiet back lanes which—despite the march of progress—is still largely rustic and timeless Breton in places.

The fourth part of the guide encompasses what is arguably the most dramatic of all France's seaboards: the Brittany Channel coast from the Bay of Saint-Michel to Brest. In between lie the most regal of towering cliffs, medieval gems like Saint-Malo and Dinan, seaside resorts of international renown and fishing villages scarcely touched by our contemporary hustle and bustle. Some of the finest seafood restaurants in the world exist here, served by colourful markets like Paimpol; itself a revelation to any fish-fancying gourmet for the quantity and variety of edible marine riches displayed and avidly snapped up.

Each area, then—distinctly different, and quite surprisingly extensive considering the ostensible compactness of the peninsula—may legitimately be considered as a self-contained touring ground in its own right. Conversely, two, three, or even all four sections may be tackled clockwise or anti-clockwise, according to personal whim and leisure time available. Whatever the options chosen, this four-way division of the country in question should ensure that none of the acknowledged scenic treasures are missed, and that transit routes to them are, where possible, the most practical yet interesting for the traveller.

Just the Essentials

On a first-time visit to Brittany, you may be overwhelmed by the sheer wealth of choices you have wherever you start. The major landmarks and places to see and visit are proposed here to help you establish your priorities.

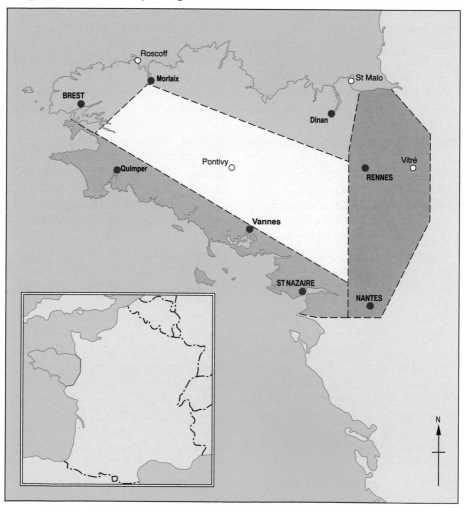

The Breton Marches

Mont-Saint Michel
Fougères Château: (reputed) largest
  castle in western Europe
Vitré: fortified township
(further afield)—la Roche aux Fées
  and fine megalithic burial site
—Dompierre-du-Chemin: Saut de
  Roland (Roland's Leap)
Rennes: church of Saint Germain
  (15th-century flamboyant Gothic)
Châteaubriant: stronghold
(surrounding area)—Carrière des
  Fusillés: World War II memorial
(further afield)—Ancenis: pleasant
  historic town
—Clisson: château ruin
Nantes: passage Pommeraye, a 19th-
  century shopping arcade
—Château of the Dukes of Brittany
(further afield)—Saint-Philbert:
  Caroligman abbey-church; original
  marble sarcophagus of St Peter

The Brittany Hinterland

Menez-Hom: highest point of
  Monagnes Noires 300 m (1,000 ft)
Huelgoat: delightful region of natural
  beauty
—Maison de la Faune Sauvage la
  Forêt in Shrignac
Guerlédan: man-made barrage lake
—Bon Répos Abbey
—les Forges-des-Salles: 18th-century
  hamlet
Kernascléden: Flamboyant Gothic
  church, 15th century
Josselin: gracious château and Gothic
  church
(surrounding area)—Saint-Marcel:
  hamlet with indoor/outdoor
  museum of occupied Brittany
(further afield)—Rochefort-en-Terre:
  Chemin des Douves
—Château de Comper
—Paimpont village: attractive Sylvan
  setting

The Atlantic Coast

La Baule-les-Pins: trees, flowers, parks
Guérande: medieval town
le Brière: designated nature park
la Roche-Bernard: ancient historical site
Vannes: 18th-century château
Golfe du Morbihan: glorious nautical
  harbour
(surrounding area)—Sarzeau: 13th-
  century château de Suscinio
—Sainte-Anne-d'Auray: 15 and 26
  July, religious *pardon*
Quiberon Peninsula: "Côte Sauvage"
Belle Ile: Brittany's largest offshore
  island
Port-Louis: harbour with medieval
  citadel
Pont-Aven: main haunt of Gaugin,
  delightful riverside walks
Quimper—Cornouaille festival: 4th
  Sunday in July
(surrounding area)—Pont-l'Abbé:
  dignified and unhurried
(surrounding area)—Pointe du Raz:
  majestic headland
Locronan: tiny medieval jewel

The Channel Coast

Cancale—oyster capital of Brittany
Saint Malo
Saint-Servan-sur-Mer: Tour Solidor
Dinard: car-free Promenade-du-Clair-
  de-Lune
Dinan: medieval gem!
—Saint-Sauveur's church
(further afield)—Jugon-les-Lacs: rural
  Breton settlement
—Cap Fréhel: dramatic headland
Montcoutour: ancient fortress château
Binic: port and traditional fishing
  village
(further afield)—la Dernière Sou: plage
  Bonaparte; beach-allied landings
Paimpol: working port, market town
Longuivy: pretty fishing harbour
Tregastel-Plage: pink (granite)
  boulders
(further afield)—Saint-Thégonnec: fine
  Breton Parish close
Brest: Oceanopolis (marine) pavilion
—Pointe de Saint Mathien:
  atmospheric 16th-century ruined
  abbey

Going Places with Something Special in Mind

Wherever you happen to travel in Brittany along main road routes, there will always be a wealth of seductive detours. Many will be signposted, indicating places or sites of special interest, while others will simply point out village place names. Here then, is a selection of Breton leisure routes, pin-pointing not only some of the more orthodox holidaymaker circuits, but many of the lesser-known regional high spots, together with the most scenic access routes. None need be followed slavishly, of course, though part of any should prove rewarding to pursue.

Parish Closes

Morlaix is the starting point for the classic religious art objectives of the region, the great majority of which are located in ancient Lower Brittany. Between the medieval stone clusters, the scenery is primarily rustic, partially alongside the river Elorn and touching upon the fringe of the Monts d'Arrée.

1 SAINT-THEGONNEC
Has a Triumphal arch, Calvary (1610)

*W*herever you go in *Brittany, you will find religious overtones, like this shrine at Port Blanc.*

and ossuary (1676). There is a fine sepulchre with carved wooden figures—one of Brittany's best.

2 LAMPAUL-GUIMILIAU
Has a triple-cross triumphal arch and 17th-century Calvary and ossuary. Interesting church interior (16th century), with carved wooden panels of St Peter and St Paul.

3 BODILIS
Enclosure with flamboyant Gothic bell tower, 16th century.

4 LA MARTYRE
This 15th-century church is the oldest in the area; the ossuary walls are imaginatively decorated with Heaven and Hell carvings.

*P*arish closes in Brittany.

5 SIZUN
A magnificent 16th-century triple-arch church gateway is found here as well as superb wall panelling. The whole lies in an impressive setting.

6 COMMANA
Once one of Brittany's most remote parish closes, the hilltop location is delightful. The church has a Renaissance porch among other treasures dating from the 17th century.

7 LA ROCHE-MAURICE
This is the most dramatic of hilltop settings, close to a ruined feudal castle. A huge 17th-century ossuary warns visitors of their mortality through carvings of *Ankou,* Breton for "death".

*H*istoric sites in the Brittany Marches.

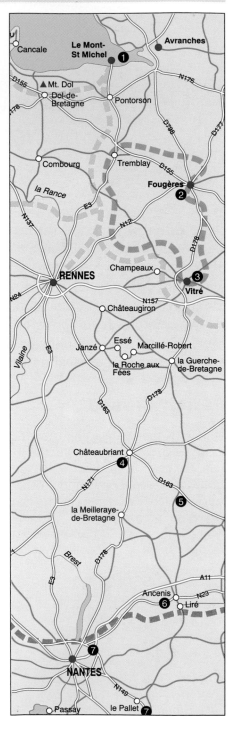

The Brittany Marches

For the student of history there could hardly be a more revealing boundary than that imaginary line between French France of the Middle Ages and the ancient, independent dukedom of Bretagne. The route is punctuated by some of the best preserved and romantic relics in northern Europe, one being rated as a world heritage site.

1 MONT SAINT MICHEL
The island fortress/abbey just inside Normandy is now treasured as one of the world's architectural wonders.

2 FOUGERES
Thirteen massive towers guard this 12th- to 15th-century fortress, a majestic example of Breton military architecture.

3 VITRE
Here is another glorious castle and a near perfectly preserved medieval town.

4 CHATEAUBRIANT
Two redoubts for the price of one here—a 13th-century fortress keep and a Renaissance château.

5 MOTTE-GLAIN
An ancient frontier fortress of the 15th century, Renaissance restored and housing many hunting trophies.

6 ANCENIS
A vital Breton defence point of the Loire during the 15th century; the river here is still a natural frontier.

7 BASSE-GOULAINE
Another ancient fortress site, reconstructed from the vestiges of medieval redoubt.

8 CLISSON
The most southerly of the old Breton strongholds. It dates from the 13th century and was once the residence of François II, among other illustrious figures of history.

The *Route des Ducs de Bretagne*

A loose-knit collection of historic high spots, collated by the French tourist office under a grand heritage trail title. Notwithstanding, they make a collective whole and seldom fail to impress the contemporary visitor through powerful architectural imagery. Below are listed some of the most exciting.

1 PONTIVY
History from the Rohan dynasty to Napoleon Bonaparte, much of it still highly visual.

2 JOSSELIN
Brittany's most celebrated fairy-tale castle. An architectural gem, and another Rohan redoubt.

3 LARGOET CASTLE
Also called the Tours d'Elven. Splendid feudal ruins, once the residence of Marshal Rieux, kinsman of François II.

4 VANNES
Here 9th-century Nominoë, founder and first Duke of Brittany, held court.

61

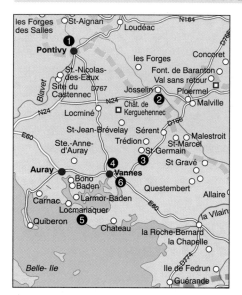

*S*ites *on the* Route des Ducs de Bretagne.

5 SARZEAU

The Château Suscinio is found here—an intimidating and massive structure and ducal residence during the 13th and 15th centuries.

6 THEIX

Château du Plessis-Josso. In this once-fortified manor lived Duc Jean III in 1330. Restored in later centuries there is much that is typical Breton here.

The Offshore Islands

With a veritable necklace of picturesque ports around the mainland of this seafaring region, it is easy to indulge in island hopping. There is a sufficiency and variety of Breton isles to fill any holiday.

1 ILE DE BREHAT

A short hop from Paimpol and very popular with birdwatchers.

2 ILE DE BATZ

For youthful leisure and an acknowledged summertime canoeist's base.

3 ILE D'OUESSANT

Brittany's most westerly territory. Notorious as a wrecker of old-time tall ships, today you can sail or fly from several points. Still largely old-world and very maritime.

4 ILE DE SEIN

A tiny beauty spot off the south Finistère coast, served by boat from Audierne in an hour's voyage which passes the rugged Pointe du Raz.

5 ILE DE GLENAN

This cluster is served by no less than four ferry ports south of Quimper. There are some nine reef-encircled islets in the group.

6 ILE DE GROIX

Big enough to boast a capital and several hamlets. Very wild and craggy but with south-facing sand beaches. Ferry service from Lorient.

7 BELLE-ILE

Brittany's biggest, most-visited island. The region in miniature, complete with a Côte Sauvage and all mod-cons for holidaymakers. Ferries ply from Quiberon.

Other sea-girt outcrops are Houat, Hoëdic, Arz, the Ile aux Moines and Molène. The dozen are known collectively as Bretagne's "string of pearls".

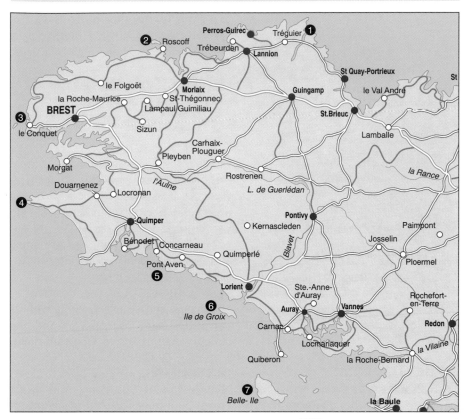

Looking at Lighthouses

The offshore islands of Brittany.

Any visitor to Brittany who has taken the ferry to the island of Ushant must have been impressed with the plethora of lighthouses and beacons dotting the potentially treacherous waters. There is a goodly selection around the edge of the Finistère mainland too. Below are just some which are either open to view, or close enough to the shore to be observed.

1 PHARE DU PORTZIC
Overlooking Brest roads, to the west of the city and close to the Tour Tanguy, arsenal and submarine base.

2 PHARE DU MINOU
Brest is 7km (4 miles) away. This lighthouse is near an old fort, orientation table and pleasant coastal footpath.

3 PHARE DE SAINT-MATHIEU
On the point of Elorn estuary, beside ancient abbey ruins and a monument to sailors lost at sea.

4 PHARE DE KERMORVAN
Nearby are sand dunes and Fort de Kermorvan, built in 1846.

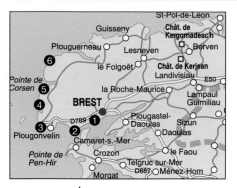

A selection of
Brittany's lighthouses.

5 PHARE DE TREZIEN

Located on the imaginary dividing line
of the Atlantic and the English Channel (or La Manche). Another memorial to lost seaman and an orientation
table.

6 PHARE DU FOUR

Warns seafarers of the notorious reefs
known as the Roches d'Argenton. It is

offshore of the tiny port on an impressive section of the Côte Sauvage.

Little Towns and Villages of Character

First-time visitors to Brittany, or those
who adhere to principal routes, frequently miss some of the best of the
venerable Breton settlements. Josselin
or Vannes, Dinard or Dinan are seldom overlooked; but here are some
less obvious scenic high spots.

1 COMBOURG

Romantic and visually exciting with its
great château, old quarter and the
mighty man of letters, Chateaubriand.

2 BECHEREL

South-west of Combourg; old textile
town on a once-fortified promontory.

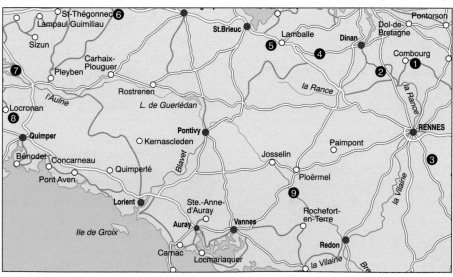

*L*ittle towns and villages of character.

64

3 CHATEAUGIRON
South-east of Rennes, with old streets and a formidable medieval keep at the heart of the cluster.

4 JUGON-LES-LACS
Rustic Brittany, complete with old church and manor house, surrounded by woodland and graced by a 100-hectare (250-acre) lake. Between Dinan and Lamballe.

5 MONCONTOUR
A beautifully located and splendidly preserved hilltop village, once fortified and still very atmospheric. Situated south-east of Saint-Brieuc.

6 GUERLESQUIN
Where ancient Léon, Tregor and Cornouaille meet south-east of Morlaix is another remnant of long-gone Bretagne. The old fortified prison, the town hall, church and fountains all reflect a bygone age.

7 LE FAOU
This tiny port on the Brest estuary was once a Roman signal station. It is very attractive at high water, with picturesque old houses and a 16th-century church.

8 LOCRONAN
Unquestionably, one of the best-preserved granite-built villages of north-western France. Lies north-west of Quimper and should not be missed.

9 MALESTROIT
More splendid remnants of medieval Brittany here, plus one of the best World War II open-air museums in France close by, south of Ploërmel.

Wine and Cider Centres

Too far north for viticulture nowadays, the four official *départements* have had no vineyards of note since Roman times. In the fifth, however (the erstwhile *Loire Inférieure*), the sun shines just that much more brilliantly and the south-facing banks of the great river are very vine-friendly.

1 ANCENIS
This extreme south-eastern corner of old Brittany is renowned for Muscadet, that most palatable of white wine.

2 NANTES
South-east and south-west vineyards flourish, producing Muscadet and Gros Plant of white, red or rosé.

3 SAINT-PHILBERT
In the heart of marais country stands this church, one of the oldest in France, and which is surrounded by Muscadet vineyards.

4 VALLET
A picturesque village devoted to the grape and a much favoured wine-tasting centre. Here the subtly different Muscadet de Sèvre et Maine is produced.

5 CLISSON
Romantically Italianate, this town on the Sèvre river centres on both Muscadet and Muscadet de Sèvre et Maine growing regions.

6 PORNIC
Inland of this seaside resort, Gros

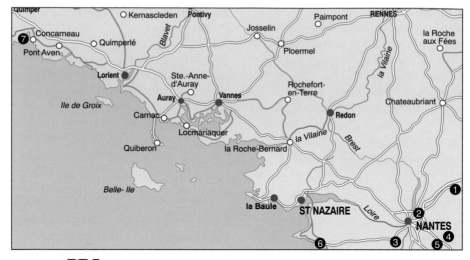

*W*ine and cider
centres in Brittany.

Plant de Pays Nantais is produced, a wine which, like the others, goes so well with *fruits de mer*.

7 FOUESNANT
Far from the Loire, in south Finistère near Quimper, is the Breton cider capital, most famous for its Fête des Pommiers held in midsummer. This refreshing (and heady) brew is popular throughout western Brittany.

Game and Coarse Fishing Water

The biggest single participant sport in France. The angling potential in Brittany is wide and handsome—salmon-fishing is available on a few rivers following two decades of pollution clean up, while fly fishing is possible in all

départements. There are 33 angling clubs in Côtes d'Armor alone, a region that contains 20 fishing lakes, large and small.

BLAVET RIVER
Between Pontivy and Hennebont—has several salmon reaches (seasonal).

AULNE RIVER
Between Carhaix-Plouguer and Châteaulin—boasts some good trout fishing stretches.

VILAINE RIVER
Between Rennes and Redon—game and coarse fish including pike.

RANCE RIVER
South-east of Dinan—some good angling stretches in scenic surroundings.

GUERLEDAN LAKE
Almost a 400-hectare (1,000-acre) inland sea, this barrage water is also traversed by pretty reaches of the Nantes—Brest canal. Mur-de-Bretagne is the principal lakeside village.

66

SAINT-MICHEL LAKE

Secluded Lac de Saint-Michel in Armorica nature park (west of Huelgoat), is a relaxing rod and line reservoir.

Gardens Open to Visitors

Some of the quieter delights of France are the many formal gardens to be found gracing château or manor house surroundings. Brittany is not overly blessed, though there are eight which are well worth seeing.

1 CHATEAU DE TREVAREZ

Many flower varieties—27 km (17 miles) north-east of Quimper.

2 JARDIN DE LA BALLUE

Imaginative floral themes and a maze—Marches, 41 km (25 miles) north of Rennes.

3 PARC DU CHATEAU DE CARADEUC

A spacious park laid out in classical style; ornamental lake—35 km (21 miles) north-east of Rennes.

4 LE MONTMARIN

A *jardin anglais*-style blended with a *jardin français* here on terraces above the Rance river—10 km (6 miles) south of Saint-Malo.

5 LE THABOR

Laid out in 1865, sculpture figures

*G*ardens worth seeing which are open to visitors.

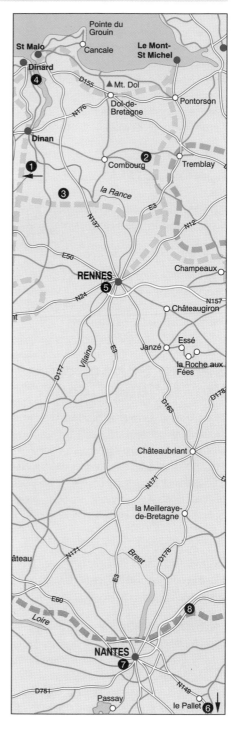

67

share traditional and exotic plant beds of the city-centre green space—place Saint-Mélaine, Rennes centre.

6 PARC DE LA GARENNE-LEMOT

A neo-classical estate created in the 19th century by local sculptor Frédéric Lemot—5 km (3 miles) south-east of Clisson.

7 JARDIN BOTANIQUE DE NANTES

Another city green space created on an historic site in rue Gambetta.

8 LES FOLIES SIFFAIT

Loire valley romantic ruins of hanging gardens and flowered terraces, with fine views—Le Cellier 25 km (15½ miles) north-east of Nantes.

Sailing School on the Holiday Coast

The Côtes d'Armor is blessed by some of the best beaches and cliff formations along the northern Brittany seaboard. Some of the resorts provide superb facilities for watersports learners, be they potential sailors, wind surfers, sea-canoeists, or sand-yacht racers.

LE VAL-ANDRE

Sailing and wind surfing are available off one of the finest sand beaches in Brittany.

PERROS-GUIREC

The La Baule of the northern coast, boasting one of the largest leisure boat harbours and super sand beaches. Every nautical pursuit may be followed here from cruising to windsurfing.

SAINT-CAST-LE-GUILDO

A municipal sailing school open all year round and catering especially for school parties.

TREBEURDEN

The sailing school here also caters to youngsters, taking boarders and day pupils.

PAIMPOL

The *Auberge de Jeunesse* (youth hostel) is also a very popular sea-canoeing school, and is open all year.

Brittany for Youngsters

Acknowledged as one of the finest family holiday regions in France, there are a number of places with special child appeal—both inland and around the extensive coastline. Many are not only fun to visit but also educational in the nicest way.

1 TREBEURDEN

North-west of Lannion is a resort almost tailor-made for children. Many supervised activities, including watersports.

2 PLEUMEUR-BODOU

Between Trébeurden and Lannion. Space-station communication centre and old-world Celtic village nearby, all very instructional.

3 SAINT-MARCEL

Near Malestroit. Brittany's finest outdoor World War II museum. Fascinating and extensive display of wartime realism.

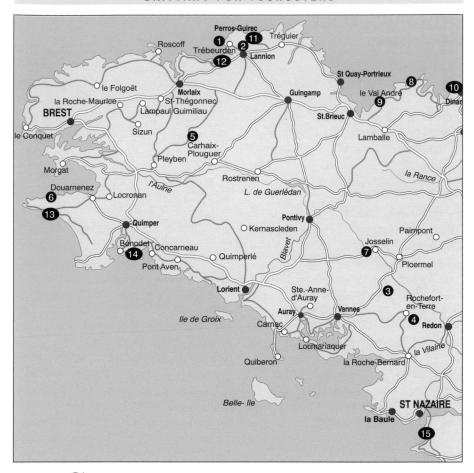

Sites for youngsters in Brittany and positions of the best beaches.

4 MALANSAC

Le Parc de Préhistoire, 2 km (1 mile) from Rocheford-en-Terre. The life of early man is re-created in the huge, lake-dotted slate quarry. There are some magnificent, realistic tableaux of hunting scenes and primitive life.

5 HUELGOAT

Armorica nature park. Le Roche Tremblante and other deep woodland attractions of a rocky nature are here. The Grotte du Diable is a favourite.

6 RESERVE DU CAP SIZUN

North-west of Audierne. Evocative wild setting and one of Brittany's finest sea-bird sanctuaries. A must for the nature-loving child.

7 JOSSELIN

All that one might expect of a typical French medieval castle with the bonus of the famous dolls museum.

Brittany's Best Beaches

There are sandy coves and sea-bathing places all around the peninsula coastline, and the waters are relatively unpolluted. Safe bathing areas are plentiful, but be careful, especially if children are in the party, for tidal flow can be strong. All the spectacular sands are in the north and west.

8 SABLES-D'OR-LES-PINS

Majestic sweeps hereabouts, backed by dunes and pine trees, on the western flank of cape Fréhel.

9 LE VAL-ANDRE

Arguably one of the finest sand beaches in Brittany, below a scenic headland footpath.

10 DINARD

Glittering sands, backed by a very swish resort infrastructure. Like La Baule, a poser's paradise.

11 PERROS-GUIREC

Largest seaside fun-centre on the Channel coast. Another beautiful sand beach on the grand scale.

12 TREBEURDEN

Fast-growing family resort. Fine sandy beaches, offshore islets, lots of appeal for children and teenagers.

13 AUDIERNE

One of the best beaches in the far west, together with the Bay of Trespasses sandy sweeps.

14 BENODET

Small (by Brittany standards), but beautifully kept and part of a grand estuary setting.

15 SAINT-BREVIN-LES-PINS

Pride of Loire-Atlantique's southwestern corner. A succession of fine sand beaches are found between here and the pretty resort of Pornic.

Exploring on Horseback

For an ever-increasing number of people, equestrian travel is now a favourite. In pastoral Brittany this great upsurge of interest is reflected by an escalating string of stables, most of which specialize in trekking. Treading the rustic bridleways, inland or coastal, can be richly rewarding. Below are some of the recognized riding centres.

COTES D'ARMOR

Saint-Cast, Trégastel, Lamballe and Plourivo (where horse-drawn carriage hire is also available).

ILLE-ET-VILAINE

Combourg, Vitré and Fougères (especially scenic to the north-west, where there are stables at Saint-Germain-en-Cogles).

MORBIHAN

Hennebont and Pontivy (canal towpath riding is on offer here) and at Elven, conveniently close to Vannes.

LOIRE-ATLANTIQUE

Clisson, Saint-Philbert-de-Grand-Lieu and Pornic. All the riding centres are reasonably close to Nantes.

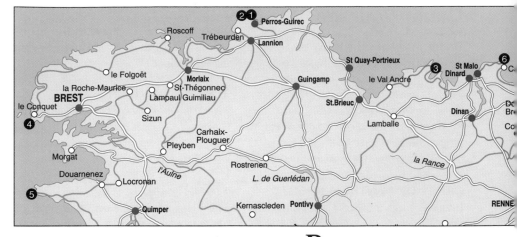

FINISTERE

Quimper, Quimperlé, Pont-l'Abbe, Morlaix and Daoulas. The latter is located in one of the region's less visited areas.

Roseate Rocks and Dramatic Headlands

A unique attraction of the north Breton coast is the blushing boulders of the Côte de Granit Rose which really do glow in certain lights and are almost as dramatic as the renowned Brittany belvederes.

1 PLOUMANACH

Now almost an appendage of Perros-Guirec, the giant pink boulders here are distinctive enough to warrant individual names, for example Napoleon's Hat.

2 TREGASTEL

The beach here, west of Ploumanach, displays more weird-shaped mighty pink rocks, notably The Thimble and The Witch.

*B*rittany's dramatic headlands.

3 FORT-LA-LATTE

Splendidly remote and rugged and setting for the film classic *The Vikings*, this is the medieval high spot of Cap Fréhel.

4 POINTE DE SAINT-MATHIEU

Close to the most westerly point of the Breton mainland, aptly pin-pointed with a fine lighthouse, a drowned seaman's memorial and an early Christian abbey.

5 POINTE DU RAZ

Without doubt the most regal of the peninsula points. Between here and the equally majestic Pointe du Van, is the Pincer-shaped Bay of Trespasses, ringed with jagged reefs.

6 POINTE DU GROUIN

Rising quite suddenly above the flat saltings of Mont-Saint-Michel bay, this specially protected headland north of Cancale overlooks a well-populated island sea-bird sanctuary.

Canal Courses

Brittany is blessed by many man-made waterways. You don't have to be a bargee to appreciate the canals. Anglers, riders, naturalists, or simply those seeking old-world tranquility, are all drawn to the more pastoral canal stretches. There are over 650 km (400 miles) of navigable waterways here.

CANAL DE NANTES A BREST
Literally links the two great cities, and links the river Aulne in the west with the Loire in the south-east.

CANAL DU BLAVET
Uses sections of the Blavet river to link the naval base of Lorient with Pontivy; Brittany's Napoleonic canal crossway.

CANAL D'ILLE RANCE
Links Saint-Malo with Rennes, and goes via the river Vilaine through La Roche Bernard to the Atlantic.

Marine Hydrotherapy

Favourable in certain coastal areas, both geographically and climatically, sea-bathing cure centres have proved extremely successful in the treatment of certain ailments. There are seven of these *thalassothérapie* centres which are expressly Breton in origin though they are now spreading to other resorts in France.

1 QUIBERON
The biggest and best in Morbihan and the first to be established at the turn of the century. Located at the very tip of the long Quiberon peninsula.

2 CARNAC
Close to the famous prehistoric site of standing stones and the fast-growing seaside resort.

3 PERROS-GUIREC
The *thalassothérapie* centre of the Côtes d'Armor. Popular with those who would combine holidaymaking with anti-stress therapy.

4 SAINT-MALO
The Thermes Marins occupies pride of place in the old port's smartest locality. The casino here is only marginally more popular!

5 ROSCOFF
Where the founder of the "thalasso" discovered the magic properties of iodine-heavy sea air and water. There are two centres: the "Ker Lena" and the "Rockroum" institute.

6 DOUARNENEZ
In the suburb of Tréboul, the Centre de Cure Marine overlooks the great bay of Douarnenez, where the sea breezes are said to be the most efficacious in Finistère.

Pardon Parades

The distinctive Breton *pardon* is the annual day when the Roman Catholic Church smiles benignly on its faithful followers, pardoning wrongs and thus warranting a procession of thankfulness. These processions are ancient, colourful and not as solemn as they may sound. The following are some of the more important or picturesque, or both.

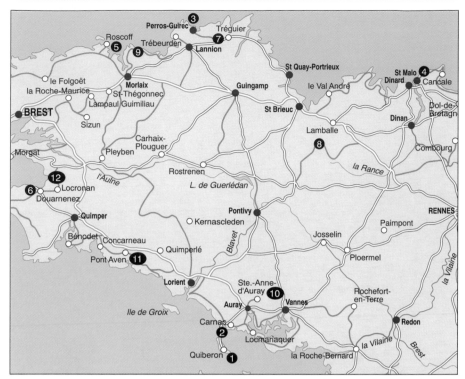

*S*ites *for marine hydrotherapy or where to experience the Breton* Pardon.

7 TREGUIER
Saint Yves procession (to the patron saint of lawyers), on the third Sunday in May. Ancient and colourful river port west of Paimpol.

8 MONCONTOUR
Film-set fortified village, off the beaten tourist track, an evocative setting for the pardon of Saint Matthew held over each Whitsun week-end.

9 ST-JEAN-DU-DOIGT
Pardon of the Fire held on the final Sunday in June. The village church here, north of Morlaix, is said to hold a strange relic—the finger of Saint John which was severed at his death.

10 ST-ANNE D'AURAY
North of Auray, this is the definitive *pardon* site of Brittany, created almost expressly as a religious centre. Hosts attend from all over France on 26 July.

11 PONT-AVEN
A *pardon* ceremony is combined with the annual Festival of Golden Gorse, held on the first Sunday in August in Brittany's most famous artist's colony.

12 LOCRONAN
One of the region's best preserved country villages of the 16th century. The Troménie ceremony is held on the second Sunday in July.

Brittany is a Super Blend of Atmosphere and Natural Splendour

Brittany embraces no less than one-third of the total coastline of France. With the healthy stimulus of a bracing climate, the rugged north-western peninsula is ideal for active holidays beside the sea. Sand-yachting or horse-riding can be enjoyed to the full in a region blessed by more than 1,000 km (600 miles) of silver sandy beaches, while inland walkers and cyclists can roam a staggering 3,000 km (1,900 miles) of bridleways.

The great French peninsula of Brittany has a landscape of outstanding natural beauty, a mild and welcoming climate, and a people with unique character; all these contribute to its great attraction as a popular yet unspoilt tourist destination. Remember also that this list omits the trio of principal holiday delights: the coastline; the cuisine; and the old-world ambience that still prevails.

A pardon *procession of thanksgiving where the traditional clothing fashions of yesteryear are always elegantly displayed.*

The province is surrounded on three sides by water, and the shoreline—which is lapped by two seas—is dramatically imposing in places and extensive enough to hold the most avid explorer. For the food gourmet the variety of seafood dishes is among the most mouthwatering to be found in France. Then there is the acknowledged aura of romance and mystery which abounds right across the hinterland. This is epitomized by Merlin the Wizard who was enchanted by the fairy nymph, Viviane. The legendary Holy Grail itself is said to lie somewhere in the forested country west of Rennes, where perhaps King Arthur and his Knights of the Round Table once held court. Lakes and legends, and forests and magical trysting places

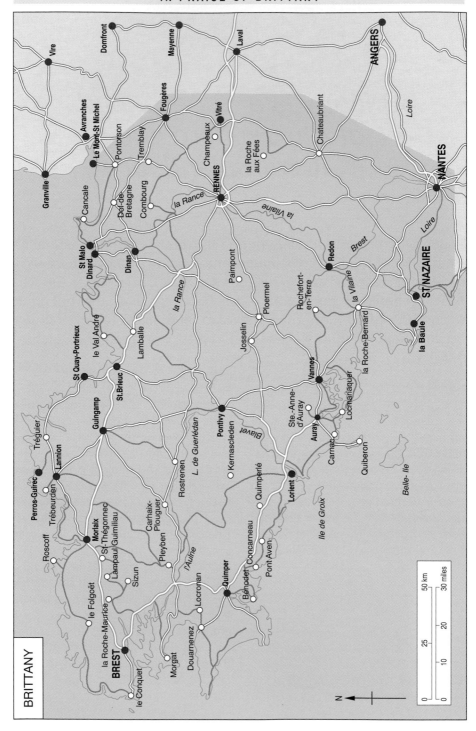

BRITTANY

N

50 km
30 miles

0   10   20   30 miles
0   25   50 km

M ap of the Brittany region showing the major towns and roads.

are an intriguing lure, where belief may be suspended awhile amid scenery that assuredly spellbound Abélard and Héloïse, and Tristan and Isolde.

Brittany is a ruggedly remote and wild land off the mainstream tracks, as invigorating and therapeutic in its way as the Western Highlands of Scotland; a region where visitors who seek genuine pastoral peace can still find it. Caesar and Charlemagne, Bonnie Prince Charlie and Gauguin, Jules Verne and Jacques Tati, Chateaubriand and Honoré de Balzac all found the Brittany peninsula strongly magnetic in one way or another and there is yet diverse allure for the contemporary traveller. This includes numerous fun places within the boundaries of a premier seaside province which might almost have been created with the holidaying family in mind.

Typical of the delights are the 5 km (3 mile) silver-sand beach of La Baule, the splintered grandeur of the Finistère headlands, or a mixture of fine sand and splendid cliffs such as may be enjoyed in the vicinity of Saint-Malo or Dinard. Concarneau and Carnac offer sun, sand and sea, while the latter is also world-renowned for its tangible and remarkable face of prehistoric France, displayed through the strange legions of standing stones, as timeless and as mystifying as England's Stonehenge.

T angible evidence of prehistoric France is everywhere on show throughout the peninsula. These strangely shaped stones are at Carnac.

Cycle touring is increasingly favourite with visitors to France, while machine hire, on a daily or weekly basis, is readily available.

For active leisure Brittany is variously blessed. The small-boat enthusiast can compete against some of the trickiest offshore sailing waters in the world at one extreme, or at the other can drift the serene canal network which includes a devious waterway link between the English Channel and the Atlantic Ocean. In between, there are countless sheltered bays where windsurfing and every other type of aquatic sport may happily be pursued. Sea angling from a boat or the fore-shore is popular and fruitful, while the game and coarse fishing potential is wide along the principal rivers and estuaries. Skin-diving and underwater fishing are promoted at many resorts along the Atlantic Coast, especially in the vicinity of Concarneau and from Belle-Ile, offshore of Quiberon.

Cyclists have hundreds of kilometres of minor country roads to explore, many of which are virtually free of motor traffic for much of the year, and which are interesting, seldom exhaustively hilly and with habitation and comfort stations in reasonable profusion. Walkers have a skein of *Sentiers de Grande Randonnée* hiking trails criss-crossing the interior and tracing the coastline, often through territory that has remained pastorally much the same for centuries. For those keen on nature study, casual rambling and camping *à la ferme*, there are many wildlife reserves, way-marked footpaths and bounteous low-cost accommodation units, often amid surroundings that are as fascinating and revealingly different as any in France.

The way in which Brittany differs from the rest of France is also emphasized through the traditional festivals, or *pardons*, which stem directly from the Middle Ages and which Brittany alone of all the official French *régions* still celebrates. These colourful ceremonies which predominate through the summer months perpetuate not only religious belief, but also a seafaring past when every Breton was said to have salt-water in the veins. The Bretons are still a maritime people at heart, with a staunch love of the sea and, by implication, of the out-doors and Nature in all her moods. This engenders an easy, uncomplicated attitude to life which most visitors find refreshingly attractive.

Apart from the unique nature of the peninsula's appeal, there is also the unmistakable stamp of France and the French, which for any Francophile is, of course, an absolutely vital ingredient. The warp and weft of Gallic influence which overlays the diligently preserved Celtic past is reflected in the high standard of traveller service,

*B*reton France of the ancien régime, *admirably displayed by the great castle of Combourg where Chateaubriand spent his childhood.*

dispensed with civilized *politesse* in the main, and coupled nowadays with an infrastructure that is as modern and efficient as any in western Europe.

As for the France of the *ancien régime,* of castles and châteaux, Brittany has but a scattering compared to the Loire or Dordogne regions; the ungiving Brittany granite, bane of the old-time stonemasons, is largely responsible for the dearth. Nonetheless, there is the Chateaubriand Trail, revealing some twenty castles and manors in Upper Brittany, along an ancient and once very turbulent frontier, the Breton Marches. If individual strongholds or stately homes are quite thinly distributed, there are some towns outstanding for their historic centres, for example, Saint-Malo and Concarneau. These contain all their architectural treasures (either restored or original) within fully walled ramparts.

In brief, Brittany offers primarily the simple and healthy outdoor life. For the majority of visitors—particularly those with children—this is enough. There is sophistication aplenty in the bigger cities such as Nantes, Brest, and swish—and expensive—resorts like Dinard. In the main, however, it is the sea, the green and peaceful hinterland and the majestic wide-sky and wide-horizon aspects of the peninsula that tug and hold an increasing number of visitors who yearn to recharge their physical and spiritual batteries. Breathing the iodine-rich ozone and winding down in some fishing village or hamlet that time has passed by, it does appear that mild Brittany bestows not only a high level of holiday enjoyment, but a health-boost bonus of the most invigorating kind.

Dream-time Brittany

Romantic and mystical, with one of its crucial eras of development totally undocumented, it is little wonder that the peninsula is shrouded in legendary mist. The very location of the sea-swept landscape—harshly forbidding in places even today—engenders myth and mysticism to absorb and fascinate all those with a receptive imagination, coupled with an affinity with the past.

In the early Middle Ages Brittany became supremely synonymous with tales of the supernatural, of dragons and drowned cities, and of gallant heroes and seductive enchantresses. There were darker sagas too, more tangible and tinged with truth, of human sacrifice perpetrated by a long-gone race, whose existence could be proved indisputably through the plethora of megaliths surviving centuries, apparently oblivious to erosion. Such is the stuff of which magic is made, more than worthy of respect for the unknown which has been instilled into succeeding generations.

The Brittany peninsula is still a land where belief can be enjoyably suspended and where, from tiny seeds of past intelligence, one can gain at least the semblance of images revealing those early tribal inhabitants, and a smattering of understanding about subsequent Breton folklore. All of this makes any holiday visit to the Atlantic-battered promontory that much richer and rewarding.

When you gaze upon one of those strange standing stones topping some hillock that may even today be distant from a modern settlement, consider that it has probably stood thus for a period of time almost inconceivable to grasp—long before the arrival of the Gauls, the first recorded inhabitants of the peninsula, and in some cases for as long as 7,000 years. Merely contemplating the logistics of transportation and subsequent positioning of these massive stones, often weighing hundreds of tons, will stir wonder in the beholder. In an era of the most primitive technology, why were these enigmatic markers erected, and why are so many confined primarily to Brittany, culminating in multi-stone circles like those at Camaret-sur-Mer and the world-renowned serried ranks of Carnac?

No definitive answer will ever be forthcoming. Not even the most intensive, prolonged and sophisticated scientific probings have produced any really satisfactory explanations. Theories aplenty abound of course, all of which bounce off the impervious granite blocks, leaving them a permanent and exasperating enigma. The best and broadest guess about the Breton megaliths—be they menhir, dolmen or cromlech—is that they were ritual or burial sites. Beyond that the experts are baffled; a heartening thought in an age when there is a compulsion to strip every vestige of mystery from the world about us and beyond. Some of the Breton megaliths are linked with Stonehenge and Druidic rites, but these claims are no more authentic than the theory of the sea-swallowed Breton city of Ys, or the forest of Paimport (Brocéliande) being the home of the Knights of the Round Table.

And yet there *are* still tiny pockets of a once mighty forest west of Rennes, where vibrations of an earlier world still tremble, if ever so faintly. Among the ancient ash and beech trees, where it is still difficult to navigate whether on foot or in a car, leprechauns and ogres lurk, merely in suspended animation according to some Breton folklore. Here too, the ghosts of King Arthur, Merlin,

Lancelot and Guinevere dwell, their outlines brought to sharper focus at shrines like the Val-sans-Retour, the spine-tingling remnants of isolated Comper château and the elusively hidden Fontaine de Barenton, where Breton rainmakers have invoked storms since the Dark Ages in times of drought—the last incidentally, early this century.

At La Roche aux Fées Celtic myth cloaks a very solid pile. These fairy rocks, south-east of Rennes, are one of the finest megalithic burial sites in Brittany, yet the site was for centuries more famous throughout rustic Brittany as a match-making place. There is also, in hinterland Finistère, and deep in the ancient forest of Argoat near Huelgoat, a location of more sinister repute. The

Carved gargoyle on a medieval dwelling in Malestroit. This one is typical of the Breton talismans which were displayed to ward off evil spirits.

moss-cloaked giant boulders of the Devil's Grotto, a watery, rock-girt fastness are intimidating even now and are where mystic sacrifices were once said to have been performed.

In short, it would be perfectly possible to spend a holiday visiting the many and varied of Brittany's legendary and fabled sites. It is not at all a bad touring objective searching for and subsequently contemplating these timeless fragments, which survive from a period when the life of man was infinitely simpler than today, yet certainly no less exciting, one way or another.

To discover something of a pastoral Breton life-style closer to your own, you have to join the multitudes of indigenous visitors who gather at all those well attended regional fête days. Many of these symbolic and colourful celebrations are held throughout the summer months and some are really magnificent displays of both religious and secular splendour, the participants resplendent in elaborate local costume. All the bigger towns and cities of Brittany hold annual carnivals (often combined with *pardon* pilgrimage processions), but so do many backwater market towns and villages. These normally sleepy and slow-paced settlements often arrange those truly authentic and surprisingly animated Breton feast days which stem from the distant past. Tressignaux near Guingamp in Cotes-d'Amour is just one example of a magnificent combined *pardon* and fête, held at the end of August.

Alternatively, for fun on a really grand scale, Quimper, capital of Cornouaille at the heart of southern Finistère, is the annual venue for one of the grandest city festivals in France. Every July, the old town is transformed by distinctive Breton music, dance and traditional costume of eye-catching opulence. The celebrations go on for a week, and are attended by thousands of people— many of whom are folklore enthusiasts—from all over Brittany, the numbers being swelled by Celtic contingents from farther afield, especially Scotland, Ireland, Wales and England's West Country.

At such events as this you can hear Brezoneg, that unique Breton tongue descended from ancient Celtic roots, a language it was forbidden to speak until very recently by the French authorities who were never totally sure of their high-spirited and proud peninsula subjects. Almost eradicated where it was once widespread, Brezoneg survives, and indeed is being actively revived, especially in areas where the most ancient and enduring of Breton festivals are still celebrated.

At the Quimper gatherings, as elsewhere, you may hear snatches of the old Breton language spoken by men and women, dressed as they might have been 200 years ago. You may also hear the plaintive skirl of Breton bagpipes, every bit as ancient as their Scottish and Irish counterparts, and accompanied by strangely unfamiliar wind instruments and the drone of the hurdy-gurdy.

Finally, for a people so reliant on the sea for survival it is fitting that annual homage is paid to the bountiful coastal waters of Brittany. Nowhere in the peninsula is this demonstrated more fervently or impressively than at the Concarneau Fête des Filets Bleus (Festival of Blue Nets) in late August. The only surprise about this massively attended event, is that it is essentially a 20th century celebration! There are, however, numerous other sea-blessing processions held at many fishing ports and villages that have been performed since the arrival of the Christian religion, and probably in pagan version long before that.

For the History Buff here is the Heritage Trail of Medieval Bretagne

This is frontier country, scenically gentle compared to the north and western coasts, but as blood-soaked historically as any in Brittany. Punctuated by evidence of medieval splendour like Fougères and Vitré, where the echoes of clashing arms can still faintly be heard, here is a splendid field lesson of old France—especially for the back-lane driver travelling between Mont-Saint-Michel and the Loire.

Ille-et-Vilaine

A telling clue to the type of terrain that predominates throughout the great swathe of country that is the Breton Marches is unmistakably revealed on entry from neighbouring Normandy. Approaching Brittany via the Freedom Road south of Avranches where the kilometre posts commemorate World War II liberation, the landscape

As with everywhere else throughout France there is every type of eating house ready to give its service in most towns, often in delightfully atmospheric settings.

becomes increasingly flat and treeless, while looming ever present, ever more clearly and tantalizingly close, is that priceless treasure of the western world and the most visited site in France: **Mont-Saint-Michel**.

Indeed, the Mont appears at certain times and in certain light, as if it could be touched from the circuitous road that winds around the eastern end of the vast Bay of Saint-Michel. This is a deceptive illusion, however, for the most direct approach is from Pontorson, just inside the Normandy boundary, where the holy isle is just 9 km (5 ½ miles) away. Ruthlessly commercialized now, wondrous to some and an over-ornate rock pile to others, the magetism of the shrine exerts less of a pull on religious travellers than it

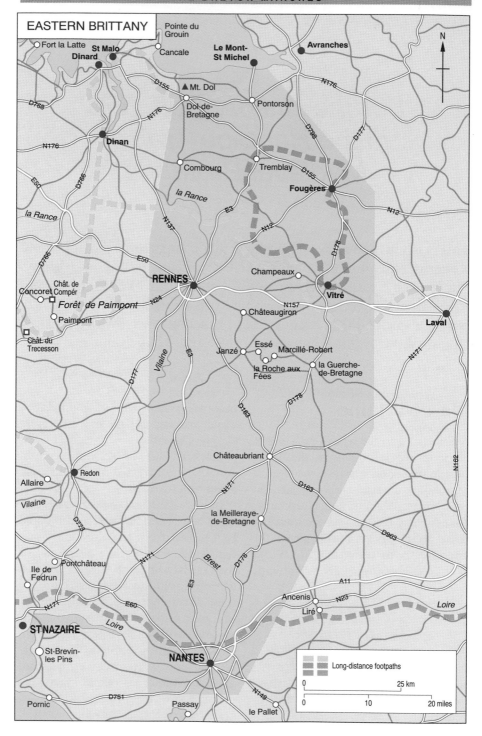

EASTERN BRITTANY

Pointe du Grouin
Fort la Latte
St Malo
Dinard
Cancale
Le Mont-St Michel
Avranches
N176
D155
Mt. Dol
Pontorson
D768
Dol-de-Bretagne
D798
D177
N176
N176
Dinan
Combourg
Tremblay
D155
Fougères
la Rance
E3
N12
N12
N157
la Rance
D766
E50
Champeaux
Vitré
Laval
D766
Chât. de Compér
Concoret
RENNES
N24
Forêt de Paimpont
Paimpont
Châteaugiron
N157
D177
D163
Chât. du Trecesson
Vilaine
E3
Janzé
Essé
Marcillé-Robert
N771
la Roche aux Fées
la Guerche-de-Bretagne
D178
D163
Châteaubriant
D163
N162
Allaire
Redon
N771
Vilaine
D775
la Meilleraye-de-Bretagne
D963
Ile de Fedrun
Pontchâteau
N771
Brest
D178
E3
A11
Ancenis
N23
Liré
Loire
ST NAZAIRE
N171
E60
Loire
St-Brevin-les Pins
NANTES
Pornic
D751
Passay
le Pallet
N149

Long-distance footpaths

0   25 km
0   10   20 miles

86

once did. It is still an almost obligatory objective for any first-time visitor to the area, so find your way to the causeway car-park and pay your dues for a memorable ascent to a memorable place.

The granite islet, at the mouth of the Couesnon river, lies almost 1.5 km (1 mile) offshore, but is linked to the mainland by a narrow causeway and is surrounded by treacherous quicksands. It is possible to walk across the mud flats at ebb tide, for the waters recede for miles hereabouts, but it is not a venture to be undertaken lightly. There are qualified guides available for those who prefer the ancient and tricky pilgrim route. The Couesnon (which was diverted to prevent escalating dyke damage), once flowed in a more north-

*M*ap *of eastern Brittany, the Breton Marches.*

M ont-Saint-Michel, *world famous sentinal of history on the Normandy/Brittany border. Guardian and treasure house of the sweeping bay since the 10th century.*

westerly direction to form the ancient frontier between Brittany and Normandy. Thus, although officially within Normandy nowadays, the Mont is also regarded as an indisputable piece of Breton heritage—especially since the mighty warrior-knight Bertrand du Guesclin (revered hero of early Breton history) used the monastic pile as his home and command post in 1366. His house, named after his wife Tiphaine, is now a museum.

The history of the shrine goes back a good deal further than the Middle Ages however. It was during the 8th century that a bishop of Avranches had a vision of the Archangel Michael, who commanded the creation of a chapel on the nearby sea-girt outcrop. Thenceforth this became sacred to pilgrims—principally from the British Isles. There is, of course, a monastic link between Mont-Saint-Michel and St Michael's Mount on the Cornish coast.

In due course something grander than a chapel was called for, and the resulting fortress-abbey was constructed from huge granite blocks quarried and transported from inland Brittany. Lying in the fiercest tidal estuary in France where the difference between high and low water can vary by as much as 14 m (46 ft), Mont-Saint-Michel is one of the greatest monuments to religious architecture anywhere in the world. It is more remarkable still since the principal construction of the massive monastery decreed by Richard, Duke of Normandy in 966, was located on the most precipitous flank of the islet. Predictably many of the early religious treasures and relics which filled the new centre of worship came from England as plunder following the Norman Conquest exactly 100 years later.

The dominant Gothic abbey, occupying the islet summit, is the culmination of 400 years of staged medieval construction and is still as much a pilgrim shrine today as it is a secular scenic magnet for others. The old part of Mont-Saint-Michel dates back to the first half of the 13th century, as evidenced by the famous Merveille (marvel) buildings. These are the architectural gems of the islet, and are half- fortress and half-residential, with the cloister being of the most sublime harmony and timeless elegance. Below the splendours of the abbey, a winding main street ascends within machicolated and turreted ramparts, reminding the visitor that the Mont was once as important militarily as it was a centre of religion. It was fought over and occupied by the armies of both France and England during the Hundred Years War, while earlier still, in 1203, the monastery was fired by Philippe-Auguste (King Philippe II of France) as part of a scorched earth policy directed against King John of England who held powerful sway at the time in this part of France. Much later in history, during the Wars of Religion, Protestant forces made many attempts to storm the fortified islet, but never succeeded.

Unquestionably, Mont-Saint-Michel is one of the most impressive of all the northern France landmarks, its glory accentuated by the uniform flatness of

Present-day Pilgrims

Invasion of Mont-Saint-Michel is benign nowadays, foot traffic inside the ramparts and along the summit road route being sustained and more or less continuous throughout the summer months. Many of the medieval houses are now souvenir shops. Like its inland counterpart, Rocamadour (the second most visited site in France), Mont-Saint-Michel has been a pilgrimage centre for countless kings and commoners throughout the ages, including Saint Louis, Louis XI and Henri IV. The religious zenith of the islet declined in the 17th century, reaching its nadir in the late 18th century when the abbey was used as a prison. It was not until the mid-19th century that a programme of extensive restoration was instigated by the state, to be subsequently executed with a degree of skilful ability for which the French are now renowned.

the surrounding coastal plain. Happily for the lcisure traveller, it is not the only gem of history which graces the one-time frontier country of the Breton Marches. Indeed, it is predominantly the historic legacy that is the great visitor attraction, for the landscape between the English Channel and the Atlantic is not exciting. A glance at any map of France will reveal no exceptional high country hereabouts, no extensive forests and mighty river courses—apart from the Loire estuary—spilling into the Atlantic at the southern extremity.

Although there is no natural grandeur here, it is a restful and pleasing country for all that—predominantly green, rustic, well tended and crisscrossed by a seemingly endless network of finely-surfaced minor roads serving a host of farming villages and hamlets. If time is available, it is possible (and distinctly pleasurable), to span the Channel–Atlantic land bridge without touching a single major traffic route. Since the terrain is gentle and settlements are so abundant and in close proximity to each other, it is eminently suitable for cycle-touring, particularly since motor traffic is light away from conurbations like Rennes and Nantes.

What is today a highly civilized and totally tamed agricultural plain country, was once very stern wilderness covered in deceptively benign looking *marais* (marshes), which appeared almost as an open door to those in the east who coveted the lands of Brittany. The area formed a natural, if not obvious, hazard to potential medieval invaders of eager avarice, for example the warlords of neighbouring Normandy, Maine and Anjou. In the Middle Ages, the countryside was far more afforested than it is now, but there were scarcely any roads, no easily navigable rivers and the whole region deteriorated into a dangerous quagmire during winter, created by undrained inlets from the Bay of Mont-Saint-Michel in the north and the great basin of the Loire in the south.

It was this inhospitable no man's land, supplemented by a string of guardian frontier strongholds, that helped to keep Brittany independent from her mightily powerful French neighbours through several turbulent centuries, even defeating wily and usually successful invaders like William I, the conqueror of England. Knowing this somehow makes any explorative journey south through these Breton Marches much more intriguing, while the significance of those fortified defences of old, which stand at intervals to this day, is not lost upon the visitor. Over the Normandy boundary, then, just west of Pontorson, you will find the first of those fascinating stone piles of the past.

Dol-de-Bretagne

One of the most exposed of all the eastern Brittany frontier posts in the Middle Ages, Dol-de-Bretagne was a fortified town constructed on a low-rise bluff, which was tide-washed until the sea receded around the 12th century. A tiny settlement, even by today's standards, the cosy and colourful old town is hugely dominated by its oversize and austere 13th century **cathedral**. Such a mighty structure looks almost out of place today, though it does emphasize the little town's erstwhile importance, for it was once the religious

89

Dol-de-Bretagne cathedral dominates the old town still. It was here that the Breton chieftan Nominoë was crowned duke of Brittany in the 9th century.

capital of the whole of Brittany province, arising from very early beginnings, when Saint-Samson left England to build a monastery on this spot, some two centuries before the founding of Mont-Saint-Michel in the 8th century. It was here that Nominoë, Celtic scourge of the Normans and hero duke of Brittany in the 9th century, was crowned. Close to Saint-Samson's is an interesting **museum** of local history, open from Easter to the end of October.

Heavily frequented by British visitors (since it is also a very strategic base for both Mont-Saint-Michel and

Saint-Malo), Dol exudes a warm and welcoming ambience, amplified quickly for strangers, because it is a compact enough town to ensure rapid orientation. There are some delightful 16th- and 17th-century houses, primarily in the **Grande-Rue des Stuarts** which also boasts a 15th-century **Maison de la Guillotière**, now an antique shop, and once a Knights Templar inn.

From the tree-lined **Promenade des Douves,** close to the main thoroughfare, there is preserved evidence of the stout medieval **ramparts** and once-deep **moat**, while to the north there is a good view of **Mont Dol**, an isolated, wooded mound, rising with exaggerated prominence from the surrounding flatlands. This granite outcrop, not dissimilar to Mont-Saint-Michel, was just an inland bluff like its more illustrious counterpart until the sea encroached around the 5th century. Unlike Mont-Saint-Michel, however, it regained its dry location when the waters finally receded. Its summit is merely graced by a restored **windmill**, but the outcrop is a valued repository of prehistory, for mammoth and other early animal remains have been unearthed by archaeologists. Early man left evidence of his existence by erecting the **Menhir du Champ-Dolent** a few kilometres

> **Mont Dol**
> To the north, the distinctive Mont Dol is crowned quite handsomely with trees, arboreal ancestors of the once vast Scissy Forest, which was swallowed by the sea during the Dark Ages. On and around the granite outcrop many tree fossils were excavated during the transforming of the marshland into fertile farming land. There are wide views of the horizon from the summit above Mont Dol village which is clustered around its 12th-century Romanesque church. You can drive around the Mont and there are easy pedestrian routes to the windmill which graces the summit of this 65 m (213 ft) high knoll.

south of the town. This massive standing stone, a 9.5 m (31 ft) pillar of granite is the first of these enigmatic, prehistoric relics to be found inside the Brittany boundary, but by no means the last!

Well able to administer to the comfort of visitors, Dol-de-Bretagne is served by some eight hotels (four with restaurants) and five *chambres d'hôtes*. There is a municipal touring site too in the rue de Dinan, close to the centre. A variety of restaurants, brasseries, and pizza parlours dispense quality fare and Dol is renowned for its seafood (the mussel beds of Mont-Saint-Michel are world-famous). And while *crêperies* are ubiquitous in Brittany, nowhere are these pancake-houses more in evidence than in the *département* of Ille-et-Vilaine. The town is a good source of leatherware souvenirs, especially footwear, including the traditional and almost indestructible wooden-soled *sabots*.

Dol, in truth, is a very popular base for short holidays—especially for

Dol museum provides an illuminating backward glimpse into medieval Bretagne, especially upon armaments and costume of that era.

visitors from the UK as it is conveniently close to the ferry ports of Saint-Malo and Cherbourg, both of which have good train connections with the historic town. Away from the hub and heart of the old town with its quaint houses and rampart remnants, there is (almost inevitably), creeping commercial and residential development, while the traffic flow (principally of heavy lorries) is irritatingly heavy at times. Despite the urgently needed bypass, this is an intriguing base which makes a pleasant and memorable impression on most Brittany explorers.

Land reclamation throughout several centuries has created marvellously fertile country around Dol, congenially inhabitable terrain which has much in common with the Dutch polders. This land-taming has only occasionally been interrupted by periods of human conflict, when fortified settlements like Dol suffered considerably. Their blackest hour was during the French Revolution when royalist sympathies were very widespread in Brittany; during one savage battle fought here, some 14,000 men were killed. Nowadays such grand-scale tragedies simply add colour.

The Dol tourist office is open all year round and dispenses useful brochures, some of which are in English, giving details on the general attractions of the town and its environs, together with information on specialized pursuits. There are, for example, a number of lakes (*étangs*) and rivers within easy reach to interest anglers, while for pedestrian explorers the long-distance GR34 footpath traverses a popular coastal link between Mont-Saint-Michel and Saint-Malo; it may be joined about 8 km (5 miles) north of Dol. Bicycles may be hired from a sports shop in the rue de Rennes.

For southbound leisure travellers, the first obligatory target along the D795 is **Combourg**, some 17 km (11 miles) from Dol. For those not unduly pressed for time, there are a couple of worthwhile detours off this pastoral and not too heavily used country road. The **Musée de la Paysannerie** (Farm Life Museum), is two minutes' drive south of the Menhir du Champ-Dolent—simply turn right towards the hamlet of Baguer-Morvan. Here you will find lots of rustic relics displayed over 2,000 m (6,500 ft) of exhibition space, creating a telling picture of pastoral life as it has evolved over a century or so. There are many implements, farm tools and materials, and an accurately reconstructed peasant farmhouse. The museum is open daily from May until September.

Further south, and on the eastern side of the D795, is the 15th-century **Château Landal**, reached by signposted minor roads. The pedestrian approach—taking about 15 minutes—is quite imposing and follows a lake and a venerable tree-lined drive. The wonderful view of the medieval fortified manor with its ramparts and round towers that this walk provides, is reward enough for most visitors. This defensive cluster is just one of many half-hidden feudal strongholds scattered throughout Ille-et-Vilaine; more testimony to the turbulent uncertainty of the Middle Ages, especially for settlements within frontier territory which were only partially protected by seasonally marshy terrain.

Combourg

For an even more impressive example of military masonry on the grand scale (combined with a blend of later, more aesthetic residential design), there is the ancient town of Combourg, gloriously lauding the landscape above a large and gracious lake. Thrown up around the time of the Norman Conquest, there are also remains of the 14th-century structure, while the main **façade** and great **Crusader Tower** date from the 15th century. Two of Brittany's most illustrious names are connected with Combourg; the du Guesclin dynasty (the first recorded owners) and, during the 18th century, the Chateaubriand family, responsible for one of France's greatest romantic writers.

Francis René Chateaubriand, Vicomte de Combourg, spent only a short period of his early life here, but much of the author's later melancholy was said to have stemmed from his time living within the cold and gloomy walls, with eccentric parents and cut off almost entirely from the outside world. Now partly a museum, the **Tour de Chat** (Cat Tower) is still owned by the Chateaubriand family and was once the boy's living quarters. It is reputed to be haunted and illustrates how depressing such a vast home must have been (particularly in winter), surrounded as it is by deep and then virtually silent woods. In the sunlight, however, and viewed from the tree-lined waterside of the castle lake, it is an impressive building, justifiably one of the great architectural prides of the *département*, along with Fougères and Vitré.

Just a short stroll from the towering walls of the castle, the township of Combourg is, by contrast, cosy and compact, retaining a vestigial patina of medieval France through old buildings like the **Maison de la Lanterne**, which now contains the *Syndicat d'Initiative*. This office is kept busy during summer, dispensing information about Combourg's most illustrious son, to a steady stream of visitors—understandably, for Chateaubriand led a very colourful life.

Born in 1768, he was urged towards the church by a mother afflicted with religious mania, but chose the army instead, perhaps to escape the oppressive atmosphere of his home life which included a morose and reclusive father. After a brief military career, he became an explorer, and following a spell of living with North American Indians, his gifted literary talent became increasingly apparent. Despite his high-born status (he was made a Knight Templar at the age of 22), he was initially in favour of the Revolution, only changing his views after his whole family, including a much-loved sister, perished during The Terror. Married in 1792 to a bride who brought with her a rich dowry, Chateaubriand himself nearly died of wounds in Belgium after fighting with the Royalists. He survived and escaped to the Channel Islands with the help of friends, and from there found his way to London, where he lived for a while in straitened circumstances

Returning home to France in 1800, he was at last lauded as a literary lion and was appointed to the French consulate in Rome by Napoleon, whom the writer eventually offended, comparing him to Nero. His life threatened, he wandered east to the

Holy Land, but his writing remained diverse and prolific, covering a swathe of subjects from romance to the fall of the Roman Empire. Subsequently much admired by his peers and even Louis XVIII after 1814, the writer was sent to several European capitals as plenipotentiary, becoming more active politically and again making more enemies than friends, including the king. His most famous mentor was his mistress of many years, Madame Récamier. He died, an octogenarian, in 1848. Despite colossal conceit, his talent was unquestionably immense and he will be remembered for his most enduring work, *Mémoires d'Outre-Tombe* (*Reflections Beyond the Grave*).

Combourg wears its mantle of national fame well, and remains a friendly and welcoming little town, modestly proud of its castle and heritage. It enjoys pleasant if not spectacular surroundings, amid dairy and cereal crop farms, the landscape one of gentle undulations dotted by sporadic stands of trees. A *Station Verte*, as befits a place of high tourist appeal, there is a choice of four comfortable hotels (one overlooking the lake), a camping site open from May to mid-September and a wide choice of bed-and-breakfast houses in the vicinity.

Like the lake below the great château, Lac Tranquille, the Maison

The legendary Lantern House of Old Combourg, now the tourist office. A fine piece of 16th-century architecture, purpose-built to lighten the medieval darkness.

de la Lanterne is also aptly named, since this distinctive 16th-century building *did* house a great lantern, which was kept burning faithfully throughout the duration of the celebrated Combourg market fairs, held annually throughout the Middle Ages. Such illumination was necessary to prevent people stealing goods from the stalls during what were otherwise extremely dark nights.

Combourg is served by the SNCF (Saint-Malo–Rennes line), and in addition to sports facilities like a heated indoor swimming pool and tennis courts, there is a popular horse-riding centre, the **Domaine de la Bouteillerie**, some 4 km (2 ½ miles) west of Combourg off the Dinan road. The centre is scenically sited and has a varied programme of equestrian activities suitable for both novice and expert riders. There is also a very good golf course at **Le Tronchet**, some 16 km (10 miles) to the north-west, while at **Becherel**, an ancient hilltop village some 15 km (9 miles) to the south-west, there is good walking along way-marked circuits, through forests over hill crests, and varying from one to six hours in duration. Some of these paths provide fine distant views, the magnificent landscaped park of nearby **Château Caradeuc** which is close by, is open to visitors during the summer.

There are two options for drivers southbound from Combourg: the first is to go directly to Rennes via the D795 and N137; the second is to go eastwards and then south, to take in Fougères and Vitré. The latter is, of course, the classic tourist route and the obvious choice of all but the most time-pressed visitors.

Fougères

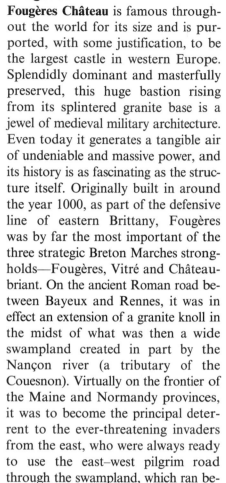

Fougères Château is famous throughout the world for its size and is purported, with some justification, to be the largest castle in western Europe. Splendidly dominant and masterfully preserved, this huge bastion rising from its splintered granite base is a jewel of medieval military architecture. Even today it generates a tangible air of undeniable and massive power, and its history is as fascinating as the structure itself. Originally built in around the year 1000, as part of the defensive line of eastern Brittany, Fougères was by far the most important of the three strategic Breton Marches strongholds—Fougères, Vitré and Châteaubriant. On the ancient Roman road between Bayeux and Rennes, it was in effect an extension of a granite knoll in the midst of what was then a wide swampland created in part by the Nançon river (a tributary of the Couesnon). Virtually on the frontier of the Maine and Normandy provinces, it was to become the principal deterrent to the ever-threatening invaders from the east, who were always ready to use the east–west pilgrim road through the swampland, which ran between Chartres and the equally rich religious centre of Dol-de-Bretagne.

The first castle, partially constructed of timber, was burned down in 1166 by Henry Plantagenet, king of England, only to be rebuilt on the orders of the ducal knight, Raoul II, who was determined to make the resurrected castle the biggest and most fiercesome in Brittany. So far as size was concerned he succeeded, but the low-lying location was decidedly suspect and distinctly tempting to potential

A section of Fougères castle, massively constructed, superbly preserved and still partially moated.

aggressors. Despite this drawback it was never a walkover. Even though now largely a shell ruin, 13 massively stout towers punctuate ramparts that are studded with siege-gun platforms, sentry walks, machicolations and copious narrow firing slits for archers.

All these towers are named (one after Raoul of course), but the Melusine Tower, close to the remnants of the original keep, is the most awesome of aspect. The medieval military engineers built a formidable fortress here, even diverting the narrow Nançon, to create an islet. This was later to be linked to the upper township by rampart spans, which could be blocked in times of war.

The old part of **Fougères town**, to the south-east of the castle, boasts a number of attractions, including a handsome **public garden**, from the terraces of which there are splendid views over the ancient settlement. The gardens are close to the **church of Saint-Leonard**, first built in the 15th century but with a much later Gothic façade. Also nearby is the old **Maison de Ville**, still intact and largely dating from the 15th century. The **place du Marchix** (the old cattle market), has a number of medieval houses and the **church of Saint-Sulpice**, built in the flamboyant Gothic style, has a distinctive 15th-century slate-covered **bell tower**. The **town belfry**, built in 1387, is one of Fougère's oldest civil structures and can be found in the rue du Belfroi.

All along the river banks, close to the comforting protection of the great castle, commercial enterprises flourished, especially the tannery trade, the manufacture of paper, flour mills and

A Massive Marches Guardian

The area around Fougères castle, enfolded by arms of the Nançon river, is very attractive and since it is really quite separate from the busy town, there is usually parking space in the immediate vicinity, notably in place Raoul II. As already stated, the castle location is almost uniquely unusual since it lies not above, but below the town. In olden times it was only the encircling river and the granite base (almost impossible to tunnel through), plus the surrounding water meadows and quagmire marshes that ensured its survival. As it was, Fougères castle was stormed successfully on several occasions, either by stealth or after protracted sieges. Among other invaders, the English took it in 1448, but the most famous warrior-knight to break in was Bertrand du Guesclin.

World War I, and which led to rapid and extensive commercial development and diversification following World War II. Evidence of this industry, much of it bland and some of it downright ugly, surrounds old Fougères in a wide swathe. The modern centre, however, is appealing in parts, particularly around the elevated **place Aristide-Briand**.

Semi-pedestrian precincts, playing fountains and a number of nice focal points like the the the **place du Théâtre** attract visiting strollers. This area is spacious, airy and very nicely renovated—much of the spaciousness was created in 1710, when a disastrous fire almost destroyed the ancient centre, and from

weaving. It was the later expansion of the leather industry that made Fougères one of the leading shoe manufacturing towns of Europe, a source of great municipal wealth up to

*F*ougères town centre *and part of the old quarter around place Aristide Briand. This area has also been diligently restored.*

that date, granite rather than wood was used for all new buildings. This is a good area for people-watching, with its popular pavement cafés and choice of quality shops. The **rue de Pinterie** is the most venerable of Fougère's streets, its name derived from the tin mugs (1pt measures), made here in profusion by artisans. The street did, however, suffer some wartime bomb damage during 1944.

For those wishing to make the town a base, the tourist office is located in place Aristide-Briand and is a good source of local knowledge. There are nine hotels in town, five with restaurants. There are a dozen recommended restaurants, together with numerous eating houses offering speciality dishes from Tunis to Vietnam, plus the ubiquitous *crêperies* and pizza houses. For self-catering visitors there are hypermarkets along the **Route de Paris** and a good choice of food stores in the centre. Fougères is served by the SNCF and is a rail terminus. There is a municipal camping site in the **Route de la Chapelle Janson**, on the eastern perimeter.

North of the town, the **Forêt de Fougères** is a much-favoured leisure area with locals. It is studded with regal beech trees among which are several megaliths and truly ancient Gallic ruins. There is also a huge cave dug in the 12th century, the **Cellars of Landéan**, where religious treasures were secreted during the Hundred Years War. There are 1,700 hectares (4,200 acres) of woods here which are criss-crossed by a number of a marked footpaths. There is also an outdoor leisure centre in the forest, **La Ferme de Chênedet** near Landéan, which has full amenities

including horse-riding, lake swimming, and a health and fitness circuit.

South of Fougères the countryside is a patchwork of neat farm fields for the most part, relieved now and then by partially wooded valleys like that of Couesnon and the other watercourse which lends its name to the *département*, the Vilaine. Of these agreeable pastoral pockets, one surrounds Vitré, the most easterly of all the old Brittany fortified towns and unquestionably the most outstanding.

Nowadays the TGV whisks through this terrain *en route* from Paris to Rennes at a speed that would have appeared quite unearthly to medieval eyes. To extract the maximum delight from this area, however, conjuring the past is more rewarding than watching the products of contemporary technology, especially hereabouts on the acknowledged Route of Castles and Châteaux.

On the modern map of France, Brittany's boundary is marked by just two neighbouring *régions*—Basse Normandy and Pays de la Loire. In the Middle Ages, around the 14th century, the dukedom was bounded from north to south by four ancient provinces—Normandy, Maine, Anjou and Poitou. The Normans of this period were still very conscious of their Viking ancestors, those founders of Normandy who were renowned for their aggressive territorial claims. Their descendants, under warrior leaders like William the Conqueror, subsequent king of England, were ever keen to expand their duchy westwards—particularly into a land of alien Celts. Normandy suffered heavily during the Hundred Years War, becoming accustomed to pillage and plunder and thus as eager to bestow as it had received.

Maine, with its important and influential capital city of Le Mans, was as keen as Normandy was to extend its territory. Anjou was for centuries little short of a permanent battlefield, more sinned against by the warlike dukes of Brittany than sinning itself, but it was a threat nevertheless, since the countship changed hands frequently (and invariably bloodily), every new takeover fuelling burning territorial ambition. Poitou, after the Treaty of Bretigny in 1360, fell under the English crown as part of greater Aquitaine, a vast region stretching from the Pyrenees almost to the Loire. Thus all the lowland territory of ancient Brittany south of the river was in constant peril from invasion, real or imagined, by the forces of perfidious Albion, as England was aptly dubbed.

From the time of 9th century Nominoë, however, Brittany always managed to have a powerful and protective champion, none more timely or courageously successful than Bertrand du Guesclin, a man who dominated the military fortunes of Brittany through some of the most dangerous years of the Hundred Years War.

Waged throughout the reigns of five English and five French kings between 1337 and 1453, the conflict started over disputed lands of France which were English-owned through the marriage of Eleanor of Aquitaine to Henry Plantagenet, future king of England. The English triumphed at first, destroying the French fleet off the Dutch coast and winning the great Battle of Crécy in 1346. The treaty of Bretigny gave France some breathing space and

then, in 1369, Charles V declared war on Edward III of England for breaking the terms of the truce, and the forces of du Guesclin won two significant battles in 1370 and 1373. During this period Charles tried to annexe Brittany to France but failed, principally because du Guesclin (who had fought so successfully for the French king) refused to attack his Breton compatriots. A personal profile of this valiant warrior-knight will be found elsewhere.

During 1341 Brittany was ravaged, for the great armies of England and France were locked in conflict, principally on account of the claims and counter-claims of Charles de Blois and Jean de Montfort to the succession of the great duchy. Charles de Blois was supported by the French king, Montfort by the English. It was the eastern side of the peninsula which was the most ravaged, not only by the greater war between France and England, and the parallel struggle for the Brittany succession, but also through destructive enmity between political and religious factions which flared frequently along the trio of troublesome Brittany neighbours—Normandy, Maine and Anjou. In 1364 Montfort finally won and was proclaimed Duke of Brittany, but his reign was far from peaceable.

His successor-dukes, determined to instil order and stability, created a standing army which did at last largely keep the peace throughout much of the 15th and 16th centuries. Before this, the Breton Marches were fraught with danger and no settlement of note could be created or maintained unless it was powerfully protected and vigorously defended.

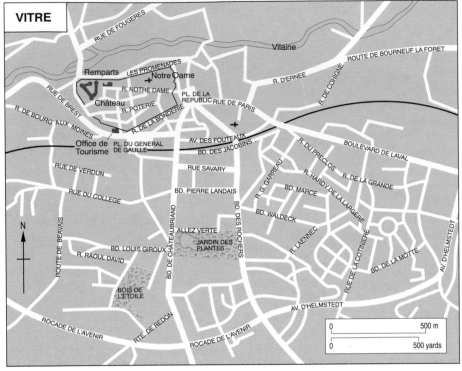

Town plan of Vitré.

Vitré

Nowhere in Brittany is this need for protection more revealingly illustrated than by the **fortified township** of Vitré. Marvellously exposed to the visitor on approach from the north, the aspect is not too dissimilar from that which the medieval pilgrim traveller might have experienced. After the spectacular splendour of the Combourg and Fougères castles, one might think that there could be no more shining gems of ancient France along this classic route, and yet there in all its preserved glory basks one of the finest medieval relics to be found in the Republic outside the *bastide* country of the Dordogne.

The skyline of the place is impressively striking on the approach from the Fougères road—a tight-knit cluster of castle towers, pepper-pot cappings above massive ramparts of blue schist stone, rising like a Gothic creation on its granite bluff above the Vilaine river. Just to amble along the **rue Beaudrairie** or the **rue Poterie**, is to transplant oneself back in time through six centuries.

The riches of the ancient buildings which grace Vitré are almost embarrassing, for there is not only the great castle built in the 13th century—and the *raison d'être* for the preserved old town in its shadow—but a wealth of individual dwellings and narrow streets within surviving protective walls. The 15th-century **Notre-Dame church** facing the photogenic **market place**, is just one of two fine Gothic churches within the municipal boundary. Surprisingly, considering its extremely close proximity, the suburb of **Faubourg-du-Rachapt**, on the northern river bank, was an English stronghold at one time during the Hundred Years War, although the real prize—Vitré with its defiant castle—was never breached by the invaders. The town fathers eventually paid a kind of Danegeld to regain Faubourg, hence the tag *rachapt*, which translates as "buy-back". It is a friendly irony then that today Vitré is twinned with Lymington in Hampshire and is a place about which Henri IV declared at the turn of the 16th century, "Were I not King of France I would be a citizen of Vitré". Such sentiments might be expressed by any visitor (about the old part of town at least), even today.

For this reason Vitré is selected as the first major touring base inside the Brittany boundary, for it is in itself a fascinating town, not yet overwhelmed by too much peripheral development, and with a number of interesting places within easy reach, by either road or rail. While the population has almost doubled within half a century, it is still comfortably compact, while the facilities and amenities for residents and visitors alike are pleasingly modern and comprehensive thanks to a revived economy since World War II. Vitré has a very active agri-industry, supplemented by textile, electronic and mechanical equipment plants, located in the heart of a rich rural region.

The history of Vitré is long and illustrious, the town and castle springing up around an 11th-century monastery bequeathed by a kinsman of William the Conqueror. Early in the 13th century, the growing town was walled, for the castle alone was not sufficient protection against the escalating, and ever more daring brigandage which plagued this frontier country. Doubly protected, Vitré thus grew in power and wealth, largely through the canvas trade which made the town (together with nearby Fougères) increasingly affluent, and eventually one of the most important of Brittany baronies. It became a favoured residence of rich merchants who exported sailcloth (made from locally grown hemp) to customers near and far including those in India. Most of the more opulent and interesting medieval houses were built by these merchants during the late 15th and early 16th centuries. It was at this time that Vitré became a strong Protestant centre, and the town was besieged by Catholic forces during the Wars of Religion. Hemp supplies dwindled, prosperity declined and for over two centuries the old town was metaphorically coated in aspic. It was this total suspension of all progress that preserved the best of the settlement for prosperity. During the 17th century even the castle itself was deserted by the ruling lords for more comfortable, purpose-built mansions, of which there are many scattered throughout Vilaine. Among 19th-century visitors, Victor Hugo was just one to be captivated by Vitré's genuinely medieval aspect.

The railway, also constructed in the 19th century, replaced Vitré on the map and was responsible for restoring life and prosperity into the old place, but only at the cost of some drastic alteration and some inevitable destruction of the ancient walls. The castle was listed as an historic monument in 1872 though, and restoration work was completed just before World War I, and another period of long stagnation.

Modern Vitré dwarfs the original town and lies to the south of the Paris–Rennes railway line, although happily the town planners have been astute in the segregation, so that the world of contemporary industry and commerce does not encroach too much, as is often the case with many French towns or cities with equally ancient hearts. While the great southern ramparts have been eliminated, large sections of the northern walls still stand, partly encircling the rich tapestry of 15th- and 16th-century dwellings. Some of these are beautifully half-timbered, with arched entrances and upper storey balconies—some of the latter are fancifully gabled, with one or two being of most curious design, for example, that of the ancient inn constructed in 1513, the **Bol d'Or.**

Walking along the **Promenade du Val**, then entering old Vitré through the arched **Potern Saint-Pierre**, one can truly capture a vibration of the intimate, familiar and secure permanence which living in the shadow of such a mighty fortress must have instilled in the medieval inhabitants. They would have assuredly counted their blessings in the church of Notre-Dame, the huge building bizarre in parts and typical of Breton Gothic design of the 15th century, with its many imaginative gargoyles.

A one-time hostelry of ancient Vitré, constructed in 1513, the odd-looking pilgrims' halt, Bol d'Or inn.

Vitré castle, triangular in outline, is much more compact than that of Fougères; it is still formidably imposing, however, and has a regal grouping of round towers with machicolations, the most impressive being the 14th-century **Tour Saint-Laurent**, which houses a **museum** of local historic artefacts. The **fortified gatehouse**, with massive close-set towers, is one of the best preserved in all France. This is located in the **place du Château**, and it leads to a fine courtyard, part of which is now occupied by the **Hôtel de Ville**.

Conveniently sited right in front of the castle is a large carpark, which usually has spaces for visitors. For an extensive bird's-eye view over the town and surrounding country, make your way to the viewing belvedere of the **Tour de Montafilant**. Guided tours of the old town and castle are organized from the tourist office during high summer.

For up-to-date attractions, Vitré enjoys its fair share too. As in the rest of France, culture and leisure form as an important part of life as industry, while sport and gastronomy also share a top billing when it comes to popularity. The town boasts two swimming pools (indoor and outdoor), six tennis courts, gymnasiums, athletic tracks, two football grounds and local associations devoted to every outdoor sport from cycling and horse-riding to rambling and angling. It is therefore a most agreeable base, with a good selection of hotel and alternative accommodation, plus a nice variety of restaurants and cafés, both within the old town and the modern quarter.

Rated one of the best-preserved ancient towns of Brittany, the location of Vitré is just as strategic for the modern traveller as it was to defenders of the old-world frontier. Less busy—and much less crowded—than Fougères, and not so frenetically concerned with workaday business either, Fougères castle and old town can comfortably be visited in a day out from Vitré—it is only 17 km (10½ miles), as can Rennes—some 35 km (22 miles) to the west. Lastly, while the landscape in general is somewhat bland, there are appealing pockets in eastern Vilaine, and these are most prominent in the Vitré area.

From September to June the covered swimming pool, the Piscine Caneton, is open in Vitré in boulevard Louis Giroux. During July and August the open-air pool in the boulevard des Rochers is open. There are two sports complexes and numerous sporting associations, some of which welcome temporary visitors, particularly anglers, cyclists and horse-riders. There are a number of way-marked routes in the region (notably in the Forêt du Pertre to the south-east) for riders and ramblers, while the long-distance GR37 takes in both Vitré and the Château of Les Rochers. Sail-boarding is popular on nearby Lac de la Chapelle Erbrée; golf at the Château of Les Rochers Sévigné. Further details are available from the *Syndicat d'Initiative*.

Not officially designated as a *station longue durée*, none-the-less the updated town facilities and amenities plus the surrounding attractions now assuredly make Vitré worthy of the accolade; certainly for eastern Brittany, it is an appealing base from which to set forth and return to, in addition to being a rich relic of ancient France in its own right.

On the town doorstep, as it were, there is pleasant strolling, particularly along the banks of the Vilaine river, which takes in three local attractions. There is neighbouring Faubourg-du-Rachapt where, at **Les Tertres Noirs** (the Black Hillocks), there is a panoramic view from a favoured picnic spot, and off rue Pasteur lies the imposing 15th-century **monastery of Saint-Nicholas** with its adjacent chapel and museum.

A few kilometres south, via the Boulard des Rochers, the municipal touring site is located in the grounds of a château ruin, immediately adjacent to Vitré horse-racing circuit. The facilities here are attractively housed in part of the ancient courtyard buildings and are maintained in pristine condition. The town deserves bonus marks for this clean and well-run touring site, which is directly on the road to one of the major visitor magnets of Vilaine *département*, the Sévigné's château of **Les Rochers** some 5 km (3 miles) off the D88.

This superb château, created during the 14th century as a fortified manor house, was restyled with graceful elegance some three centuries later and is a perfectly proportioned example of Renaissance art in architecture. L-shaped wings fan out to either side of a massive, yet shapely corner tower, and these are capped by pepper-pot towers and steeply pitched roofs of glistening slate. The whole structure is linked to a sturdy octagonal estate chapel with a domed roof, utterly contrasting with the mansion, yet somehow retaining an integral appearance. Les Rochers would of course, appear exactly as it was when the château was the home of its national celebrity, Madame Sévigné, yet another of the perceptive and talented essayists of ancient France, who lived there during the 17th century.

Marie-de-Rabutin-Chantal was born to a rich family in 1626, her Burgundian father being a pugnacious and persistent duelist who was killed by an English adversary a year after his daughter's birth. The girl's mother died six years later and her uncle, an erudite *abbé* became the orphan's guardian

*T*he château of Rochers Sévigné. In the foreground is the imposing family chapel, handsomely domed. There are fine woodland walks in the grounds.

Where History and Sporting life combine
Les Rochers is not only visited today for its splendid architecture or for its former illustrious owner, but also for its fine 18-hole golf-course laid out amid the extensive grounds which embrace some regal beech woods. These grounds are now freely available to all and are much appreciated by locals and active visitors alike, for the jogging course is along ancient rides and footpaths, where once Madame Sévigné strolled, even naming some of the forest paths after her much-loved daughter. The whole enclave is a pastoral haven of green delight, elevated enough in its setting to give wide views across the Rochers lake and the distant Vilaine countryside. Although the château is now in private hands, there is visitor access to the tiny chapel and parts of the mansion containing Sévigné memorabilia.

and was largely responsible for educating his young ward into such a famous woman of letters.

Spirited, beautiful, intelligent and observant, she married into an old Breton family, becoming the wife of Henri, Marquise de Sévigné, when she was just 18 and taking up residence at Les Rochers. Her husband, raffish and profligate, was also an ardent duelist who quarrelled once too often (over another woman), and he was killed in 1651 leaving his wife with two small children. Though many suitors pursued the desirable young widow, she never remarried, remaining magnanimously regretful (in the circumstances), of her husband's passing. Now totally independent, she was able to devote herself to writing which, in later years, made the Marquise world-famous as the author of those celebrated "letters". Her talent, expressed through volumes of

letters to family, friends and acquaintances (as was the fashion of the era) possessed the quality of what we would now describe as reportage.

The letters, although primarily personal, contained a wealth of vivid word pictures—priceless vignettes to future historians—about life in France during the 17th century, including country and court news gleaned from Vitré, Paris and Provençe among other places. She was the queen of letter-writers, and her vivacious, illuminating and often pithy style was much emulated in later decades. Nicolas Fouquet, Minister of Finance to Louis XIV was rumoured to have been her lover, but she strenuously denied this potentially dangerous liaison, claiming only platonic friendship. Nonetheless she lobbied hard for the corrupt Fouquet, whose eventual death sentence was commuted to life imprisonment. Marie herself died of smallpox in 1696 and her son went on to become the king's lieutenant in Brittany.

Continuing south and then east from Les Rochers through Argentré-du-Plessis (and passing another, privately-owned, feudal château), the D33 minor road will take you to **le Pertre**. This little town has very ancient origins and was a monk's haven during the 9th century; it was another frontier township often under threat, this time on the borders of Maine. The whole area was a notorious hiding place during the French Revolution for Royalist supporters, know as *Chouans* (screech-owls) after their secret identifying calls. **The forest of Pertre**, together with that north of Fougères (both of which were much more extensive then), still have surviving caves of the *Chouans,* who began their opposition honourably but later deteriorated into bands of unscrupulous brigands.

Directly east of Vitré, some 10 km (6 miles) distant, is **la Chapelle-Erbrée**. Here there is good scope for windsurfing on a barrage lake of the Vilaine, and there is also scenic walking and horse-riding, a bathing beach and a *plage*. To the north of town, and reached directly via the D178 is **Chatillon-de-Vendelais**, another warm-weather target with Vitré inhabitants. Like countless other barrage waters in France, the 100-hectare (250-acre) lake here has been cleverly landscaped, thus providing not only a vital reservoir, but an outdoor leisure base with wide appeal — again with a bathing beach, picnic spots, sailing facilities and angling waters.

Just north of this lake is **Dompierre-du-Chemin**, a village 6 km (4 miles) south of Fougères, with a particularly handsome buttressed **church** of the 12th century. The village, however, is most visited for the nearby **Saut de Roland** (Roland's Leap), a half-hidden ravine site above the narrow river Cantache, a tributary of the Vilaine which literally forms the border between Brittany and Normandy. One of ancient France's most romantic, half-mythical heroes, Roland, is said to have died at this lonely spot (as opposed to the fictional demise in the Pyrenean pass of Roncesvalles as recounted in the medieval *Chanson de Roland*). The *Saut* is probably just as apocryphal as the hero's burial place—said to lie beneath the Vauban citadel at Blaye, on the Gironde estuary—but it makes for intriguing speculation. The view from the rocky outcrop is dramatic enough to deserve an accompanying tale of Roland's last breath. There may even be a grain of truth in the story, for it *was* the old frontier between Brittany and Normandy and not the spectacularly mountainous one between France and Spain that was the original source of the Roland legend.

Finally, some 9 km (5½ miles) along the D29 north-west of Vitré, on the fringe of Chêvre forest, is the village of **Champeaux**. Surrounded by pleasant countryside is a cluster of delightful medieval buildings including a splendidly preserved 14th-century **collegiate church** and the dwellings of Renaissance churchmen. This is an appealing and contemplative backwater graced by lawns, chestnut trees and a dome-capped drinking well, which has fish-scale tiles and has been lovingly restored.

La Guerche-de-Bretagne

About 23 km (14 miles) south of Vitré is an acknowledged holiday base of inland Brittany, much appreciated by those who enjoy their leisure amid the tranquillity of pastoral France. Designated an official *Station Verte* on several counts, Guerche is a popular objective with country-loving visitors. There is the visual attraction of the town itself, natural magnets like the river Seiche (a good angling water), the Guerche forest, covering some 3,000 hectares (7,400 acres) with its good horse-riding and rambling potential, plus a number of prehistoric monuments, of which the Roche-aux-Fées is an outstanding example.

Add to this the whole skein of medieval churches, chapels and stately châteaux which grace this area, and the appeal of the eastern Vilaine border country again becomes apparent. As a country town, La Guerche has charm without pretension and is subtly interesting rather than overtly dramatic. The half-timbered old houses and shops in the centre are cosy-looking and inviting, and some have projecting upper storeys. They create an atmosphere which is friendly, easy and unhurried. Most towns in France which possess a long history seem to generate a slow tempo which is as infectious as it is delightful and were it not for the internal combustion engine, one might still quite legitimately experience the saner pace of earlier centuries.

Founded sometime in the 10th century, La Guerche grew slowly around a crude wooden castle, replaced and walled into a fortified town during the 13th century, when it became a centre of Knights Templar and thus grew in importance. Indeed, the mighty knight du Guesclin was appointed overlord of this particular barony, one of just four orders of Breton knighthood, the great fortress strengthened expressly to fend off attack from across the frontier.

Inevitably, the town was fought over repeatedly, being sited in acknowledged bandit country, and the castle was eventually razed, but not until early in the 18th century. The picturesque, part-chequered dwellings in the **place de la Mairie** are evidence of the renewed prosperity the little town enjoyed during the latter part of the 18th century. The town **church**, originally built in the 13th century, is now largely of 16th-century construction, though there are some elegant stained-glass windows of earlier origin. The tower, with its massive abutments, is typical of grandiose medieval Breton church architecture.

The weekly high spot of La Guerche is the Tuesday **market**, a colourful and traditional affair, which has been held almost without interruption since 1181. At the beginning of September the **annual fair** takes place, one of the most popular (and again most ancient) gatherings in this part of Brittany which is still dominated by farming and country matters. Amid the fertile, low-lying **marches,** which hereabouts seldom exceed more than a few metres above sea level, La Guerche and the surrounding villages are rich sources of the famous Breton cider, *cidre artisanal*, of goat's cheese, cream and speciality duck dishes.

To the west of La Guerche, between the villages of Esse and Retiers, stands the biggest megalithic monument in Brittany and the second largest in all France. Its name, **La Roche-aux-Fées**,

---

A Mystery Never To Be Fully Solved
Who *were* the people who selected, transported and then assembled such mighty stones? Once covered with earth and thus deliberately concealed, there is a staggering total of 42 blue schist stones, all of them individually gigantic, and one of which—the heaviest—weighing some 45 tonnes. (To find out how these great boulders might have been shifted by primitive man, *see* the chapter, Rochefort-en-Terre.) Why this porticoed tunnel structure was created will never be fully understood, but the best scholastic guess is that it may have been the final resting place of a more than usually important Celtic chieftain or, more chillingly, a pagan sacrifice site.

La Roche-aux-Fées, not far from La Guerche de Bretagne. As enigmatic as the standing stones of Carnac, and as timelessly enduring.

may be inappropriately twee (Fairies' Rocks), but there is nothing fanciful about the Goliath proportions or the massively solid reality of this landmark. In all probability a neolithic burial place (although this has never been proven positively) and constructed around 2500 BC, it is as enigmatic as the *alignements* of Carnac. Even today, in its remote setting on slightly elevated ground, shaded by trees and surrounded on all sides by farm country, it evokes a degree of awed puzzlement in the viewer.

Sacrifice of a lighter kind is perpetuated by the inevitable legend, dreamed up in a more superstitious age than our own, which surrounds the lonely monument. Prospective marriage partners supposedly walked around the dolmen when the moon was new, counting the great stones as they went. If their respective additions coincided, all augured well. A reasonable alliance could still be expected if they were only two stones adrift in their sums. More, however, and the partnership was doomed to failure. Cynics claimed that the more devious potential husbands deliberately miscounted!

This whole rustic and rather charming region of backwater Brittany is known as Roche-aux-Fées country, and among other attractive high spots there are several lakes (*étangs*), accessible for sport or leisure. The **Étang de Carcraon** (near La-Guerche-de-Bretagne) is a favoured angling water, while the **Étang de Marcille-Robert**, which covers almost 90 hectares (220 acres) offers most aquatic sports, together with quieter waters reserved for wildlife, bankside footpaths, picnic spots and a camping area. The village of Marcille-Robert is quite interesting and is dominated by a 19th-century **château**, which lies in a very ancient location. There are also the remnants of an 11th-century castle here.

Among others, the market towns of **Bais, Janze** and **Esse** are typically picturesque, the first for its unusual 16th-century church which has a three-gable entry, still known by its revealing name coined in the late 16th century, **Leper's Porch**. Janze boasts a number of well-preserved medieval vestiges, including a fine example of a **turreted house** in the main street. Esse, the nearest village to the Roche-aux-Fées megalith, has a small **ecomuseum** containing bygones of yesteryear, fascinating examples and illustrations of a rural France now gone forever.

La Guerche-de-Bretagne caters well to visitors who enjoy active leisure, with its heated swimming pool, tennis courts, rambling and cycling circuits in the vicinity, and its municipal camping ground. There is also a wide choice of hotels and *gîtes ruraux* in the area, befitting a *Station Verte*. There is a regular coach service from La Guerche to Vitré and Rennes, and it is a recommended country base for those who find even Vitré almost urban by comparison. There is a helpful and well-stocked *Syndicat d'Initiative* which is open only during the summer, after which it transfers to the nearby *mairie*.

Rennes

For genuine urban bustle and crush, travel west from Vitré for 35 km (22 miles)—those without private

Architecture that still reflects a proud independence. The parliament building, Rennes. An interesting example of Renaissance stonemasons' art.

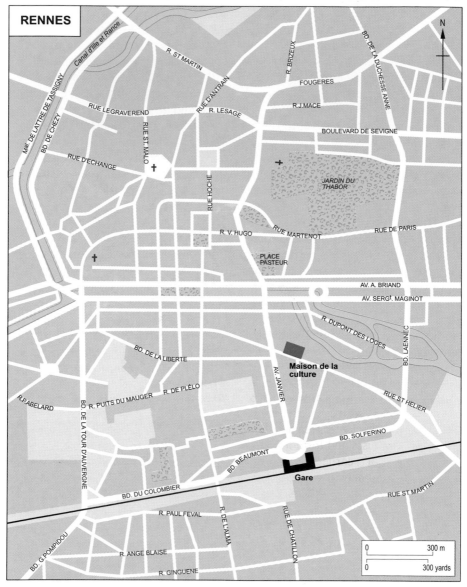

*T*own plan of Rennes.

transport can take train or coach—to the regional capital of Brittany and the *préfecture* of Ille-et-Vilaine. Since Rennes is located in the centre of the *département*, why not use it as a long-term base? The answer is simply that Rennes does not hold much appeal for holidaymakers or leisure travellers. The city has a well-earned reputation as a hive of industry and commerce and is an acknowledged business conference centre, but its aesthetic charms are

sparse. It is a good excursion target from a Vitré base for all that; especially on a wet day.

This very untypical dearth of visual delight is largely due to a catastrophic fire which raged for a whole week in 1720 and utterly destroyed the essentially Breton character, reflected by the half-timbered houses and tortuous cobbled streets of earlier centuries. Phoenix-like, the new town arose and expanded greatly during the 18th century, but the imprint was entirely French, classical and elegant—definitely not Breton. The Hôtel de Ville, Saint-Georges Palace and the Breton Parliament building are striking examples of classic French architecture. For the Celtic Rennes of old, however, one must be satisfied with quite tiny remains.

These will be found primarily in the **rue Saint-Georges**, where timbered houses of the 16th century do survive, along with the **church of Saint-Germain**

Rennes city centre, where a lively and varied programme of entertaining events are played out every summer.

(15th century flamboyant Gothic), and remnant walls of a once-fortified city. Another ancient landmark is the **Tour Duchesne** in the rue Nantaise which was constructed in the 15th century, while the **Porte Mordelaises** was the grand entry point into the city for those all-powerful dukes of Brittany. This ceremonial gateway is close to the relatively modern **Cathedrale Saint-Pierre** which was completed during the 19th century. Additionally, there are imposing 17th-century buildings in the **place du Champ Jacquet**, while the market place of **Les Lices**, is a colourful gathering of private enterprise commerce every Saturday morning. The *place* itself has some interesting features, including many ornate building façades.

For the rest, Rennes is much afflicted with high-rise concrete, almost insufferable traffic congestion at times, with all parking places seemingly permanently full. Walk, cycle or use public transport to explore the centre at leisure, but don't expect to discover much beauty, character or colour in the rest of the metropolitan area. Flaubert, author of *Madame Bovary*, travelled in Brittany during 1846 and commented that Rennes was a place of no interest. Admittedly he was a melancholy character who hated everything ordinary and bourgeois, and his dismissal was a mite abrupt, for there are a few nice pockets. Perhaps the proliferation of dark granite used in place of timber for the reconstruction of the old capital had something to do with Flaubert's acid assessment; the stone does seem sombre and even depressing on a wet day. This greyness does tend to act as a hasty spur to many visitors during indifferent weather, and they then miss the historic nuggets revealed along the few winding streets that did survive a conflagration that destroyed a thousand dwellings.

No city in Brittany, has a more turbulent or exciting past, which can be traced back to the earliest period of recorded history when it was the chief city of the Gallic Redones tribe. Rennes, then called Condate, became the hub of a Roman province after subjugation by Caesar's legions. Some sections of the many radiating military roads of that era may still be traced in this region. From the 10th century, it was the capital of the dukes of Brittany after long power struggles between rival dynasties. During the savage Hundred Years War, the bold Bertrand du Guesclin broke an English siege of the fortified town in 1357 (and found time to engage in solo combat with an English knight, one Thomas of Canterbury). The long sought-after Brittany Parliament was finally created in the mid-16th century. A revolt against royal taxes by the Rennes citizens in 1675 was brutally put down with widespread massacres, while during the Revolution there was more wanton blood-letting, although Rennes did not suffer quite so much as Nantes during the subsequent Reign of Terror.

A city of constant turmoil from the time of its creation, Rennes eventually

Old Cars and Ancient Woods

There are two other attractions, in the vicinity of Rennes which are of contrasting interest. The first is the Musée Automobile de Bretagne, off the N12 and about 4 km north-east at Cesson-Sévigné, now really a suburb of the capital. A fascinating collection of some 70 vehicles is on show here, ranging from the dawn of the motor age, to cars of the 1920s. All the exhibits are lovingly restored and maintained in tip-top condition. From here, the day visitor might consider continuing north-east to the Rennes forest, some 4 km (2½ miles) further on, eventually returning to Vitré via Champeaux. The delightful mixed woodland of the forest, with its wealth of oak, chestnut and beech trees, is a much-favoured area with Rennes citizens in summer. The woods extend over some 31 sq km (12 sq miles) in all, presenting a very scenic state forest which is traversed by the GR39 long-distance footpath.

prospered during the 20th century, despite horrendous casualties during the Great War, and suffering infamy as a headquarters of the Gestapo during World War II. Latterly, the expansion of industry, particularly in parts of inland Brittany, has attracted more and more people to the regional capital and the population of the city has increased explosively to twice the 1945 total. Rennes has some 45 hotels, many on the left bank of the Vilaine, the "new" Rennes, which is functional but uninspiring.

To capture the whiff of an earlier age, visit the **Musée de Bretagne** and the **Musée des Beaux Arts,** both of which are located on the quai Emile-Zola. The first exhibits a handsome collection of sculpture, costumes and furniture; while the fine art museum is rich in French culture, with over 1,000 paintings by early and Renaissance masters, one or two of which are true national treasures.

A good starting point for city centre exploration is the **place de la République**, where the tourist office is situated, and it may even be possible to find car-parking space if your arrival is timely (Sunday morning is recommended). All the best of the old city is thus close to hand as it were, with the famous **Jardin du Thabor**, an agreeable place for a picnic lunch if the weather is fine. Filled with flowers and formerly landscaped, the gardens, created partly on the site of an ancient abbey, now extend over some 10 hectares (25 acres); a genuine green oasis in a sea of concrete.

One final worthy objective in the vicinity is an area of curvaceous reaches on the river Vilaine, about 15 km (9 miles) south-west of Rennes off the D117 and around the elevated village of **Le Boel**. There are some rugged granite outcrops here, amid rich woodland above the water bends, and a barrage dam and watermill make impressive landmarks. Again, there are some nice riverside walks hereabouts.

Loire-Atlantique

South from Vitré for the final time, beyond the expansive Forêt de La Guerche and the narrow river Semnon (a tributary of the Vilaine) the boundary line in the Forêt d'Araize heralds entry into the *département* of Loire-Atlantique. The first town of note in this new territory is Châteaubriant; the spelling not *quite* the same as the name of the celebrated Breton author, who nonetheless claimed connections with the ancient and once-fortified town.

Châteaubriant
A majestic stronghold still dominates here, indicating yet again the defensive line of independent Brittany during medieval times. A huge hilltop town, Châteaubriant was built to combat the long-standing threat from the rapacious barons ruling the old province of Anjou, yet another mighty redoubt that kept Brittany independent of France until 1532.

Châteaubriant, like most other towns in this area, has grown considerably, but since the old part graces a low hill it is still possible to visualize the medieval layout, despite the encroachment of modern development. Even today there is a wealth of

P ractical information display boards like this are to be found on approach to most Brittany tourist targets; usually adjacent to free parking.

gracious woodland ribboning the banks of the river Chère. The **château** is really two distinct structures: the original fortress first constructed around the time of the Norman Conquest of England, and the Renaissance château—16th century—which is prominently impressive, though not so imaginatively stirring.

Two tales about the early inhabitants are perpetuated. The first (probably apocryphal) relates how the wife of a 13th-century knight flung herself into the arms of her returning beloved and promptly died from sheer happiness. The second, concerning Jean de Laval, the Count of Châteaubriant, is much more a recorded truth. The count's wife became the mistress

of François I (after some devious subterfuge on the part of the monarch) and paid for the infidelity eventually, being murdered by her husband in 1537 after ten years' incarceration in the castle. Gazing at the vestigial shell of the old castle keep, it is not difficult to envisage the gloomy, damp existence of Madame de Foix, after the opulence and excitement of life with the royal court.

Remnants of early fortifications, including towers, ramparts and the massive keep, even yet paint a picture of indomitable strength, which during the Middle Ages kept Châteaubriant largely immune from attack. Guided tours of the Renaissance apartments, and the Italian-style gallery and pavilion are conducted from mid-June to mid-September and there is access to the terrace gardens all year round. While much of the rest of modern Châteaubriant is uninspiring, there are pockets of old-world charm, including a few medieval houses and the 11th-century

The Carrière des Fusillés *hostage memorial ground, just outside Châteaubriant. The honey-comb base contains earth from the execution places.*

church of Saint-Jean-de-Béré, at the northern end of town. On the N171 Pouancé road, some 2 km (1 mile) distant, is the **Carrière des Fusillés**, a poignant memorial to World War II victims and a powerful reminder of the brutality which war always uncovers. This surprisingly spacious and now hallowed place of execution is kept ever green by a France determined never to forget the 27 non-combatant fellow countrymen who were shot as reprisal hostages in October 1941.

A less harrowing landmark of conflict—and softened by the passing of centuries—lies to the west of Châteaubriant. Take the D34 to **Grand-Fougeray**, a little market town with a distinguished and ancient claim to fame. Just before entering the town, turn left off the road (the D54 on the Vilaine side of the boundary). Here, in a still evocative setting of parkland among shady trees and rising from a grassy knoll, is the remnant of another once-mighty **castle** stormed and occupied by English forces during the Hundred Years War. Once more, the name of that illustrious Breton warrior-knight, Bertrand du Guesclin, is synonymous with success in battle and perpetuates the pride felt locally about the medieval remains of this hugely sturdy keep. On this spot in 1356, the same year the great knight besieged and captured Rennes, he penetrated the castle defences of Fougeray with imaginative guile, disguising himself and his men as woodcutters. Once inside, the 30 innocent-looking load-carriers suddenly dropped their wood bundles to become soldiers, and the English garrison was slaughtered at this ancient frontier post between Brittany and Anjou.

South of Châteaubriant, a faint but quite detectable difference in ambience becomes apparent as Loire-Atlantique is penetrated progressively. The atmosphere becomes slightly drier, the not *quite* so lush landscape undergoes a subtle change and there is the merest *frisson* of southern France. This almost always stirs a touch of excitement and expectation within the southbound

*A*ncenis castle, another splendid remnant of the 15th century on the banks of the Loire. This was once the most threatened stronghold of the Breton Marches frontier.

traveller, as the wide river Loire and the Atlantic Ocean gradually grow nearer.

This pleasure is compounded by the old-world delight of **Meilleraye Abbey**, where the builders of the medieval cluster seemed more concerned to protect the inhabitants from the sun, than the wind and the rain. Close to the town of Meilleraye-de-Bretagne, the Cistercian abbey and the surrounding dwellings occupy a lovely setting on an arm of the river Erdre, which here forms a wide, natural pool. First constructed in the 12th century, this is

another once-militant redoubt of the Breton Marches, and it is strongly appealing now for its stubborn resistance to the passage of time, weather and human depredation. Just to the south of Meilleraye-de-Bretagne, there are two popular visitor attractions, the **Vioreau reservoir** offering watersports of every description in scenic surroundings and the adjacent **Vioreau forest**, extending over almost 1,000 hectares (2,500 acres), which is traversed by rides and footpaths.

To the north-west is one more visitor magnet, the **Château de la Motte-Glain**. It is another frontier fortress of old, built towards the end of the 15th century and later converted to an elegant Renaissance residence amid regal woodland and placid lake waters. There is visitor access to the abbey church only, but Motte-Glain is open daily (except Tuesday), between mid-June and mid-September. The château is most famed nowadays for its extensive, if out-of-fashion, collection of hunting trophies.

The south bound traveller can drive directly to Nantes from Châteaubriant along the busy but uninteresting D178, although dedicated followers of the designated Route-Touristique-des-Marches-de-Bretagne will surely opt for the old frontier-hugging road, which takes in not only Motte-Glain château, but also historic **Ancenis**, straddling the river Loire. Another town deserving of its *Station Verte* status, Ancenis lies 40 km (25 miles) north-east of Nantes and it certainly does generate a subtle air of the south, as do a number of places along the lower Loire valley. The landscape hereabouts is virtually devoid of hill ranges and the sun-average is consequently high. The summer sun indeed is strong enough and constant enough to encourage viticulture (especially the production of Muscadet) on a grand scale for this part of France.

Well-tended gardens grace the river banks here, adding to the colour and

A Remnant of Frontier Fortification

Of particular significance in the long history of Brittany, it was at Ancenis, within the still-regal shell of the 15th-century château, that François II, Duke of Brittany, and the king of France, Louis XI, signed a peace treaty in 1468 which was to lead eventually to the creation of a unified nation. Acknowledged as one of the most ancient gateways into the Brittany province, the town today is a quiet and rather charming backwater, partly commercial, cleanly attractive and dominated still by the castle ruin, a 15th-century church and the great river bridge spanning the Loire.

character which Ancenis, in part, already possesses. The château is open to visitors during high summer and guided tours are conducted daily except Monday. Conveniently on the Paris–Nantes main railway line (TGV), the town provides good local leisure amenities, including horse-riding, riverside walking (partially along the GR3 long-distance path), a heated swimming pool and six tennis courts. Cycles may be hired from a centre in the rue du Château, while there is a helpful tourist office in the place du Millénaire. Across the river bridge, at **Lire** on the southern bank, is the birthplace of the 16th-century Breton poet and critic, Joachim du Bellay. A small museum is devoted to this classicist who was fervently keen to promote the French language to the level of classical Latin and Greek, which were used during du Bellay's era for poetry and prose.

Below the wide river, in the far south-eastern extremity of what is now the *région* of Pays-de-la-Loire, is the last frontier post of those ancient Breton Marches, handsomely represented by the château of Clisson. To get there from Ancenis, the road traveller using the D763 from Lire, must first cross a corner of the Maine-et-Loire *département* before coming upon the small town of **Vallet** which, together with nearby le Pallet, is an interesting objective. The first, occupying an important cross-roads site, is the centre of Brittany's celebrated, and only wine-producing region, the Muscadet and Gros Plant vineyards. While the landscape around Ancenis, along both banks of the Loire, produces Muscadet-des-Coteaux, the Vallet vintages enjoy the tag of Muscadet de Sèvre-et-Maine, which the local growers, not unnaturally, maintain is the finest of all. The celebrated white matures quickly within one season, and is bottled rapidly to capture the special bouquet of what is really a quite delicate wine. It should be drunk when freshly bottled, and preferably it should be chilled. In addition to the much-acclaimed Muscadet and Gros Plant whites, red and rosé vintages are also produced around Ancenis and to the south-west of Vallet.

The town of Vallet itself, like most others in recognized wine-producing regions of France, is much-visited and is proud of its reputation as the capital of "Sèvre-et-Maine". As a result, this old settlement which commands a strategic road-crossing of ancient eastern Brittany, is now classed as a *Station Verte*. Conducted tours around the vineyards are very popular and there are, of course, a number of cellars and wine-tasting stations readily open to visitors. Located some 24 km (15 miles) south-east of Nantes, there is a choice of hotel, auberge or campground accommodation. A heated swimming pool, open and covered tennis courts and a choice of marked footpaths along the river valleys of the Logne and the Sanguèze, are the prime leisure amenities. There is also, a rather

V isually unremarkable but a student shrine; the village of le Pallet and the birthplace of Pierre Abélard, a gifted but tragic figure of history.

118

impressive l9th-century manor house, the **Château de la Noé-Bel-Air**, the grounds of which are open seasonally. The Vallet *Syndicat d'Initiative* is located in place de Gaulle.

If time allows, do not drive direct from Vallet to Clisson if southbound, but make the modest detour to take in **le Pallet**, a short distance to the southwest and lying on the bank of the river Sèvre. Here there is a permanent exhibition devoted to viticulture (which is hardly surprising) and to pastoral folklore (which is apt considering the setting); there is also a small museum perpetuating the memory of a very famous Frenchman born in this tiny backwater village—Pierre Abélard. Hero of that most moving and tragic love story of the medieval age, Héloïse and Abélard, Pierre was born at le Pallet in 1079, of notable Breton parentage.

Showing exceptional early intelligence, which was eventually to earn him a name as a brilliant philosopher and scholar, Abélard was quickly and universally acclaimed for his original expositions on realism and logic. He reached the pinnacle of his fame in his early twenties, being awarded the chair of philosophy in Paris in 1115. His eventual *femme fatale*, Héloïse, was not only young and very beautiful, but was also talented and highly intelligent, being fluent in both Latin and Greek. Of noble birth and under the protection of her guardian uncle, a powerful church canon, she became first a student and then the mistress of Abélard. The couple eloped to Brittany, where an illegitimate son was born. Willing and indeed eager to marry Héloïse, Pierre was at first rejected by

his lover for the most noble of reasons—she wished him to retain his independence and his burgeoning career success within the church. Marriage was finally agreed upon, although the teenage Héloïse adamantly denied her new status publicly.

The girl's guardian, vengeful in the extreme at what he saw as devious seduction on the part of Abélard (who was some 22 years his bride's senior), eventually stormed the philosopher's chamber at the dead of night in the company of confederates. Abélard was overpowered and brutally castrated. Héloïse, almost inconsolable, became a nun, while her shamed and mutilated husband had no other recourse but to become a simple monk, sometime within the great monastery of Cluny. He continued to write about theology and philosophy, incidentally making many more enemies because of his revolutionary theories, was charged eventually with heresy and died miserably near Chalon-sur-Saône in 1142. All this time Héloïse remained staunchly faithful, penning letters which to this day epitomize unswerving devotion and passionate love. In death, the bones of the tragic couple were finally joined, and they still lie side by side in a Paris tomb. Abélard's enduring fame was assured by his contribution to the medieval acceptance of Aristotle as the greatest of all Greek thinkers and authority on logic, ethics and morals. That he was also destined to be one of the most tragic lovers of history is, however, his more unfortunate epitaph.

A short distance south of le Pallet lies **Clisson**, and the prettiest approach is via the minor road which runs largely alongside the river Sèvre, "prettiest" being only a comparative term in this case, since in general the countryside south of the Loire is no more scenically remarkable than the flatlands of most great river basin estuaries. It is primarily the man-made features which highlight such plain country, and Clisson is certainly an impressive example, being at once colourful, atmospheric and architecturally dramatic: a fitting final objective in fact, at the most southerly end of the Breton Marches medieval defensive chain.

Another recognized centre of Nantais vineyards, specializing in Muscadet de Sèvre-et-Maine and Gros-Plant du Pays Nantais, this distinctly Italianate town originates from the Middle Ages, part of the impressive **château ruin** stemming from the 13th century. The château was the seat of the ancient warrior family of Clisson, the most famous member of which became constable of France, succeeding no less an illustrious predecessor than Bertrand du Guesclin.

Much of original Clisson, together with the mighty **château**, was razed during the Vendean uprisings of 1792–3, and subsequently reconstructed to the orders of a rich sculptor owner, strongly influenced by Italian Renaissance architecture. Hence the quaint and somewhat misplaced semblance of Tuscany, deep in an ancient part of Brittany, which in some respects makes for a charming 18th-century scene, now of course warmly mellowed on the banks of the Sèvre-Maine river confluence.

A fine Gothic bridge spans the Maine, while the town and château

---

Du Guesclin's Worthy Successor

Olivier de Clisson, son of a knight executed for collaborating with the English in 1343, was born in 1336 and raised in England. He returned to Brittany and at first sided with Jean de Montfort in the English cause, fighting at the Battle of Auray in 1364. Disillusioned with this alliance, he changed sides to support the French king, and thus joined forces with the redoubtable du Guesclin, whom he fought alongside in all the subsequent battles of the great warlord against the English. When du Guesclin was killed in 1380, Clisson inherited the dead hero's title as constable of France. Among Clisson's other military exploits, he made an abortive attempt to invade England in 1389. Like his father, Olivier lived dangerously, surviving an assassination attempt in Paris, and falling out periously with Charles VI of France. In 1399 there was a reconciliation with the monarchy, and constable Clisson became protector of the Brittany duchy, to die wealthy and acclaimed in 1407 in the Josselin château; his widow was Marguerite, a member of the Rohan family, who own the Morbihan castle to the present day.

---

occupy both banks of the Sèvre in a naturally pretty, and slightly elevated location.

Another worthy recipient of *Station Verte* status, Clisson lies 28 km (17 miles) south-east of Nantes and is on the main railway line between Nantes and Poitiers. It is much visited and enjoyed primarily for its visual historic delights like the château, the picturesque bridges, a splendid 15th-century timber-built **market place** (now a national monument); a number of early-19th-century villas; and the very Italianate churches—the Romanesque

Saint-Jacques and the 12th-century **Notre-Dame de la Madeleine** occupying the high ground. With bell towers, Knights Templar chapels, a predominance of white stone and terracotta roofs, Clisson *is* Italian—especially in bright sunlight. Only the language of the locals reminds the visitor that this is, in reality, very much French France.

Above charming terraces, the massively forbidding round-tower keep of Clisson château still stands almost as intact as it was during the Middle Ages. It is open to visitors daily except Wednesday, and *son et lumière* displays are held twice weekly during the summer season. Clisson has that enviable air that makes it attractive to people of all ages, and on a summer evening it is much favoured by leisure strollers who throng the attractive Italian-style terraces and landscaped park area of this comfortable and still partly medieval settlement.

It is still pronounced with pride on local signposts that this is the first (and last) town in Brittany; despite its new bureaucratic classification as part of Pays-de-la-Loire *région*. Clisson boasts two hotels, the Auberge de la Cascade being in a particularly scenic position, and there are several quality restaurants together with traditional *crêperies* and cafés. There is a nicely located camping ground close to the river and town centre, from which there are waterside walks. A number of *gîtes ruraux* exist in the vicinity. Sporting facilities include a heated swimming pool, a canoe and kayak centre, an archery centre and riding stables which lie some 4 km (2½ miles) distant. There is a tourist office in the place du Minage (open seasonally), otherwise contact the *Syndicat d'Initiative* at the Clisson *mairie*. Clisson is a favoured town for visiting Nantes by those who prefer city exploration from a semi-rural base.

Nantes

Rennes may be the current capital of Brittany, but for those who seek that older France, Nantes retains that indefinable but unmistakable stamp of a true capital—which it was when the ancient province was self-governed. As if to prove to the world its great significance within the Republic, it constitutes the most important and the most populated metropolis and commercial river port in western France. Nantes' strategic location at the junction of three major provinces—Brittany, Anjou and the Vendée—is reflected in its huge expansion since World War II, which makes it one of the most industrious cities in Europe and one of the most prosperous, the wealth founded on a maritime past that built upon each and every sea-going activity from whaling to slave trading. During the 17th and 18th centuries, the tidal Loire below the massed clutter of the Nantes wharves, was almost permanently crowded with tall ships coming and going on their perilous but very lucrative voyages to countries half a world away.

More French than Breton, the great city was founded by a very ancient Celtic tribe, the Namneti, some 500 years before the birth of Christ, but it was Julius Caesar who transformed the primitive riverside settlement into a great harbour. Nowadays a thriving commercial port, Nantes is capable of

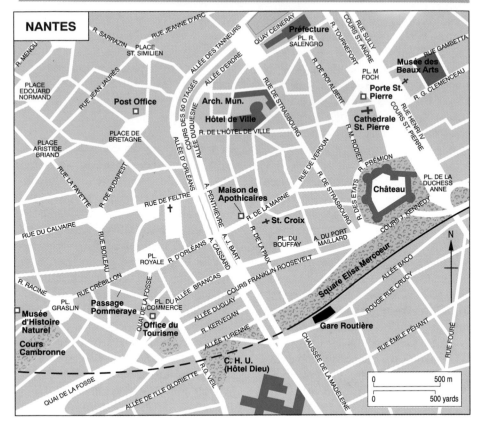

NANTES

T own plan of Nantes.

accepting ocean-going ships in the 20,000 tonnage range.

Since 1988 and somehow symbolizing the Nantes salt-water connection, a decommissioned navy destroyer, the *Maillé-Brézé*, has been secured off the quai de la Fosse, a most impressive floating naval museum which is open to visitors daily during the summer save Mondays. Appropriately, the warship is named after a 17th-century maritime hero and nephew of Cardinal Richelieu. The Marquis of Brézé was a brilliant naval strategist who fought in eight sea battles during a brief career, became an admiral at the age of 24 and was killed in action at 27. The *Maillé-Brézé* is armed heavily with contemporary anti-aircraft and anti-submarine weaponry, plus a surface-to-surface missile launcher.

The floating museum is one part of the Nantes marine association, formed to re-create the spirit of 18th-century enterprise of French shipbuilders, merchants and sailors. The whole of the **quai de la Fosse** is destined to become a national maritime and cultural centre, mirroring Nantes illustrious past. The setting, where the Loire is split into two wide arms by the Ile Beaulieu, could not be a more apt location.

*T*he novel way to see Nantes city centre; these tourist trains are almost an obligatory feature of most French cities and towns now.

Like most cities that have endured since earliest recorded time Nantes' historic centre is compact and really quite small. Thus almost all the ancient gems can be enjoyed within a day of easy strolling in the vicinity of the cathedral and the magnificent château, both of which are but a short distance from the railway station, the coach station and, of course, the river. All the principal treasures of old Nantes are on the north bank of the Loire, within a square kilometre cluster really, which may seem improbable to any car driver approaching and entering the city heart for the first time. Nantes *is* now a vast metropolis, with massive and

ever-expanding development which must be negotiated along all the approach roads. Happily, the road-builders have kept pace with escalating modernization and there are excellent throughways, ring roads and high-speed traverses, coupled with clear signposting and peripheral car-parking places. The majority of city centre streets are one-way (another reason for exploring on foot, by bicycle or on public transport). Three road bridges link the north bank of the Loire with Ile Beaulieu, and two more join the island to the south bank.

In summer, special mini-coach tours of historic Nantes are organized through the tourist office, while for those who prefer to explore independently, the **cathedral** is a natural and dramatic starting point. Built in the 15th century, the cathedral of St Peter and St Paul is a soaring monument to Gothic architecture, much of which is

N antes cathedral. An imposing, almost overwhelming structure which totally dominates its surroundings above the château of Nantes. The ornate Gothic south-facing entrance arch.

acknowledged to be the greatest of all Breton sculptors. The interior, with its supremely beautiful nave and vaulted roof higher than that of Westminster Abbey, is breath-taking.

Outside, there is the medieval **Port Saint-Pierre**, originally a Roman gateway in the ancient city wall, **place Saint -Pierre**, fronting the cathedral, is gracious, spacious and colourfully atmospheric, as is the nearby **place Maréchal Foch**, distinguished by the tall Louis XVI column. The latter, incidentally, has a car-parking area adjacent, but you have to arrive very early in the morning to find a space. This is the locality of some very large and elegant mansions, the erstwhile homes of merchants made rich through maritime industry of the French empire, which, like other dominant nations of the western world, pursued a vigorous and highly profitable slave trade, tagged euphemistically as the "ebony trade".

After the abolition of slavery, the turbulence of the Revolution, and the expansion of home-produced sugarbeet (which drastically reduced sugarcane import), the fortunes of Nantes began to wane rapidly. This was further accelerated by the silting up of the Loire estuary and, by the middle of the 1800s, the emergence of nearby Saint-Nazaire as a serious commercial rival. Saint-Nazaire became a burgeoning port right on the Atlantic seaboard at the mouth of the Loire, and was able to take all the deep-draught ships now unable to navigate upriver to Nantes (of which there was an ever increasing tonnage).

Adapt or die became a desperate clarion cry among the Nantes city

a masterful work of restoration after the disastrous fire of 1972. Outstanding features include the five intricately decorated arched entrances, some superb 15th-century carvings and the tomb of François II, the last Duke of Brittany, a masterpiece carved in the early 16th century by Michel Colombe, fathers, and the metropolis responded by diversifying in the time-honoured manner, producing vast quantities of biscuits, canned foods and agricultural chemicals. Eventually there came also maritime revival with the dredging of the river estuary and the building of a canal to bypass shoal waters downriver of the city. This did much to restore flagging trade, especially during the latter years of the sailing ship era. Meanwhile, the new industry established Nantes as the prime warehouse and food larder of western France.

Massive and continuous civil engineering projects ensured major expansion through the last half of the 19th and the whole of the 20th century, including the diversion of river waters. The Erdre was channelled underground north of the château, while to eliminate Loire tributaries holding up city development, whole reaches were sealed off and filled.

Today, Nantes is a recognized centre of advanced technology, largely reconstructed after much World War II damage; again a busy port with a thriving ship-building industry, many other essential commodities are produced and distributed worldwide, from refined sugar to nuclear power propulsion systems for sea-going vessels.

Despite its status as one of the leading modern workshops of the new Europe, the past is still much in evidence within that square kilometre or so of the old city centre—singularly evidenced by the great **château** of the dukes of Brittany, an easy stroll down towards the Loire from the cathedral. The château now houses three museums devoted to art, folklore and maritime history, but it was once a mighty

fortress dominating a wondrously defensive site, being flanked by two rivers—the Loire and the Erdre. The position was fortified by the Romans, and later embellished to embrace the walled city between the 10th and 12th centuries, with the most enduring redoubt being built during the 14th and 15th centuries, as the recognized power centre of the dukes of Brittany. At that time, the castle was located literally at

A quiet haven amid the city bustle. The château formal gardens (popular for lunchtime picnics), laid out where once moat waters flowed.

the water's edge, the swift-flowing Loire forming a naturally defensive moat around the western and southern ramparts.

The first lady of Brittany province (held in the highest esteem even today) was of course Anne, born in the château in 1477, and the daughter of François II and Margaret de Foix. It was she who later retained the sculptor Colombe to create her father's tomb, and she also supervised the completion of the Nantes château, begun by François in 1466. An imposing cluster of round towers, moat-lapped ramparts and elegant if flamboyant inner courtyards, the château today is a fascinating multi-museum, and a quiet green oasis where sunken lawns and flower gardens have replaced ancient moat waters. The château is open daily except Tuesdays, and you should allow a good hour or two to see it properly.

From the place de la Duchesse Anne to the **place du Bouffay** is just a short step, but one that keeps time with history, for the latter is the oldest square in Nantes, around which are some fascinating narrow streets and alleys, together with their old dwelling houses. The **rue de la Juiverie** (medieval Jewish quarter), the **Maison des Apothicaires** (a half-timbered 15th-century house in the place du Change), the **Maison des Palefrois** (ancient stables) and the 17th-century **church of Sainte-Croix**, the belfry of which is a relic from the once-magnificent Chateau du Bouffay, can all be found nearby. The tourist office itself in the place du Commerce, is housed within a particularly fine half-timbered 16th-century residence. During the Reign of Terror which followed the French Revolution,

place du Bouffay was also the place of execution.

The **place Royale** with its fine statue-topped fountain is handsome, while nearby **passage Pommeraye** is strikingly dramatic and one of the great high spots of Nantes, famous for its triple-level shopping arcade created during the 19th century which is adorned with mirrors, columns, gracious stairways and a whole variety of statues and wall carvings. Opulent and elegant, the arcade accurately reflects the heyday era of what was once the premier port of France.

A little west of here in the place Graslin is another building equally imposing, the **Grand Theatre**. The Corinthian styling of the majestic façade is a perfect example of 18th-century grand architecture; at once simple and four-square, yet regally impressive. There are a number of other buildings in the vicinity still redolent with 18th- and 19th-century wealth and style, especially in the **Cours Cambronne**. Close to the theatre there are two celebrated museums and the most famous café in Nantes, **La Cigale**; behind its portals you enter authentic 19th-century France. The **museum of natural history** in rue Voltaire is considered to be one of the most beautiful in the Republic, while the **Thomas Dobrée museum** place Jean-V (partly in a 15th-century mansion), displays rare books, manuscripts and the shrine casket containing the heart of Anne of Brittany.

Back towards the city centre, the arm of the Loire which once created the ancient Ile Feydeau is now largely a tarmacadam bordered garden strip, while the ait itself still retains strong 18th-century overtones, particularly along the **Cours Olivier-de-Clisson**. The illustrious reputation of this one-time constable of France is now upstaged, if not virtually eclipsed, by a more contemporary and far more famous Nantes hero, Jules Verne, who was born here in 1828. The **Verne Museum**, devoted to memorabilia of the great science fiction writer who wrote such well-known books as *Around the World in Eighty Days*, is in the rue de l'Hermitage, just north of the quai de la Fosse.

Two other city centre treasures are the **fine arts museum** and the **Jardin des Plantes**, just to the east of the cathedral and château. The first has a splendid collections of paintings from Renaissance to Impressionist artists, including works by Tintoretto and Courbet, while the botanical gardens— which were laid out in 1805—display a superb variety of flowers in season, among tree-shaded ponds and paths which are dotted with sculptures, including one of Jules Verne. This is a much-favoured promenade and picnic spot, particularly by potential train travellers, since the gardens are adjacent to the imposing SNCF station.

For the gourmet, Nantes has a high reputation as a seafood centre as might be guessed; there are also any number of freshwater delicacies on offer, for example, pike prepared as the once-favoured royal dish, *brochet beurre blanc*—comes with the unusual white butter sauce that was invented in Nantes. Invariably on offer at the city's leading restaurants, this is a feast for the gastronomically adventurous; others may opt for the equally popular *canard Nantais*, a succulent and rich duck dish.

Home of the French biscuit industry, with outlying districts providing a constant flow of fine fruit and vegetables, plus a huge annual volume of Muscadet, Gros Plant and Gamay wines from over 12,000 hectares (30,000 acres) of fertile vineyards, Nantes offers eating and drinking pleasure as imaginative and variable as any in the Republic. In general, meals will be found agreeably satisfying and certainly generous and tasty, although they do err on the plain side for France. *Haute cuisine* exists, of course, but if that is what you desire, then you must select your eating house carefully. On a simpler level, there is no better place than Nantes to sample some of the best-known of Breton fast food, the ubiquitous *crêpe* in all its forms, savoury or sweet.

For those wishing to dwell awhile in Nantes, there is a truly staggering total of more than 100 registered hotels within the city environs—over 60 lie within the centre city confines, and half of these can be found in the vicinity of the historic heart itself. Four are in the luxury class, headed by the Hôtel France in the rue Crébillon; the Graslin in rue Piron, and the Jules-Verne in place Fleuriot-de-l'Angle. Suggested two-star hotels are the Amiral in rue Scribe, and the Duchesse-Anne in the *place* of the same name. A popular one-star hotel (among a wealth of others) is the Hôtel de la Bourse on the quai de la Fosse. There is an *auberge de jeunesse* (youth hostel) at the oddly-named Manufacture des Tabacs (off the boulevard Stalingrad), which is close to the SNCF station.

For caravanners and campers, there is a permanently open municipal touring site some 3 km (2 miles) north of the city centre. Covering 8 hectares (18 acres) of ground in an attractive setting by the sports centre and hippodrome (horse-racing circuit), there is plenty here for the sporting enthusiast including a bowling alley and a swimming pool. To get there, follow boulevard Guy Molletto to the Complexe du Petit-Port on the banks of the river Cens, a tributary of the Erdre.

As for the wide sprawl of greater Nantes, it must be said that despite its very impressive heart and hub, much of the modern city is architecturally poor. There are, however, occasional bright spots like the famous experimental housing unit built by Le Corbusier at Rezé suburb. The old centre and the banks of the Loire are locations from which to glimpse the glorious and sometimes very turbulent Nantes of long ago.

Two events especially, one famous and one infamous—mark the exciting pages of Nantes' history. The first occurred in 1598 in the great château when that document of enlightenment, the Edict of Nantes, was signed by King Henri IV, extending to all citizens freedom of religious worship, and thus ending (for a while at least) the open enmity between Catholics and Protestants. After some 35 years of Huguenot persecution (which flared periodically into savage civil war) peace was at last to pervade Brittany and all France. That was the theory; in reality Henri renounced his Protestant faith, became Catholic and the edict of good intention was eventually revoked, in 1685.

The second episode concerns one of Brittany's more infamous sons of the past (although by no means the most notorious), Joseph Fouché, born just outside Nantes in 1763. Destined to become a fanatical revolutionary and early confederate of Robespierre, he quickly rose to high office within the Convention. When the counter-revolt of royalist Brittany peasants (and those from neighbouring Vendée) threatened the Convention forces, Fouché was the man responsible for crushing the uprising with brutal savagery through an equally callous appointed deputy, Jean-Baptiste Carrier. Both men were ardent Jacobins—the political society largely responsible for the ultimate success of the French Revolution.

Fouché attempted to extinguish Christianity throughout France and in 1793 many churches were ransacked, the spoils being commandeered for the National Convention treasury. The feared atheist narrowly escaped the guillotine himself at one period of The Terror, but went on to high office and served under Napoleon and even Louis XVIII—which says much about the man's devious flair for self-advancement and survival! He was eventually heaped with honours, titled as the Duke of Otranto, and died peacefully and immensely wealthy in 1820.

As for his deputy Carrier, his career was also brutal, but far shorter. Charged with the task of finding ever more space for political prisoners in the Nantes region, he emptied the overflowing prisons by drowning the inmates in the Loire. This wholesale slaughter, supplemented with *en masse* executions by shooting or the guillotine, without even the pretence of individual trial, was too much even for the harsh revolutionary Convention.

He was recalled to Paris to face a tribunal and was subsequently guillotined, just one year after instigating the Nantes atrocity, aged 38 years. He was certainly a brutal fanatic, although perhaps no worse in some ways than his superior Fouché, who was totally amoral in his final support of royalty and renunciation of sworn Jacobin allegiance.

To understand something of the bitter opposition to the Revolution which prevailed in Brittany and neighbouring areas of western France, one must visualize the population of that era. Essential peasantry, the revolutionary fervour which blazed ferociously across most of the country (and especially in urban areas like Paris), left the people of Brittany, and elsewhere, singularly unimpressed. Many were ardent loyalists, while nearly all viewed the revolutionary supporters as religious heretics.

Stirred from apathy to opposition by the Church, there was widespread insurrection in 1793, principally in the Vendée (the struggle afterwards became known as the Vendée Wars), but also in many places in Brittany. Like all civil wars, this was a savage clash which lasted for less than a year, but which even today is a source of bitter memory. Nantes itself was almost taken by the Catholic Royalists during the battle for which a principal leader of the uprising, a humble pedlar named Jacques Cathelineau, was killed. The white cockade, symbol of the defeated but defiant peasant army, is still displayed with pride in parts of Brittany, Poitou, Maine and Anjou.

River boat excursions on the Loire, Sèvre or Erdre, reservations and tariffs, tel: 40-20-24-50. Scenic river cruises often with on-board meals, duration 3–4 hours depending on water chosen. The Erdre is popular with watersport enthusiasts, especially canoeists. There is a city centre heated swimming pool (the Leo Lagrange), quai de Tourville, and the esteemed Vigneux golf-course (18 holes), 15 km (9 miles) distant and due north of the city. There are numerous horse-riding centres in the vicinity of the city—information from the Poney-Club Nantais, 32 rue Lanoue Bras de Fer (five minutes' walk from SNCF station), tel: 40-48-49-72. For local footpath exploration Topo-guides are available from the tourist office, which can also advise on city and suburb cycle hire.

To the south-west of the old capital city, there is an intriguing area of Brittany, which is sporadically explored by foreigners. This is partly because the area south of the Loire estuary is (if only psychologically) difficult to get at, and partly because the terrain itself is principally flat, ostensibly a *marais* of little interest. In truth, hereabouts there are a number of fascinating objectives and one in particular which will make the blood run cold.

The first of these is a natural gem of true delight and a total contrast to the feverish urban bustle of Nantes which, almost unbelievably, lies only 20 km (12½ miles) to the north. The **Lac de Grand Lieu**, one of the largest natural expanses of inland water in France, is best explored from Passay, a cul-de-sac fishing village at the water's edge. The lake has been a designated nature reserve since 1980; a wonderful haven of wildlife, now jealously protected, it has some 4,000 hectares (9,900 acres) of

Lac de Grande Lieu. Aspect from the atmospheric fishing village of Passay. An excellent base from which to explore the celebrated bird reserve.

marshy shallows which are invaded by encroaching vegetation to create a land and waterscape which resembles the Norfolk Broads in some places and the Florida Everglades in others.

Grand Lieu has dominated this ancient south-eastern corner of Brittany since the prehistory era when, according to the records, the extent of clear water was twice that of today. Certainly it was a much-favoured area of human habitation from earliest times, as copious finds of megalithic monuments, flint tools and bronze axes have proved. It is a rich source of archaeological treasures still, providing tangible links between pagan times and the earliest Christian period when some of the first monasteries of the western world were established in the vicinity.

The contemporary and proud claim to fame of Grand Lieu is that it is the largest heronry in the Republic; situated on an established Atlantic migration route, the lake is something of a bird-watcher's paradise, with more than 220 seasonal bird species recorded. The waters are rich in aquatic life, with an abundance of tench, carp, pike and eels. Freshwater fishing has been a way of life in **Passay** from the dawn of recorded history, the village recorded in the 9th century as Paciacum, though today there are only a few families still pursuing the craft with special wicker cages and traditional flat-bottomed boats called *yoles*. These few remaining professionals are the only ones now allowed to fish the lake.

The village of Passay is quaint and as atmospheric as the great sweep of reed beds and water it borders; a shimmering, silent expanse of nature, mysteriously beautiful at sunrise when mist exaggerates the fragmented outlines of reed beds and bird calls echo timelessly. There is easy car-parking for visitors, except during the height of summer, and from the village there is a 5 km (3-mile) way-marked walk—pedestrian wanderers should take care not to stray from the routes for obvious reasons. Passay now boasts a small folk museum and an observation tower—the **Maison du Pecheur**—which provides an appropriate bird's-eye view of the clear water and the huge expanse of surrounding marshes.

*T*he 9th century miraculously preserved. The interior of Saint Philbert abbey church on the edge of ancient marshland. One of the oldest places of Christian worship in all France.

On the southern shores of the water, fed here by the river Bolougne, is another of those half-hidden gems of the past that no traveller in this region of ancient marsh country will want to bypass. While it is true that **Saint-Philbert-de-Grand-Lieu** is a *Station Verte,* once again it is a tucked away holiday resort, acknowledged mainly by the citizens of Nantes as a peaceful green haven only 25 km (15½ miles) from the city. Reached via minor roads off the D117 immediately south of the lake, Saint-Philbert possesses an enviable and striking relic of antiquity; one of the oldest surviving places of Christian worship in France.

The **Carolingian abbey-church** dating from AD 815 is one of the most prestigious examples of religious architecture in existence anywhere in western Europe. Apart from the building itself—which has miraculously remained almost intact across 11 centuries—its stout walls also contain the original marble sarcophagus which held the body of Saint-Philbert (Saint-Filbert), during the middle years of the 9th century. The interior of the outwardly unimpressive structure is memorably beautiful, if deceptively simple. A series of arches and columns, constructed of alternating white stone and pink brick stratas, create a subtly sublime and perfectly proportioned whole.

Of course, any building of such venerable age has had to pay the price for surviving so many years, particularly one that was only fully restored and re-opened as a place of worship in 1936. The detritus of time had to be cleared—almost 9 m (30 ft) in depth—to uncover the original nave floor level, while the ravages of weathering had to be made good and the roof (at one period crudely holed and glassed over to create a covered market) replaced. Happily, there is still a wealth of 9th-century treasure in stone remaining, the quality of the workmanship still drawing gasps of admiration from visitors. In its simple beauty, Saint-Philbert is assuredly as majestic and atmospheric as any vast grandiose cathedral.

Around the church the town of Saint-Philbert is small, but it boasts a good choice of visitor accommodation including a hotel, some half-dozen *gîtes ruraux* and a similar number of *chambres d'hôtes* in the near neighbourhood. There is also a riverside municipal campground. The river and lake are the natural magnets, while there is also an interesting folk and natural history museum. For the active, there is a heated swimming pool and a sports complex providing tennis and miniature golf, or one can hire a boat to explore the Bolougne river. There is a cycle hire centre—Cycles Blanchard—in the rue Sainte-Barbe. The tourist office is located in the museum building in the rue de l'Abreuvoir. The vicinity of Saint-Philbert is popular with both leisure walkers and anglers; the former have a 3 km (2-mile) waymarked route starting from behind the church, while the latter have the adjacent river (fishing tickets are available from the shop, Pêche et Chasse, in the rue de l'Hôtel de Ville). There is also a market held in the town on Sundays.

A short distance to the north-west of Saint-Philbert is the village of **Sainte-Lumine de Coutais**, where there is more evidence of longevity— a 2,000-year-old box tree marking the site of a one-time Roman encampment. Close by is the 16th-century church, its bell tower doubling as an observatory which, as the brochure states, "lays out Lac de Grand-Lieu at one's feet". The lofty belfry, some 40 m (130 ft) above ground level, provides remarkable views across the water and the distant landscape to the spires of Nantes, and is open regularly, except during any religious ceremonies.

From Saint-Philbert the D117 winds westwards towards the Atlantic, passing through more pleasant if undramatic countryside. The land here is primarily concerned with wine production and market gardening—these are found on either side of the forest of Machecoul, before the town of the same name is entered. Today, this is a popular Pays-de-la-Loire resort which is colourful and lively, yet compact. There was a short time during the Middle Ages, however, when it was a place with a dark and terrible secret. **Machecoul** is the ancient capital of the Pays de Retz, a massive and fabulously rich area of old Brittany, and it was one of the medieval dukes of Retz that put Machecoul on the map for the most devilish infamy.

The life of Gilles de Retz began honourably enough. He was born in 1404 in Chamtocé-sur-Loire, destined for a brilliant early military career. He was fiercely loyal to the cause of Joan of Arc, and actually fought at the Maid's side during many battles, rising to the rank of Field Marshal at the age of 24. However, after Joan's death in 1431, he just as swiftly frittered away his vast family fortune, at the same time descending to the depths of depravity as a seducer, torturer and murderer of children, mainly boys, in his castle at Machecoul and other strongholds in the region. The exact number of his victims is not known, but is soundly estimated at between 150 and 200. His equally evil accomplices scoured the surrounding countryside abducting children ever more frequently to satisfy the monster's increasing blood lust. A devotee of the Black Mass, Gilles also held to a mad belief that gold could be conjured from the blood of children by some strange alchemy.

The heinous crimes were of course finally uncovered and not surprisingly the subsequent trial became almost as celebrated in medieval France as that of Joan of Arc. Inevitably found guilty, Gilles was not burned at the stake, as is sometimes claimed, but was simply hanged at Nantes in 1440, aged 36. It was Gilles de Retz and his vile crimes which inspired the fictional demon Bluebeard, a story written some 200 years later by Charles Perrault (1628—1703). This gifted author, who had created *Sleeping Beauty* after seeing the delicate inspirational architecture of Usse château near Tours, was compelled to put pen to paper for very different reasons when he wrote *La Barbe Bleu.*

The still-evident shell of Machecoul castle is gauntly vestigial and somehow fittingly, it is not open to visitors. It can just be glimpsed through the trees on the approach road from Saint-Philbert as one enters Machecoul town. Even on the sunniest of days this stark landmark cannot fail to evoke a shiver.

The fictional killer created by Perrault, almost a petty criminal by comparison, is much more celebrated in Machecoul (and elsewhere in the region) than Gilles de Retz, the name bandied about mainly for the benefit of tourists, as that of Cyrano de Bergerac is displayed in the lower Dordogne area. Bluebeard is a bogeyman about whom no one is uneasy; indeed the gory legend has helped promote Machecoul considerably, another officially designated *Station Verte*. It has a convenient SNCF station, a large, two-star hotel, six *gîtes de France* and a municipal camping site. The leisure facilities are also wide and varied, with a heated swimming pool, tennis courts and horse-riding nearby. There are way-marked pedestrian routes in the Bois de Céné and the Machecoul forest which covers over 350 hectares (860 acres), plus cycle-touring circuits over easy terrain (cycle hire is available from Cycles Gitane).

There is a useful *Syndicat d'Initiative* in the place du Port, and the market is locally renowned for quality fruit and vegetables; market day is on Wednesday.

Across the expanse of fertile flatland to the north-west, known as the Marais de Machecoul, the Brittany border is followed to the Atlantic shoreline at Bourgneuf-en-Retz. From this point, a string of pleasing if predictable seaside resorts punctuate the coastal strip all the way north-westwards to the Saint-Nazaire bridge. Of these, **Pornic** is the most attractive and most frequented. A holiday town with a difference, Pornic is celebrated not only as a delightful small-boat haven, but also for its well-preserved 15th-century château called (what else?) **Bluebeard's Castle**.

Colourful bustle pervades Pornic throughout the summer, much appreciated by holidaymakers demanding all the modern seaside amenities, although on a cosier and smaller scale than that provided by the super resort of this Jade Coast, La Baule.

Pornic, situated between the Vendée boundary and the Loire estuary, is a natural deep-water harbour, still backed by green and pastoral countryside. Served by the railway, Pornic has been a sea-bathing station and health spa since the mid-19th century, gaining comparison to Deauville and Trouville for its lively casinos and eminent patrons like Georges Sand and Gustave Flaubert.

To the north is Pointe-de-Saint-Gildas, the Land's End of southern Loire-Atlantique, which together with neighbouring Préfailles, is a new nautical centre for leisure sailors in a location that provides some fine views of the open Atlantic. The area may be flat and fairly featureless inland, but the succession of coastal resorts are all lively with up-to-the-minute amenities, and the climate is particularly temperate being humid, equable and enjoying a mean annual average of 13°C (55°F).

The quaintly named Saint-Michel-Chef-Chef vies with its two-part neighbour, Saint-Brévin (l'Océan and Les-Pins respectively). Hereabouts is the sandy foreshore and backing dunes so beloved by children, pine trees and holiday homes occupying the higher ground above the 8 km (5 miles) or so of beaches, in about equal proportions. Saint-Brévin is expanding steadily,

being only 58 km (36 miles) west of Nantes, and now boasts a choice of hotels, a youth hostel and a string of touring parks.

The landmark which commands the skyline above Saint Brévin is the mighty Pont de Saint-Nazaire, the longest road bridge in France and the gateway to Brittany's Atlantic seaboard. There could not be a more dramatic entry point.

*P*ornic harbour.
Predictably for this area, the château in the background is called "Bluebeard's Castle" after the famous fictional character. The truth about nearby Machecoul is far more sinister.

135

A Woman of Destiny

The last and much-loved sovereign of an independent province, there are no significant places in the peninsula that do not in some way pay homage to Anne, Duchess of Brittany. Even today, she is held in reverence not only for her devout faith, but for the staunch support she maintained for the peninsula's right to rule itself; and when this became impossible, for her efforts to gain the best from a very powerful neighbour. The name of Anne is held in the highest regard by most Bretons, since it has become synonymous with political-astuteness.

That she died comparatively young also contributes to feelings of fondness on the part of succeeding Breton generations. For the somewhat more pro-French eastern area of Brittany, La Duchesse Anne is also a shining heroine, her image eternally bright for the part she played (largely through the eventual marriage of her daughter), in making the autonomous dukedom a permanent part of the French nation.

In an age when constant court intrigue was the norm, the young girl Anne was buffeted hither and thus by fate and the devious machinations of medieval power-game players. She was born in 1477, daughter of François II, Duke of Brittany, and Margeurite de Foix. This was an age of great change and uncertainty in western Europe, scarcely twenty-five years since the end of the destructive Hundred Years War, and some fifteen years in advance of Christopher Columbus's voyage and discovery of the New World. There was optimism too—within the ruling-class circles at least—reflected by a flowering of art and culture in cities like Nantes, where massive depredations left by the

La Duchesse Anne. Although she died relatively young, Anne of Brittany is recognized as having been an able administrator to the duchy.

War of Succession were made good by humane and conscientious ducal dynasties.

François II of the Montfort dynasty ruled from 1458 to 1488 and was one ruler who left a beneficial mark upon the province. Determined to resist any attempt at a French takeover of Brittany, he wooed the English court, led by Edward IV, as part of a defensive strategy, offering his daughter in marriage to the Prince of Wales. There were other ardent suitors with political motives, however, one of whom was the Emperor of Austria in waiting, Maximillian. The records indicate that Anne was not at all averse to an alliance with the emperor, although she was only twelve years old when her father died. She was apparently a charming and vivacious person, afflicted with a slight physical disability in the form of a limp. The proxy marriage to Maximillian was performed in

1490, but was never consummated. Meanwhile, the desirable heiress was being eyed again by Charles VIII of France (1470–1498). Weak of intellect and easily led, Charles had a slack-mouthed and dumpy appearance, and showed no interest in the affairs of state until his twenty-first year, when he decided to make up for lost time. He was also betrothed to Margaret of Austria, but both contracts were conveniently annulled and Anne became the wife of Charles, and queen. The marriage joined Brittany to France at last, and there was even a clause in the marriage contract that declared that if anything happened to Charles, Anne would have to marry his successor! This was a very shrewd proviso on the part of the king's advisers, as once absorbed into the kingdom of France, the French ruling class had no intention of allowing the dukedom to regain its independence.

History records that much to everyone's surprise, the royal newly-weds found their arranged alliance most agreeable; at the very least it was an amicable partnership which appeared set fair to blossom into long-term happiness. Alas, after only seven years together (during which Charles pursued grandiose and ludicrous dreams, setting off at one stage to proclaim himself Emperor of Constantinople and the East), the hapless monarch suffered a fatal accident at his beloved Amboise chateau. Possibly in his cups, he stumbled, fell heavily and hit his head, dying a short time afterwards. Anne was filled with remorse—but not for long.

Since no children survived the alliance, the rightful heir to the French throne became Louis XII (1462–1515). He too was married, but the continued dominion over Brittany was, of course, far more important. Much horse-trading at the highest level ensued between Rome and *éminence grise* figures behind the French throne. Eventually, in return for massive military aid to Italy (at that time heavily embroiled in several internal wars), the Pope, a wily negotiator called Cesare Borgia, granted an annulment. Anne was thus married for a second time in 1499, this time to a frail, prematurely aged king—one destined to be mated to afflicted partners, it appears since his first wife had been known as Joan the Lame.

From her second marriage day, right up to her death in 1514, at the relatively young age of thirty-seven, the Breton-born queen filled her days with the personal administration of the Bretagne duchy. In 1504 she signed a treaty which she thought would ensure security of the province's future independence. This she engineered through an alliance with Austria via the future marriage of her new daughter, Claude, born in the year of her betrothal to Louis. This treaty was subsequently broken, however, and Claude was eventually married to the future François I of France in 1532—and thus the permanent absorption of the peninsula duchy into the French fold was secured.

Anne's greatest surviving monument is the mighty chateau of Nantes, one of the finest in all France. The construction of this stone masterpiece was begun by her beloved father, and Anne was determined to see it completed after his death; which it was in the year she married Charles VIII. For her first husband this strong-willed and capable princess had affection, and for her second she had much developed respect. Louis, despite ill-health, was a good husband and an able king, as kind to his subjects as he was ruthless with his enemies. After Anne died, Louis married Mary Tudor (sister of Henry VIII of England), but he survived his Breton spouse by only a few months, dying on New Year's Day, 1515.

The Warmest, Sunniest Seaboard; Plus the Loire Estuary and Regal Western Cliffs

Two contrasting nature parks, a Nice of the North, a world-renowned prehistoric treasure and a breath-taking western landfall. Where Gauguin painted and Tati filmed, there is invigorating variety all along this south-facing seaboard. It is now manicured to provide gold-standard holiday amenities like those at La Baule and Bénodet, with oases of venerable Bretagne highlighted by Vannes, Quimperlé and Quimper.

Loire-Atlantique

Appropriately, this section begins with a near-aerial glimpse of the Atlantic from the impressive height of the **Saint-Nazaire toll bridge**. The bridge is a rainbow-arch of elegance rising 60 m (197ft) above the Loire estuary. The open sea lies below and beyond, while ahead are the wartime U-boat pens and the most important of France's naval dockyards. Completed in the

Quiberon's Côte Sauvage; very dramatic to observe when the sea is lively, but no place to take an impromptu dip. Disregard the warning notices at your peril.

mid-1970s, the toll charge is comparatively excessive, but the payment is worth the view and the exhilarating experience of actually traversing the massive fretwork steel structure which spans over 2.5 km (1½ miles) of tidal waters.

Saint-Nazaire

In all honesty the great bridge is one of the few attractions of Saint-Nazaire for the leisure visitor—unless he or she is passionately interested in the shipyard industry. There are the submarine pens, but since, by their very nature, they were designed to be not only bomb-proof but distinctly unobtrusive, they are in no way architecturally stimulating. For those who want a closer view than that provided by the toll

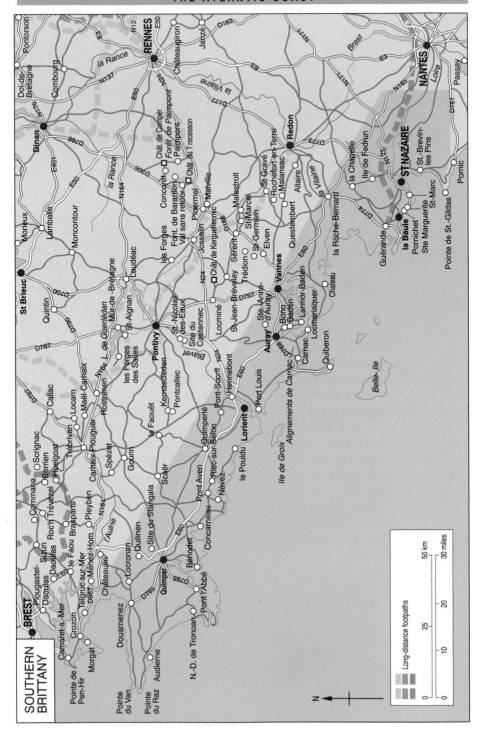

SOUTHERN BRITTANY

Long-distance footpaths

| 0 | | 10 | 25 | | 50 km |
| 0 | | | 20 | 30 miles |

N

bridge, there is dock access and a viewing platform. The great port is still, in part, a base for submarines, though it is now primarily concerned with deep-sea cargo vessel production. There is an illustrative **ecomuseum** in quai des Fregates, with car parking adjacent to the lock. In season, minibus tours of the shipyard basin are organized by the tourist office which is in place François-Blancho.

The town of Saint-Nazaire is virtually all new, save for the dolmen relics of prehistory, attractively displayed in a city centre square. The old town was almost totally destroyed by allied air and ground attacks in the latter stages of World War II. Nothing remains of the fishing village of medieval times, nor indeed of the 19th-century port and town expansion which followed

*M*ap of Brittany's Atlantic Coast.

*T*oll bridge approaching Saint-Nazaire. There are some breathtaking Loire estuary views from Europe's longest span of steel arch.

the demise of neighbouring Nantes' fortunes. The new town is laid out in a grid pattern around a town hall which was completed only in the late 1960s. Commercial and residential life proceeds smoothly, if blandly, from clean, straight streets relieved only by rare visual high spots, like the **Jardin des Plantes**, off the outer harbour, and the striking **Lagrange sports stadium** just to the north-west, constructed imaginatively in concrete and steel and aptly named the "flying saucer".

It is not surprising that the whole of Saint-Nazaire is pristine and modern, for it suffered particularly violently during the War. It was here, in 1942, that a daring British and Canadian commando raid was responsible for the partial closure of the port when the destroyer *Cambeltown* rammed a vital lock gate and was then blown up to seal the entrance. Despite subsequent saturation bombing on a massive scale, much of the German submarine base survived intact, many of the structures today being civilian workshops. Unique in one respect, Saint-Nazaire does possess the one submarine in France which may be seen by the public; what is more the *Espadon*—now the centre piece of that ecomuseum— was the first French vessel to sail beneath the polar ice-cap.

While beyond the port there is little of historic interest, the town does have excellent sporting facilities, principally in the **Parc Paysager**, which boasts a lake, a swimming pool, tennis courts, participant amenities for children and adults, picnic areas and several large car parks. The fine central feature is a futuristic stadium which can seat 4,500 spectators. Sports-conscious Nazairiens can enjoy healthy fun at a number of gymnasiums and parks equipped with jogging and cycle tracks, squash and basketball courts, plus specialized centres for gymnastic and martial arts enthusiasts. There are no less than three city swimming pools, 22 tennis courts and an 18-hole golf-course.

Culture vultures are equally well served, with a wide choice of multiscreen cinemas, theatres, a full programme of classical and jazz concerts, plus numerous art exhibitions and a grand summer fair. There are 25 hotels within the city confines and two camping parks, while a whole range of gourmet and ethnic restaurants are ready to give service, along with quickfood bars and *crêperies*. Comprehensive shopping outlets provide for every possible need and the main food market days are Tuesday, Friday and Sunday mornings at the place du Commerce. Saint-Nazaire is served by the SNCF, of course, and has an important coach station, and there are also direct flights to Paris (Orly) from Saint-Nazaire airport. Admittedly all those hotels cater mainly to conference cohorts of business people, while the first-rate sports and leisure facilities are patronized mainly by the local population. Nonetheless, for those who actually enjoy holidaying in cities of commerce and industry (and there are some), Saint-Nazaire could be an agreeable choice. Those seeking a more orthodox leisure base will certainly continue westwards to the real funstrip of the Côte d'Amour, the centre of which is La Baule, otherwise known as "the Nice of the North".

La Baule

The comparison with that most famous of Riviera resorts is in many ways justified. La Baule is big, both brash and exclusive, expensive, very crowded in the high summer, and in its way delightful. It also possesses superfine sand beaches, washed daily by Atlantic tides, thus ensuring a low pollution factor and actually scoring points over its Mediterranean counterpart. As a seaside resort, La Baule has been particularly blessed by nature. Situated in the centre of a sweeping, south-facing bay, and flanked by the smaller suburbs of Pornichet and Le Pouliguen, there are some 9 km (5½ miles) of silvery beach, the great

waterside attraction claimed to be the finest in Europe. The area also enjoys an exceptionally high annual sunshine average, while the iodine-laden air is said to be an invigorating tonic.

Behind the long beach, which becomes densely thronged in July and August, serried rows of dazzling stone and glass hotels and apartments form man-made cliffs above the wide promenade, invariably filled with an almost ceaseless procession of slow-moving cars. In between, sunburned pedestrians dodge from the beach to pavement cafés and back again. La Baule is not only a family fun centre, it is also a poser's paradise.

Since the late 19th century the town has been something of an up-market resort, and traces of *belle époque* architecture have not yet been totally eradicated by contemporary building. Indeed, parts of the centre are distinctly pleasing where, back from the opulence of the frontal boulevard,

*T*he beach at La Baule; the fun-strip offers every kind of seaside facility and is dubbed the "Nice of the North".

smart shopping streets and tree-shaded residential enclaves exist in a happy profusion amid camellia and mimosa blooms, emerald-green lawns and semitropical trees and shrubs.

There is more than a touch of Mediterranean ambience here when the sun shines brightly through the branches of the countless pine trees which thrive abundantly between new houses and apartment blocks. They give the whole conurbation an atmosphere of a formal, landscaped park which is effective and easy on the eye. It is a purpose-built seaside city then, created expressly for holidaymakers. You either love or hate the conception, but it must be said that La Baule is a shining example of the marque.

Linear in configuration, now virtually embracing Pornichet to the east, there are in effect three town centres, all of which are to the south of the railway and the two SNCF stations. Around the place de Victoire is one hub, around the place des Palmiers another, and around the place Notre-Dame a third. In all these locations the La Baule bustle is at its busiest in season, where residential and shopping precincts overlap and intermix. The main market place is off the avenue des Ibis, just to the north of the imposing Hôtel de Ville. The main tourist office is in the place de la Victoire near Gare Escoublac, and there is a high-season annexe office in place des Palmiers, close to Gare Les Pins.

A canal (once a busy commercial access waterway to the salt-pans) separates La Baule from Le Pouliguen at the western end of town. It is on the other side of this narrow divide that those seeking slightly less expensive accommodation or holiday facilities will look. There are over 50 hotels in La Baule, ranging from four-star luxury palaces like l'Hermitage, through a choice of *logis de France*, to modest bed-and-breakfast-houses. For campers and touring caravanners there is a choice of touring parks—municipal and private—on the northern outskirts of town amid agreeably green and predictably quieter terrain.

The beaches, bright lights and smart shops are magnetically attractive to countless thousands during the summer, together with the marvellous

Up-market opulence prevails at the smartest resort in western France, reflected by the Hôtel de Ville.

variety of leisure and sporting facilities. La Baule boasts some of the best in France, whether your particular interest be sailing, windsurfing (or any other watersport), horse-riding, tennis or golf (the Bretesch course, adjacent to a glorious 15th-century fairytale château, is scenically splendid). For those simply wishing to tone up physically, there are two *centres de thalassothérapie* (sea-bathing stations).

The Definitive "See and be Seen" Resort
Renowned for its grand casino, country clubs, swish hotels and prestigious shopping arcades, La Baule could very quickly deplete the biggest holiday budget, so if you fall into the explorer or traveller bracket, you may not wish to linger too long. On the other hand, this seaside centre of French high life can be seductive! Horses and high-powered cars are a major interest, with *concours hippique* events as popularly thronged as the resort's most swanky show, the annual *Concours d'Elegance á l'Automobile*, held annually since 1924 not far from the harbour. There are no less than four yacht clubs at the harbour, where personal wealth is ostentatiously displayed. Now less than three hours from Paris thanks to the TGV extension, the resort is increasingly a playground of the capital's well-to-do, whisked at 300 kph (190 mph) from the Ile de France for a tonic of *calme et repos*.

The inner body is also pampered at La Baule. For those who like to experiment gastronomically, there are some 50 restaurants within the city confines, from gourmet establishments like l'Espadon, through ethnic speciality houses as varied as Mandarin and Moroccan, down to fast-food counters and *crêperies* which proliferate in certain quarters. In addition to the casino, there are half a dozen night clubs, discotheques, four cinemas and a theatre, while a dozen galleries display permanent exhibitions of painting, sculpture and pottery.

Official market days are Tuesday, Friday, Saturday and Sunday morning, although every day is market day in the summer.

There is plenty of pleasant walking in and around the resort; most popularly perhaps along the esplanade Benoit (vehicle free), across the canal bridge into Pouliguen, returning via pine-shaded avenues to the town centre. In **La Baule-Les-Pins**, there are many venerable trees, some over 100 years old, flower gardens and the Parc des Dryades, with children's play areas and open-air theatre; and nearby Bois d'Amour, a favourite with strollers and picnickers.

Back on the sea front and at the eastern end of town, Pornichet has its new small-boat harbour and horse-racing circuit, while westwards, at the other end of the 9 km (5½ mile) beach, **Le Pouliguen** is the major port area, both for commercial fishing and pleasure craft. There is pleasant woodland walking immediately inland, plus a stretch of rock-girt and cave-studded coast, traced by an old customs lookout route, the *Sentier des Douaniers*.

Just north of Le Pouliguen are the extensive honeycomb pools, the celebrated Loire-Atlantique **salt-pans**, once a major industry of the area. **Saillé** is the central village, still displaying some old-world houses and a church museum exhibiting evidence of this one-time source of pastoral prosperity. You can still buy fine, fresh sea-salt direct from roadside sellers hereabouts. There is a bus service from Saillé back to La Baule centre, about 5 km (3 miles) distant. One of the best views over the salt-pan network is from the picturesque village of **Careil**, about 2.5 km (1½ miles) east of Saillé, which has a preserved 15th-century chapel and an ancient château, which is open to visitors.

The most historic part of the La Baule region lies at the extreme western end of the finger peninsula, past Batz-sur-Mer, on the arm of the natural harbour. There are some venerable 15th- to 17th-century fishermen's houses lining what is still partly a working port. A good source of fresh-caught fish is Le Croisic—especially crab, lobster and bass when in season.

For cycling enthusiasts there are a number of recommended local excursions and bikes may be hired on a daily or weekly basis from several La Baule centres. You can consider the easy 25 km (15½ mile) coast road route around the Côte Sauvage peninsula to Le Croisic, overlooking **Grand Traict lagoon**, or explore those intriguing salt-pans at close quarters. It is easy riding between the vast jigsaw shapes of shallow reservoirs which were created through centuries of painstaking labour, and which resulted in miles of clay retaining walls. The resultant "pans", dug with clever cunning to form progressively shallow containers, hold decanted sea-water which is finally collected in *oeillets* (literally "eyelet holes"), where the residue water evaporates to leave crystallized salt deposits. Marsh managers—*paludiers*—collect the valuable crop and cultivate the delicate system much as they have done since earliest times.

From fringe settlements like Le Pouliguen and **Batz-sur-Mer** (which amid modern bustle still retains a 10th-century chapel and an authenticated record of Norse population during the Dark Ages), there is easy access to quieter bathing beaches, like those of Port-Lin and Valentin. **Le Croisic** boasts an interesting **naval museum** and an excellent **aquarium** housing many fish species including voracious piranhas and a stuffed version of the almost-extinct coelacanth. Open all year, this is a good wet-weather objective. In fine weather, Le Croisic and Pouliguen are popular skin-diving centres where underwater fishing is much practised. For even more exotic (and expensive) sport, you can learn to fly or indulge in parachute jumping at La Baule aerodrome, d'Escoublac.

More prosaic but just as pleasurable, is the pastime of walking or cycling east of Pornichet. There is undulating countryside here and a coast road revealing a succession of sheltered beaches and rocky spurs, backed by woods and with islets and a lighthouse offshore. The scenic cove of **Saint-Marc**, which was the location of the classic Jacques Tati film, *Monsieur Hulot's Holiday*, is a popular objective, and lies about 10 km (6 miles) from La Baule centre. Indeed the whole coastline from tiny Saint-Marc to Pointe du Croisic at the western tip of the Côte Sauvage, is dotted with visual delights; a variety of caves, inlets, viewpoints, ancient menhirs and half-secret alcoves of nature within a stone's throw of a seaside strip which is one of the busiest in France.

Slightly further afield there are two more attractive visitor targets for those based at La Baule, one man-made, the other natural. They are Guérande and the Briére nature park. **Guérande** is a distinctly well-preserved medieval market town, still proudly display moat-washed ramparts, almost as intact as they must have appeared when they were first built around the town in the 15th century. A really quite small plateau settlement, marginally elevated from the surrounding salt marshes, Guérande is unspoiled by excessive outlying development. Entering through the tower-flanked Porte Saint-Michel (one of four fortified gateways), it is possible to capture a faint vibration of a past age along the cobbled streets and alleys lined with a number of 17th-century houses, particularly close to the collegiate **church of Saint-Aubin**, parts of which date back to the 12th century.

The **ramparts** are, however, the most impressive remains, despite partial filling of the town moat in the 18th century. Incredibly, no less than ten defensive wall towers still stand. Because of the town's erstwhile importance as guardian of the precious salt-pans, it is the capital of Guérande peninsula, though now vastly outgrown by its coastal neighbours. A small museum is housed within the castle gatehouse, containing artefacts, pottery and period costume reflecting the salt-industry heyday of Guérande which owns a past studded with traumatic interludes. One of the worst was in 1344, when the ramparts were

M ain street of the medieval Guérande; interesting, quite small and faintly disappointing when compared to Vitré or Josselin, but a mellower contrast to nearby La Baule.

breached and the town captured by the forces of Charles de Blois, duke of Brittany, savagely disputing the duchy succession with Jean de Montfort. The occupation was short-lived, however, Charles being killed at the Battle of Auray two years later.

Below the modest Guérande peninsula plateau, the sea encroached in Roman times, far more than it does today, forming a huge gulf above what are now the salt-pans. Some historians argue that it was offshore here, rather than in the Bay of Quiberon further to the west, that the destruction of the Veneti sailing fleet by Caesar's war galleys took place. Certainly the contemporary location of fortified Guérande seems oddly, if only fractionally, misplaced. Assuredly, the Atlantic shoreline was strategically closer when the fortified settlement was first constructed; a conjecture of substance really, since there *was* a drastic fall of water level following the last ice age. This does not detract from Guérande's interest, although in truth the town cannot be compared to majestic Vitré.

Just to the east of Guérande's walls is the boundary of the **Brière nature park**—one of 25 such areas now established across the Republic. The GR3 long-distance footpath takes in a traverse of the park, and some enthusiasts explore the route from a Guérande base, with the aid of Michelin map No. 63. The Brière has the distinction of being one of the largest of all wildlife preserves in western Europe.

Created by government decree in 1970, the total area extends over 40,000 hectares (100,000 acres), at the heart of which is a 7,000-hectares

(17,300-acre) marsh, now actively protected and maintained through a nationally financed programme. Freely accessible to visitors, the Brière is also an open-air school of nature, where thousands of children from urban France learn about the pastoral heritage of their country. Two places which reveal the *Marais de Grande Brière* to its best advantage are Kerhinet village (off the D51 north-east of Guérande), and the Ile de Fédrun, located virtually at the centre of this marshy world.

Kerhinet, lovingly and meticulously restored, is a typical marsh-dweller's settlement of thatched cottages, together with a folk-museum of rustic clothing and everyday artefacts, a weaver's workshop, a craft house and an exhibition centre. It is certainly a deliberate tourist magnet but nonetheless is nicely executed and operated. Not far distant, the whitewashed walls and thatched roofs of **Ile de Fédrun** village create a delightful picture of an almost vanished pastoral life-style in surroundings where marsh reeds and peat are still cut, and fish still netted, although of course on a very much reduced scale nowadays. Guided tours by boat, canoe, bicycle or on foot are organized throughout the summer season (details are available from the Maison du Parc, 180 Ile de Fédrun, 44720 Saint-Joachim, tel: 40-88-42-72). At the village of **Rozé**, there is a 1 km (½ mile) nature trail and a lock-keeper's house which is partially a museum of fauna, flora and geology. The short nature walk reveals lots of indigenous plant life and, if you are lucky, a wide variety of birds, both resident and migratory.

One might think that after the Lac de Grand-Lieu near Saint-Philbert, the Brière world simply reveal more of the same. Not so, for this marsh area encompasses some 22 cantons, all of which collectively own the area, and have done since the time of François II, Duke of Brittany, in the 15th century—a long-established right similar to that enjoyed by the verderers of England's New Forest. The Brière is similarly varied of aspect, where rural workaday life continues much as it has done for centuries, despite encroaching commerce and the daytime exodus of many of the inhabitants to modern factories around Nantes.

The Brièron's true home is one of canals, narrow reed-bordered channels, and open expanses of still water where great flocks of wildfowl find a safe haven. It is watery world of natural silence and wide horizons, a fascinating region which was once a mighty forest as evidenced by the 5,000-year-old fossilized tree trunks that have been dredged.

Despite the encroachment of civilization and the inevitable draining and taming of the marsh areas, an older way of life has been revived, or still survives in pockets—for example, the **Maison du Sabotier** at La Chapelle-des-Marais, where the clog-maker's craft can be admired, and the **Bridal House** at Fédrun, where among other folklore exhibits, there are bridal dresses decorated with wax orange blossoms. These life-like corsages were once a prominent source of marsh-dweller's income during the 19th century, when the women made the flowers and the men poled their flat-bottomed boats (*chalans*) to transport livestock, to lay

wickerwork fish-traps, or to spear eels. The Brière, even yet, is a delightful—and total—contrast to the fun-city of La Baule, so near, yet so very distant in some respects.

Two other coastal towns of interest to the north-west of La Baule, are **La Turballe** and Piriac-sur-Mer. Both are partially commercial fishing ports, though with a growing predominance of pleasure craft intermingling with work boats. **La Turballe** is renowned for its prolific sardine catches and for its 8 km (5 mile) sandy beach which extends from the artificial harbour, which is itself now backed by increasing building development. Northwards, the coastline becomes prettier and rockier, before rounding the point, wich is much visited for its viewpoint, to Lerat and the natural haven of **Piriac-sur-Mer**, as popular with amateur fishermen as it is with professionals. There are vestiges of 17th-century France here, displayed by atmospheric wooden-framed houses alongside the harbour-facing church. These little townships now enjoy resort status, and are much favoured by those who like La Baule amenities, though on a somewhat smaller scale. Classified pleasure ports, they are popular family centres, with a range of medium-cost accommodation and some seven caravan and camping parks between them.

La Baule, and the whole of the Côte d'Amour, is quintessentially French France, as are neighbouring Saint-Nazaire and Nantes nowadays. The countryside around may be dotted with prehistoric menhirs, but of the Breton Brittany of the Middle Ages, there is not much noticeable within a region once such an integral part of the proud duchy. Loire-Atlantique, however, embraces a wealth of that which is beloved by roaming Francophiles—not least a superb infrastructure, backed by dedicated service and leisure facilites which make touring such a delightful pursuit.

After swishy La Baule, much of what follows is noticeably rustic by comparison; no better, no worse, simply different, as the Breton influence is increasingly felt the further west one travels.

Just beyond the north-western boundary of the huge Brière nature park, the regional boundary is crossed. After the salt-marsh flatlands, La Roche-Bernard comes as quite a scenic surprise. The location, on the lip of a gorge makes a stimulating starting point to this traditionally Breton *département*.

Morbihan

Much of the *marais* country of Loire-Atlantique is cloaked by a distinctly soporific blanket of heavy air in the summer months. This humidity is quite agreeable, especially for those leisure visitors deliberately seeking a holiday area in which to unwind. Fewer regions of France could be more relaxing. The contrast, therefore, is all the more marked upon entry into eastern Morbihan, for not only is there abrupt landscape elevation (if only a brief one), but an invigorating breeze often aerates the wide and wooded Vilaine river valley.

La Roche-Bernard

Small, venerable and mellow is La Roche-Bernard, with a long and violent history which records the existence of a strategic stronghold of the 10th

century. Bernhardt, the founder, was a Viking, whose descendants created a feudal dynasty by commanding what was then an important crossing point of the Vilaine river. In the mid-16th century, the promontory town became a Protestant centre, and the influence of the reformed religion spread widely westwards. This, of course, was bound to create strife and the town was frequently attacked by Catholic forces during the Wars of Religion. Fortunes waxed after the Edict of Nantes (1598), and prosperity reigned. When the *ancien régime* ended, La Roche-Bernard was one of the most powerful baronies in the duchy—at least until the Revolution. It was then that a large section of the populace in this region again came under threat since they were not only Protestant, but Royalist to boot. Violence was meted out once more and it was by no means all one-sided. During one savage battle of 1793, when thousands of royalist troops stormed and took La Roche-Bernard, there was surprisingly stiff resistance from the Republican Catholics (numbering under 200), led by their brave mayor Joseph Sauveur who, defiant to the end, was shot in cold blood. Later that year the town was renamed La Roche-Sauveur in honour of the courageous revolutionary, reverting to La Roche-Bernard once more in 1802.

Viewpoint over the river Vilaine at La Roche-Bernard; in the background is the old bridge accidentally dynamited by the Germans in World War II.

Once a prosperous commercial freshwater port, it is now a successful and scenic pleasure boat haven with pontoon or buoy moorings for 300 craft, together with full cruising amenities including petrol, water and mains electricity. High above the water there is a viewing belvedere of the magnificent modern suspension bridge (built 1960), beside which is the stubby remnant of the 1839 original, destroyed accidentally in 1944, when lightning struck mines laid by the German forces of occupation. For 15 years a temporary crossing point was created from Normandy invasion beach pontoons. The first bridge incidentally, was the longest ever built in France at the time and was 193 m (633 ft) long.

Birthplace of the French Man-of-War Sailing Ships

The Vilaine gets its name from the Latin *Visnonia*, (literally, "river of rusty water") as the Romans called it, for with each tide, the churned sludge turned the waters opaque. Now barraged above and below La Roche-Bernard, the river has been transformed into a huge, elongated freshwater lake extending over some 1,000 hectares (2,500 acres), no longer tidal of course, and with La Roche roughly in its centre. The town remembers its one-time sea-going days of glory through a viewpoint plaque commemorating the first triple-deck warship to be constructed in the Republic. It was ordered by Cardinal Richelieu in 1629 and was a massive vessel for the period, weighing 1,200 tonnes and carrying an eventual crew of nearly 650 men. This floating fortress constructed from local timber was called *La Couronne (The Crown)*, which was apt for she became something of a prototype for future French fighting ships of that era.

Today there is little left of what was a hive of maritime industry in the 17th century. Remnants of the old port remain reflected by the venerable warehouses and the quay. To see the other main historic high spots of the town takes about an hour, starting from the tourist office, itself a fine example of late-16th-century architecture. Parts of the imposing **Chapelle Notre-Dame** survive from the 11th century, while the **Château des Basses-Fosses** is a splendid and typical example of a rich merchant's residence of the 17th century, of which there were a good number in La Roche-Bernard. This house is now a folk museum containing a collection of rustic and maritime memorabilia. Of the ancient town streets, **rue du Tour de l'Isle** was a 17th-century Protestant enclave, honeycombed by secret connecting cellars. In the **Place du Bouffay** executions by guillotine were carried out during The Terror.

The river Vilaine rises in the Mayenne valley (north of Laval) and winds its way south over a course of some 220 km (137 miles). La Roche-Bernard, located at the heart of one of the most scenic and widest reaches, is nowadays appropriately recognized as a sporting and leisure centre with a choice of homely auberge hotels noted for their cuisine, and a three-star camping park beside the river. The town has excellent watersports facilities including a canoe and kayak centre, an all-weather swimming pool with solarium, while anglers have a wide choice of coarse fish quarries. Boat cruises are also popular, both on the river and on the canal system. At Arzal, some 5 km (3 miles) downstream, you can cruise the 21 km (13 miles) of water known as La Rivière des Ducs de Bretagne, aboard the sleek river boat, appropriately called *Anne de Bretagne*. Market day at La Roche is Thursday, and the charming town is in a pleasing setting and makes a promising beginning to any exploratory journey through Morbihan.

This is really no more than the traveller might expect, since this region— the name translates as "Little Sea", *Mor Bihan* in Gaellic—has the reputation for being one of the most picturesque in Brittany, and one of the most equable in terms of climate. Mild all the year round, it is a hot and sunny region from late May to early October, thus boasting a wide variety of plants normally rare at such a latitude. It encompasses a landscape of variety too—of gentle valleys, forests and plains, lakes and rivers, and with the great convoluted Gulf of Morbihan the unmistakable central feature.

Driving westwards from la Roche-Bernard—itself at the extreme eastern end of the Lanvaux Moors ridge—this near-distant Morbihan 'high country' north of the N165 is scenically green and interesting. Most travellers, however, will probably find the gulf more immediately attractive after La Roche. Fear not, for the Lanvaux ridge is described in detail in THE BRITTANY HINTERLAND chapter. Just past Muzillac, some 15 km (9 miles) distant, there is an agreeable halfway stop beside the barrage lake of **Pen-Mur**. Here is a well-signposted **zoo park** extending over 50 hectares (123 acres), the home of animal and bird species from 5 continents. The park is famed for its kangeroos and ibis. Consider also the Moulin de Pen-Mur and a guided tour of a **paper mill** where traditional paper-making can still be seen as it was in the 13th century. The Muzillac mill is open all year.

Vannes

One of the oldest and most stimulating of the southern Breton cities (and thankfully unharmed during 20th-century conflicts) is Vannes, the prefecture of Morbihan *département*. The ancient capital of the Veneti, wrested from them in 56 BC by the legions of Julius Caesar, it was originally called Darioritum. Even then, this wonderfully

T own plan of Vannes.

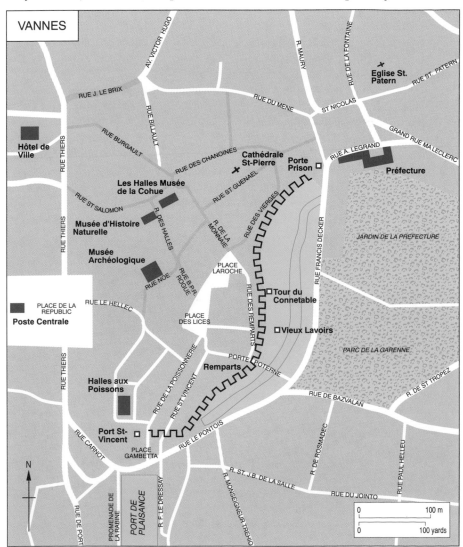

VANNES

AV. VICTOR HUGO
RUE J. LE BRIX
RUE BILLAULT
RUE BURGAULT
RUE THIERS
RUE DES CHANOINES
RUE ST SALOMON
RUE THIERS
R. DES HALLES
RUE NOÉ
R. DE LA MONNAIE
RUE ST GUENAEL
RUE DES VIERGES
RUE B.P.R. ROQUE
RUE LE HELLEC
PLACE LAROCHE
PLACE DES LICES
RUE DES REMPARTS
RUE THIERS
PLACE DE LA REPUBLIC
RUE DE LA POISSONNERIE
RUE ST VINCENT
PORTE POTERNE
RUE CARNOT
RUE LE PONTOIS
PLACE GAMBETTA
RUE DE PORT
PROMENADE DE LA RABINE
PORT DE PLAISANCE
R. F. LE DRESSAY
R. MONSEIGNEUR TREHIO
R. ST. J.B. DE LA SALLE
R. DE ROSMADEC
RUE DE BAZVALAN
R. DE ST TROPEZ
RUE PAUL HELLEU
RUE DU JOINTO
R. MAURY
RUE DU MENE
ST NICOLAS
RUE DE LA FONTAINE
Eglise St. Patern
RUE ST. PATERN
GRAND RUE MA LECLERC
RUE A. LEGRAND
Préfecture
RUE FRANCIS DECKER
JARDIN DE LA PREFECTURE
PARC DE LA GARENNE

Hôtel de Ville
Cathédrale St-Pierre
Porte Prison
Les Halles Musée de la Cohue
Musée d'Histoire Naturelle
Musée Archéologique
Poste Centrale
Tour du Connetable
Vieux Lavoirs
Remparts
Halles aux Poissons
Port St-Vincent

N

0   100 m
0   100 yards

sited and fortified settlement at the head of the huge Atlantic inlet, was not easily subdued, for the Veneti were warlike and stubborn, and they had surrounded their home with formidable defensive walls. Nominoë, the 9th-century warrior chieftain who united the Breton tribes into a powerful entity (and who was crowned at Dol-de-Bretagne), chose Vannes as the capital of his new kingdom. Over 700 years were to pass before the independent state he created proclaimed loyalty to France and was itself rewarded with duchy status. The province thus became a veritable state within a state, governed from its own parliament, and raising its own taxes and protective army. The decisive oath of allegiance to King François I, Duke of Brittany, was sworn at Vannes in 1532, and not until the Revolution of 1789 did Brittany become an integral part of the French nation.

Always a city of commercial, administrative and strategic importance before the waters of the Gulf of Morbihan receded, it is today a medieval kernel of delight, surrounded by increasing development, although this has not been allowed to encroach too much. Vannes' connection with the open sea—some 16 km (10 miles) distant now—is tenuous, but it still retains the feel of a bustling maritime port, imparted through its narrow Port de Plaisance harbour, which provides access to the gulf and ultimately the Atlantic.

Vannes also has the short, aboveground ribbon of the ancient Rohan

*V*annes, the famous *ancient washhouses and the castle ramparts; the* Tour de Connetable *is the central feature.*

stream, which flows below the remains of impressive rampart walls. From this watered level, one must walk uphill to the south-facing town centre, which again evokes a seafaring atmosphere when seagulls wheel overhead. Before ascending, some of the most precious of Vannes' architectural treasures must be admired from the Porte Poterne; they are the splendidly preserved medieval wash houses with their curious dormer roofs, which lie in a real bygone setting between the Rohan stream and the old castle ramparts.

The ducal **château** in the background (circa 1800), is now a seat of learning and is enhanced by formal flower gardens which extend across the rue Francis Decker. It is an attractive scene by day or night, since the area is floodlit at dusk. At the northern end of the remaining city walls, is the **Prison Gate**, distinguished by its stout, machicolated tower. Adjacent is the

The old town of Vannes is littered with a delightful array of unusual historic architectural features. A gratifying place to stroll and observe.

Cathédrale Saint-Pierre, which was erected during the 13th century, although only a small part of the somewhat forbidding structure (the north tower) is original. Nonetheless, this flamboyant Gothic building has one or two interesting features, not least an Italianate rotunda chapel (16th century)—very unusual in this region. There is also, the church treasure, housed in the old chapterhouse, and which includes a 12th-century chest and a holy cross with receptacle. The cathedral is revered for containing the tomb of Saint-Vincent-Ferrier, who was canonized in the 15th century for his miracle cures.

The atmosphere of the Middle Ages is retained, with just a little visitor imagination, in **place Henri IV** close by Saint-Pierre. Now at the centre of a pleasant pedestrian precinct, there are a number of magnificently preserved 16th-century houses hereabouts, with steeply pitched roofs, gables and tiny windows. The rue Salomon is rich in venerable town houses, as is the rue des Halles, where there is an entrance to the medieval covered market, **La Cohue**, now a museum. The **Musée Archéologique**, housed in Château Gaillard, a 15th-century mansion and erstwhile parliament building, exhibits some splendid specimens of prehistory gathered in Morbihan *département*, including bracelets and other adornments, weapons and primitive tools. There is also a **museum of fine art**, which contains paintings by Breton artists and a collection of *objets d'art* and sculptures.

Other pleasing buildings will be found in the rue Saint-Vincent, in particular: the Hôtel Dondel; the gracious 19th-century crescent of classical elegance which is place Gambetta; the street with ancient Welsh connections, rue Saint-Gwenael, where a 14th-century dwelling with overhanging eaves survives; and in the place Valencia, number 17 where Saint-Vincent-Ferrier died in 1419 (the house was restored in 1574). One of Vannes' celebrated buildings will also be found just here at the corner of rue Noë, an ancient dwelling decorated with carvings of two jovial peasant gargoyle faces known as **Maison de Vannes et sa Femme**. The tourist office, located at the corner of rue Thiers and rue du Drezen, is itself an attractive 16th-century building, which seems very appropriate.

As a base, Vannes must be awarded high marks, for not only is the town an interesting, lively and compact area to explore on foot (at least in the centre), it is also adjacent to one of France's most magnificent Atlantic inlets. The **Golfe du Morbihan**—a glorious natural harbour—extends across some 12,000 hectares (30,000 acres) of almost totally landlocked waters, the sea flowing in and out through one miniscule gap at the Pointe de Bourgneuf. Within the land arms, the tidal waters run fast and bountiful; high water at spring tides often reaches in excess of 5 m (16½ ft). The gulf is studded with a scattering of islands and islets—364 in all, or virtually one for every day of the calendar as the locals claim—forty being inhabited, of which the Ile aux Moines and Ile d'Arz are the largest. Cruise and ferry boats explore all the most interesting parts of the gulf from landing stages at Vannes, Locmariaquer, Port-Navalo at the gulf's southern extremity, or Auray.

For small-boat enthusiasts the Gulf of Morbihan is a mecca, while bird-watchers and naturalists will certainly wish to visit the **Falguérec Nature Reserve**, some 4 km (2 ½ miles) south of Vannes at Séné, where a host of resident and migratory wildfowl throng the saltings. The reserve is open from April to August and there is a small admission charge. Close to Vannes town centre there are more attractions for nature enthusiasts within the confines of Vannes' eminent

Zone de Loisirs, just to the south of the town centre off the Conleau road.

Two of these attractions, both recommended wet-weather targets, are the **butterfly museum**, and the nearby **Vannes Aquarium** in the Parc du Golfe. The first displays a collection of over 1,500 *papillons*, most of which are exotic tropicals; while the second, occupying a huge multi-storey building, is claimed with some justification to be the biggest and most comprehensively stocked aquarium in Europe. The layout and decor of this aquatic centre is superb, containing over 400 specimens housed in 50 pools, many of which are linked by cascades. Open from 9 a.m. to 11 p.m. (unusually with no lunchbreak), and from June to August, this is an educational fun place for children. For those who prefer man-made rather than natural movement, there is a **museum of mechanical dolls**, 300 of them in all, which is opposite the aquarium and which is open from Easter to October.

For visitors *sans* car, Vannes is particularly blessed for it is served by the railway, a first-rate local coach service to all points of the Gulf of Morbihan area, and by ferry or cruise boats from the town port. In addition, good information for pedestrian explorers is available from the *Fédération Française de la Randonneé* at number 11, allée du Grador, or from the *Amis des Chemins de Ronde* (details are available from the tourist office). Bicycles may be hired from the SNCF station or at 118, boulevard de la Paix (M. Trébossen), or on both the larger gulf islands of Ile aux Moines or Ile d'Arz. On the doorstep, as it were, there are 8 km (5 miles) of promenade at Vannes, where you can stretch your legs by walking or cycling.

To reach the gulf islands, the bigger ones of which are quiet havens of sandy beaches, woodland and megalithic monuments (these are especially prominent on Ile d'Arz), the Navix fleet, Vedettes du Golfe, operates a wide service with 21 modern, fast and safe vessels, which ply between all the major islands, plus daytrips to distant Belle-Ile, the Ile d'Houat and the Loire-Atlantique coast. Their office in the Parc du Golfe can provide full details and sailing schedules (tel: 97-63-79-99).

The accommodation choice is wide and handsome in and around Vannes, as one would expect. There are some two dozen hotels in town and a similar number in outlying districts together with a spread of *chambres d'hôtes* (B&Bs) both on the mainland and on the main offshore islands, the latter also having camping grounds. Nearest to Vannes centre is the municipal caravan and camping park on the Séné road (D199), which is open from April to November. The facilities do not match the three-star rating, being primitive and hard used; the setting is pleasant though.

Compact, like every medieval city worthy of the name, Vannes is easy on the feet for those who enjoy a culture ramble combined with a shopping and/or eating foray. There are a number of smart shops here which are frequently dovetailed into venerable buildings with quaint overhangs along the narrower, cobbled streets, all of which adds to the interest. For antiques, try the rue des Halles, and for pottery, try the rue Carnot.

Including those ubiquitous Brittany *crêperies*, there are almost 50 eating houses in Vannes, dispensing the widest variety of fare, including every conceivable fish dish, as one would expect. For the best of Breton traditional cuisine, just one of several good restaurants is La Varendre in the rue de la Fontaine. The Piazza d'Italia in the rue Thiers is noted for its pasta specialities, as is the Restaurant l'Andaluz, in the rue Vierges, for its paella. All three, like most of the others (which offer dishes from Vietnam to Alsace) are decorous and atmospheric.

While making a short list of restaurants, you will certainly come across some delightful corner of Vannes, or pause to admire its more obvious landmarks, like the **Tour du Connetable** (Constable's Tower). That constable of France, Olivier Clisson, was once locked up here at the end of the 14th century. Or you'll come face to face with the most ostentatious of 19th-century town hall buildings in the place Maurice-Marchais. What is impressive here is a splendid lively statue, massive of proportion and depicting the mighty warrior Duc de Richemont—he who led the French army to final victory against the English in the Hundred Years War.

Finally, for self-catering visitors, the **market place** (on the Vannes shopping front in the place des Lices) is open every Wednesday and Saturday and is renowned for its fresh produce, while the *Continent* hypermarket in Vannes Commercial Centre boasts a 50-shop foyer. It is open daily, *sans interruption*, as they say, except Sunday.

For entertainment, there are three cinemas in Vannes, two of which (the Garenne and the Eden) have three screens. There are two discotheque-/night clubs, which are open late until 4 a.m. and which can be found just outside town. Le Spinaker is on the route d'Auray, while l'Atlantide is on the route de Sainte-Anne. A number of bars (some with cabaret entertainment or dancing) remain open until the small hours; one, the Pub le Glasgow in avenue de Verdun, stays open until 2 a.m.

Leisure largely revolves around watersport in the Vannes district; principally within the huge natural harbour that is the Gulf of Morbihan. Sailing is the number one pursuit, and boat or sailboard hire is available from many locations, plus tuition courses on a daily or residential basis. Vannes is a major stop-over port for vessels competing in the annual Tour de France à la Voile. For anglers there are a number of waters, both sea and fresh, while there is horse-riding and golf in the vicinity.

During summer there is a well-filled programme of spectacular events, including an annual fair with a colourful medieval procession of ingenious authenticity, military ceremonies on the town ramparts, and a jazz festival held at the end of July which grows in reputation year by year.

Delightful though Vannes town centre may be, car parking is difficult in the extreme especially in the tourist season; almost enough to be off-putting for the car-driving visitor unfamiliar with the town layout. If you do arrive at a busy time, try the area around the port initially, but be prepared to leave your car on the town perimeter. There is usually space in outlying streets for those ready to walk 500 m (555 yd) or so.

Those not fond of traffic hassles might prefer to base themselves a short distance away, then walk or ride into town on public transport or on a hired bicycle. One place well situated for exploratory trips to Vannes and other gulf high spots is **Larmor-Baden**, some 12 km (7 ½ miles) south-west of the prefecture. It is an attractive and tranquil fishing village located on an indented mini-peninsula, with an indigenous population of about 1,000 which swells to four times that number in high summer: an indication of its popularity. Outside July and August it is a settlement of maritime industry, minus the hectic holiday pace, with modest but comprehensive visitor amenities. These include a variety of accommodation (three hotels, self-catering apartments, camping and so on), restaurant and snack bars, two market days (Wednesday and Sunday) and utilities such as cycle hire.

A premier source of Brittany **oysters**, there are a dozen or so oyster-bed specialists here (*ostréiculteurs*) along with both amateur and professional fishermen, as evidenced by the boats in the picturesque port, Lagaden. A scenic route for pedestrians traces its way around the Larmor foreshore, the port area and the neighbouring cove, Anse de Locmiquel; while just to the northeast is **Pen en Toul**, a land-locked inlet and *marais* much inhabited with wildfowl, herons and egrets at times.

Exploring the surrounding gulf water is popular too; one of the most impressive of all Brittany megaliths lies just a 15-minute boat trip from Larmor port—that of **Gavrinis Tumulus**.

This massive landmark is 50m (165ft) in circumference and 6m (20ft) high. The prehistoric monument contains a great gallery of slabs with carved supports, the centre piece topped with a giant slab some 4m (13ft) square. Thought to be the burial chamber of a druid chieftain; it carries an air of mystery still.

Just to the south-east of Vannes there are two minor roads both worth pursuing, the first down the short peninsula to Séné and the bird sanctuary already described, the second via the D780 to the Rhuys peninsula (Presqu'ile de Rhuys), to the small township of **Sarzeau**, which boasts a largely 16th-century church and square with Renaissance houses, and which is today served by half a dozen caravan and camping sites in the vicinity, plus a choice of seasonal hotels. There is a large and interesting sweep of the Gulf of Morbihan just to the north which is reserved for wildlife, while on the seaward side of town is the **Château de Suscinio**, which has stood on this grandly wild coast since the 13th century. This stone treasure has been partially rebuilt and transformed into a museum which is open to visitors from April to September. Enough of the original survives, however, to impress the viewer, for here stood a proud fortified redoubt, which was the seat of the Dukes of Brittany, and which is still powerful in outline with six defensive towers and massive ramparts.

Birthplace of the Duc de Richemont (who won the last decisive battle of the Hundred Years War, and whose statue dominates the place Maurice-Marchais in Vannes), the still moated Suscinio castle contains the ghosts, if not the bones, of many English soldiers who were killed when the fortress was stormed by du Guesclin in 1373—the year when the warrior knight liberated all Brittany, save for Brest. Heavily damaged during the Wars of Religion, and almost destroyed during the Revolution, it is a near-miracle that Suscinio in its Atlantic-battered location survives at all. That it does is a source of real delight to those who see it at close quarters.

Two more high spots along the exposed peninsula are the 12th-century **Saint-Gildas-de-Rhuys monastic church**, where Pierre Abélard tried to resume his study after being brutally castrated by Canon Fulbert, the Parisian guardian of Héloïse; and the celebrated tumulus named **Caesar's Mound** where, it is claimed, the emperor stood surveying the decimation of the Veneti sailing fleet by Roman war galleys. The latter, being rowed and not sailed, attacked when the Veneti were becalmed, and the Roman short-sword did the rest. The view from this ancient barrow, both seaward and inland across the gulf, is splendid and it is worth the 20-minutes walk from the car park to this elevated spy point.

At the peninsula tip, the expanding Port du Crouesty now competes with neighbouring Port-Navalo, which boasts a south-facing beach. This area is becoming very popular with families seeking orthodox seaside holidays. Just across the dividing narrows lies **Locmariaquer**, a settlement since earliest times as its cluster of megaliths testify. The **Grand Menhir**, the biggest ever recorded in France, now lies broken into slabs, though it once stood 30 m

(98ft) high and weighed an estimated 350 tonnes. The village itself has a **church** built originally in the 11th century (the chancel and transept being genuine), but it is really the dolmen and menhirs hereabouts that are the magnets, at least for those keen on antiquity. Others find the sandy beach the great Locmariaquer attraction, together with the Navix sightseeing boats (Vedettes du Golfe), which ply from the harbour to all corners of the gulf and up the Auray river between April and August. There is a good hotel here, and three caravan and camping sites nearby.

Where the river Auray becomes the river Loch (or Loc), west of Vannes, the water which bisects **Auray** town is still tidal, even though it is 12 km (7 ½ miles) from the open sea. Much modernized and developed industrially and commercially on the right bank, it is blessed, today if that is the word, with a convoluted and almost confusing road network. The interesting heart of Auray is the quarter of Saint-Goustan, approached via a fine 17th-century stone bridge and the quai Franklin. Benjamin Franklin, the first ambassador to France dispatched by the newly independent America, disembarked here in 1776; there are parts of old Auray, including the bridge, which would still be immediately recognizable to Franklin.

The port and town of Auray was old long before the arrival of the gifted American, as can be seen in the 15th- and 16th-century half-timbered houses, the steep streets and the alleys around the once-bustling medieval port. Once partly fortified, the town is a prominent landmark of Breton history, for

nearby, Jean de Montfort defeated Charles de Blois in the final and decisive battle for succession to the Duchy of Brittany in 1364. At the head of Charles's forces was the redoubtable Bertrand du Guesclin, while Jean de Montfort's army was commanded by the Englishman, Sir John Chandos, a brave and brilliant soldier who had saved the life of the Black Prince at the Battle of Poitiers in 1336, and who had fought with great distinction at the Battle of Crécy, ten years later.

Despite the prowess of du Guesclin (who personally battled with stubborn ferocity), the Breton hero was to be on the losing side for once. Charles was killed and du Guesclin captured, but was treated with magnanimous chivalry for his display of courage. Jean de Montfort, now the undisputed Duc de Brittany, had a monastic

Le Bono, an ancient oyster port south of Auray. Here the river Bono spills into the mighty gulf of Morbihan to create a typical Brittany scene.

chapel erected on the battlefield just to the north of Auray, at **La Chartreuse d'Auray**,which still retains a monastic landmark and church. There is also a reliquary chapel to the last of the *Chouans* (Royalists), executed after the abortive counter-revolution battle of Quiberon Peninsula in 1795 (see under CARNAC).

The **Maison de Ville** in the place de la République at Auray was built just prior to the Revolution, while adjacent, the old **covered market** dates from the 12th century; only remnants are left, for it was virtually demolished in the early part of this century. **Saint-Gildas church** (17th century) has a fine portal, and the **Holy Ghost chapel**, which was built originally in the 13th century, has the old prison nearby, with its grim dungeons still illustrating how the unfortunate prisoners were kept chained to the walls. On the site of the old Auray **castle** (circa 1200), there is a terraced walk above the slopes of the lake waters, all of which is worth exploring on the right bank of the river. Guided tours are organized by the tourist office (which may be found in the place de la République), during July and August.

It is, however, **Sainte-Anne d'Auray**, 6 km (4 miles) north-east, that holds the greatest appeal for those in search of the traditional Brittany, for it is here that the definitive religious *pardon* is held on the same dates every year—25 and 26 July. This is indisputably the most important pilgrimage of the *région,* though others, almost as impressive and well-attended, take place at frequent intervals throughout the summer, beginning on 7 March. This interesting centre of the *Grand Pardon* still manages to retain the quiet atmosphere, and even the pleasingly rustic appearance in part of a country village. However, superimposed, and not seemingly too much out of place, are some very grandiose monuments in stone, all of which are dovetailed

T he impressive war memorial and expansive setting; just one of the memorable features of the pilgramage centre of Saint-Anne d'Auray...

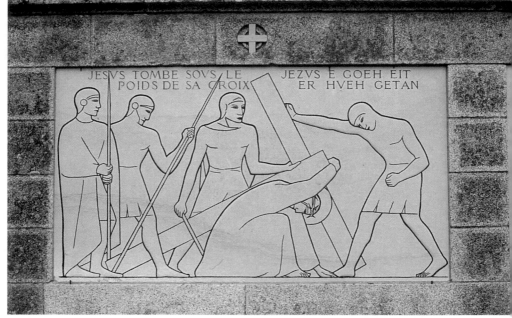

JESVS TOMBE SOVS LE
POIDS DE SA CROIX

JEZVS E GOEH EIT
ER HVEH GETAN

*...Another being the
Stations of the Cross wall-inserts
which decorate the approach
route walls. The wording is
in both French and Breton.*

sympathetically into what is really a
pastoral enclave of France.

This is the impression created, at
any rate, for the winter visitor. During
the season of *pardons,* and particularly
during the principal pilgrim influxes,
there is unavoidable bustle, a crush of
cars and coachborne humanity, and a
significant increase in commercial overtones. Don't miss Sainte-Anne-d'Auray
though, whatever the month, for it *is*
impressive with the mighty 19th-century
basilica with its Versailles-like setting
dominating the town. There is an old
convent next to the basilica with medieval cloisters, the **treasury** displaying
Sainte-Anne relics, the **Fountain of**

Miracles, and a **war memorial** which is
certainly the most remarkable and
imaginative in western France. The
memorial is approached through formal gardens which are flanked by
walls inscribed with the names of the
fallen and the Stations of the Cross,
and within the great cupola vault there
are dedication alcoves for each of the
Brittany *départements.* The monument
was raised originally through public
donations in remembrance of the
250,000 Breton servicemen who died in
the Great War of 1914–18. Now it has
become a national shrine, honouring
all the war victims of this blood-
soaked 20th century.

The sanctuary complex is built upon
the site where Sainte-Anne is said to
have appeared before a peasant farmer
named Yves Nicolazic in 1625, commanding him to build a chapel of
dedication. The dwelling where the vision first occurred—the **House of**

Nicolazic—is preserved and there is a museum. There is also the **Sainte-Anne Diorama** which, together with the basilica treasury, is open to visitors throughout the summer. There are several other chapels in the immediate vicinity and even a memorial to the valiant *Chouan* Royalists killed in the Battle of Quiberon. The whole area is suffused with an air, which though sombre, is in no way miserable or depressing. This is perhaps befitting a place dedicated to the mother of the Virgin Mary and the patron saint of Brittany.

There is a two-star hotel at Sainte-Anne d'Auray, the Myriam, which opens seasonally, and a municipal camping ground 1 km (½ mile) from the centre, open mid-June to mid-September; Auray is the main base for pilgrim visitors, however, since the accommodation choice is wider and the town amenities more comprehensive. More than a dozen hotels (headed by the three-star Hôtel Les Voyageurs) and over 30 restaurants, bistro-bars, cafés and *crêperies*, indicate the popularity of Auray as a Morbihan long-stop and tourist attraction. The appeal of the place is multiple, since it is itself a significantly historic centre, while the waters of the Gulf of Morbihan and-Sainte-Anne d'Auray are both close by. The gastronomic reputation of Auray is also a main attraction. Renowned for its oysters, the waters of the gulf are also a rich source of crayfish, lobsters and scallops, while the Atlantic bass and tuna-fish are some of the best to be found in France—as are the humble but tasty grilled sardines taken offshore along the Quiberon peninsula. It is south to the coast, Carnac and the vast sweep of Quiberon bay that is the next logical objective of the leisure traveller.

> **Yet another Medieval Gem of Stone**
> Some 15 km (9½ miles) north-east of Vannes and half-hidden in a wooded valley setting, squats the Tours d'Elven, or the Largoët castle ruins as they are sometimes called. Part of a formal park now, these remnants are truly feudal, once a great stronghold of the Lord of Rieux, one-time tutor of the duchess Anne. Stormed and all but destroyed in the 15th century by the forces of Charles VIII, the French invader king of Brittany, the sturdy keep and entrance gates (one of which is 13th century) remain standing today. Henry VIII of England also stayed here, but as a prisoner for a short time before his enthronement. An impressive *son-et-lumière* show is performed regularly in season and the château is open daily throughout the year. For reservation for this spectacular, Tristan et Yseult (Tristan and Isolde), tel: 97-53-52-79.

Carnac

The approach to Carnac is via the the ruler-straight D768, the course of an ancient Roman road. It slices through a landscape south of Auray that is now only semi-rural, although patchwork small-holdings and stands of trees do survive between villages which are patently bent on modernizing and expanding. The Roman era may be very distant, but it is almost recent compared to the timeless treasure of Carnac, which displays the most concentrated gathering of prehistoric monuments in Europe, the incredible centrepiece of that southern Brittany seaboard which is appropriately known as the **Côte des Mégalithes**.

The Menhirs stand to the north of Carnac town (reached directly via the D119 from Auray), a silent legion of massive standing stones, clustered in three main groups and littering the open heathland above the seaside resort. These petrified avenues run roughly east to west and are as much a mystery to archaeologists as Britain's Stonehenge. There is a staggering total of almost 3,000 stones, erected around 4,500 years ago, the single stones being supplemented with dolmen graves and cromlechs.

It is conjectured that the menhirs originated as symbols of worship, as individual memorial stones to warriors killed in some vast and unrecorded battle, or collectively as some complex, astronomical calendar reference. Whatever they might represent, they are profoundly impressive; even more so for their setting which is in a very Celtic corner of France. The stones still baffle scientific experts, which is somehow very comforting in a high-tech, know-it-all age!

Les Alignements de Kerzerho around Ménec, Kermario and Kerlescan, cover an area of 3 km (2 miles), the serried ranks being 100 m (330 ft) or more wide, and assuredly represent ing countless hours of back-breaking labour on the part of prehistoric man. To walk these strange avenues, especially early or late in the day, is an

Carnac and part of the Kermario alignment obscured by the multi-lingual preservation notice directed at visitors.

absorbing and almost eerie experience. Protected by law, the area has been left as natural as possible, but it may not be long before some restriction on access is imposed. The signs are already there, the surrounding heathland is hard-trodden and permanently impacted, and even the great megaliths themselves are showing signs of mortality. It will not be long before the Alignments of Carnac like Stonehenge will have to admired from a respectful distance.

Currently, there are several viewing areas freely accessible along with recommended pedestrian routes to them. One of the favoured starting points is the **Saint-Michel Tumulus**, a prehistoric burial chamber archaeologically excavated, and lying at an elevated viewpoint just to the north-east of Carnac town centre. From here, there is nice walking northwards across wooded heath, taking in traverses of the most

*C*urrently there is free access to this unique pre-historic site, but there will assuredly soon be restrictions. This is the Menac alignment, megaliths once hidden by dense forest.

extensive stone avenues, those of **Ménec** and **Kermario**. A pamphlet describing this walk (Promenade No. 2), is available with others from the Carnac tourist office. This walk is 7 km (4½ miles) in length through woodland and heath country, and taking in the hamlets of **Cloucarnac** and Kermario. It is signposted with yellow markers, and the walking time is approximately two hours.

For more detailed information about the megaliths, there are nicely displayed artefacts of ancient times in the **Carnac Museum of Prehistory** including necklaces, stone weapons and implements, and sculptured animal talismen. The museum was found in 1882 by a Scot called James Miln, an amateur enthusiast of antiquity, who spent much of his life trying to unravel the enigma of the Carnac stones.

While Carnac is unique for its wondrous relics of Europe's distant past, it is equally celebrated among French people (and an escalating number of foreigners) for its reputation as a seaside resort. The variety and quality of its bathing beaches alone put it close to the top of the popularity poll. There are six in all at this fine location on Quiberon Bay, the principal strand— **Grande Plage**—being a magnificent sweep of south-facing fine sand fronting the smart resort, which is nowadays being tagged with some accuracy as a mini La Baule.

Expansion is inevitable, and the Carnac area is almost certainly destined to be transformed from a semi-rural enclave into an urban spread ere long, if current development continues unchecked. At present, however, the balance between natural and man-made is still pleasantly agreeable—a mix of linear built-up areas but with the blue sea and green hinterland remaining prominent natural features. For those who desire beach-lazing and lotus-eating, with excursions into a fascinating and mystical past, few resorts in France could compete with Carnac.

Small enough to be administered efficiently, but large enough to provide all the recognized leisure and sport amenities associated with the turn of the 21st century, there are signs of things to come here. A sea-bathing station (thalassothérapie) is considered an obligatory complex to restore or pep up the visitor's personal health, while no dogs are permitted on Grande Plage; not even on leads. Children, of course, are particularly well catered for through organized beach entertainments during high summer. Beach tents can be hired here now (in the light of contemporary medical findings), for those wishing to avoid too much sunshine.

The beach is backed by a wide **boulevard**, with tennis courts at the eastern end just inland from Pointe Churchill, and the purpose-built small-boat harbour and yacht club at the western end, seaward of the heated swimming pool and sea-bathing station. A short stroll from the foreshore, past the old salt marsh lagoon (salines du Breno), is the town centre. A pleasing network of narrow, shady streets cluster here, the whole exuding an air of easy-going Breton life at the heart of an acknowledged leisure township.

The tourist office, in place de l'Eglise, is well stocked with local literature dispensed by a helpful staff, while Carnac commerce bows to an illustrious past, though not in a boring, exploitive manner. There is a supermarket in the avenue des Druides called—what else—Des Druides, and this is well patronized by self-catering visitors, partially for its easy parking and slightly lower priced petrol outlet. This store opens seasonally, from March to September.

For others travellers, there is the usual wide choice of holiday accommodation, ranging from a four-star luxury hotel to a whole range of caravan and camping sites; one of the

MUSÉE

A favourite with the children at the top end of the Quiberon peninsula. A replica galleon, actually a sea-shell museum, opposite Penthièvre fortress.

largest concentrations of coastal France. As for sailing, golfing, tennis, horse-riding, fishing or cycling, the Carnac environs together with the Quiberon peninsula, offer a full range. This is a family holiday region of high repute, located where the warmest of Brittany sun shines, with the widest possible variety of leisure attractions including two stretches of Côte Sauvage—one on the long finger of jutting mainland, the other on Belle-Ile, 45 minutes' sailing time from Quiberon.

 In season the **Quiberon peninsula** will probably only appeal to those who enjoy an excess of togetherness, for the

15 km (9 miles) access road to the tip and Quiberon port is narrow and liberally punctuated with traffic lights where minor roads make their lateral traverses to the Côte Sauvage. This route becomes congested at times with a fair percentage of the 100,000-plus summer volume of visitors. Called the "wild coast" for its one-time remoteness and jagged contours, and because in winter Atlantic storms lash the promontories and inlets. During July and August, however, the coastal road is inevitably crammed with cars and the cliffs, though impressive, are not at their visual best in calm weather for car-bound viewers.

Like so many other natural splendours of France, you have to use your feet to see and appreciate the best of the scenery which lies seaward of the tarmac. The 18 km (11-mile) motoring circuit provides numerous places where the active pedestrian explorer can discover the rugged coves and weirdly shaped rock formations which tower above postage-stamp beaches. Some of the seascapes are also spectacular, across the water to Belle-Ile and beyond. Incidentally, all swimming is strictly prohibited due to some very dangerous tidal currents.

At the narrowest point of the peninsula, **Fort de Penthièvre** dominates on one side while a mock-galleon museum of shells and maritime artefacts lies on the other. The fortress guardian of the landstrip was modernized after the abortive royalist invasion of 1795, when a force of 10,000 exiles were landed at Carnac by the English navy, hoping to stir a national counter-revolution. This force was much smaller than its organizers hoped for and convention troops under Général Hoche, engaged and vanquished the invaders at the peninsula extremity. Rough weather prevented any complete evacuation, the English ships lying off Quiberon being unable to approach

the treacherous shores. Those not killed in battle were later executed (many *Chouans* among them) at various points around Morbihan gulf. In another, even grimmer struggle, French Resistance fighters were shot here *en masse* during 1944. Even on a sunny day the fort is grim of outline; but the small town of Penthièvre boasts nice sand beaches either side of the road and railway, which runs straight down the peninsula centre to Quiberon.

From Port-Maria in **Quiberon** town leisure boats ply to Belle-Ile and the sister islands of Houat and Hoedic. Served by French railways, Quiberon is another fast-expanding resort,

An outdoor pottery display at Penthièvre; some of Brittany's better souvenir buys will be found at such craftsmen outlets.

*T*halassothérapie *rejuvination hotel at the tip of Quiberon peninsula. A super-modern health centre, one of the most visited in the region and very contemporary in appearance...*

justly famous nowadays for its tha-lassothérapie complex in addition to a full bill of holiday fare, including lively after-dark entertainment at the height of the season. Market day is on Saturday.

The port is picturesque, the main beach (Grande Plage) being another south-facing strand of silver. The town centre is really quite extensive, spilling over into neighbouring Haliguen, and with a good choice of shops, restaurants and hotels between Port-Maria and Port Haliguen. There are more than 20 hotels, double that number of eating houses and some eight caravan and camping sites. The Côte Sauvage

is, of course, the principal natural gem. To see it properly make your base in the vicinity of the town, then walk or cycle (there are three hire centres in Quiberon) along one of the recommended routes between Quiberon and Saint-Pierre. These are colour-coded circular walks of two or four hours duration, which touch upon some of the most impressive coastal high spots. Again, do not venture too close to the sea cliff edges, for the incoming tide can be not only spectacular but dangerous to those who get too close.

While Quiberon itself is an extremely magnetic resort which manages to absorb a huge total of holiday-makers each summer, **Belle-Ile** still enjoys much of the remoteness which has prevailed for centuries. Brittany's largest offshore island, some 17 km (10½ miles) in length, it is nonetheless popular, though many of its visitors are day-trippers. It is a windswept island, its central plateau devoid of trees, supporting only 4,000 souls, compared with the summer population of Quiberon. Le Palais is the port and the principal township, famous for its **defensive citadel** modernized in 1650 by Vauban, the master of military architecture, for the wily Nicolas Fouquet, minister to Louis XIV. The structure was extended and strengthened from an original castle, built for Henri II in the mid-16th century. Today the stout ramparts house a **museum**.

The building of this massive coastal redoubt was, however, fully justified, as Belle-Ile was considered fair game for marauding men-of-war of all nations for some time, and was twice occupied by English forces in the mid-18th century. Later, the island became a fashionable summer watering hole with artists, Claude Monet among them; the great actress Sarah Bernhardt bought a house here. For visitors wishing to stay a while, there are a number of good hotels, many B&B houses, *gîtes*, a youth hostel and some nine camping sites. Sport and leisure facilities are good, they include an 18-hole golf-course; tennis courts; two swimming pools; horse-riding; boat hire; and a sailing school.

Le Palais is quaintly attractive (as are many of the coastal sections),

... While only a few yards distance is the truly traditional Brittany epitomized by this fisherman's cottage overlooking Pointe du Conguel.

dotted with valleys and much friendlier and lusher than the stern upland plateau. There are some fine viewpoints worth exploring, notably the **Pointe des Poulains**, the nearby **l'Apothicairerie grotto**, a dramatic rock fissure, and the **Aiguilles de Port-Coton** needle rocks—all highly scenic places of Belle-Ile's own Côte Sauvage. The **Grand Phare lighthouse**, one of Europe's most brilliant and which throws a beam 130 km (80 miles) seawards, and Les Grands Sables, Belle-Ile's best beach, are two other visitor attractions. Bicycles may be hired at Le Palais, though wanderers should exercise caution near the wild cliff edges of the southern coast. Proof that Belle-Ile was discovered early by Christian settlers is found at **Bangor** village, which, as the Celtic name suggests, stands on the site of an ancient monastery.

Westwards of the Quiberon peninsula, the traveller is obliged to follow the D781 to Port-Louis, traversing the wide estuary of the river Etel *en route*. Access to the Morbihan foreshore is virtually forbidden (save for a short stretch below Plouhinec), the whole section being a military firing range (*champ de tir*). **Etel** fishing village and port enjoys a pleasant setting in an island-dotted tidal region. It is very marshy hereabouts, although much of the land has been reclaimed and developed—especially the 12 km (7½ miles) strip which separates the Etel waters from the even wider Blavet estuary, the entrance to which is guarded by Port-Louis.

As the name **Port-Louis** suggests, this is a harbour with royal connections, since before Louis XIII ruled, it was called simply Blavet; the city

fathers were apparently more than pleased to adopt the more grand-sounding title in 1635. The new name went well with the new enterprise, called the French India Company, first established here and partly financed from the royal coffers at the urging of the king's first minister, the astute Richelieu. It was the master military architect, Sebastien Vauban, who later fortified the port to create a formidably protected citadel. As a commercial venture, however, Port-Louis was not a success for several reasons, and the lucrative (and fast growing), import-export trade finally went to the purpose-built maritime complex rapidly expanding on the opposite bank of the Blavet. This bustling new docks site was dubbed "The Orient" by its builders, creating the rich link between their homeland and China and India. "L'Orient" it has remained, although the contemporary port is now more famous for its submarine base and commercial fishing harbour.

The Port-Louis **citadel**, stark and functionally rectangle, is inhabited nowadays only by ghosts of that long-gone medieval age and visitors anxious to catch a whiff of a colourful past. The fortress area is atmospheric and there are fine views across the water to neighbouring Lorient. There is a small **maritime museum** housed in the entrance keep, together with other exhibition enclaves in town showing military impedimenta, lifeboat relics and historic documents relating to the commercial connections of France with the Orient. It is a spacious and intriguing remnant of history, now landscaped to provide beach access, picnic and leisure green spaces, and plenty of car-parking facilities for visitors wishing to explore the adjacent town still partially encompassed by 17th-century ramparts. There are two hotel-restaurants in Port-Louis and a two-star municipal camping site which is open from mid-June to mid-September. Market day is Saturday.

From either Port-Louis or Lorient there is a ferry service to **Ile de Groix**—Belle-Ile's smaller neighbour, though with a coastline just as wild and craggy in places. With a population of 3,000 (considerably swelled in July and August). Ile de Groix has a couple of hotel-restaurants, an *auberge*, a youth hostel and a three-star camping site. Sailing, skin-diving or horse-riding between menhirs and sandy beaches are the main leisure pursuits on Groix. For more information contact the tourist office (tel: 97-05-53-08).

Lorient, like Saint-Nazaire, has limited appeal for most holiday visitors as it is also a thriving commercial and industrial town which was totally rebuilt after World War II. Its major industry is centred upon the naval dockyards and the fishing port, which is the second largest in France. There is still a submarine base here, though it is out of bounds to foreign visitors. Since the port area is really the Lorient highlight, the interesting and leisurely way to see it is by hopping on one of the regular ferries which plies across the estuary from Port-Louis (the sailing time is about 30 minutes). Lorient's fishing port *is* bustling and colourful, while **Larmor-Plage**, at the southern end of town, boasts a sandy beach and an interesting 17th-century church with strong maritime connections. Market days are Wednesdays and Sundays.

From Port-Louis, follow the banks of the Blavet inland for 10 km (6 miles) or so and cross the river at **Hennebont**, another Morbihan township well worth going out of your way to see. One of the heaviest fortified river ports of the Middle Ages, there are still some imposing remains of the 13th-century **ramparts** and **watch-towers**; once a very real necessity, principally during the long occupation by the English during the Hundred Years War. Hennebont's hub, around the massive 16th-century flamboyant Gothic church, is a stroller's delight. **Notre-Dame-du-Paradis** dominates a magnificent Place Maréchal-Foch and some extensive botanical gardens. There is a revealing rampart walk, (about 1½ hour's duration), while another impressive landmark to look out for is the multi-arched bridge. The Blavet and its tributaries are popular with anglers, while bankside paths are also well trodden by leisure walkers and horse-riders.

While much of the town has been modernized and rebuilt, there is still charm to be found in the old centre and the steep valley flanks which remain visually pleasing. Hennebont is now the horse-breeding capital of Morbihan, the national stud farm being established here in 1987; it is also quite famous for its weekly market, one of Brittany's biggest, which is held every Thursday. There are good visitor facilities, ranging from the four-star Château de Locguenole hotel, to a municipal caravan and campsite on the banks of the Blavet which is open from June to September. There is a wide choice of eating houses too, many specializing in traditional Breton dishes. It is also yet another good seafood and cider centre.

Like so many other old industrial towns of western Europe, Hennebont has had to adapt markedly to our new age. This once-great iron foundry workshop of western France (it employed over 3,000 workers, and produced, among other things, millions of sardine tins) has changed out of countenance. High-tech industry and electronics is now the name of the game at Hennebont, and has been since the forges finally closed in 1968. A smokeless modern industry now thrives unobtrusively on the industrial estates of the town's outskirts. Much that is old and good remains, however. Hennebont was a favourite of Madame Sévigné, who enjoyed the riverside walks here. She would still find the **Esplanade du Bois du Duc**, and the **Chemin de Halage** distinctly pleasing, while some of the ancient **Ville Close** would still appear largely as it must have done in the 17th century.

From Hennebont, the prettier, less-used route westwards, is via the D769 and the D26, to Quimperlé. This landscape is sparse heathland in the main, but there is a scenic halfway mark at **Pont Scorff**, on the river of the same name. A comfortable *logis de France* hotel-restaurant can be found here amid a nice landscape blend of river and woodland which is popular with canoeists. About 3 km (2 miles) south is Scorff Zoo (signposted), where big game species, such as lions, and some exotic birds may be seen. This is the last little township in Morbihan—the Finistère boundary lies just ahead, the *département* considered by many to contain the best of rugged Brittany.

Finistère

Quimperlé

Finistère is holiday terrain *par excellence* for all who like their coastal resorts surrounded by natural, often wild beauty. Quimperlé embodies attributes that make Finistère subtly different from neighbouring Morbihan. There are stronger Breton overtones, most noticeably reflected by the church architecture which, though just as strong and impressive of scale, is marginally less flamboyant.

In truth, travel-brochure Finistère is glimpsed at Quimperlé, and even though the location is a considerable distance inland, the maritime influence still exerts a sturdy pull, via the waters of the Laïta river and its tributaries. Here is the Brittany where those colourful regional costumes are worn proudly on high days and holidays, among a society of people who are still countryfolk at heart. It is where Calvaries and lace *coiffes* are commonplace in a landscape that is often stern—even stark—but where water-fed arbours of shady tranquility can be found. It is, above all, France's "land's end", the whole peninsula assaulted thunderously at times by crashing Atlantic breakers which hurl themselves against granite cliffs after an uninterrupted journey of some 3,000 miles The sound of the sea is never far away in Finistère.

Quimperlé, though really quite a small town, is mightily crowned by the great **church of Saint-Michel**, or Notre-Dame-de-l'Assomtion, known colloquially as the "sugar loaf". This dominant 13th-century cluster of stone is supplemented by the **church of Sainte-Croix**, raised a century earlier and a testimony to the devout character of the town's medieval citizens. The latter building, almost a carbon copy of Jerusalem's Holy Sepulchre, is said to have been erected as a tribute of thankfulness by returning knights of the Crusade. The apse is a superb example of Romanesque architecture and is the only 12th-century remnant, the remainder of the church being rebuilt after a partial collapse in the 19th century.

There are many other interesting corners of this gateway to Finistère, which geographically commands the crossroads of three valleys. In the **rue Dom-Morice** and the **rue Bremond d'Ars** there are some lovely old dwellings with exaggerated upper-storey overhangs, where the 15th and 16th centuries can still be glimpsed outside **La Maison des Archers**, once the domicile of town defenders, now an interesting Breton **folk museum**. There are seven hotels in this attractive town of split levels, created between the arms of the Laïta tributaries l'Isole and l'Ellé, a dozen restaurants, *crêperies* and cafés, and a municipal camping site beside the sports stadium.

Car-parking space is usually available in the place de Gaulle (across the river bridge from the tourist office), there are local coaches which serve the nearby coastal resorts and inland villages, and the town is served by the SNCF. Visitor amenities are good and include a municipal swimming pool and tennis courts. The *Syndicat d'Initiative* is in the rue du Bourgneuf; for hotel reservation or other information, tel: 98-96-04-32.

The most alluring attraction found near Quimperlé is the **Carnoët forest** and the D49 road which leads to the Atlantic foreshore and Le Pouldu, some 12 km (7½ miles) distant. Here, after crossing a lush river-valley greensward which spreads across a wide wedge of some 700 hectares (1,700 acres), and which is networked by pedestrian paths and equestrian ride, **Le Pouldu** occupies a pleasing location—the first coastal spot in eastern Finistère—on the fringe of the wide Laïta estuary. This was a favoured watering hole of Paul Gauguin, where today the **Maison Marie Henri** presents a well-constructed replica of the *auberge* frequented by the great artist and his fellow painters. There is a popular horse-riding centre here, Equestre de Cotenard (tel: 98-39-90-79), and a choice of hotels and a camping site will be found a short distance inland at Clohars Carnoët.

There is another destination worth visiting from Quimperlé; or worth considering as a country base, since it is a *Station Verte*. **Le Faouët**, some 20 km (12 ½ miles) north-east, is located in an attractive area of the Ellé valley, and is particularly popular with anglers and walkers, since there are a number of way-marked paths. There are some nice wooded stretches hereabouts provided by the **Sainte-Barbe forest**, with the **Roches du Diable** (a waterside outcrop of rock and a local beauty spot) lying roughly at the halfway point, east of the D790.

Le Faouët is famed for its imposing 16th-century covered market and a unique monument in the square dedicated to the youngest ever army volunteer of France in the Great War, one Corentin Carré, aged 15 years. There is a comfortable two-star hotel, a *gîte d'étape*, furnished accommodation and a three-star municipal campsite open from March to mid-September. A popular leisure water is Lac du Bel-Air-Priziac which lies north-east of town, while Le Faouët itself has a heated swimming pool, tennis courts and riding stables. The *Syndicat d'Initiative* is in rue de Quimper, (tel: 97-23-23-23).

North and south of town respectively are the chapels of **Sainte-Barbe** and **Saint-Fiacre**. Both are charming and unusual, and both have 15th-century origins. The first has a pilgrim's stairway ascending a rocky escarpment, and the second is graced by one of the finest medieval bell towers in Brittany, flanked by buttressed towers of great delicacy. The GR83 long-distance walk passes by here.

A scenic return to Quimperlé is via Scaër westwards (another place famous for its Breton wrestlers), then south-east through green and pleasant country flanking the river Isole. Scaer is also a *Station Verte*.

The main haunt of Gauguin in this region was **Pont-Aven**, some 15 km (9 miles) west of Quimperlé. Descending from the valley flank road into the tiny, close-knit community, the traveller will at once realize why this riverside settlement held so much appeal for the artist during the latter half of the 19th century. Even today, Pont-Aven is a real charmer. Car

T here are some delightful waterside walks around Pont-Aven, not surprisingly an artists' colony since the Gauguin era.

parking is not always easy here; beside the church is probably better than place Paul Gauguin in high summer. This little river port which once enjoyed a lucrative trade with Ile de Groix was busy with loaded coasters during the 18th century, dealing mainly in cereals and fresh-milled flour, hence the number of old mills in the area. The town centre, above and below the picturesque bridge, retains something of an earlier, more gracious age, enhanced by a number of **art galleries**. Just off the attractive place de l'Hôtel de Ville, is the **museum** which displays exhibitions of work by the Pont-Aven school. Beside the bridge is the old *auberge* (now a newspaper shop), where Gauguin stayed.

The riverside walks around the town are delightful, and they include way-marked routes which actually identify locations of paintings which are now world famous, for example, the

Some of the way-marked paths actually pass by scenes now immortalized in oilpaint, while preserved old mills like this are graphic reminders of times past.

magnificent *Haymaking in Brittany*, completed by Gauguin in 1888. This and other masterpieces, were created in the riverside area known as the Bois d'Amour. There are three principal pedestrian routes tracing the town's artistic era: the Bois d'Amour; the Town Walk; and the Roz an Bidou. Trail. Leaflet guides are available from the tourist office in the place de l'Hôtel de Ville (tel: 98-06-04-70), and extended cycle routes are also provided. Also worth seeing is the 16th-century **chapel of Tremelo** containing the crucifix which was the model for

Gauguin's *Le Christ Jaune*, the splendid little chapel and Calvary cross at **Nizon**, just to the north-west of town. The Calvary cross in the village square inspired the master's *Christ Vert*.

Those wishing to stay for a while in Pont-Aven will find comfortable accommodation in three hotels, or from a wide range of B&B houses or holiday flats—the latter number more than 100 in the vicinity, and serve 100,000 people who visit the town museum alone every summer. There are five restaurants all dispensing typical regional delights from butter cake to *crêpes*, accompanied when requested by the potent but thirst-quenching Breton cider. **Bélon** oysters are often served in Pont-Aven too. These came to fame during the l9th century when Parisian gourmets found the flat, local variety superior to those from Ostend. The mix of fresh and salt-water, peculiar to the Bélon river, imparts the much sought-after flavour. The town of Riec-sur-Bélon, just to the south-east, has an epicurean reputation, while the Bélon Fort pedestrian route, is a fine 10 km (6-mile) circuit walk.

Cycles may be hired in Pont-Aven for those wishing to extend their local exploration, and for other active visitors there are tennis courts (indoor and out), and the Aven river is much enjoyed by both anglers and canoeists. Predictably, Pont-Aven endures very heavy patronage throughout the summer, particularly around the time of the annual *pardon*, the *Fête des Fleurs d'Ajoncs* (Golden Gorse Festival), held on the first Sunday in August. There are, of course, a number of alternative bases in the area, located amid quieter and less busy Finistère.

Nevez is one which lies close to the Atlantic coast south-west of Pont-Aven and which has some excellent bathing beaches. Within the Nevez commune there are picturesque thatched cottages dominating quaint pastoral villages, old flour mills, prehistoric sites and an intriguing coastline where the rural way of Breton life is still not much affected by the summer influx of people. Yet facilities for visitors are modern and all-embracing, including hotel-restaurants of a high standard, many *chambres d'hôtes*, and a dozen caravan and camping parks close to, or on the coast. There are several fine sand beaches—totalling over 6 km (4 miles) in length—between the Aven estuary and Pointe de Trévignon; one of the best being Raguénès plage. Nevez is compact, and friendly, and offers good shopping to self-catering holidaymakers, including a supermarket. There is good country and coastal walking in the neighbourhood, lots of watersports, cycle hire and, in yet another acknowledged seafood and cider centre, there is a helpful *Syndicat d'Initiative* which is open only during the high season (tel: 98-06-87-90).

Concarneau

Boulogne is France's number-one fishing port, Lorient the second, and then Concarneau, arguably the most photogenic, and also the most romantically historic. The magnificent *Ville Close* fortified island town, is one of the most visited in Brittany. Strategically sheltered in the Baie de la Forêt, Concarneau became affluent through the historic treasure of its medieval islet, stoutly ramparted within the inner harbour since the 14th century.

Stroll along the elevated **parapet walk** (for which a modest charge is made) to capture a faint echo of turbulent times long past, when guards scanned their surroundings in earnest through granite spy-holes. The industrious Vauban improved the fortifications of this precious settlement for Louis XIV in the 17th century. The narrow rue Vauban, which runs for much of the islet's length of 350 m (380 yd), commemorates the master military engineer, but devotes almost all its energy nowadays to tempting the tourist with souvenirs of one kind or another. The former barracks is now the **Musée de la Pêche**, and contains a first-rate display of maritime life, including many aquarium tanks, many species of fish and some of the very first sardine cans ever manufactured in France.

*C*oncarneau harbour.
In the background the ramparts of the Vauban citadel. This Villa Close *is still completely walled as it was in the 17th century.*

Concarneau's **fish auction** is one of Brittany's most famous—see it at its most dynamic at around 7.30 a.m. Later strollers will no doubt enjoy the parade of smart shops in the town centre, or take to the Concarneau beaches about a kilometre distant, the Plage des Sables Blancs being the best.

Served by the SNCF (there is a coach link with Rosporden, the nearest railway station), Concarneau and the surrounding bay area is a popular bee-line target for many family holidaymakers, as the town's 19 hotels,

7 caravan and camping sites in the area and a youth hostel (place de la Croix), indicate. There are more than 60 restaurants, *crêperies*, café-bars and pizzerias, in addition to a wide selection of food shops—especially in Les Halles and the *Criée* (fish market), on quai Carnot.

Concarneau is also a very popular base for those who enjoy coastal exploration by boat. The Vedettes Glenn company does brisk business throughout the summer months ferrying sightseers to the offshore Glénan island cluster, and up the Odet river to the west. The first is an archipeligo rich in flora and fauna, some 20 km (12½ miles) distant, while the second is a 70 km (43-mile) round trip around the coast and along one of France's prettiest rivers. Trips may be booked direct at the company office (17, avenue du Dr Nicolas, tel: 98-97-10-31), or through Concarneau tourist office on the quai d'Aguillon (tel: 98-97-01-44). Other holiday attractions here are the sailing school, tennis courts, cycle hire, and the bar-dancing night spot, Taverne des Korrigans. Concarneau's grand festival, that of "the Blue Nets", is held on the third Sunday in August. It is one of the region's most impressive festivals—a riot of colour, processions, much bagpipe music and a splendid exhibition of Breton maritime tradition.

Town plan of Quimper.

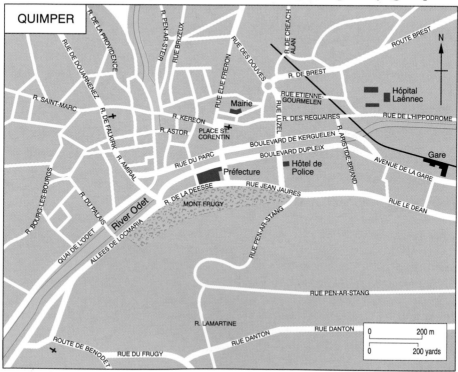

180

*T*he lofty elegance of Quimper cathedral. The 19th-century spires have been dovetailed to the original 15th-century structure—but you can't see the join!

Quimper

Quimper, the *préfecture* of Finistère and one of Brittany's most definitive Breton cities, lies 24 km (15 miles) inland of Concarneau. The approach along the D738 is through slightly more voluptuous countryside now that the long *marais* traverse of the coastal Morbihan plains has been left behind. The capital itself snuggles cosily in a quite steep-sided valley cleft of the river Odet, the main river being supplemented by the Steir tributary. The settlement is just as attractive on arrival as the approach is promising. Quimper carries the accolade "City of Art" with justified pride, particularly in view of the fine quality pottery which has been produced here for over three centuries.

A superb museum of fine art and another devoted to Breton folklore, make this one-time capital of Cornouaille something of a pilgrimage for Brittany people. Here in the great cathedral, services are still conducted in Celtic at times, while the old town centre, befitting such an ancient city, is a hub of charming cobbled streets, alleyways and medieval dwellings like those in the place Terre-au-Duc or rue-du-Sallé.

Casual car visitors will probably find it best to park to the north of the centre beside the river Steir, where there is room for 1,000 cars. Alternative prospects are the place de la Tour d'Auvergne, or off the rue de la Providence. If you wish to make Quimper a touring base, the welcome you will find is as practical as it is friendly— there are a dozen hotels, a youth hostel and an attractive camping ground (open from May to mid-September)

alongside the river Odet. Six of the hotels have restaurants, and there are also two dozen other eating houses, serving traditional or exotic fare, a selection of which can be found along or alongside the rue du Parc, the principal boulevard overlooking the tree-lined, if rather canalized, Odet. The Grande Café de Bretagne is a central and congenial meeting place for both locals and visitors, either at the pavement tables or within the brasserie of high repute. The choice of *fruits de mer* here is wide and handsome—as it is at most other restaurants in coastal Brittany.

Conveniently, the interesting part of Quimper is quite closely confined within a square kilometre of the cathedral, thus orientation is quick and simple for the newcomer, with pedestrian exploration easy on the feet. The splendid granite **cathedral of Saint-Corentin** which is begun in the year 1240, is the unmistakable central landmark of the compact city, its twin spires soaring majestically—confirmation in stone that here indeed is the chief seat of administration in Finistère. A magnificence of Gothic stonework and stained-glass windows, the building is claimed to be the most beautiful medieval place of worship in western France. Certainly the Quimperois skyline is totally dominated by the regal edifice and there is much to admire, inside and out, of 13th- to 15th-century craftsmanship. Alas, the spires themselves are but 19th-century additions, but the grafting is cunning and the effect graciously enhancing, a rare success of afterthought architecture.

Between the towers there is a statue of the 6th-century king, Gradlon, thus creating an intertwining of religion and legend which is often so naturally expressed by the Breton psyche.

Gradlon—if he existed at all—was ruler of the mystical city of Ys, which was said to have stood offshore of Cornouaille somewhere in the region of Douarnenez bay. According to Bretan tales, the city was so enchanting that the inhabitants named their home *Par-Is*, which is Celtic for "beautiful". Thus the capital of all France was eventually christened! The legend goes on to relate that Ys (or Is) was swallowed beneath the waves, together with the king's daughter who was a bit too fun-loving and had made a pact with the Devil—supposedly, it was Old Nick himself who opened the flood gates. Gradlon, seeking an alternative capital in his vast domain, chose Quimper. Hence the mounted monarch who stands guard to this day in front of the cathedral.

From this spot, it is but a short step to some intriguing old Breton streets and alleyways which are lined with medieval houses—like the rue Guéodet, or the rue des Gentilhommes. Follow the restored **rue du Sallé**, and you come to the **place au Beurre**, where salted butter once stood in profusion in huge earthenware jars. The splendid, newly-built covered fruit, vegetable and flower market, with the tourist office adjacent, lies off the colourful quai du Steir, while in rue Élie-Fréron, there are typical dwellings dating back to the Middle Ages, as there are in several places beside the Steir.

Amid a welter of old France, there are two treasures that no serious visitor will want to miss. The first is the fine **art display** in the Hôtel de Ville,

containing works by Rubens, Corot Velasquez, Picasso and Emile Bernard (he who so profoundly influenced Gauguin and the rest of the Pont-Aven school). The second is the **Musée Départemental Breton**, off the boulevard de Kerguelen at 1, rue de Roi Gradlon. There is a wonderful collection devoted to Brittany's past here, from Gallo-Roman remains, to 16th-century carvings, pottery, artefacts and regional costumes.

There is also a summer exhibition of pottery, Trois Siècles de Faïences, at the **Fine Arts Museum**, 40, place Saint-Corentin, which is open daily except

The old town centre is attractive in parts, celebrated for its art and Breton architecture. This is the rue Kéréon.

Tuesday, from May to mid-September. Presented here is a display of ten generations of Breton potter's art, including the most delicate and delightful chinaware depicting traditional Brittany. Ever since 1690, when a Provençal potter set up the first factory and kilns, Quimper has been famous for its earthenware art. Several potteries in the area may be visited, the H.B. Henriot works on route de Bénodet, in the suburb of Locmaria being the closest to Quimper centre. For hand-painted souvenirs of high quality one might well consider the Quimper **school of pottery**, especially the limited editions of painted earthenware which genuinely reflect Cornouaille art, coupled with French flair and technical excellence.

Dwell awhile in Quimper and you will quickly learn to love the old place; the pace of life is sane, the natives are friendly, and there are contrasting delights of smart shops and ancient rampart walks to enjoy between Finistère culinary pleasures. Be in the city during the annual Cornouaille Festival (fourth Sunday in July) for a true Breton extravaganza of culture, involving upwards of 2,000 participants in traditional processions of music and dance.

The town is only 15 km (9 miles) from the coast, which beckons visitors alluringly, particularly when the weather is hot. Seawards, both sides of the Odet are dotted with interesting scenery and man-made objectives, and those who enjoy boat trips can see a variety of châteaux amid their formal garden settings. There is a daily riverboat service (Quimper to Bénodet) during the summer season. For those who prefer to explore by road, the D34 to the east of the river winds to Fouesnant and/or Bénodet.

Fouesnant is both a countryside and a maritime attraction, liberally dotted with wooded sand dunes, which are criss-crossed by footpaths and well sheltered from the prevailing westerlies. There are a number of safe bathing beaches in the vicinity of the old town, which is famous for its *pardon* of Sainte-Anne (last weekend in July), its apple tree orchards and, of course, its cider, said to be Brittany's finest. **La Forêt-Fouesnant** just to the east is located snugly at the end of a deep bay and, as the village name implies, is blessed by a surrounding wealth of woodland. This is another popular sailing area, with a well-patronized marina. It is also a recognized walking area; more information and footpath guides can be obtained, from the *Syndicat d'Initiative* in rue du Port, or at the Fouesnant tourist office in rue Armor.

Bénodet, on the Odet estuary, is really something of a purpose-built resort, complete with casino and smart, smoked-glass hotels and apartments. It is frenetically busy during the brief high season, but tranquil and easy-paced (by comparison) for the main part; in early June or September it is very agreeable. The silver sand beaches and the sailing centre (of international repute) are the big draws, the harbour being a stop-over point for the around-France yacht race. Like Fouesnant, this up-market resort is surrounded by prettily wooded river valley terrain and is especially pleasing to cycle tourists. There is a ferry boat which crosses the estuary to Sainte-

Marine (no vehicles), thus providing a circuit route link for cyclists based at Quimper.

All recognized holiday facilities are available at Bénodet and there is every form of accommodation, including 16 hotels and 7 caravan and campsites. Fouesnant (with La Forêt-Fouesnant) has 24 hotels, the same total of campsites, plus numerous furnished apartments and *chambres d'hôte*. This will give some indication of the popularity of both seaside fun spots. The sporting and leisure amenities are comprehensive too. From Bénodet you can take a boat trip up the Odet river, or to the

Bénodet, a small-boat haven par-excellence on the Odet river estuary. A panorama from the lofty Pont de Cornouaille road bridge.

offshore Iles de Glénan. You can also learn to sail, hire a bicycle, go horseriding, or play golf over one of the best 18-hole courses in Brittany, at nearby Clohars-Fouesnant. Bénodet is yet another resort which boasts a thalassothérapie centre. The tourist office is at 51, avenue de la Plage, tel: 98-57-00-14.

West of the Odet, via the D785 from Quimper, there is a quieter and more traditional Brittany, as displayed by **Pont-l'Abbé**, which straddles a narrow river of the same name. A mellow and elegant market town and port with a choice of quality hotels, it is dominated by a 14th-century **castle**, now much restored and once the seat of power of the Bigouden region, neighbour to the adjoining Cornouaille.

Dignified and unhurried, Pont-l'Abbé is very different from Bénodet, though equally appealing to those keen

A Glimpse of the Old Breton Argoat

Before we say a final goodbye to Quimper, there is another natural gem in the vicinity to be considered, and which is a total contrast to the sweep of wild Atlantic coast. As if to confirm that the Odet is indeed one of the region's most beautiful rivers, the Site du Stangala waits, where a fine bird's-eye view from a granite outcrop high above the flowing water is made yet more dramatic by the distant panorama. Across the richly-wooded slopes of the valley one can see the chapel on the summit of Locronan hill to the north-west, and beyond, one can see almost to the coast. It is a very pleasant walking and picnic area hereabouts. To get there, make for the village of Quéllenec (north-west of Quimper off the D15), and then follow the signs to the viewpoint.

to avoid holiday crowding. This is one of those little townships of Brittany where the ancient head-dress, the *coiffe,* is still worn by the women and not just on fête days. Alas, this is increasingly rare now, and is only done by ladies of more mature years. There is, however, something a little special about seeing such an attractive habit, worn not for the tourist, but for preference.

In addition to the capped-tower castle of Pont-l'Abbé there is **Notre-Dame des Carmes**, a medieval monastery chapel, and the remnants of an ancient church on the opposite bank of the river. There is also a **folklore museum** housed within the castle, displaying Bigouden costume, furniture and artefacts, many of which have seagoing, connections. Close by, the heart of the little town is the place de la République, which is a nicely atmospheric spot for an aperitif. There are also some scenic strolling areas around the quai and the leisure park beside the barrage lake.

A pretty road leads south, alongside the estuary and largely through market gardening country, to the small port **Loctudy** and several other bijou fishing harbours and inlets westwards. For the main part, this coastal section is not particularly remarkable, although it does culminate with the massive and lofty **Eckmuhl lighthouse**, which landmarks the southernmost point of vast Audierne bay.

Unlike the northern extremity spectacular coastline is not too evident here, yet it still holds much fascination for the *aficionados* of seaside Brittany, as the number of camping and caravan sites testify. A great sweep of sand and shingle over 20km (12 miles) in length dominates a stern foreshore, where eroded dolmen stand watch and seabirds wheel over marshy inlets. The lonely **Notre-Dame-de-Tronoën** graces its desolate dune setting, a 15th-century chapel still markedly isolated in what must have been a true medieval wilderness. Beside it, the time-worn Calvary of granite is the most ancient in Brittany. There is an annual pilgrimage *pardon* to this windswept place of worship on the last Sunday in September.

Illustrating an even earlier period of human habitation is the **museum of prehistory**, close to the fishing village of Saint-Guénolé. This is surrounded by collected megaliths and exhibits relics from the Neolithic to the Gallo-Roman era. Most carborne visitors then complete this excursion circuit of the peninsula by continuing north to **Penhors** whose *Grand Pardon,* held early in September, is one of Brittany's biggest), to **Plozevet**, a settlement of 13th-century origins with nice walking in the vicinity, and then back to Quimper via the D784.

The Bay of Douarnenez

Drive due west from Quimper along the D784 for yet another subtle change of landscape which occurs as the Goyen river is crossed. Here the coast truly begins to live up to its name of Sud-Finistère, the most westerly part of France which, on the map of the Republic, is said to look like the head of a snarling dog defying the menacing Atlantic breakers. Audierne is the first sizeable town amid a Brittany terrain that in places retains more than a tinge of the ruggedly untamed, and where the echoing Atlantic becomes more accentuated as the peninsula gradually narrows.

Audierne is very different from the cosier fishing ports and soporific clime of the Morbihan, although this in no way detracts from the attractive setting of the port on the Goyen estuary. Most famous for its lobster and crayfish catches, it is also a ferry port for the **Ile de Sein**, this treeless patch (less than a kilometre square) at sea-level, still being inhabited. Once infamous for its wreckers, the island has a most honourable World War II record as the embarkation point of Free French volunteers escaping to England. There is a miniscule village, a perilously-sited lighthouse and hosts of sea-birds, which thrive on the island's fish waste. Ile de Sein lies 1½ hours' sailing time westward of Audierne.

Audierne, a comparatively tranquil fishing port on the Goyen river estuary of south-western Finistère, in an interesting setting.

Audierne beach, roughly 1 km (½ mile) from the busy little harbour, is one of the best in the district, and is thronged by sun-seekers, skin-divers and small-boat enthusiasts throughout the summer. The area is also popular with walkers, bird-watchers (there is scenic wooded hill country above the town) and cyclists, who can hire bicycles in town. A popular holiday base with families, there is a wide accommodation choice and varied leisure amenities. The *Syndicat d' Initiative*, place de la Liberté, tel: 98-70-12-20.

Across the Goyen estuary are the **Pointe du Raz**, the **Baie des Trépassés** and the **Pointe du Van**, a trio of majestic natural splendours. Like the westernmost tip of England, the terrain is networked by minor roads, and is studded with many villages and hamlets, yet it still manages to evoke an air of untamed grandeur, where the impact of centuries of civilization has made but a slight dent. A storm-tossed granite and sand spectacular on approach from the east, it is no less exciting on arrival.

On the surface, western Finistère, once so very remote and inaccessible, is tamed by scatterings of white-walled houses with uniform charcoal-coloured roofs. Surprisingly green and well-wooded in parts, there are excellent access roads and many of the villages have impressively modern facilities, including supermarket shopping. Timelessly unchanging, however, is that powerfully evocative scene of the adjacent sea and the wide sky—a grand

In regal isolation, the first—and last—hotel at Pointe-de-Raz. Alas not all of far-flung western Brittany is now so gloriously remote.

horizon aspect which unquestionably stimulates a sense of freedom and well-being. It is a landscape for pottering by car or by cycle, since traffic is blessedly light most of the year east of Audierne, with crowding a rarity.

However, you do have to pay to park a car at the commercialized cliff-top of **Raz Point**—an imposition of sorts, as it is a national heritage site. It has to be said though that this is a sign of the times, when access is only available to fee-payers, and not only in Brittany but throughout Europe. If you don't pay you don't see, a dilemma only the individual can resolve.

*B*ay *of Trespasses. Majestic, super-fine sands and sweeping stretches of rugged coast dominate hereabouts. This is one of the most invigorating parts of Brittany.*

It is best to visit Raz Point, the most westerly landfall in France, early in the day, or better still early in the season.

The dramatic, sheer flanks of the splintered granite cliffs beyond the shopping and car-park complex, and the signal station, lead the eye westwards across a necklace of reefs to Vieille lighthouse and Ile de Sein, some 12 km (7 ½ miles) distant. The point is heavily trodden, but caution is prudent when traversing around chasms with names like Hell's Mouth—stick strictly to the obvious marked paths especially if youngsters are in your party. To be in this spot when the sea is rough is an awesome privilege.

Return inland through the hamlet of Lescoff and turn towards the coast, again this time descending the narrow, view-revealing hill to the **Baie des Tré-passés**. This provides yet another glorious panorama across the sweep of silver sands where, it is said, Druid burial

ceremonies were once performed before the corpses were transferred to Ile de Sein. There is a hotel-restaurant here but not much else (unlike Point de Raz), and the Finistère authorities must be commended for keeping this delightful place as natural as possible. It is under the waters of this "Bay of the Dead" that the mystical city of Ys, the legendary capital of King Gradlon's Cornouaille, is said to lie. Again,

The bay at Douarnenez reveals some of the wildest coastal cliffs and highest surf in the region. This is Point-du-Van.

there is some fine walking potential here at sea level and along the cliff-tops, coupled with an emotive atmosphere of mystical Brittany around the bay, which was assuredly redolent with magic when the Breton world was young.

Less frequented than Raz, the **Pointe du Van** is perhaps not quite so thrilling visually, though it is dramatic enough and is certainly on a grand scale. It is another area much favoured for its walks over the handsome expanse of wild headland, again faithfully traced by cliff-top footpaths. There is spacious, free car parking (although it is much used by coaches during the high season) just above a weather-beaten 15th-century sailor's chapel. Once more, it is best either to arrive early or late in the day to explore in comfort.

A minor road, the D7, meanders picturesquely from Pointe du Van to Douarnenez, with a number of seaward lanes turning off to the coast, 2–3 km (1–2 miles) distant. One of the most interesting of these leads to the wild bird reserve at **Cap Sizun** (spring and summer access only). The reserve occupies a promontory some 75 m (245 ft) above the waves, and the springtime nests of guillemots, cormorants and puffins may be studied amid surroundings of regal natural splendour.

Douarnenez is essentially a working port, but it has some redeeming features for the leisure visitor. Located on a steep hillside, there are a number of colourful streets between the port and the town centre, the older and more interesting part of which is now a semi-pedestrian area. There are some characterful 17th- and 18th-century houses,

*D*ouarnenez, *port Rosmeur. One of the biggest fishing and canning towns in Brittany, especially of sardines.*

and two churches of the same era. The port itself—or rather both ports, since old Douarnenez is now linked to neighbouring Tréboul by an estuary viaduct—is part of an amalgamation that today forms the third busiest fishing harbour in France, at the heart of the largest stretch of sheltered tidal water in the country. Appropriately perhaps, it also boasts one of the best boat museums (close to the quayside fish market) in Europe.

Tréboul is the recognized holiday resort section, with a choice of small beaches opposite Tristan Island (named after the romantic lover of Isolde, in honour of his wronged uncle, King Mark). There is a scenic shoreline road which encircles Douarnenez port above two bathing strands, and from which there are pleasing views across Tristan Island and the cluster of old Tréboul.

This is a much-patronized amateur fishing and boat-trip centre, with frequent summer excursions around the bay and across to Morgat (1 ½ hours' sailing time). Many summertime activities are organized here too, from *pardon* processions to small small-boat regattas. All sports and leisure amenities are well publicized, there is a wealth of accommodation (a dozen hotels, many apartments and four camping sites) and, not surprisingly, there is yet another thalassothérapie centre at Tréboul, open all year. The tourist office is in rue du Docteur-Mével (tel: 98-92-13-35). Bicycle hire is simple and reasonably priced, and the GR37 long-distance hiking trail begins here, winding its way north to the bay of Morlaix and the English Channel. There is pleasant local walking, too, in the

vicinity of Port-Rhu estuary, between the Mole du Biron and the diminutive Plage des Sables Blancs, close to the "thalasso".

About 10 km (6 miles) east of Douarnenez—and in considerable contrast to the seaside scene—is the tiny township of **Locronan**, an aspic jewel of ancient France, which has almost miraculously survived the march of progress since the Middle Ages. If you find yourself anywhere near, make it your business to visit the town. A *cité d'art et d'histoire* to the French, it is in reality not much more than a country village, but a perfectly proportioned cluster of the 16th and 17th century, supporting a population of just 800 .

Like the ready-made stage setting that Locronan is, you have to pay to gain entry, through a modest but obligatory parking fee. In this case, however, the levy is justifiable as the funds go towards municipal upkeep. As old as recorded history, there was a Druid settlement where the village now stands, below a green hill-crest trodden by countless *pardon* processions throughout the centuries. The sombre but striking beauty of the aged granite and slate-roof houses is most pleasing as one traverses the main street, the rue du Prieuré, culminating with the 15th-century **church of Saint-Ronan**. Strongly four-square and almost a mini-cathedral, the adjacent chapel houses the tomb of Saint-Ronan. The church interior is headily atmospheric.

All around the main square—which is dominated by the church and chapel—**La Grande Place** is enclosed by steep, pitched roofs and rows of capped dormer windows which

The 15th-century church of Locronan, in a splendidly preserved medieval village of Finistère and delightfully atmospheric. There is a famous pilgrimage path from here to the summit of Locronan hill.

constantly delight the eye, while the sweeping expanse of the hillside cobbled square forms a hub from which narrow streets and alleyways radiate. All of these contribute to a genuine glimpse of olden times. Locronan still retains much of the richness it was meant to reflect when the houses were occupied by influential members of the royal household and merchants made wealthy through trade with the Indies.

There is another chapel in Locronan, a 16th-century building of interest off the rue Moal, which, with the adjacent Fontaine Saint-Eutrope, is typically Breton. There is also a **folk museum** in the place de la Mairie, where paintings by regional artists are exhibited. There are two two-star hotels and a two-star municipal camping site for those wishing to explore extensively. Locronan mountain is capped at 290 m (950 ft) by another ancient religious house, **Chapelle Plach-Ar**, a focal point for penitent pilgrims about 2 km (1 mile) above the town.

Those with time will certainly want to circumnavigate Douarnenez bay close to the shoreline, not only for the varied countryside and the fine beaches close to villages like **Telgruc-sur-Mer**, but because it is here that the Brittany of legend and slow-changing tradition can be found, where the *coiffe* is worn as naturally as the Scottish kilt, and where the sea can be calm and friendly one moment, and ferocious and dangerous at the next. Telgruc is old world, its centrepiece a 16th-century enclosed chapel amid a situation that is tranquil, yet with good pastoral amenities. The one hotel is supplemented by several furnished apartments, a *gîte d'étape*, and five caravan and camping sites in the neighbourhood. There are two nice sand beaches, a tennis club, a small sailing centre, and some 15 km (9 miles) of low cliff and beach footpaths. Those wishing to know more about traditional Breton cider can visit the **Musée du Cidre** at nearby Argol, open daily in summer and complete with free tasting.

Despite encroaching modernity, there are strong vibrations of the distant past all around the bay, confirmed by monastic remains, megaliths and museums displaying long-buried artefacts of a still-mysterious past. This is unsurprising, for like the wildernesses of Ireland and west Wales, the peninsula was a Druid stronghold long before the birth of Christ.

The intelligensia of their time, novice druids underwent a protracted period of training and enlightenment (rather like the chivalrous order of knights of a later era), often lasting up to 20 years. Thus they became the most learned of ruling classes, and despite a penchant for human sacrifice, they truly earned the name Druid, which means "wise" in Gailic.

Crozon lends its name to the mini-peninsula which separates the waters of Douarnenez bay and the Rade de Brest (Brest roads). It is not an exciting town historically or architecturally, but it caters well to holiday visitors, with a choice of hotel-restaurants and some half-dozen caravan and camp sites within the commune. Two supermarkets serve the inhabitants (one is open 7 days week, with a 24-hour petrol service). There are cycle hire centres at Crozon, sailing and horse-riding at nearby Morgat, and plenty of paths to explore, individually or on

---

Ancient Bretons who were also Ancient Britons

As lawmakers, priests and nobles, Druids paid no taxes and were exempt from military service—little wonder the movement was popular with ambitious youths of the time. It was, however, thought that they could foretell the future, make powerful magic and turn themselves into other creatures or even stone. All of this strongly influenced the superstitious Gauls of Brittany, as it did the Celts of the British Isles. The sect did not, however, hold the Romans in awe, and the latter systematically eliminated the sect as a potential threat to the empire. The Druids' mysticism and transmitted knowledge, particularly about obscure subjects like astronomy and science, left a lasting impression of admiration among Celtic races though, which is still acknowledged to this day. Since the Romans found difficulty in penetrating hinterland Armorica (as Brittany was then), pockets of Druidism did linger, notably in the vicinity of Douarnenez bay, the whole western extremity of the Brittany peninsula, and on the isolated offshore islands, as the liberal scattering of dolmens, menhirs and cromlechs testify. If the ancient Celtic city of Ys did in fact exist, Douarnenez bay must surely be a likely location.

guided walks organized in the summer. The **Pointe de Dinan** is a fine cliff-top viewpoint, providing stunning panoramas above the natural sea arch known as the **Castle of Dinan**. The peninsula point is flanked to either side by long, sandy beaches. The tourist office in Crozon is in boulevard de Pralognan, tel: 98-26-17-18. There is another tourist office in Morgat (a pretty port and resort sheltered by cliffs), in the boulevard de la Plage, tel: 98-27-07-92. Some 7 km (4½ miles) south of here there is another natural spectacular, **Cap de la Chèvre**. This was a strategic German lookout station during World War II—understandable, for there are sweeping Atlantic vistas between the bay extremities of Raz Point and Penhir Point. There is spacious car parking at the road end, and some splendid sandstone and

The definitive Breton scene, mirrored by Camaret-sur-Mer. In the centre, are the distinctive heritage treasures of the Vauban fortifications and the Notre-dame-de-Rocamadour sailor's chapel.

quartz cliff formations can be admired from the lofty footpaths. The spectacular sea grottoes and cliffs between Morgat and Tas de Pois, can be admired from the Vedettes Sirenes sightseeing craft which operates from Morgat port daily in summer.

The whole hammerhead-shark outline of this rugged peninsula tip, Presqu'île de Crozon—almost an island, as it aptly translates—is rightly included within the boundary of the huge Armorique Regional Nature Park which encompasses a staggering 95,000 hectares (235,000 acres) and is one of the biggest of the 25 national parks of France. True, this vast area includes offshore islands like Ouessant (Ushant), but it also embraces a magnificent swathe of inland Brittany, as will be seen later in the guide in THE BRITTANY HINTERLAND.

The area around Crozon and Morgat is pretty enough to justify inclusion within the park, but bonus marks for character plus visual reward must be awarded to **Camaret-sur-Mer**, the most westerly of all Brittany townships and commercial fishing ports. From Crozon, the approach is via a good road through quite lush woodland patches (considering the generally harsh terrain of the sea-girt landscape), coppices alternating with open heath, stretches of bay and estuary waters to either side in advance of a quite steep descent to the foreshore, and a fine elevated preview over Camaret.

Old world, slow-paced and oozing with friendly ambience, this is one of those definitive Brittany holiday spots in any month outside August. It has all the ingredients to make it so, for the gourmet will go for the lobsters (Camaret being France's number-one port for this crustacean), and the sun-seeking family will be lured by the Plage du Corréjou. The nature-lover will make it a base for the headland walks and the wealth of sea-birds, while the lover of medieval France will surely appreciate the Tour de Vauban fortifications and the delightful sailor's chapel, Notre-Dame-de-Rocamadour. Finally, for the prehistory buff there is a mini-Carnac at **Lagatjar**, 1 km (½ mile) south and high above the town centre,

where nearly 150 menhirs are grouped, as strangely mystical as the countless others found in such profusion throughout the province. A little further afield, the **Pointe de Penhir** is certainly one of the most dramatic headland highlights, and the aspect of sheer cliffs above the reef rocks of Les Tas de Pois is majestic.

Modern Camaret, though well patronized, somehow manages to remain a simple working port with good, though incidental facilities for visitors—how thing should be for any settlement under national park protection. It is the relatively unsophisticated character of the place that is a major attraction. Most visitors seem to prefer it this way, for there are countless other places where the tail has long since swung the cat. There are three hotels in Camaret, a youth hostel, a holiday apartment block and two campsites within 3 km (2 miles) of town. There are half a dozen restaurants, snack bars and *crêperies*, lobster, of course, being the speciality. Sailing, sea-fishing and skin-diving enthusiasts are well catered for at Camaret as they are at most other Finistère resorts. The tourist office is in quai Kléber, tel: 98-27-93-60.

Camaret's historic high spot is clustered around the end of a natural dyke, some ½ km (⅓ mile) in length and now walled, to form a sweeping pretective harbour mole. At the seaward extremity stands the 17th-century restored chapel, on the site of an original 12th-century shrine and resting place of pilgrims *en route* to Rocamadour—hence the name association with distant Quercy province. Old paintings illustrate how remote the setting of this charming chapel once was; in medieval times it was isolated amid windswept sand dunes and accessible only with great difficulty as most pilgrimage centres frequently were. **Notre-Dame-de-Rocamadour** still manages to stand fractionally aloof from the group of commercial port buildings and that other fine legacy of the 17th century, the **Tour de Vauban**, which now houses an interesting maritime museum.

This is the most westerly of Vauban's defensive works, and was erected in 1689. It is yet another massive fortress among a total of over 600 which once guarded the frontiers of France, from Finistère to Alsace, and from Montreuil (near Calais) to the foothills of the Pyrenees. A surprising number of these citadels have survived as a testimony to their builder's prowess. The mighty redoubt on the **Pointe de Sillon** at Camaret is one of many standing memorials to Vauban, a man with an amazing life story.

Born in 1633, this impoverished orphan rose to become marshal of France and the greatest military engineer in the history of the Royalist regime. As a young man he sided with the anti-Royalist *Fronde,* fighting with conspicuous gallantry and exhibiting a flair for siege warfare. Captured in battle, he eventually gave allegiance to Louis XIV, and fought just as courageously during many subsequent battles, in which he suffered multiple wounds. No mere soldier, his knowledge of military engineering was uncanny, and during service with the Sun King he tirelessly created a ring of impregnable bastions right around the kingdom.

The structure at Camaret has all the hallmarks of the master builder's proficiency—massive scale, inherent strength and incredible durability. Sebastien le Prestre de Vauban was an innovative genius, and equal credit must be accorded to Louis XIV for realizing the potential of his military engineer. In later years Vauban, also a prolific writer, became increasingly uneasy about his country's poverty, and he more or less reverted to the politics of his youth. He was prophetic in foreseeing the advent of the French Revolution, and he died virtually out of royal favour in 1707.

Where Myth and Legend Reign— Highlighted at Huelgoat and Within Paimpont Forest

Unique parish closes, Calvaries and *crêpes*. Industry and infrastructure are encroaching into the ancient hinterland, but happily pastoral Brittany prevails. The "Valley of No Return" is still a half-hidden location in Paimpont forest, while the woods of Huelgoat revealed recently a Celtic settlement. On the peninsula's highest point, Menez-Hom, you can stand upon what was the only land in France above the waves (apart from the central Midi-Plateau and the Ardennes), as a result of the second Ice Age after-flood.

Finistère

Everyone is aware that the coastline of Brittany is its most exciting terrain. Nearly every first-time visitor to the *région* opts for those seashore resorts and beauty spots because they accept this general opinion, and because most of us anyway are drawn irresistibly to unfamiliar water—a magnet pull acknowledging the embryonic beginnings of the human race.

*L*e Gouffre (chasm), *Huelgoat forest. Hereabouts is remnant evidence of prehistoric Argoat landscape, in places almost imprenetrable.*

After the long drive to the extremity of Finistère, however, you may find a change from blue sea to green countryside welcome, and there is much to see if you take the inland road from west to east in Brittany. A happy start is made directly really, from the Presqu'île de Crozon, where at once a majestic hinterland gem lies close—the celebrated **Menez-Hom**. Menez means "mount", and this is the highest point of the Montagnes Noires, its summit over 300 m (1,000 ft) and appearing much more pronounced in the plains country surroundings. It is a very dramatic landmark dominating the southwestern section of the Armorique nature park, and epitomizing quite grandly a lesser-known aspect of rustic Brittany.

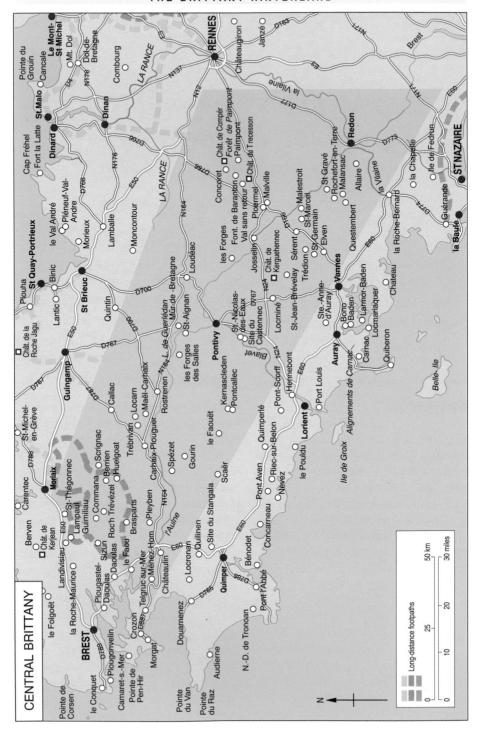

Armorica Regional Nature Park

Menez-Hom may be approached from Crozon town via Landévennec and Argol, since both places appropriately mirror the face of a long-gone rustic life. The first, nestling at the end of the hooked spit of land known as the Sillon des Anglais (English Ridge), is reached after a steep hill descent. **Landévennec** guards the entrance to the Aulne river estuary and enjoys a growing reputation as a relaxing little resort for its sheltered location, its woodland provided by a *département* forest and its choice of low-water sandy beaches.

There is a *gîte d'étape* here, close to a very ancient abbey remnant, the oldest in the Armorica park. Founded in AD 485, the Benedictine **Abbaye de Landévennec** church is largely a restored cluster of original walling, not to be confused with the modern abbey which was constructed during the 1950s. This venerable centre of sanctuary and learning, was established by the Welsh St Gennole. The museum displays a number of artefacts illustrating the spiritual, artistic and economic way of life during centuries long gone, in this atmospheric corner of Crozon peninsula.

Argol (between Landévennec and Telgruc-sur-Mer) is the location of an active craft centre, *Ar Micheriou Coz*, which translates as, "The Ancient Trades". Throughout the summer season special activity days are organized, based upon the old crafts of this pastoral and maritime region, including open-fire forging of waggon wheels (truly a master-craft), basket-weaving, clog-making and primitive furniture production, using only the simplest of authentic tools and passed-on expertise. Many other once-vital processes may be seen here, from butter- and charcoal-making, to the traditional manufacture of fishing lines and the processing of nut oil. The centre is open every Wednesday and Thursday afternoons through July and August. A salutary lesson is learned here by the visitor—if nothing else, about the ease and comfort of contemporary living!

And so to that rounded giant, **Menez-Hom**, one of Brittany's natural pilgrimage places. It is reached via a minor road detour off the D887, near the **chapel of Sainte-Marie**, which is worth seeing for a fine Calvary in the churchyard and some notable 18th-century carvings of religious figures inside. The ascent to the summit of the isolated hill is made not only by many tourists eager to enjoy the distant views across Douarnenez bay and the Crozon peninsula, but also by an ever-increasing army of hang-gliding enthusiasts, just as keen to catch the thermals which swirl almost ceaselessly above the hilltop crown. At the summit, there is a large car-parking area and a viewing table, pin-pointing distant features. Menez Hom is also the ancient site of a midsummer religious festival, still held annually, though rather more secular nowadays. The visitor to this as with all prominent hilltops in Brittany—not overly blessed with high country anywhere within its extensive boundaries—stands where earliest man must also have stood and gazed in wonderment at the silent

*M*ap of the Brittany *Hinterland.*

world of land and sea about him. The distant panoramas, especially on hazy days, are not drastically changed over the centuries through development (except of course in the direction of Brest); certainly they are still soberingly impressive.

All of this is very fitting as an opening scene to Brittany's singular regional nature park. Like designated protected areas of other nations, the entire land mass of the park remains an inhabited area; its qualification as a park is simply the variety of landscape and natural features worthy of special notice and therefore of special care. The Armorica park charter defines its objectives as: the protection and development of the cultural heritage within its boundaries; the instillation of a wider awareness of all natural and historic attraction; and the aid to local projects while maintaining careful respect for the balance of nature.

A code of visitor conduct is encouraged and officially overseen across some 32 rural communes, which support over 40,000 inhabitants. Within the Armorica park are offshore islands like Ouessant and Sein, and the rolling mainland hill country of the Monts d'Arrée. Since the purpose of the park is to provide a congenial region where town meets country, there is a gentle though unobtrusive emphasis upon education of urban-dwelling visitors—in other words, the ones who form the bulk of the summertime throngs. Consequently, at most of the park's acknowledged beauty spots or places of historic interest, there is an abundance of useful information which is broadcast via detailed notice-boards, or through local *Syndicat d'Initiative* literature. All of this ensures that the stranger obtains the most from any visit, and it adds a certain piquancy to learn, for example, that much of the park terrain is located on very ancient terrain, dating back geologically to the Primary era. In some places—like the Crozon peninsula for example—the rock layers reveal a past so distant as to be contemporaneous with the very genesis of our planet, and with the origin of life itself.

Unlike the coast, the inland hill country of this central Finistère swathe produces a micro-climate with rainy winters and steeper year-round temperature fluctuations—a lot harsher than the mild, almost Mediterranean atmosphere of the seaboard.

Across country and north-east of Crozon, the Breton moorland extends austerely, yet at once intriguingly and sometimes quite beautifully since light luminosity is high. This gives way in and around the many river valleys to greenwood coppices and half-hidden villages which are invariably interesting, if not picturesque. It is this fascinating inland nature park that we now traverse.

From Menez-Hom, it is necessary to leave the park momentarily, for **Châteaulin** on the southern park boundary. This is no hardship though, for it merely means a continuation of the scenic, and lightly used road which winds all the way from Camaret. Châteaulin is a sedate and comfortable old town, not remarkable of aspect, but solidly straddling both banks of the river Aulne between steep and well-wooded hill flanks.

Now officially a *Station Verte*, the town lies 28 km (17 miles) north of Quimper and the SNCF Quimper- -Brest line. It is a recognized entry point for tourists intent on tackling the Argoat scenic circuit. Full holiday facilities are provided with a choice of hotels (a couple of which are adapted for handicapped visitors), numerous apartments, a youth centre and a municipal camping site. There are also five tennis courts and a heated indoor swimming pool. This is a popular horse-riding area and there are several stables in the vicinity, while game fishers cast optimistically for the annual run of salmon—often prolific in this part of the Aulne valley. There is a seasonal tourist pavilion in the quai Cosmao, tel: 98-86-02-11. Out of season, information can be gained from the *mairie*, tel: 98-86-10-05.

Drive north from here via the D770, and a succeeding stretch of country lane will take you past an interesting **Maison du Parc** (off the D342) and so, eventually, to Sizun. Very nice countryside prevails hereabouts, with the Menez-Meur *maison* located in a 420-hectare (1,000-acre) estate, which was developed by an old gold prospector in the heart of natural woodland. Around the buildings a forest trail leads to a number of wild animal enclosures and farm stock paddocks. There is also a horse museum here, with organized carriage rides, a children's play area and a refreshment café.

This is the starting point for several heathland and forest walking routes. Detailed information can be obtained from the park office, tel: 98-21-90-69.

*T*he 19th-century pastoral Breton attire. Figures in the parish close chapel museum at Sizun.

To reach **Sizun**, 8 km (5 miles) to the north, you pass the western foothills of the Monts d'Arrée, through another pretty stretch of landscape and into the heart of the park and **parish close** country. The greatest concentration of parish closes are found is here in Lower Brittany. They are a direct throwback to the once-fierce religious rivalry between villages which reached the zenith of its artistic expression during the 17th century, when each settlement strove to produce in stone the ultimate tributes to the Deity. As an example, the close at Sizun, boasts one structural feature that unmistakably resembles a scaled-down version of a Roman triumphal arch, while the charnel house is handsomely arcaded and the adjacent 16th-century church is adorned internally with intricately carved panels. There are some 20 villages in the locality famous for their closes (*enclos paroissiaux*), plus a number of others both north and south of the park boundary. Sizun market takes place on the first Friday of each month. A highlight for anglers is the **Moulin de Vergraon** river museum which can be found here. A recommended side trip from Sizun (itself another *Station Verte* is that to **Le Faou** , which is about 15 km (9 miles) south-west and which overlooks the Brest roads at the head of the Faou estuary. The cluster of old houses and the 16th-century church are impressively attractive at high water. About 9 km (5½ miles) east of Sizun along the D964 is **Commana** village, in an elevated and once isolated location. The close here is another example full of character and loving workmanship, and lies beside a 16th-century church. There is also an ecomuseum here—the **Moulin de Kerouat**, tel: 98-68-87-76. For those wishing to stay here for a while, there is a *gîte d'étape* which has 36 beds. Going south-east of here for 3km (2 miles) takes you to another popular viewpoint, the **Roc'h Trévézel** which lies 365 m (1,198 ft) above sea level. It is a granite outcrop affording vastly distant views across the Brittany plateau and access to it is via a footpath and a 15-minute walk, well worth the effort.

One of the best parish closes on the south side of the park boundary is that of **Pleyben**, some 10 km (6 miles) east of Châteaulin, via the scenic Aulne valley road. It is a very pleasant little country town, with arguably one of the most complex of Calvaries. This one is a splendid group carving, not only of the Last Supper, but also depicting the ceremonious Washing of Feet. The ensemble—around the 16th-century flamboyant Gothic church and charnel house—is a marvellous example of stone carving and the richness and variety of the carving is a testimony to the relative affluence of the agricultural communities living in 17th-century Finistère and religious devotion here at the time. All the parish closes in this uniquely Breton enclave of France reflect the symbolic connection between spiritual awareness of the devout living, and the hallowed legions of the dead.

There is comfortable accommodation at Pleyben, with a choice of three hotels (two with restaurants) and a two-star municipal campsite on the bank of an Aulne river tributary, open from June to mid-September. There are also a couple of high reputation *crêperies* here dispensing traditional fare. Those wanting to see old Pleyben in context with parish close importance should visit during the first Sunday in August, when the imposing *pardon* ceremony is held.

Driving north from here on the D785, park territory is re-entered via the odd-sounding **Brasparts**, a village also proud of its parish close, which again has an ossuary and mid-16th-

P leyben parish close boasts one of the oldest and most crowded calvary; the size and complexity also reflected the secular wealth of the town.

century Calvary. There is a regional **craft museum centre** here (La Maison des Artisans, tel: 98-81-41-13),where some 250 skilled artisans produce and exhibit their handiwork during the summer season. For active nature-lovers this is a good area, with numerous hiking and horse-riding trails, and even waggon-trekking on horse-drawn gipsy caravans through the hill country above the Saint-Michel reservoir and around the hilltop **chapel of St-Michel de Brasparts** just off the D785. Some fine pastoral heights of the Monts d'Arrée are found here in the centre of the Armorica park.

Just south of Brasparts the D14 winds its way eastwards along the nature park boundary, to that acknowledged hub of natural beauty—**Huelgoat**. It is unquestionably the most strategic—and delightful—base for the forested region of the park, although for some visitors (particularly those relying to an extent on public transport) Carhaix-Plouguer some 20 km (12½ miles) to the south-east may be preferred.

The Huelgoat environs are a marvellous mix of pine and and deciduous forest swathes, gentle hills, clean fast flowing rivers and one or two quite spectacular water courses which have scoured some dramatic ravines. The whole area is truly a mecca for leisure walkers, with many carefully way-marked trails to follow.

Appropriately the one-time chief settlement of the ancient Argoat,

M ain street Huelgoat; charm and atmosphere pervade where wooded hills encroach right into the little market town perimeter.

Huelgoat is still very much at the heart of deeply wooded country and is, for Brittany, a township of altitude located within the southern foothills of the Monts d'Arrée—the average altitude is 200 m (660 ft). The town itself is quite tiny and the surrounding country encroaches nicely on all sides; it is a handsomely preserved enclave of ancient Finistère and a visual credit to the parc Armorique.

Huelgoat also manages to retain something of the atmosphere of a period when the most imposing building was called, deferentially, l'Hôtel Anglais. For this was a recognized stopping place of the affluent few who were able to indulge in the Grand Tour of Europe around the turn of the century, when Huelgoat really was "The Pearl of the Argoat". Just one wide, spacious and gracious main street forms the original centre, now part of a one-way system which runs beside the attractive town lake some 15 hectares (37 acres) in extent and very popular with coarse anglers.

Around the hill-town there are vestigial signs of the silver mining carried on industriously here during the 18th century, although it is the natural treasure rather than industrial archaeology that appeals to visitors. Tourist promotion is directed primarily towards outdoor-life pursuits, the single—and almost the only—source of local income nowadays. Visitor facilities are therefore pristine and comprehensive.

There are four hotels, two camping sites, a number of holiday apartments and *gîtes ruraux* in the vicinity, plus, of course, a wide choice of restaurants, *crêperies*, cafés and bars. There is a new municipal heated swimming pool and a tourist office dispensing comprehensive literature about the locality for walkers, cyclists, horse-riders, anglers and those who may wish to explore, the area by horse-drawn caravan.

Around the town the choice of footpaths is extensive, from long-distance hiking trails like the GR34 and GR380, to circular strolls of an hour or so in duration along romantically named paths like the Allée Violette and the Chemin des Amoureux. **Camp d'Artus** and **Roche Tremblante** are just two among many fascinating rock formations where mighty granite boulders have been shaped by aeons of water erosion. The first was recorded in the annals of Julius Caesar, and was indeed a camp, uncovered only in 1938 by an archaeological team led by that outstanding wizard of the science, Sir Mortimer Wheeler. It was found not to be a Roman camp, however, as was first surmised, but rather a much earlier Celtic settlement. The Roche Tremblante (logan-stone), is a 100,000 kg (220,500 lb) mass of granite which can be set rocking with the gentlest of human pressure, despite its immense weight.

More scenic objectives, among a host in the surrounding woods and alongside the swift-flowing river Argent, are the **Grotte du Diable**, the **Chaos du Moulin** (a chaotic scattering of smooth boulders), and the **Théâtre de Verdure** (a natural forest glade

amphitheatre of sublime character). Oak trees as old as 300 years are grouped around the village church of **Locmaria-Berrien**, 6 km (4 miles) south-east of Huelgoat, and form the centre piece of another golden area for walkers and anglers. At **Berrien**, 6 km (4 miles) north of Huelgoat, the setting is even more scenic, immediately below the main ridge of the Monts d' Arrée and appreciably off the beaten tourist track. There is a 24-bed *gîte d'étape* here (tel: 98-99-73-09) which is popular with hill-walkers, one of two dozen such rest-house centres for walkers and horse-riders which are scattered throughout the national park. The Huelgoat tourist office is at place de la Mairie and is open from June to September (tel: 98-99-72-32; out of season, ring: 98-99-71-55).

There is more pleasing countryside in and around the extreme eastern end of the parc Armorique, all of which is within easy reach of Huelgoat for the pedestrian, cyclist, or car driver wishing to potter along the network of minor roads and farm lanes separating villages and hamlets. There are two *département* forests, the Saint-Ambroise and the Freau, which are criss-crossed by narrow valley streams and dotted with time-worn settlements that reflect the way of life of rustic Brittany in a quietly delightful way.

Scrignac, for example, which lies between two designated sections of the great nature park some 12 km (7½ miles) north-east of Huelgoat, enjoys an elevated location and is typical of the small farming towns of the region. The dominant heathland all around has only recently become habitable and rewarding—not long ago it was an area guaranteed only to provide the lowest of subsistence-level existence. As a result it bred hardy Bretons who could compete in a particularly exhausting form of wrestling!

Scrignac became widely acclaimed for the number of strong-armed champions it produced for the essentially Breton contests, still practised at Berrien, a short distance to the southwest. Wild boar still roam freely in this part of the country too, where original and regenerated forests border the dozen or so tributaries of the principal Aulne and Argent rivers. For more information about the wealth of wildlife and where to see it, call at the **Maison de la Faune Sauvage la Fôret**, located in Scrignac's now disused railway station (tel: 98-78-25-00).

North-east of Huelgoat the countryside is, even today, largely unknown to most regional visitors, French nationals and foreigners alike. It is hill country still sparsely populated, slow-paced and restful. Those who like discovering less-trodden France may still find a Breton craftsman here producing hand-carved *sabots,* may come across deserted hill-top chapels, or may be confronted by some massive and timeless standing stone, the legacy of prehistoric habitation. The lanes of the Finistère/Côtes d'Armor boundary reveal many charming surprises.

Carhaix-Plouguer

Carhaix-Plouguer, though somewhat distant from the sea, is now something of a holiday resort where visitors are looked after in an efficient and friendly manner. The town is compact, with a high-quality shopping area and an obliging tourist office which is housed within a most handsome dwelling. History records that Carhaix was a very important Roman command centre, overseeing a complex military road junction, but its greatest claim to fame is as the birthplace of the celebrated soldier who was commonly named Corret, but who was more widely known as La Tour d'Auvergne.

Back to Roman Carhaix, it must be remarked how adept those empire

---

Old Soldiers Do *Not* Fade Away in France
Born in 1743, Corret was so passionately intent on a military career that he presented a false certificate of nobility and entered the king's service bearing a rather more grand-sounding title. In fact he was half entitled to do so, since he was distantly related to the powerful Turenne family of medieval Perigord. He proved to be a brilliant soldier and was valiantly courageous, especially in his unswerving loyalty to the crown during the Revolution. Many times wounded during the Napoleonic Wars, his audacious bravery was coupled with a disarming modesty (particularly in view of his early exploits), and he consistently refused promotion to a rank more senior than Captain. He left the army in 1795 after being captured and held for two years by the English, and he wrote *Origines Gauloises*, reflecting his passion for the Celtic language. He re-enlisted as a Private when in his mid-fifties, volunteering in place of a student about to be conscripted. His reputation blossomed and he became a national hero, finally being honoured as "The First Grenadier of France". He was killed in action in 1800, but to this day his name is revered by French army regiments. In Carhaix there is a ceremony of honour held for La Tour d'Auvergne annually on the last Sunday in June.

---

builders were at selecting strategic military locations. So much so that many of them, throughout what was that ancient empire, have retained their importance ever since. During the 1st century AD, the fortified Carhaix oversaw no less than six military roads. Today, the town is still the hub centre of five public access routes, though now shared by rail and bus services. This does make it a good excursion centre for central Brittany, since it also happens to be at the crossroads of three neighbouring *départements*: Finistère; Côtes-d'Armor; and Morbihan.

For the active explorer, the GR37 long-distance trail passes close to the town along the Nantes–Brest canal on its east–west course between Huelgoat and Rosporden.

There are also a number of advocated cycle tours in the area and no less than three cycle hire locations in Carhaix, operating on behalf of the local cyclists' club. These circuit routes vary in duration and degree of difficulty, and last from 1 ½ to 4 hours. All are colour-coded and a descriptive leaflet, with a map, is available from the tourist office.

For lovers of very ancient France, Carhaix offers one or two vestigial remains of the Roman era, when the town was known as Vorganium. Among these are traces of the **Pont Gaulois** and the remnants of a once-massive aqueduct which extended from Sainte-Catherine, some 3 km (2 miles) north of the town and lying beside the river Hyères. Still well watered, Carhaix is bounded by the Aulne river to the east and the Nantes–Brest canal to the south, both of which are perennially popular with anglers.

The **church of Plouguer**, which is now designated an integral part of Carhaix as the double-barrelled name implies, was built around 1175. It still retains massively Romanesque origins although it was partially rebuilt during the 16th century and virtually reconstructed in the 20th century. The Gothic **church of Saint Trémeur** has a tower dating from the 15th century, commemorating Tremeur, a 6th-century Christian martyr.

During the Middle Ages, major-domos were appointed by all powerful warlords as regional administrators. These were known as *sénéchals*, and were akin to those one-time colonial residents who ruled regionally for the British Empire. They were all-powerful local overlords, answerable only to their omnipotent superiors. Thus the delightful **sénéchal's residence** still in existence at 3, rue Brizeux in Carhaix is at once imposing yet inviting, as the best of French Renaissance town houses always are. The fine 15th-century building is today the tourist office and exhibition centre. There are a number of other old houses too, which are interesting, if not quite so compelling. Among them is one where La Tour d'Auvergne was born—or to give him his official name, in full, Theophile Malo Corret.

There was much damage and vindictive punishment meted out to the people of Carhaix in 1675 during the reign of Louis XIV, when the abject poverty of many rural areas of western France became endurable no longer. The peasant rising of this era was known as the Revolt of the Red Bonnets, after the imposition of yet another grossly unfair tax imposed by

Colbert. The savage repression which followed was just one more injustice to be added to the suffering of country-folk at the time, and which exploded in that final national revolution over a century later.

In general, however, throughout the medieval and Renaissance period, Carhaix enjoyed relative peace and stability, not least because it was a major Brittany market centrally located within a wide and lucrative cattle and dairy farming enclave—as it remains to this day. For the visitor, the prevalent workaday atmosphere, genuine and free of frills, is all part of the old town's attraction and is an added incentive for some to stay perhaps longer than intended.

There are half a dozen hotels here, of which the two-star Le Gradlon, in the boulevard de la République, has a recommended restaurant dispensing a full range of traditional cuisine. There is also a *gîte d'étape* at Port de Carhaix and three bed-and-breakfast houses in town. Full lists are available from the elegantly-housed tourist office, tel: 98-93-04-42. There are also several restaurants specializing in regional dishes, while La Racletterie in the place de la Mairie serves Swiss *raclette* (melted Gruyère over roast potatoes) and *Fondue Savoyarde*, equally mouth-watering.

*I*nland high points like *Trévezel or Toullaëron (shown here), still reveal wide, near-wilderness vistas in parts of western Finistère.*

Appropriately for such a geographical hub, there are attractive excursion targets at almost every point of the compass, many of which are perhaps most enjoyably (and healthily) visited by bicycle. This is possibly why there are three cycle hire centres, in the rue des Martyrs, avenue Victor Hugo and rue Ferdinand Lancien respectively. North-west of town lies Huelgoat and the Monts d'Arrée (a scenic route is via the D769 and Poullaouén), while to the south-east, along quiet minor roads, **Mael-Carhaix** and **Rostrennen** are worth seeing, particularly the latter for its pretty setting and hilltop location. There is also lake fishing here, canal-side walking and a section of the GR37 which may be walked over the 22 km (14 miles) between Carhaix and Rostrennen.

To the south of Carhaix, the **Montagnes Noires** slumber rounded and gentle, still quite remote and indeed almost isolated in places. Approach them via the westerly route through **Spezet** if possible, for there is a particularly fine 16th-century chapel-church here, the **Notre-Dame-du-Crann**, now classified as an historic monument for its exceptional interior and stained-glass windows. An annual *pardon* takes place here in May.

Another singular viewing point in the Montagnes Noires (like Trévèzel in the Monts d'Arrée) is the **Roc de Toullaëron**, rising some 326 m (1,070 ft) above sea level. It lies off the D17 north-west of Gourin, again along a scenic and lightly used road, but it is not well signposted, so keep a sharp eye for the lay-by parking approximately 4 km (2½ miles) north-west of Gourin. The summit route to the highest point of the Montagnes Noires is reached by a path which traverses a gorse-covered hillside, and which takes about 15 minutes to negotiate. The panoramas are impressively wide and sweeping on a clear day, across Morbihan in one direction and north-west Finistère in the other. Another long-distance trail, the GR38, tracks across the high point.

Gourin, an old slate quarrying centre, is now primarily a dairy farm country town of moderate size, which is situated around a 16th-century church. There are a number of stud farms in the district, which is becoming increasingly popular with horse-riding enthusiasts. There is nothing very remarkable about Gourin, but like so many small settlements in this part of Brittany, it emanates a comfortable atmosphere and the inhabitants seem ever ready to smile at visitors.

A full-day excursion from Carhaix awaits those ready to journey some 20 km (12½ miles) north-east, largely along the D54 and skirting the Armorica nature park once more, to **Callac**. This little *Station Verte* township, landmarked by an intriguing ancient church ruin, is a strategic spot for exploring the **Corong Gorges** in the wooded river valley of the Forêt de Duault to the south-east of town. Callac itself is now blessed with a hotel, a number of *gîtes*, and furnished holiday apartments and a municipal camping site, aptly named Verte Vallée (open mid-June to mid-September). Good sporting facilities are here for the asking, including angling, miniature golf, tennis and cycle hire.

Visitors who are based at Carhaix can make an interesting return from the forest and gorge scene using country lanes, via Locarn and Trébrivan, on the D20.

Morbihan

Guerlédan

The principal swathe of the central Brittany hinterland is unspectacular yet absorbing. Still largely a triangle of genuinely pastoral terrain, it lies between Carhaix, Guingamp and Saint-Brieuc to the north-east, itself within a greater area of north-western France. Much of this one-time semi-wilderness has become predominantly industrial now, with ever-growing and over-populated towns and cities, massive development projects and high-tech nuclear centres, the land itself over-scarred by a seemingly excessive number of high-speed roads.

It is not easy to visualize a land that was almost completely pastoral only some four decades ago. It was even quite primitive outside a handful of major cities and towns at the beginning of this century, and almost totally untainted by any industrial revolution. The traveller in this particular Brittany backwater, however, may capture more than a fleeting glimpse of an earlier era by meandering along the byways. Here the countryside is calm and still natural looking. The secluded farming villages may appear deserted, but are really quite active socially,

*G*uerlédan, close to Mur-de-Bretagne, where the river Blavet becomes a lake and a watery diversion forms the Nantes–Brest canal. Now an acknowledged beauty area.

where comfortable, time-worn café-bars are open all hours and the little shops are well stocked with fresh produce. In short, this is a countryside most pleasurable to explore, seemingly a million miles away from the frenetic urban whirl which now afflicts most of western Europe.

One of the brightest scenic jewels of inland Brittany—and it does possess one or two dramatic landscapes—is that centred upon Mur-de-Bretagne. One could almost describe this area as a natural jewel too, save that the centre piece expanse of water is a man-made barrage lake. However, even this has acquired a softening patina of nature around its 60-year-old shoreline. Indeed, the first-time visitor might assume that **Lac de Guerlédan** has been thus for the past 600 years, so effective is the original landscaping and so luxuriant is the subsequent flora.

Almost exactly equidistant from the English Channel and the Atlantic, the lake and its surroundings are the acknowledged premier outdoor playground of the Brittany hinterland. Certainly the attractions are magnetic, for here—appropriately at the heart of the Argoat—it really is a world of woods and watercourses, interspersed with a number of handsome river gorges and high granite crests. Traversed by the Nantes–Brest canal and richly enfolded on the southern side by the vast Forêt de Quénécan, there is no sizeable town within the recognized confines of the lake district, Mur-de-Bretagne itself being only a modestly-sized village.

The whole area is networked by narrow lanes, long-distance hiking trails and way-marked circuit footpaths to delight any walker, cyclist, or horse-rider, and sailing and canoeing enthusiasts have the lake and canal/river system to enjoy respectively. Within the environs of the lake there are also some picturesque hamlets and picture-postcard landmarks, like the Bon Repos abbey ruins and Les Forges-des-salles, where iron ore was once smelted over charcoal furnaces. There is excellent accommodation to suit all pockets in and around Mur village, with a choice of hotels, a *gîte d'étape*, a modern, well-appointed youth hostel at nearby Saint-Guen, two camping sites (the very pleasant municipal ground at Rond Point overlooking the lake), and a holiday village which is also a horse-riding centre in the summer.

Approaching from the west, the most interesting route to the heart of the holiday area is via the minor road system south of the N164, which is reached by turning south at the well-signposted **Bon Repos Abbey**. You might consider the rugged escarpments which form the Daoulas Gorges (to the north of the N164), as a separate excursion, for the delightful scene of the abbey enclave will almost certainly take precedence. The river Blavet is partially restricted here with an old locking system, and there is a sturdy, buttressed pack-horse bridge of ancient vintage. Beside a hotel of the same name lie the ruins of the 12th-century Cistercian abbey (founded by Alain Duke of Rohan, in 1184). It was all but destroyed during the French Revolution, yet there is still an air of dignified grace about the monastic cluster which was originally built to a very grand scale. Guided visits are available for those wishing to explore the ruins

The beautiful Blavet river adjacent to Bon-Repos abbey on the western side of Guerléden lake.

at close quarters, and the aspect here on a sunny day epitomizes all that might be expected of an acknowledged rustic beauty spot.

Going south of the abbey, along a narrow winding road through a belt of rich woodland, you will traverse part of the 3,000-hectare (7,400-acre) **Quénécan forest** which blankets the undulating plateau country above the Blavet river valley. There is a predominance of pine here, but there is also a liberal growth of beech, spruce and other deciduous trees. This makes for rich variety of flora which in turn supports a healthy fauna—there are deer and wild boar here in the forest

enclosures that are least trodden by humans.

Amid this beautiful wooded country, **Les Forges-des-Salles**—only a couple of kilometres or so from the abbey— appears for all the world like a medieval hamlet on approach, although the low tumbledown buildings are primarily 18th century with only remnants of much older habitation. Here you are actually within the ancient fief of the ducs of Rohan, as evidenced by the once-great fortified **château of Les Salles** and the adjacent lake, accessible only to pedestrians. There is a small local history and folk **museum** at Les Forges-des-Salles, which opens to visitors sporadically throughout summer. A particularly scenic section of the GR41 crosses this area, a well-marked trail winding east to Mur-de-Bretagne. It is popular with walkers since there is a convenient *gîte d'étape* roughly at the halfway point, between Forges and

Mur, along the 25 km (15½ mile) stretch.

For car drivers there are a number of lanes leading to the lake as one progresses eastwards, and parking and picnic spaces are provided at the water's edge. These are well signposted, as are the woodland footpaths which ascend the overlooking wooded banks. There are a number of elevated viewpoints from which you can see the great barrage, especially as you approach and then detour around the

Early industrial history reflected by the long-deserted workers cottages at the hamlet of Forges-les-Salles. Iron ore was once smelted on charcoal furnaces here.

village of **Saint-Aignan**—pause awhile here to admire the endearing little 12th-century church. The Guerlédan dam is a masterpiece of civil engineering, created in 1929 to provide the region with electricity. The lake itself covers some 400 hectares (1,000 acres) and stretches for approximately 12 km (7½ miles) between Mur and Gouarec in the west.

There is more tranquil towpath walking alongside the Nantes–Brest canal, which here links the rivers Blavet and Aulne. To remind you that this is still very much traditional Brittany, there are a number of prehistoric megaliths in the vicinity, including Gallic burial places and menhirs, plus a full share of medieval chapels and churches in surrounding villages. **Saint-Gilles-Vieux-Marché**, north of Mur, is

reached along a notably impressive road which runs through the **Gorges du Poulancre**, a *ville fleuri* of charm. A short distance north-west of here is **Saint-Mayeux** and the Gallic burial place known as La Lande Rohan, which is located on one of the several cycle circuits advocated in the area. For those more inclined towards the relaxed method of sightseeing, Guerlédan lake may be viewed from the motor launch which plies it regularly in season from a *base nautique* close to Caurel village on the northern shore of the lake, at the Beau Rivage embarkation point; the round trip lasts three hours.

Mur-de-Bretagne exudes a certain Breton charm with little concession to tourist dressing, and is quaintly pleasing. The 17th-century **church of Sainte-Suzanne** is rightly the principal building to one side of the spacious village square called, of course, place de l'Église. The interior is graced by some notable coloured panels. A slightly elevated setting, coupled with preserved pastoral surroundings, add to the aspect of the village which was much admired by the 19th-century painter, Corot. Opposite the church, there is a scattering of essential shops together with a modern, but nicely designed tourist information pavilion dispensing comprehensive literature about the barrage lake and adjoining leisure areas. It is open seasonally, and English is spoken by the staff (tel: 96-28-51-41).

*N*ot built for beauty but strictly for Middle Ages military purposes. The enduring Rohan château at Pontivy. There is pleasant towpath walking close by along the canal Napoleon built.

Canal Country

During the Dark Ages of the 7th century, an English monk named Ivy embarked on a long and dangerous pilgrimage from Lindisfarne off the Northumberland coast, to the quieter sanctity of central Brittany. There he created a monastery beside the river Blavet which was later bridged at the same spot—thus the settlement became known as **Pontivy.** It remained so for some eleven centuries, until a ruler of France, with the easy arrogance of most despots, renamed it Napoléonville. It was a very temporary arrangement, the original and venerable title being restored at the fall of that short-lived empire.

It was, however, no mere whim that induced the Little Corporal to rechristen the town, but part of a vast national military project, which included linking the two major sea ports of Brest and Nantes with an inland canal system. This was created to avoid

P ontivy and place Martray in the old town centre. There is a pleasant semi-pedestrian precinct here; a popular base for touring central Brittany.

coastal confrontation with the English Navy, which was formidably active at this time. Pontivy, roughly equidistant between the two ports, was to be the strategic headquarters of Brittany. A huge rebuilding programme was instigated by Napoleon in 1805, which resulted in a not unpleasant mix of barracks and boulevards, administrative grandeur of the 19th-century kind, and landscaped squares. Much of this once-urgent redevelopment is still on view.

The original **old town** was left more or less intact, huddled in the shadow of a mighty 15th-century **château**, the control centre built for another powerful warlord, the medieval Duc Jean

II de Rohan in 1485. This majestic construction, dry-moated and now a partial ruin, is still a marvellous example of Breton military architecture of an earlier era, part of which is now used for periodic cultural exhibitions. Below the ramparts there are a number of colourful, narrow streets lined with 15th- and 16th-century houses, notably around the Place du Martray, which is now principally a pedestrian precinct.

Today, Pontivy is a lively and very pleasant town of two quite contrasting ages, much enhanced by the tamed river and the canal arm dug during the l9th century to link the Blavet with the Aulne to the west. A major market town of the region, there is an inevitable expansion of commercial development around its periphery, much of which is devoted to light industry. The centre, however, retains its venerable character, especially in the vicinity of the waterside. There is an excellent, ruler-straight main shopping avenue, the rue Nationale which runs into the rue General de Gaulle. The canal towpath runs directly into the surrounding countryside via a spacious sport and leisure area, and offers easy and tranquil walking or exploration by bicycle.

This is another popular centre with the horse-riding fraternity and there are stables with riding schools close to town at Fontaine-Faven 2km (1 mile) west, and at Guerlogoden, off the D191, 8 km (5 miles) to the north. Both of these establishments specialize in trekking ventures for riders of all ages and abilities, along the canal towpaths and in the wooded country around Malguénac.

In town, there is a good selection of accommodation, with eight hotels, a number of *chambres d'hôte*, a conveniently located youth hostel and a two-star municipal camping site. In the environs a good choice of farm *gîtes* and holiday apartments are on offer, as one might expect from such a central touring base. The gourmet is well catered for too, since four of the hotels are also restaurants, and these are supplemented by *crêperies*, pizzerias and traditional Breton eating houses. There are also Vietnamese dishes on offer for those who enjoy more exotic food. There is a market which takes place on Mondays.

In short, Pontivy is an historically interesting place, a recommended base for any visitor who enjoys staying in a working town in preference to a purpose-built holiday resort. A principal stop-over on the celebrated route des Ducs de Bretagne, Pontivy occupies the extreme north-western corner of an historic triangle embracing a wide area of Morbihan and Ille-et-Vilaine. Market day Monday.

The lower section of the Blavet river valley is one of the first scenic targets to consider, for here the river reaches are wide and pleasing, and the woodland which cloaks the valley flanks is lush in parts. By using the secondary roads close to the water the traffic is light, even at the height of summer. There are a few saw-mills and other light industrial pockets, but in general the aspect is rural. This route takes in the pretty little town of **Saint-Nicolas-des-Eaux** and further south another fine view of the river and surrounding country can be gained from the Castennec belvedere where the Blavet loops tortuously. Again, this area epitomizes inland Brittany at its most peaceful, where Calvaries and chapels landmark that is primarily a rustic world, scarce changed since the last century.

Driving south-west from Pontivy you traverse more farming terrain which can include (by detouring modestly), two of the most delightful villages of northern Morbihan. The first is **Quelven**, a photogenic settlement of appealing character with an ancient chapel, now classified as an historic monument. Some 20 km (12½ miles) further west, via Guern, Persquen and Lignol, lies **Kernascléden**, part of a country estate once owned by the medieval Rohan dynasty. The flamboyant **Gothic church** here, built in 1423, boasts two decorated porches instead of the usual one, thus displaying all twelve of the Apostles, instead of a mere selection, the more usual practice where room was restricted. Inside, there are graphic 15th-century frescoes, including visions of Hell and Damnation, plus a wealth of intricately carved statuary. This is rated as one of the best of all Breton chapel-churches, for the fineness of its architectural design and meticulous attention to building detail. There is a handsome **château** and lake close to the village, and the château grounds are open to visitors seasonally. For those wishing to stay overnight in the vicinity at modest cost, there is a *gîte ruraux* at Guern (tel: 97-51-40-50), and a *gîte d'étape* at Kernascléden (tel: 97-05-61-31).

East of Pontivy there is green and tranquil countryside along and alongside the Nantes–Brest canal, which loops to link with Rohan. In between, via the D2, there are the visual pleasures of **Noyal-Pontivy parish church**, which is impressively grand and a sturdy example of 15th-century Breton building, plus the natural allure of picturesque wooded banks above the canal water, just to the north-east around Gueltas, in the forest of Branguily. There is nice canal-side walking between Gueltas and Rohan.

Of the mighty Rohan dynasty, there is nothing much within the little town itself. **Rohan** town grew close to a castle which was built in 1104 on the orders of Alain, first Duc of Rohan, to

---

Ally of Elizabeth I

The feudal Rohans, once rulers over most of Morbihan, were among the most illustrious and colourful families of ancient France, and all-powerful in this part of Brittany between the 13th and 16th centuries. Principally Protestant, Henri, Duc-de-Rohan (1579–1683) was actually a leader of the Huguenots, and as a consequence was much favoured by Elizabeth I of England. Being of that particular religious persuasion in medieval France meant that all the duke's strongholds had to be constructed to the highest possible standards.

Thus the great château of Pontivy survives as the only remaining example of authentic 15th-century military architecture in Brittany. Surveying the incredibly stalwart ramparts and towers—as forbidding now as they were in the feudal era—it is possible to understand why the dynasty made such formidable adversaries and lasted as rulers for so long. Although the family no longer reigns, it thrives to this day and occupies another Rohan creation in stone, one of the most regal in Brittany or indeed anywhere else in western France—the château of Josselin.

take advantage of the strategic terrain and the nearby hunting forest of Lanouée. Les Forges on the western fringe of this forest incidentally, is a starting point of a scenic traverse along the D117, into ancient woodland served by rides and footpaths and with several locations marking early Celtic and Roman occupation. Just to the north of Rohan town, is a dynastic legacy, the **Notre-Dame-de-Bonne-Encontre Chapel**, built by Jean de Rohan in 1510 on the banks of the river Oust.

This is a recognized relaxation enclave for the inhabitants of both Pontivy town and district, with a choice of camping grounds, purpose-built leisure areas, boating water and way-marked footpaths. There are also a number of prehistoric sites, and the 19th-century Abbeye-de-Timadeuc, which is not open to visitors but which does occupy a scenic wooded setting. Access is only allowed to the gatehouse at the entrance, which is also an information centre.

Here is the fairytale stone-pile of Josselin also held by the all-powerful Rohan family. Set aside a day to see it.

About 20 km (12½ miles) south-east of Rohan, **Josselin** is very different from the duc's redoubt at Pontivy. This is no squat, belligerent-looking fortress, but one of those definitive fairy-tale constructions of opulent majesty, rising high above the Oust river and Nantes–Brest canal. Enhanced by a splendid trio of dunce-capped towers, the powerful rampart walls enclose what is really more of a gracious château now still fortified and of imposing presence—not nearly as austere as the 15th-century original. The early version did not boast the architectural refinements which can be seen above the medieval battlements— the tower cappings and the ornate dormer windows, which were added during the Renaissance period. The most drastic conversion of castle to residence was carried out during the 19th century.

Nonetheless, from the riverside at least, the whole complex manages to appear half chivalrous in the grand manner, and half intimidating in the best tradition of French châteaux of the Middle Ages. Once the home of celebrated constables of France, like Olivier de Clisson and Jean de Beaumanoir, in the mid-14th century, Josselin castle (which had already been partly destroyed and rebuilt during the tail-end of the Hundred Years War) was once again at the centre of turmoil, this time through the Brittany War of Succession.

The Rohan dynasty supported the French royal household, and as a consequence, the Duke of Brittany, François II, stormed Josselin in 1488 and razed it once again. At a later time of reconciliation, the great and good duchess Anne, daughter of François, restored the castle to the Rohans and aided generously with the cost of reconstruction. It is, however, the Battle of the Thirty—a bloody clash of arms even by medieval standards—which took place some 5 km (3 miles) from the castle, that epitomizes knightly valour and places Josselin among the most respected of chivalric sites in France.

At the height of the war for mastery of Bretagne, Jean de Beaumanoir was the Josselin warlord and marshal of Brittany for Charles de Blois, who in turn supported the French king. Only a few miles distant at Ploërmel, an English knight, John Bramborough, was in command of his respective castle and was supporting the cause of the Blois rival, Jean de Montfort, who was in turn championed by the king of England. Both factions clashed frequently during marauding forays and the situation eventually became intolerable. In fact Bramborough's men ignored a pledged truce, and continued to pillage the surrounding countryside until Beaumanoir's patience finally ran out.

He issued a challenge of personal combat, in which 30 men picked from either side would fight hand to hand for a final resolution of supremecy. Bramborough accepted the challenge and the resultant skirmish resulted in one of the most ferocious set-piece tournaments of medieval history. The Breton knights and their squires under Beaumanoir eventually won against an equal number of English knights supported by a handful of German mercenaries. With battle-axes, swords and daggers, the carnage continued all day on 25 March 1351, and at dusk all the

*O*n *this spot in 1351, the bloody Battle of the Thirty was fought. The victor on that day was Charles de Blois, but it was Jean de Montfort who finally won the war—and the Brittany succession.*

combatants of both sides were dead (including Bramborough), or badly wounded. A quote uttered at the height of this merciless struggle has since been immortalized. When Jean de Beaumanoir, who had been seriously wounded, cried out for water, an embattled Breton knight by the name of Geoffroy du Bois, retorted, "Drink your own blood Beaumanoir—that will quench your thirst!"

Following the custom among highborn warriors of that era who would not hesitate to massacre their low-caste adversaries, the few survivors on the losing side were courteously treated and quickly released after the usual ransom payment had been made. The spot where the slaughter took place, the **Obélisque de Trente** at **Pyramide**, can be seen where the dual carriageway divides, halfway between Josselin and Ploërmel. A stone column is inscribed with the names of the Breton knights, but of the equally courageous vanquished—since the struggle was virtually a pyrrhic victory—there is no mention.

After Beaumanoir's death, his widow Marguerite, herself a member of the Rohan family, married Olivier de Clisson who thus became the owner of Josselin castle. He in turn died there as constable of France in 1407, and his statue may be seen on the ground floor of the château, one of the sections open to visitors. Today, the Rohan **collection of dolls** through the centuries is almost as famous as the château itself. This is a unique and unusual display of some 600 period models, dating from the 17th to the 19th centuries, all of them in the most remarkable state of preservation. They are housed in the ancient castle stables, within what must surely be one of the most elegant courtyards in the land. Like the château, the doll museum is open seasonally.

As with the château, so with the town of Josselin, another collection of medieval France around the once-walled centre, where a number of half-timbered 17th-century dwellings surround the flamboyant Gothic church of **Notre-Dame-du-Roncier**. ("Our Lady of the Rose Bush", as the name quaintly translates). A centre of worship since the 11th century, the great church mainly dates from the 16th and 17th centuries, and is decorated with a number of impressive flying buttresses and hugely extended water-spouts with gargoyles. The area around this church, networked by narrow alleys and archways, and flanked with charming slate-roofed houses, is a photographer's delight.

There is a choice of comfortable hotels in the old town, the prominent Hôtel du Château, perhaps providing the closest, and best, view of the Rohan ancestral home from the banks of the river Oust in the rue Général de Gaulle. Among recommended restaurants, the Duchesse-Anne, in the *place* of the same name, serves traditional Breton fare. Each summer, in September, an elaborate *pardon* ceremony is held in Josselin, which fully justifies the five hotels, six restaurants, the 20-bed *gîte d'étape*, various *chambres d'hôte* and the pleasant camping site that the tiny town provides as part of the good visitor service.

For those intent on sampling an atmospheric glimpse of France past, there is a really revealing footpath walk which begins from the entrance to the Bas de la Lande campground on the western fringe of town, just off the N24 Lorient road. There is an easily accessible towpath here, bordering a stretch of the Nantes–Brest canal, which becomes the river Oust as one approaches Josselin, a couple of kilometres distant. Actually a section of the long-distance GR37, the path leads directly to the foot of the towering ramparts and is by far the most romantic approach. There is a *base nautique* here, the embarkation point for many in summer, and boarding point for the sightseeing river cruisers.

The direct route back to Pontivy, via the D764 is 28km (17 miles) long, and takes you to the start of another contrasting excursion. Take the D767 south-east from Pontivy, an arm of the route des Ducs, and after 23 km (14 miles) you will reach **Locminé**. A monastery created here in the 6th century exhibits only vestigial remnants today of a 16th-century church, adjacent to a house of contemporary worship. There is a surviving 16th-century chapel, however, which is as attractive as one or two of the old houses in the small town centre.

For another example of modernity built around a venerable centrepiece, take the D1 minor road from Locminé to Bignan, and then to the signposted château of **Kerguéhennec**. Around an 18th-century mansion, amid a well-tended botanical garden landscape, there is a permanent exhibition of modern sculpture, some of the pieces by artists of international repute. This is a government project which was established to promote regional works of art, and is one of many such projects found nationwide, which the French execute so well through a Ministry of Culture. There are some nice walks on this estate, which also boasts a large lake. Kerguéhennec is open daily from April to September.

Among the Moorland Hills of Lanvaux

Continue south-east along the Dl/D10 from Bignan for yet another intriguing stretch of inland Brittany. This is a traverse of the northern flanks of the **Landes de Lanvaux**, along a route seldom explored by the sea-oriented majority of Morbihan visitors. While the scenery may not be spectacular, the ancient moorland ridge rises so abruptly from the surrounding plains in places that it frequently appears quite lofty.

Well-wooded nowadays through a national forestry planting programme,

---

A Morbihan Elevated Hiking Trail

Not long ago one of Brittany's most impoverished areas, the Lanvaux region has only recently been reclaimed by the diligent application of modern husbandry. Healthy woodland swathes now flourish where once tree growth was abysmally sparse across the succession of rocky spurs where topsoil was so meagre. Bare or broom-covered flanks remain between forestry enclosures, while evidence of prehistory is amply evident through the number of megaliths, notably around Saint-Germain, between Trédion and the Tours-d'Elven, just to the south of the GR38. *En route* from Locminé, there are a number of country villages, like Saint-Jean-Brévelay, Pumelec and Serent—all settlements of character—with access roads into the nearby Lanvaux hills.

---

the long ridge—which extends eastwards for about 60 km (37 miles) across the Morbihan *département* above Vannes—has a continuous pedestrian trail (the GR38) winding its way across heath and through forest. The densest, most scenic area of woodland is considered to be that to the south-east of Baud, within the *département forests* of Camors and Floranges. For long-distance walkers, villages and refreshment points are encountered frequently. The Lanvaux ridge is an odd geological feature, primarily of granite, in an otherwise flattish landscape and this is part of its allure to leisure walkers.

Towards the eastern end of the traverse route lie two more places of interest to travellers, namely **Malestroit** and **Rochefort-en-Terre**.

The first of these is one of those nuggets of ancient France which is preserved in aspic, and certainly one of the most picturesque market towns in Morbihan. Around the **church of Saint-Gilles** (built originally in the 12th century) there are many 16th- and 17th-century buildings which are a delight as much as they are a surprise to the unsuspecting traveller. These are half-timbered dwellings with decorated overhangs above cobbled alleyways, many with carved wooden gargoyles gracing external corner posts and beams. The low arched waterside houses alongside the Oust river and the Nantes–Brest canal are especially memorable. This is an attractive place for any lunch-break or overnight stop, as visitor facilities are good at this designated beauty spot and *Station Verte*.

Active holidaymakers are well served too, for Malestroit and neighbouring La Chapelle-Caro (8 km, or 5 miles, distant), provide between them hotel and *gîte d'étape* accommodation, a heated swimming pool, tennis courts, a *base nautique*, and boat, canoe and cycle hire There are also way-marked circuit footpaths for keen walkers. Incidentally, Serent, some 10 km (6 miles) west, has one of the nicest landscaped municipal camping sites in the area, which is open all year round. Just north-east of La Chapelle-Caro, is the **Château du Crevy** on the banks of the Oust, a truly splendid fortified redoubt dating from around the 14th century with an even older history, traceable right back to the 3rd century. The interior houses an elegant display of period costumes, from the 17th to the 20th centuries.

For many visitors to this area, Malestroit old town is not the major attraction—delightful though it is—because for students of contemporary history, the hamlet of **Saint-Marcel**, 3 km (2 miles) west, is the irresistible target. Here, in a spacious 6-hectare (15-acre) enclosure, which was remote wooded hill-country during World War II was a secret stronghold of the Maquis, the guerilla resistance fighters of France, a most influential hidden army in Brittany and one which played an important part during the final struggle for liberation in 1945.

Appropriately located then, this is an extensive indoor/outdoor **museum**, laid out imaginatively amid woodland, and distant enough from habitation to enhance the atmosphere of the time. The scenes created are designed to simulate occupied Brittany where possible, with blockhouses, vehicles (military and civilian) of the era, field guns, a massive range-finder, an American Sherman tank and a variety of military impedimenta revealed along woodland paths. These outdoor exhibits are supplemented by indoor video displays, small arms, uniforms, documents, photographs and much other fascinating memorabilia of the 1940s. For veterans of World War II the camouflage patterns and paint used on some of the exhibits may not be *quite* authentic, but on the whole this is an interesting and instructive showground. There is spacious parking (for 100 cars), picnic and disabled visitor facilities, a children's adventure playground, a *crêperie* and drink bar, of course, and apt souvenirs for sale including real bullet key-rings! The museum is open every day during the season, and children under 12 years are admitted free.

Driving south from Malestroit you will cross the great Lanvaux ridge which, after a 22-km (14-mile) drive of gentle ascents and descents, culminates with another acknowledged high spot of the route des Ducs, the promontory settlement of **Rochefort-en-Terre**. There was a regal château here in the 14th century, but only remnants remain of the once-splendid medieval stronghold, which was razed shortly after the French Revolution. The restored buildings inside the grounds are used as a **museum**, housing a collection of medieval paintings and furniture, largely gathered by a recent American owner of the château who was himself an artist. There is also an impressive display of early porcelain, some of the pieces dating back to the 14th century. There is visitor access to the museum from April to September.

The medieval town clustered below

the castle, is one of great charm, having been carefully preserved and lovingly restored where necessary. As a result, the setting is one of the prettiest in the hinterland, occupying a commanding knoll of the eastern Lanvaux ridge, amid handsomely wooded ravines above the Arz river, and a lake called the Étang du Moulin Neuf. Bedecked with blooms throughout the summer, appropriately for a *plus belle ville fleuri*, some of the ancient château ramparts still survive, linking the town to the castle.

Stroll along the Chemin des Douves, between the inner and outer walls, for elevated views across the township roofs of the many 16th- and 17th-century houses, and distantly over the Vallée de Guezon. Picturesque, atmospheric and friendly, there is a comfortable hotel here, the Lion d'Or, noted for its traditional Breton cuisine. There is also a municipal camping ground (open from April to September) and a *gîte d'étape* (24 places) called, like the lake, Le Moulin Neuf.

Another pleasing feature of granite-built Rochefort, is the **Notre-Dame-de-la-Tronchaye church**, dating originally from the 12th century, but mainly 17th-century flamboyant Gothic now, with an interesting interior, including a statue of the Virgin thought to date from the 11th century. The tourist office is housed in an attractive pavilion, part of which was once the town's covered market in the place des Halles

*P*arc de Prehistoire at Malansac near Rochefort-en-Terre. Garish maybe, but children are very impressed by this modest Breton version of Euro-Disney. There is educational fun here.

(tel: 97-43-32-81). This is a recommended stop-over for any hiker on the GR38 trail, which passes right through the town. An elaborate *pardon* procession is held here annually on 21 August—if you stay here on this date, book any overnight accommodation. A *petite cité de caractère* Rochefort may be, but again—like Malestroit—it is not the sole magnet for many visitors. This time the attraction happens to be located about 4 km (2½ miles) to the south-east of Rochefort, and is one of the national prestige sites of antiquity, comparable to those of the Vézère valley in the Dordogne. It is the **Parc de Préhistoire** at **Malansac**.

Enterprises such as these are often unashamedly profit-motivated and frequently suspect when it comes to authenticity. The Malansac enclave, however, is no down-market theme park, being neither overly spectacular, nor wildly dramatic about life on Earth when the planet was younger. In truth, the project, the only one of its kind in Brittany and winner of a tourist trophy award in 1989, is a genuine contributor to basic knowledge of prehistory. The era is presented in a manner that is visually stimulating for adults and is a much-appreciated method of learning for children and students.

The park presents in capsulated form life and times on our planet largely during the period 25000–2000 BC, and particularly where possible, how it affected Brittany and north-western France. Scientific in conception, it presents evolutionary tableaux within an ostensibly untamed woodland area (once a slate quarry), yet which is in reality carefully landscaped with a marked-out viewing route which winds between a scattering of small lakes. The main display path has been constructed to accommodate wheelchairs.

There are naturalistic scenes of the Lower Palaeolithic period (early Stone Age) with *Homo Érectus* creating fire, making tools, and crude shelters, to the later Stone Age represented by Cro-Magnon man, hunting mammoth and reindeer or demonstrating vividly how those huge menhirs were transported (often for incredible distances), and then erected. There is also a painted cave (after the manner of the Dordogne Lascaux example), a chambered dolmen with engraved stones, pots and human remains of the period. The viewing circuit path is about 1km (½ mile) in length, with some 50 life-like human and animal figures contributing to some seventeen scenes of prehistory, all with explanatory panels in several languages, including English. Information on botanical species of the area is also provided, plus a mineral and fossil exhibition. There is spacious car parking and the Malansac site is open daily from Easter to mid-October, tel: 97-43-34-17.

East of Malansac, lies one of the great waterway junctions of Brittany, in the vicinity of **Redon**. Here the rivers Oust and Vilaine, and the man-made Nantes–Brest canal converge at the easternmost extremity of the Lanvaux ridge. Redon itself is an attractive base for anglers, canoeists and pleasure-craft sailors. Walkers, too, have the choice of a scenic way-marked pedestrian circuit, or they may explore the GR38 and GR347, long-distance trails passing through the environs.

Redon is a pleasant, quite small

The Nantes–Brest canal at Redon. Deserving its title of Ville-Fleuri, the town is ablaze with flower blooms in season.

market town, if unremarkable in the main for its old-world architecture. It becomes more attractive each summer, however, through a prolific display of flowers which decorate all the principal places, including canal and river locks and bridges. There is an old town centre, mainly around the imposing **church of Saint-Sauveur**. Founded in the 9th century, this 12th-century restoration is largely Romanesque with a magnificent 14th-century belfry. Inside there is a massive altarpiece, which was donated by Cardinal Richelieu who was responsible for rebuilding the adjacent ancient abbey during the 17th century. The cloisters here are of elegant and tranquil dignity, the whole area enhanced by a newly installed semi-pedestrian precinct, with place Duchesse Anne indicating to the visitor that this is most definitely Brittany. There are a number of attractive 17th- and 18th-century houses hereabouts, the quai Dugay-Trouin boasting some unmistakable examples of the homes of one-time rich merchants. There are also vestigial remnants of medieval ramparts in the quai Saint-Jacques, but these few preserved features apart, Redon is mainly a modern, thriving centre of agricultural industry today.

Redon is a compact and friendly town, with some nice shops and a choice of hotels, and with an escalating commercial and industrial periphery, especially alongside the now little-used canal. There are three *gîtes d'étape* in the vicinity (the nearest is at

Rieux, 7 km, or 4 miles, south), and a municipal campground which is open from mid-June to mid-September. The north–south railway line between Saint Malo and Nantes serves Redon, as does the SNCF line westwards to Vannes and Quimper. The annual high spot at Redon is the colourful chestnut fair, held during the last weekend of October. Gardening enthusiasts may care to make a 10 km (6-mile) excursion north-west, to **Saint-Jacut-les-Pins**, where there is a noted Jardin Exotique, displaying an impressive array of tropical plants and flowers, in a 3-hectare (7-acre) setting. The park is open from March to November and is closed on Mondays.

Turn north from Rochefort-en-Terre or Malestroit, and you come to Ploërmel. About halfway between this town and Rennes, off the N24, is Brittany's inland enclave of magical myth and legend, nowadays known as the **Forêt de Paimpont**. Although it is only a fraction of the dense woodland that once cloaked almost all of the peninsula hinterland, it is still large enough by contemporary standards, covering more than 8,000 hectares (19,000 acres) of forest, moorland, lakes and valleys. It is but the shrunken heart of what was in medieval times (and for a great deal longer than that), when it was one of the finest hunting forests in Europe.

Thus it is a delightful region of Morbihan and neighbouring Ille-et-Vilaine, steeped in real history and in many ways enhanced through medieval romance. Happily, through a national programme of conservation and industrious reafforestation, the area of Paimpont increases healthily year by year. Although there will never

be a full renaissance of the mighty forest which once stretched for nearly 160 km (100 miles) from Brittany's eastern border to the Black Mountains of Finistère, the expanding green enclosure is large enough, and certainly fascinating enough to fill any walking or cycling holiday. There are strategic bases both in and around the forest, **Ploërmel** being a popular choice with those visitors who enjoy town comforts and services.

Ploërmel's origin is as ancient as the nearby forest, its name being derived from a 6th-century monk, Armel, who created a settlement here. Hence *plou Armel* in Gaelic, meaning "family of Armel". The town **church of Saint-Armel**, built in the 16th century, boasts finely carved portal doors depicting the Apostles, and some splendid stained-glass windows. Inside there are statues of the ancient dukes of Brittany (John II and John III), for Ploërmel was once a ruler's residence. There are some 16th-century houses in the rue Beaumanoir (so named after the victor of the Battle of the Thirty), including a princely residence and **La Maison des Marmousets**, with a façade richly ornate and beautifully preserved. Of the great medieval castle which once ruled proudly here there remains nothing, although there is still evidence of a 12th-century tower and fractions of rampart walls, which can be seen in the place Daversin, just to the north of the church.

Old Ploërmel is nowadays almost vestigial compared with the modern complex which spreads widely from the original centre. The latter embraces much light industry and commerce which does not, in truth, enhance the immediate surroundings. Nonetheless, the town is interesting, lively and there are three hotels, *gîtes d'étape* in the vicinity, and a camping ground. The Ploërmel leisure lake is a big local draw, the second largest of its kind in Brittany and covering some 20 hectares (600 acres).The **Étang au Duc**, as it is called, is a comprehensive *base nautique*, providing windsurfing, sailing and water-skiing facilities. There is also a man-made *plage* and stretches of the water are reserved for anglers, The Ploërmel *Syndicat d'Initiative* is in place Lamennais tel: 97-74-02-70 and market days are on Mondays and Fridays. The GR37 skirts the town *en route* for Paimpont forest which lies approximately 10 km (6 miles) to the north-east, the 2,000-year-old Brocéliande even today strangely mystical in certain areas.

Land of Arthurian Legend

About 2 km (1 mile) south-east of Ploërmel via the D772, is the park of **Malleville** and its château. It is worth a short detour, if only to admire the beautiful chapel within the landscaped grounds. The scene epitomizes the elegant richness of life for the fortunate minority prior to the Revolution. The N24 can now be rejoined for the first of the forest gems, the **Château de Trécesson** and its picturesque lake near Campeneac. This is a 15th-century castle of impressive dignity where visitors are permitted to see the courtyard surroundings on request. Distinctly medieval of aspect and atmosphere, it is an appropriate mood setter for exploring the even earlier era of Paimpont forest, which may be dated to about the 5th or 6th centuries.

It was around this period of the Dark Ages that there was a chieftain of the Silures (a tribe of south-western Britain), who fought off Saxon invaders repeatedly and successfully. This warrior leader almost certainly fell in battle. From these scraps of historic fact, the great romantic cycle of Arthurian legend stems. How then were these sagas of the ancient world transferred from the British Isles to Brittany, and is there any reason to believe that the stories might at least be based on real events?

Logic of the 20th century suggests that all such tales were simply invented by story-tellers for an audience as superstitious and ignorant of the world about them as those early times dictated. And yet there are still faint clues which can be grasped about this mist-enshrouded era which give credence to some of the stories. Even if cold logic can dismiss all evidence of glorified knightly endeavour and the triumph of right over evil, it doesn't hurt to suspend belief just occasionally. Indeed, for any visit to the celebrated high spots of the ancient Brocéliande forest to the west of Rennes, it is obligatory if you are to extract the maximum enjoyment. Entering this leafy world of semi-fantasy is also made even more exciting for knowing that there may be an element of truth among a welter of fairy-tales.

From recorded history, we know that indigenous British tribes fled in increasing numbers to Brittany during the 6th to 8th centuries to escape the rapacious Teutonic Saxon and Scandinavian Viking invaders. We know too, that maritime traffic in the English Channel was quite heavy during this time, with many craft plying back and forth between the British Isles and the European mainland, albeit of small boats which carried relatively few people. The vast majority of British emigrants were of Celtic stock and it is a reasonable supposition that they took with them stories of heroic derring-do, which in time became completely intertwined with Breton folklore, and then later became elaborated upon through the lays of medieval minstrels. Fact and fiction would have become inextricably mixed, only the spell-binding quality of subsequent tales really mattering.

Certainly no heroic romances of earlier times captivate more than those of Arthurian legend, particularly the tales of the principal characters: Arthur himself; the bold knight Sir Lancelot; Merlin the sorcerer; the seductive wood nymph Viviane; (the Lady of the Lake), Guinevere; and many others. These moral tales grew in strength with the Christian church, which was much concerned with the search for and final discovery of the Holy Grail—all of which may, or may not, have been enacted on the Brittany peninsula long ago. If the great adventures did take place in France, the most likely region could have been deep within the almost impenetrable depths of Brocéliande.

There is no record of any tribal chieftain of the Silures venturing to Brittany, although there was a cult hero of the ancient Gauls named Mercurious Artaius. The boldest of the bold, he was said to have slain a ferocious giant living on Mont Saint-Michel. Was this Arthur? Certainly Tristan—sometime attender at King Arthur's court—sailed from Cornwall to Brittany (to the protection of the Duke of Hoel). He and Isolde did spend one idyllic interlude in a forest glade, which might well have been Brocéliande. Merlin's tomb can be seen in the forest too, although the master of wizardry is also said to lie beneath Castle Mound, in what is now the grounds of Marlborough College, in England.

As for Sir Lancelot, was he not raised by Viviane at the castle of Comper? The most glamorous of King Arthur's knights might have been the discoverer of the Holy Grail itself, had it not been for his illicit liaison with Queen Guinevere. The moral tales could not allow him this ultimate triumph, but they did the next best thing by having his son, Sir Galahad, find the sacred relic. This chalice, used at the Last Supper, was given into the care of Joseph of Arimathea, who used it to gather Christ's blood at the Crucifixion. Differing versions say it was then spirited away from Palestine, either to England or France.

Arthurian romance is slightly confounded by the knowledge that at Fécamp, near Le Havre on the Normandy coast, there was a relic lodged in the nunnery which was founded there in the year 658. The nunnery was built expressly as a haven for this "Relic of the True Blood", which was discovered on the foreshore, secreted in a hollow fig-tree log. It was surmised that it had drifted from the Holy Land, and it is still in the care of Fécamp church today. This seaside town is not all that far from the forest of Paimpont. Conversely, there is also the story that the Grail was brought to Britain, again by Joseph of Arimathea, to be buried at Glastonbury Tor in Somerset. Fact overlaps fiction once more here, with the discovery of a Celtic settlement dated to around 300 BC, surrounded by swamps and known as the mystical Isle of Avalon. According to monastic claims, this was the burial place of King Arthur, and hence was a place of hallowed pilgrimage right up to the 11th century. Legend has it that Joseph left his staff in the ground at Glastonbury, which afterwards became a flowering thorn bush. If he *was* in Britain, could he not also have been in Normandy—or Brittany?

Then there is Gawain (called Walwain in France), Arthur's nephew, and the epitomy of knightly courage and chivalry. His feats rivalled those of the king himself in some versions of the romance; in others he is described as treacherous, cowardly and immoral. A character as mist-shrouded as any, and known equally in ancient France, Germany, Italy and England, Gawain was said to possess the illuminated sword Excalibar, rather than Arthur. He was also said to be one of the earliest seekers of the mysterious Grail before it took on any religious connotations, in an even more distant age, when the peoples of Europe were sun-worshippers rather than Christians. One certainty is that there is no more atmospheric location to ponder questions about life and times in Brittany past,

Evocative rampart shell of the original Comper castle, a Montfort dynasty stronghold during the 14th century. There are distinct Arthurian vibrations hereabouts.

of twenty centuries or so ago, than in the leafy glades of the region's largest remaining forest.

Perhaps there is no more apt starting point for a time-travel venture into Arthurian Brocéliande, than the **Château de Comper**, claimed in fables of early Breton romance to be the birthplace of the enchantress Viviane (or Vivien). She was the original Lady of the Lake, who bewitched the wizard Merlin and was said to have raised the child Lancelot. There are three lakes at Comper, and one can easily imagine the glowing sword and ghostly white hand, breaking the surface waters. Adjacent to the medium-sized château which was restored in the 19th century, there are also some crumbled ramparts of a 13th-century castle.

The château is now the **Centre de l'Imaginaire Arthurien Musée**, containing images and artefacts to stimulate imagination, while the setting, in reality, is still wonderfully secluded— almost isolated and physically distanced from modern France. It lies off the D167 east of Mauron, about 16 km (10 miles) north-east of Ploërmel. Out of season and with only bird song to disturb the pastoral silence, tales of Merlin's prowess, Viviane's wanton deceipt, Lancelot's valour and Arthur's wisdom do not seem so far-fetched here. And if those crumbling rampart walls were once part of a proud castle owned by the powerful Montfort dynasty in the 14th century, perhaps an even earlier redoubt stood here too, its walls resounding to the clatter of horses' hooves and the clash of knightly jousting as depicted by the exhibition of *Arturus Rex* and the legend of *Table Ronde*. Certainly one can picture what a perfect forest hideaway such a castle might have been in those early times for fated lovers like Tristan and Isolde, hiding from a vengeful King Mark, or as the home of Viviane. If she existed in Brocéliande, so certainly did Merlin— he who finally revealed to Arthur that he was the true king of the Britons.

South of Comper château and reached via an attractive minor road, the D773, is **Paimpont village**, a most attractive little settlement, again in a secluded silvan setting and dominated by a largely 17th-century abbey on the site of a very ancient monastery, which was founded during the 7th century. Much damaged during the Revolution, the huge building is still the subject of extensive restoration, and it overlooks a delightful woodland lake. There is another lake some 3 km (2 miles) north-east, which is called the **Étang du Pas-du-Houx**. On its shores is a modern château named, not surprisingly, Brocéliande. The surroundings of the village are much enjoyed by walkers who have a wide choice of marked forest trails to explore.

Among the pedestrian routes are two long-distance paths, the GR37 and GR37A, both of which touch upon Paimpont, a popular and picturesque overnight stopping place. There is a comfortable two-star *relais* hotel here (yes, it's called Brocéliande) which is open all year, tel: 99-07-81-07. There are also two *gîtes d'étape* in the neighbourhood, plus a municipal camping site. A small *Syndicat d'Initiative* (tel: 99-06-80-13), close to the abbey dispenses helpful guidance to visitors— some of the recommended beauty spots are not always easy to locate. In-

deed, parts of the forest even today are a mystic maze, where the traveller seeking the half-secret locations can easily lose patience through frustration. For those who persevere, however, tantalizing glimpses of Arthurian Bretagne and an inkling of the ancient Celtic psyche may be revealed!

An example of this can be found at the **Fontaine de Barenton**, close to the oddly-named hamlet of Folle-Pensée. According to legend, should spring water be used to anoint the rock known as "Merlin's Step", at this spot, a mighty tempest will be unleashed. In periods of severe drought, and even as

One of several beautiful lakes in Brocéliande forest. This expanse is overlooked by Paimpont abbey. There are nice woodland paths in the vicinity.

late as the 1930s, the aid of the fountain's power was invoked, following the very ancient Druidic ceremonies performed here during the 5th and 6th centuries, as written records of the 12th century indicate.

About 1 km (½ mile) from the village of Tréhorenteuc, on the western fringe of the forest, is the **Val Sans Retour**. It was here, within a delightfully scenic dale redolent still with mystery, that Viviane (sometimes called Morgaine la Fée or Morgana), that most wanton of fairies, worked her magic. It was she who secretly hated all knights, and who was the half-sister of Arthur, revealing to him the infidelity of his wife Guinevere with Sir Lancelot. No maid of modesty herself, she lured all her ex-lovers (including the master wizard Merlin), to this ostensible place of bliss, which was really a prison where the doors locked for eternity.

More Arthurian fantasy may be discovered near here, in the **church of Tréhorenteuc**, which houses images of the Holy Grail and the court of Arthur seated at the massive Round Table. Legend has it that during the early days of Arthur's rule, his knights would fight to the death to gain a place at, or near, the king's side whenever court was held. To avoid this senseless slaughter, a sorcerer-carpenter from Cornwall (or Cornouaille), was commanded to solve this vexing seating arrangement. He came up with a circular table of immense size, able to accommodate more than a thousand knights in absolute equality. Ergo, with the key to restrained knightly behaviour, came comradely chivalry and order, or as we now call it, civilization.

Allegory was often used as a medium for moralizing by the medieval story-tellers, and nowhere was it found more frequently than within the Arthurian legends. Thus Brocéliande was portrayed not only as a forest, but as an irresistible seductress almost, but never quite, within grasp; as a crock of gold at the foot of a rainbow arc; or as the field of jousting, where every gallant *chevalier* was a victor. Here within the woodlands of antiquity there are over a dozen real lakes, but countless illusions and half-truths. It was a holy place of Druids, and of even earlier inhabitants, as Neolithic burial sites such as "Merlin's Tomb" indicate.

In reality there is a Roman road here and the spot where Saint Judicaël founded a monastery in the 7th century. There is also the secret trysting place of Sir Lancelot and king Arthur's wife, Guinevere. A Celtic world of woodland, with fairy glades and fairytale castles within the reality that is Paimpont forest. It will excite the imagination of all but the most staid, should they find the patience to discover that other forest within called Brocéliande, the heart of Brittany's mystical Argoat.

Corsairs and Casinos, Castles and Half-Secret Coves, plus Cancale, Oyster Capital of France

The north face of the indented peninsula coast mirrors the definitive Brittany for many visitors. A magnetic combination of rugged nature—reflected through majestic sand beaches and granite cliffs—coupled with seaside holiday amenities to suit all pockets. There is the swish sophistication of Dinard, the family-favourite of Trébeurden, and in between the retained old-world charm of fishing ports like diminutive Loguivy-de-la-Mer or Le Conquet.

Ille-et-Vilaine

The saltings which stretch as far as the horizon around the Bay of Mont Saint-Michel command the landscape west of Avranches and the Normandy boundary. As an opener to Brittany, the sudden elevation of the Cancale cliffs comes as a marked visual stimulus to the westbound traveller. This is not to say that the approach, especially along the D155 coast road, is not

*D*inan and the original *Gothic arched bridge spanning the river Rance. This is the birds-eye view from the contemporary road viaduct.*

interesting or lacking in character. Around some of the sea-level settlements like Cherrueix, Hirel and Le Vivier-sur-Mer (the champion mussel producer of western France), shellfish compete with tourism as the principal income source. The little pockets of seafood industry appear suspended, almost with an air of unreality in a certain light, between a wide sea and a wider sky.

There is, in truth, a liberating open-space ambience along the central bay foreshore, traced faithfully by the long-distance GR34, and the natural waterline as yet unsullied by alien high-rise apartments or an overkill of leisure facilities. **Cherrueix** still exhibits its ancient past through windmills dating from the 18th century and its church,

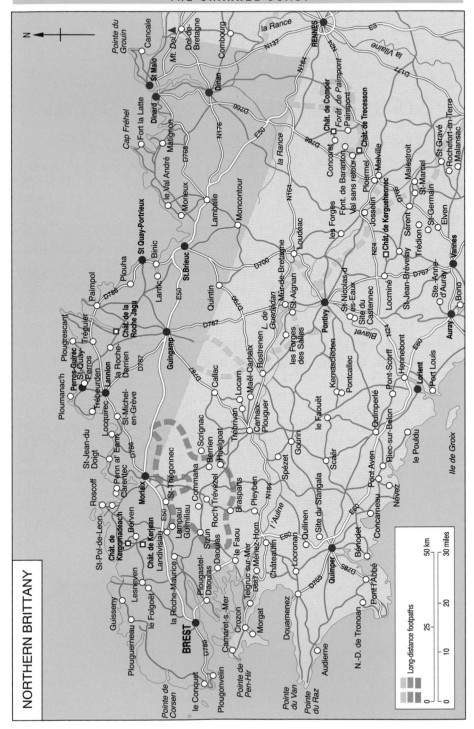

NORTHERN BRITTANY

*M*ap *of the Channel
Coast region of Brittany.*

which is of 16th century origin. The Château de l'Aumône, built in the 15th century, is now a *gîte d'étape*, popular with both walkers and horse-riders (tel: 99-48-97-28). There are numerous oyster and mussel retail outlets all along the bay edge road.

Cancale

It is cliff-hanging Cancale, however, which is the undisputed oyster capital of Brittany—if not of all France. This queen of shellfish centres is royally revealed presenting a near-aerial view spread below the heights which are traversed by the D76 on approach. At the extreme western end of the mighty bay the land suddenly thrusts upwards in

a granite cliff pinnacle, as it does around Avranches at the eastern extremity, to provide a marvellous two-level setting for Cancale which cascades from cliff-top to seashore.

The town occupies the high ground through a compact cluster of houses, shops and administrative buildings grouped closely around a dignified square. The centrepiece is a fine, stoutly-built church boasting an enormous **tower**, as if to accentuate an already imposing location. With pragmatic enterprise, the town council have opened this tower to the public. For those who don't mind stair climbing, there are views from the lofty 60 m

*T*he quality attraction *for the sea-food enthusiast at Cancale—Oyster capital of France.*

(200 ft) high belvedere, across the bay to Mont-Saint-Michel, and on a really bright day, northwards to the Channel Islands. Down at ground level there are a number of quality food shops, restaurants and cafés around the square, and just off it is the tourist office in the rue du Port.

It must be said that Cancale is a place which has managed successfully to combine being a genuine working town and an attractive little holiday resort, so that the traveller feels immediately at ease and welcome, and in no way pressurized by blatant commercial avarice as is often prevalent at many recognized coastal resorts. This self-styled "Pearl of the Emerald Coast" perhaps really does deserve the tag.

Cancale produced a heroine in the shape of the town's most famous daughter, Jeanne Jugan (1792–1879), who devoted her life to the poor of Saint-Malo and subsequently much farther afield. She became the founder of a worldwide religious order known as the Little Sisters of the Poor. Her story is depicted in the local museum housed within the old church of Saint-Méen. The museum also exhibits some fascinating folklore and sea-faring artefacts, for example, like models of the celebrated Bisquine sailing craft and details about Breton explorer captains like Jacques Cartier and other Cape Horn seafarers. The birthplace of Jeanne Jugan (a very modest cottage) is also accessible to visitors at Les Petites Croix, avenue du General-de-Gaulle, tel: 99-89-62-73.

It is the quality oyster, however, that is the leading Cancale attraction—also honoured with its very own museum which is claimed to be the only one of its kind in Europe). The oyster virtually dominates the daily life of the extensive port area and seafront promenade known as **La Houle**, which is reached via precipitous and somehow quite segregating streets from uptown Cancale.

La Houle, once quite distinctly separate from the town centre high above, is a colourful bustle of activity throughout the summer season, thronged with holidaymakers, seafood gourmets and, of course, oyster specialists of one kind or another—either producers, distributors or consumers. Until the mid-19th century, wild oysters were bountiful enough to supply demand in the bay region, but by 1850 the fame of the succulent mollusc had spread to such a degree that harvesting had reached danger point. A programme of obligatory cultivation was then instigated at a number of points around the bay, but principally at Cancale. At low water the contemporary and very extensive growing beds are revealed, where both the hollow oyster of Japanese origin, and the native flat oyster, **Belon**, are steadily brought on from spat to edible bivalve.

Nowadays all the flat variety are collected as spat from the Gulf of Morbihan, since the vital oyster sperm is no longer collectable from local waters, owing to strong currents and heavy tides. The total annual yield from the Cancale area, from both deep water and shallow growing beds, is approximately 600 tonnes from cultivation grounds which extend over some 1,000 hectares (2,500 acres). At certain times in high summer, the chain of seafront restaurants, fish merchants and direct sales kiosks along the quay and

*P*ointe du Grouin, high
spot of the Chemin de Ronde
cliff path from Cancale. A
nature reserve and favoured wild
bird haunt.

foreshore seem hell-bent on disposing
of the entire annual harvest with all
possible speed!

Apart from the magical oyster and
the delightful scenic setting amid some
15 km (9 miles) of rock-girt coastline,
Cancale has one further magnet which
should appeal particularly to active visitors: a grand coastal footpath circuit
called the **Chemin de Ronde**. Opened in
1969, it starts from the port, ascending
steeply and immediately to the Pointe
du Hock viewpoint beside an imposing
war memorial where you can gaze

down on those oyster beds (*parc à huîtres*) if the tide is out. Thenceforth, this pedestrian route traverses a fine coastal path to the headland extremity some 7 km (4 miles) to the north, known as the Pointe du Grouin encompassing some lovely wooded cliff country *en route* and revealing a whole variety of land- and seascapes. In the main, the path follows the route of an old coastguard patrol lookout trail and includes a section of the long-distance GR34.

There are a couple of agreeable camping and caravanning sites between Cancale and the Pointe du Grouin, in the vicinity of Port-Mer and Port-Pican, both of which are scenic sandy coves with good beaches and facilities for sailing and watersports. The Pointe itself is a protected nature reserve area. In practical French fashion though, this does not preclude the mainland point being provided with a very convenient car park, hotel-restaurant and even a helicopter pad. All of this is additional to the once-lonely lifeboat station, not long ago a solitary man-made sentinel on this majestic jagged rock and deeply fissured headland.

There are roped walking areas here now to prevent visitors from trampling the colourful wild flowers and other rare flora which somehow survives—even thrives—on this windswept and seemingly inhospitable height high above the crashing breakers. Just across the turbulent narrows, the **Ile des Landes** is a protected bird sanctuary, most famous for its colony of cormorants. Visitors are not allowed on the island, although close study of resident and migrant sea-birds is possible by boat. For further information telephone 99-89-63-72.

For those with strong legs, the headland walk can be continued around the cliffs to a little offshore islet which is topped by a modest but heavily fortified château. This landmark is known as the **Anse du Guesclin**, and is located just beyond a fine sand beach close to the village of Saint Coulomb, 6 km (3½ miles) from the Pointe du Grouin. On the return south-east to Cancale, pause at the very old **Chapelle de Notre-Dame-du-Verger**, a venerable sailor's chapel restored in the 19th century and the object of an annual pilgrimage of thanksgiving by the residents of Cancale every August.

There is a wide choice of other leisure pursuits in the Cancale region, and you can take to the water at the Port-Mer sailing school, enjoy a sea-fishing expedition, play tennis or mini-golf, or go horse-riding from the nearby stables of Saint-Méloir or Saint-Coulomb. Because it is largely protected from the prevailing westerlies, this extremity of the Mont-Saint-Michel bay enjoys a surprisingly equable climate considering its latitude, and there is a fair display of semi-tropical flowers and plants on south-facing residential terraces in and around the town. With a good choice of hotel and alternative accommodation and a variety of eating houses, Cancale is a favoured quiet regional base (as opposed to the more upmarket resorts such as Dinard), despite the relative dearth of sweeping silver sand beaches in the immediate vicinity. Those visitors who like leisure walking will find the old fishing port and its environs particularly rewarding.

A Man of Letters— Chateaubriand

Born at the seaport of Saint-Malo in 1768, François René Chateaubriand was the son of a Breton count, a man of sullen, introspective temperament, who distanced himself from his offspring not intentionally, but simply through reclusive preoccupation. His mother was almost totally absorbed with the Catholic church, afflicted with religious mania—patently these were not the parents to ensure a happy childhood. The brooding atmosphere of the vast grey castle at Combourg could only have intensified the restlessness and melancholy which assailed François throughout his long life—attributes which, of course, also contributed to a later talent with words.

He did enjoy a close relationship with his sister, Lucille, who was also very pious, yet equally solicitous of her brother's welfare. She had a generally happy disposition combined with gentle concern, which contrasted markedly with the frigid, formal behaviour of the count and countess. There is no doubt that Lucille nourished her brother's natural creative ability, while his environment also burnished his intense and fertile imagination. The writer was to declare in later years that it was, "In the woods of Combourg that I became what I am today".

What he became was, of course an outstanding literary and political figure of his age and a Breton hero of eternal fame. Educated at Dol-de-Bretagne, Rennes and Dinan, a pride in his Breton heritage was amply cultivated and this, coupled with a razor-sharp intellect, secured a brilliant future, not only as a writer, but as a philosopher and towering figure of influence on the 19th-century French political scene.

Not unnaturally, his parents expected—almost demanded—that François find a vocation within the church, but already the seeds of a restless and rebellious spirit were growing. Imaginative, slightly imperious and self-willed through birth and upbringing, this intensely earnest youth, faintly Byronic of visage, tried but failed to take the cloth. After a desultory study for the priesthood in and around Combourg, he became inconsolably fretful.

Resulting from earlier associations with Saint-Malo and the intoxicating atmosphere of the bustling port, François almost took ship for India in 1785. Then, quite unexpectedly, he was granted an army commission at the age of 18. During this period he was presented at the court of Louis XVI, meeting many eminent literary figures of the day. He was made a Knight of Malta and seemed poised for an orthodox career in the higher echelons of French society. This, however, was the eve of France's most traumatic era. The young soldier found himself in something of a dilemma. He was in many ways quite sympathetic towards the revolutionary movement, which was growing more threatening by the day. This was partly because in the fateful year of 1789 he was himself of a naturally rebellious age, but also because he was both perceptive and observant enough to appreciate the gross injustices that prevailed at the time for many, if not most, of the French people.

With a high-born background though, a count's son was at best impartial, at least in the beginning. As the excesses of revolutionary violence escalated, however, the young man's uneasiness increased. With his regiment disbanded, he resolved personal uncertainties in a time-honoured fashion

CHATEAUBRIAND
1768-1848
DINAN
ST PIERRE
MEILLAC
ST MALO
VITRÉ
FOUGÈRES
Centre Ville

François René Chateaubriand. Combourg's most famous son, on his well-earned pedestal above the castle lake.

by taking ship for America in 1791. He was fired by romantic if impractical ideas of exploration and discovery, not least that of the elusive north-west passage. He discovered little, save his own talent for wonderful descriptive writing about raw nature and the noble savage, the North American Indian.

In 1792 he returned to France to learn of the fall of Louis XVI. The subsequent Reign of Terror was about to begin. Fortuitously, François married Celeste Buisson de Lavigne at this time, the daughter of monied landowners. With this newly acquired wealth, the bridegroom was able to escape the very real danger facing any high-born ex-army officer of the period. His family were not so fortunate, all of them being either executed (including his favourite sister Lucille), or imprisoned.

After only the briefest dallying with his bride, François set off to join the forces of the Duke of Brunswick. In the confusion following the failure of this counter-revolution, he made his way across country to Belgium. Caught up in a skirmish in Brussels, he was wounded and left for dead in the street. After being rescued and when he had recovered, François' brother (later to die on the scaffold), helped him survive the injuries and escape again, this time to the Channel Islands. An unscrupulous sea captain left him stranded on a Guernsey beach, but once again he was succoured and subsequently sheltered by an uncle in Jersey, another escapee from The 'Terror'.

In 1793, at the height of the revolution, countless reminders of former despotism, real or imagined were ruthlessly smashed. Chateaux and religious buildings particularly were pillaged and torn apart, from that definitive fount of medieval worship, Cluny Abbey, to the beautiful cathedral of Chartres. Nowhere was inviolable. Chateaubriand wrote at this time, 'within a few short days, the civilization of twelve centuries has been destroyed'. This vengeful rape of French cultural centres only stopped when Robespierre was guillotined, on 28 July 1794.

There then followed a period of poverty for François too, as a refugee in England. It was, however, also an invaluable education proving a marvellous outlet for some epic prose poems, historical essays, literary treatises, plus some popular travel tales, especially those about North American Indians. Indeed, it was during this period that he wrote much of his enduring work. As the new century dawned, the life of Chateaubriand was increasingly devoted to social observation of the contemporary scene.

Returning home to France in 1800, he was at last recognized for his brilliant—and powerful—literary talent, and was appointed to the French consulate in Rome by Napoleon Bonaparte, whom the writer eventually offended by comparing him to Nero. This was certainly not a wise thing to do, but it illustrates the characteristic boldness of the man. His life under threat from this penned indiscretion, François took himself abroad again, this time wandering east to the Holy Land. His writing remained diverse and prolific, however, covering a wide range of subjects from religion and romance, to the fall of the Roman Empire.

Subsequently much admired by his peers—even Louis XVIII after 1814—the great writer was once again sent to several European capitals as plenipotentiary, becoming more and more active politically and again making more enemies than friends, including the monarch. His most famous mentor was his mistress of many years, Madame Récamier. He died an octogenarian in 1848. Despite his colossal conceit, his talent was unquestionably immense and he will be forever remembered, especially in France at least, for his most enduring work, *Mémoires d'outre-tombe* (*Reflections beyond the grave*).

Saint-Malo

For most of the distance from Cancale to Saint-Malo the landscape is delightful, provided that the traveller keeps to the coast road (the D20). A series of charming coves and inlets—some verged by bright sand beaches—are revealed, culminating with picture-postcard **Rothéneuf** Haven which transforms itself into a super sand beach at low tide. On the headland just west of this spot are the celebrated **carved rocks**, sculptures of the powerful Rothéneuf family dynasty, painstakingly carved by a local priest over 25 years during the latter part of the 19th century. A token fee is levied from visitors at the Rochebonne site, which also boasts a small aquarium. Incidentally, nearby is a popular and reasonably priced touring ground for caravanners and campers, the municipal Le Nicet is 6 km (3½ miles) from Saint-Malo centre and located directly above a beach. It is in the avenue de la Vard (tel: 90-40-26-32) and is open throughout the year.

Town plan of Saint-Malo.

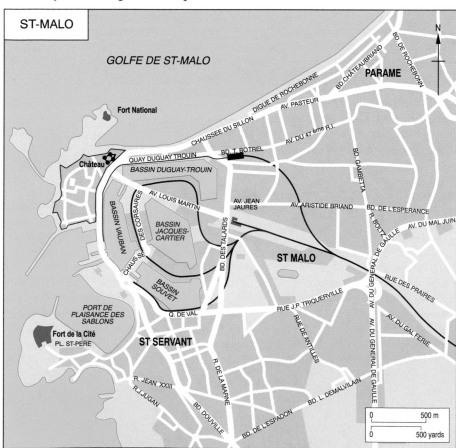

The heart of the granite city of Saint-Malo is ostensibly little different today from that of the Corsair era, when those much-feared worthies buccaneered foreign shipping relentlessly on behalf of the French king. Duguay-Trouin, one of the most successful of all these legalized pirates, captured over 300 vessels around the turn of the 17th and 18th centuries—most of them British. His name is remembered today by quay and dock basin names. The total number of ships taken, with official and indeed grateful approval, ran to thousands, resulting in vast wealth for this glorious "City of the Sea".

From the bulging coffers of original ill-gotten gains, the one-time uninhabited islet was transformed yet again during the 17th and 18th centuries from a medieval stronghold into one of the most successful and lucrative sea

*R*othenéuf Haven and *the celebrated carved rocks, hewed out during the 19th century by a local priest.*

ports of France. The complex dock system was begun by Vauban, the genius military engineer of Louis XIV (who also created the offshore island defences), while the island was finally linked to the mainland by the *sillon* (causeway) in the 18th century.

Today, the fifth largest port in the Republic is an overture of delight at the start of a visit to Brittany. In sunshine, Saint-Malo is a sparkling anchorage amid a skein of tiny islands, lording it over the beautiful Rance estuary. Here at once is all the stunning

Rance estuary and the port of Saint-Malo the most impressive ferry port in France. The medieval Solidor tower of St-Servan can be seen in the background.

impact of the Brittany seaboard at its best. Something of a natural jewel on the Emerald Coast (reflected in the varied green waters), it also boasts a wealth of man-made elegance. It is a splendidly preserved walled city and it is only slightly disappointing to learn that the original was all but obliterated during World War II and that here, once again, is yet another miracle of restoration completed during the second French Renaissance. The maze of thronged and narrow streets within the great rampart walls are a perfect re-creation of medieval to 18th-century Saint-Malo, while the seascapes across

the Rance are splendid. Indeed there could hardly be a more exhilarating disembarkation point for visitors arriving here by ferry.

For those approaching from the east by road, the prospect is not *quite* so romantic, for the Saint-Malo of the 20th century is by no means confined within the enclosing granite walls. Indeed, there is much commercial and industrial escalation on approach through the Paramé suburbs and the driver is scarcely aware at journey's end that a great causeway—the Chaussée du Sillon (a link of build-up and tarmac that was once just a sandbank)—revealed only at low water is being crossed.

It is difficult, if not impossible, to envisage the rugged deserted island that stood offshore of little Saint Servan in the 6th century, when Saint-Malo (or Maclow), arrived from the British Isles to convert the Gallo-

Roman tribe to Christianity. **Saint-Servan-sur-Mer**, now just an adjunct of greater Saint-Malo, still boasts a distinctive and proud landmark, the 14th-century **Solidor Tower**, which stands sentinel at the south-western perimeter of the great port, and which now houses a fascinating museum devoted to the derring-do of those rumbustious Corsairs and Cape-Horners. It was hereabouts that Jeanne Jugan from Cancale served the poor of the town.

Saint-Servan should not be missed for despite traffic congestion and a degree of unpromising commercial clutter around the fringe of the old town and port, the signposting is good and the area around the tower and little harbour is charming. The whole presents a most pleasing if low-key picture of maritime France of old, again masterfully preserved though shyly half-eclipsed by the more obvious splendour of Saint-Malo, its dominant château, tall ramparts and the sophisticated city bustle within.

On most days—at least during the recognized holiday season—the drivers crossing *le Sillon* may wonder where on earth parking space will be found. Surprisingly, there are gaps, often in the vicinity of the quayside tourist office which is well signposted from Paramé, and is close to the château and port centre. If not here, the vast harbour area will usually reveal a few spaces among the cars, for the walled city (though allowing vehicle access), should be visited on foot.

The first obvious objective is the massive 15th-century **castle**, now partly town hall and part museum. It houses paintings, model ships, artefacts and records of Saint Malo's most famous sons, from the Corsair Duguay-Trouin, to Jacques Cartier, navigator and discoverer of Canada, and to that most gifted of writers, Chateaubriand. The latter's tomb can be seen from the rampart walls on the island of Grand-Bé, and can even be visited on foot at low water.

Outside and high above place Chateaubriand, there are fine elevated views from the rampart watch-towers, not only in the vicinity of the castle, but all around the walled town. A walk around the **ramparts** is one of the best ways of seeing Saint-Malo. Offshore, to the north of the castle, lies **Fort National**, a second fortified islet built to guard the sea approaches as does Tour Solidor to the south. Fort National was constructed by Vauban during the 17th century and again can be reached on foot at low water. It is a forbidding stronghold, containing a grim dungeon. Petit Bé is another fortified islet accessible at low tide.

After looking down on the crowded and narrow streets from the rampart walk, ground-level rambling will be no less fascinating. As is so often found with French towns built during the Middle Ages, ancient and modern styles are blended with imaginative flair to present attractive images. Thus with Saint-Malo it is cobbles and *haute-couture*, old-world hotels providing super service, and restaurants and pavement cafés set within façades that would not be out of place on a film set for the *Tale of Two Cities*. Just a couple of the most ambient gathering points are **place Chateaubriand** immediately below the castle walls at the city's principal entry, Porte St-Vincent, and **place Jean-de-Châtillon**, which fronts the great cathedral of Saint-Vincent.

Built originally in the 11th century, the cathedral reflects the architecture of the ages from the 12th to the 20th centuries, being of course heavily restored after wartime devastation. The stained-glass windows, both medieval and modern, are interior high spots, while the elegant spire stands proud and high above all other buildings of Saint Malo *intra-muros* (within the walls).

Other visitor objectives are the **waxwork museum** housed within the castle tower which is known as the Quiquengrogne, and which was built on the command of Duchesse Anne (16th century); the multi-pool **aquarium** ingeniously built into the ramparts in place Vauban, and containing over 1,000 sea creatures from the English Channel to the waters of the tropics; and the **doll museum** in the rue de Toulouse. Slightly further afield, there is the mansion of Jacques Cartier, Limoëlou manor, at Rothéneuf; and just south of Saint-Malo centre is the **Corniche d'Alet**, a pedestrian path which winds around the headland at Saint-Servan close to the distinctive triple-tower of Solidor. This walk begins from Place Saint-Pierre close to the cathedral ruins of Alet (as Saint-Servan was called during the Dark Ages), and reveals some impressive harbour and estuary views.

For leisure and pleasure, **Paramé** has high holiday appeal, with its hugely extensive Grande Plage—over 3 km (2 miles) long—and the centrally located Grand Hôtel des Thermes (four-star), one may take the sea-water cure amid full luxury trimmings.

This is one of Brittany's renowned *thalassothérapie* centres. By contrast, there is an authentic English fish-and-chip shop, serving genuine *poisson et frites à l'anglaise*, at the junction of la Digue promenade and Boulevard de Rochebonne.

There is something for everyone in Saint-Malo including, of course, a casino at the western end of the Grande Plage, and a wide selection of high-standard hotels (over 100 in all with and without restaurants), most of which are located in the Paramé district. For those with shallower pockets, there are plenty of low-cost alternatives in the area, from a host of *chambres d'hôtes*, to half a dozen touring sites, some with holiday caravans for hire, plus a youth hostel in the rue Umbright, Paramé. For full information and free accommodation lists, contact the tourist office, Port des Yachts, 35400 Saint-Malo, tel: 99-56-64-48. For visitors without cars, Saint-Malo is well served by public transport—land, sea and air—and by the high-speed TGV from Paris (SNCF, avenue Louis Martin, tel: 99-56-08-18). Market days *intra-Muros* are Tuesdays and Fridays, and *extra-muros* are Wednesdays and Saturdays.

Dinard

While Saint-Malo and its environs are colourful, interesting and rich in history, there is much commercial and industrial escalation which spreads widely outside the walled original. If you like dense crowds and almost continual car congestion you'll love it; if not, you may well prefer to choose Dinard as a base for this part of north-eastern Brittany.

Discovered by British and American tourists around the turn of the century, this purpose-built holiday resort now basks contentedly in the knowledge that it is one of the best examples of the marque in Europe. Dinard, like Saint-Malo on the opposite side of the wide Rance estuary, is also much afflicted with the modern curse of traffic congestion, though more seasonally, and from private rather than commercial vehicles. Finding a parking space in high summer anywhere near the hub of the town around the Grande Plage (or Plage de l'Écluse as it is also known), can be a frustrating business. You must persevere, however, even if you only plan to stroll the car-free promenade-du-Clair-de-Lune, which skirts the beautiful Bay du Prieuré.

From this vantage point, one can see why the ancient and once-secluded, little fishing port held so much appeal for American high society and English aristocracy during the *belle époque* era. An American millionaire had a mock castle constructed here and was quickly emulated by others who created individual villas and mansions across the headland heights. Many of these together with their immaculately landscaped gardens, still remain to impart an Edwardian air of elegance.

The alluring white sand beaches are still there to enjoy, the water is still blue (if not *quite* so pollution-free) and much of the resort's architecture still reflects the ornate opulence prevalent at most playgrounds of the rich around the turn of the century. There is now, however, a preponderance of

The elegant esplanade and fine sands of the Plage de l'Ecluse at Dinard. A Brittany mecca for those who like to see and be seen.

modern building, while contemporary municipal wealth is reflected in the swish casino and Palais des Congres.

A bonus feature—and another reason for the resort's popularity—is that Dinard benefits from the influence of the Gulf Stream, which ensures not only an equable climate, where tamarisks and camellias thrive and where trees grow almost to high-tide level around the estuary foreshore, but above-average water temperatures for this latitude. Indeed, the Rance estuary, which is often compared to the Bosphorus, is certainly the most regal river mouth in France and Dinard really does justify its claim as the "Gem of the Emerald Coast".

Certainly there is grace and style here, with numerous smart shops, up-market promenades, much floral decoration, and bright white buildings bordering squeaky-clean beaches. It is great fun to explore as a pedestrian, but is often exasperating for car drivers anywhere around the town centre or sea-front. Dinard's most spectacular focal spot is **Pointe du Moulinet** (not to be confused with the more mundane, but similar sounding Pointe de Malouine). It is a lofty and luxuriantly wooded height on the rocky headland where the neck waters, landward of a final geological bulge, have been contained to create an imaginative municipal sea-water swimming pool.

On the opposite side of this headland is the **Musée de la Mer**, a magnificent aquarium and natural history museum containing some two dozen pools to house local species of marine life, plus other Brittany coastal fauna. The museum is open from Whitsun to October and is in avenue George Cinq. There are three main beaches, all of which are classified as safe for bathing, and there are organized beach games for children during high summer. In traditional seaside style, beach bathing tents or cabins may be hired. Apart from beach bathing—supplemented by two open-air sea-water pools—there is also a heated indoor pool of splendid design and Olympic proportions (heated of course), which is open all year round, save for January. The facilities for other watersports, especially sailing and windsurfing, are exceptionally good, as one might expect, with competitive yacht races being held offshore almost daily during July and August. Several approved sailing and wind-surfing schools exist to provide every level of tuition. Other nautical attractions are sea-fishing expeditions, sightseeing boat trips on the Rance or along a very impressive coastline to rugged cape Fréhel some 22 km (14 miles) westwards, or simply the ten-minute ferry ride to Saint-Malo. Details of these are available from Emeraude Lines, 27 avenue George Cinq; tel: 99-46-10-45.

Those preferring terra firma can exercise strenuously by playing tennis or horse-riding virtually within the town environs. You can also play golf on one of Brittany's best courses 8 km (5 miles) away. Others may opt for the gentler pursuit of exploring the designated walks around the Dinard beaches, headlands, or the Port-Riou gardens (detailed information can be obtained from the tourist office). Whatever your preference, the potential for outdoor sport and leisure could not be bettered, as one might expect from the most sophisticated fun-city in northern Brittany.

After dark, choose between roulette or black jack at the casino, a cinema show or night-club after a leisurely dinner at a traditional or ethnic restaurant. In between, you can watch firework displays laid on in July and August, or one of the light-and-music parades (*spectacle d'ambiance*) on the promenade Clair de Lune, which are held five nights a week from June to September. While Dinard is very definitely part of Brittany, it doesn't *feel* as Breton as Cancale or Saint-Malo. When the summer sun blazes on the dazzling sands and bright blue waters of the bay it is almost a mini Riviera, and this is compounded by the sleek architecture, the prevalence of high fashion and an atmosphere of *joie de vivre* which makes it all a positive French France enclave.

A Hidden High-tech Marvel

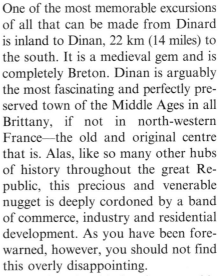

Driving from Saint-Malo to Dinard, every car has to cross the **Rance dam**. This is no ordinary barrage, though it may appear so. It is in fact the world's first wave-power generating station. The *usine maremotrice* as it is called, is totally concealed, far beneath the tarmac and concrete finger which spans the estuary waters. Silent and unseen, it produces in excess of 500 million kilowatts of electricity annually. Park at the western end, where there is usually plenty of space, and take a closer look at this engineering masterpiece. Opened in 1967, both ebb and flow tides are utilized, while there are six sluice gates and an ingenious swing-bridge which allows maritime traffic to pass. The power station is open to the public, and entry is free. Incidentally, from the parking area, there are fine views of the Saint-Malo roads and old city ramparts.

Côtes d'Armor

Dinan

One of the most memorable excursions of all that can be made from Dinard is inland to Dinan, 22 km (14 miles) to the south. It is a medieval gem and is completely Breton. Dinan is arguably the most fascinating and perfectly preserved town of the Middle Ages in all Brittany, if not in north-western France—the old and original centre that is. Alas, like so many other hubs of history throughout the great Republic, this precious and venerable nugget is deeply cordoned by a band of commerce, industry and residential development. As you have been forewarned, however, you should not find this overly disappointing.

Go when the old place is reasonably quiet if you can—on a Sunday morning, for example—and park in the place du Champ. Set aside at least three hours for pedestrian exploration, for there is much to see and admire. Not least is the **place du Guesclin** immediately adjacent, the gathering place for the vibrant Fête des Remparts held annually during the last weekend of September. This magnificent spectacular involves some 5,000 local participants, both equestrian and pedestrian, in stunningly authentic period costume. It is a pageant that really does transplant the onlooker back to the Middle Ages. Belief is convincingly suspended

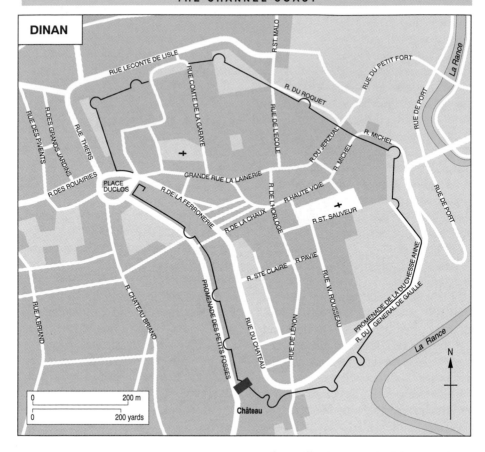

Town plan of Dinan.

during the fête, for the 15th- to 17th-century houses, churches and château of old Dinan make a totally legitimate backdrop.

Place du Guesclin is, appropriately, dominated by the towering statue of Bertrand du Guesclin on horseback, a hero-warrior who lived in France in the 14th-century and was a local boy born at La Motte-Broons château (long since destroyed), some 20 km (12½ miles) from Dinan. He was apparently a most unprepossessing youth, illiterate, surly, quick-tempered

and repellent—even to his parents—because of his facial ugliness. This probably accounted for a developed aggression and ambition, which led him to hire a suit of armour and promptly defeat a succession of famous knights. He did this in the lists at the wedding tournament of Charles de Blois at Rennes in 1338, with singular ferocity and dispatch.

From then on the ugly duckling became a lauded eagle, who swore allegiance to the monarchy and distinguished himself brilliantly, first at the siege of Vannes in 1342 in the fight by Charles against Jean de Montfort for the Brittany Succession. When Charles

was captured by the English, Bertrand was sent to England to arrange the ransom payment and the release of the duke Charles de Blois in 1354. From that time he was almost constantly embroiled in war, against the English in particular, and in a most personal manner on occasions. Just one of his famed exploits was the single-handed duel which he fought (and won) against an English knight, one Thomas of Canterbury.

Following the successful siege of Rennes, Bertrand was made Lord of Pontorson, at which period he made a home, briefly, with his wife Tiphaine (a Dinan girl) at nearby Mont-Saint-Michel. Subsequently his life was spent warring. He won many battles, was captured more than once and, as the ultimate honour, was created High Constable of France. He was killed while fighting in battle near Le Puy in the Auvergne, in 1380. Under his liege (King Charles V who died in the same

*D*inan's ancient river port snuggling deep in the Rance river valley in a splendid, film-set location.

year as his able constable), du Guesclin was largely responsible for wresting most of France from the occupying English. In the year that he and his king died, the only remaining towns under English domination were Bordeaux, Bayonne, Brest, Cherbourg and Calais. France herself was wartorn and woefully impoverished but she was free, due in no small measure to the exploits of a military leader who effected a kind of peace for almost the next 50 years. The heart of du Guesclin, this most illustrious of Breton soldier-knights, is entombed in **Saint-Sauveur's church**, just beyond which, ironically, is the neatly terraced Jardin Anglais.

A Breton Man of War

Destined to rise to one of the higher offices in the land, Bertrand du Guesclin, warrior of outstanding bravery, began life very modestly. He was born of well-endowed though not high-born parents, probably in the year of 1320. The birth was not registered, despite a venerable lineage that the family seat of La Motte Broons castle near Dinan indicated. Such omissions were common in the Middle Ages.

From the limited factual records of the boy's early life which do exist, it appears that—true to form with most who later become expert in the martial arts—he was a very poor scholar. In short, he was a confirmed outdoor boy whose early loves were hunting and hawking, while his admiration was reserved exclusively for those who exhibited physical prowess. Throughout his entire life he remained steadfastly and totally illiterate.

What is recorded are his youthful efforts to develop physically, the spontaneous and sustained search for extra muscle power embarked upon early in life by almost every natural fighter of any era. In the case of this particular Breton hero-to-be, the enthusiasm could well have been a burning one, fired remorselessly by a distinctly repellent appearance. In du Guesclin's early youth this exceptional facial ugliness must have proved a constantly depressing psychological burden, yet at once an indomitable spur. He was apparently repulsive even to his own father and mother, who more or less shunned their offspring, giving him little or no instruction and leaving the increasingly wayward lad to his own devices. This repugnance on the part of the parents could well have honed the son's latent aggression which, when nurtured, was soon to become fiercesome—the requisite hall-mark of every conquering war lord.

Evidence of his fighting skills came in early manhood, and in the most spectacular manner. In 1338 at Rennes, Bertrand made his indelible mark through a remarkable display of skill, power and almost suicidal bravery, and all this before the highest in the land. With a borrowed horse, armour and lance, he unseated a whole succession of skilled and battle-hardened knights at a great tournament organized to celebrate a royal marriage: that of Charles de Blois and Jeanne de Penthièvre. The young commoner's audacious prowess was duly noted by the high born and influential, not least by Charles himself, who may well have marked his young contemporary for future office. Bertrand's father was so surprised and impressed that he ensured from that day forth, that his gallant son lacked for no accoutrements of the medieval warrior. This was a wonderfully auspicious start then for the burgeoning man-at-arms.

Charles de Blois (1319–64) was the son of an eminent Breton count, while through his new bride (who was the daughter of Guy de Bretagne, count of Penthièvre) he could claim rightful succession to the duchy. On his marriage day it appeared that Charles would succeed without let or hindrance, however, three years later he had good reason to count the young du Guesclin among his most loyal followers. It was then that Jean III, reigning Duke of Brittany, died and Charles's claim to the succession was disputed by the old duke's brother, Jean de Montfort. Inevitably, the dispute deteriorated into deadly rivalry and war between the two factions broke out in 1341. The struggle escalated much wider than the original participants could have envisaged, since Charles

Bertrand du Guesclin, the mightiest of Bretagne warrior-knights.

soon had the support of the king of France, while Jean de Montfort was championed by the king of England. The War of the Succession became, in effect, a bloody side-show of the Hundred Years War.

Predictably, Bertrand du Guesclin fought for the cause of Charles de Blois, although not as a baron with a private army at his command as was usual, but as the undisputed leader of a partisan band, swearing loyalty to Charles despite all their mercenary proclivities. Bertrand now began to display his extraordinary talents as a soldier using strategy, guile and ferocious combat zeal in many early skirmishes, particularly during the siege of Vannes in 1342, when he eventually won the day in a set-piece battle, demoralizing the opposition to ensure a swift and lucrative victory.

There is a twelve-year blank in the record of du Guesclin's career following the Vannes siege, although it would not be unreasonable to assume that during this time, with a faithful and increasing band of followers, he was consolidating a power base of sorts as a roaming trouble-shooter with a proven success record. Such men were needed frequently and were often sought in medieval France. What is certain, however, is that he officially entered the French king's service in 1354, being knighted as a reward for his valiant deeds at Montmuran castle (between Dinan and Rennes). After this he was promptly dispatched to England to negotiate for the release of Charles de Blois, who had been captured after being defeated in battle and who had been held to ransom by the English since 1347.

Back again in France after a successful conclusion to the negotiations, the now experienced warrior defeated the forces of the Duke of Lancaster who had assaulted both Rennes and Dinan.

The siege of the former was raised through du Guesclin's efforts, while at the latter, in 1359 Bertrand fought his famous single-handed duel with Sir Thomas of Canterbury, at the same time winning the heart of a local girl, Tiphaine, who was not the least put off by her hero's unfortunate visage. The couple enjoyed a very happy marriage according to accounts, up to Tiphaine's death in 1371. Bertrand remarried two years later, but left no children from either marriage.

Bertrand's service to the French royal household was by now being acknowledged with ever-increasing honours. He was several times wounded, captured twice but released on payment of ransom, and from the date of his marriage was almost constantly on campaign, mostly against the English.

Even the most brilliant of warriors suffer set-backs, however, and one of the worst for du Guesclin was at the Battle of Auray in 1364—the decisive combat in the struggle for the Brittany succession—when Charles de Blois was slain, Jean de Montfort triumphed and Du Guesclin, apparently after tigerish but hopeless resistance, was overwhelmed and captured.

His adversary was almost as skilled militarily, was equally brave and was just as honorable. Sir John Chandos was a brilliant soldier, battle-hardened like Bertrand, and who had fought at Cambrai, Crécy and, most significantly in the English cause, at the battle of Poitiers in 1356 when astute leadership won the day, and when the death of the Black Prince was narrowly averted. Chandos was made Knight of the Garter by Edward III. Like his French counterpart, the birth year of Chandos is unknown. Also like Bertrand, the English knight was destined to die in battle, after being mortally wounded near Poitiers in 1370.

With the war of the Brittany succession finally over, thousands of mercenary soldiers were left idle, and the need for a strong hand on the situation became imperative. Du Guesclin was quickly ransomed again (reputedly for a vast sum to the English), and commissioned to lead a potentially threatening host of soldiery away from Brittany. The old warrior chose Spain, and killing two birds with one stone as it were, he allied his large, new army with Henry of Trastamara against Pedro the Cruel.

This king of Castile was as merciless as his name implies, and was being challenged as ruler by his illegitimate brother, Henry. Pedro had once been an ally of the Black Prince, but Edward was quickly appalled by the Spaniard's gross cruelty coupled with his cowardice and left Spain utterly contemptuous of his erstwhile ally. Thus the tyrant, with little support left, had decidedly bleak prospects. Henry, ably helped by du Guesclin's forces, soon overwhelmed Pedro and his diminished guards. The vanquished king was actually killed by Henry at du Guesclin's battlefield quarters early in 1369.

Bertrand enjoyed a number of military successes in this region of western Europe, not least against the king of Navarre, an area embracing part of south-western France and a province much in dispute as it was claimed by both the Spanish and French royal houses. The French territory actually survived as an independent state until annexed to France by the Bourbons. At the Battle of Cocherel, Bertrand captured a much-famed war lord, Jean de Grailly, who held a high title, was a champion of the English cause and advisor to Edward the Black Prince. Bertrand treated his captive with courteous honour; which was prudent behaviour as it happened, for Jean

became Bertrand's captor after a subsequent battle, that of Navarette. Once again, the Breton knight was soon freed to return to France.

In 1370 Bertrand du Guesclin was already entitled Duke of Trastamara and King of Granada. After more military victories (notably at Le Mans and in Perigord) the much-honoured knight was promoted to High Constable of France, by command of the French king, Charles V. France was once more at war with England and Bertrand became embroiled in another decade of warring against this old enemy. Gradually under his leadership much of the precious homeland territory was reclaimed, especially that of Poitou and Guinne (part of Aquitaine), together with occupied pockets of the Auvergne. By now very battle weary, there were still heavy demands to be made of the old soldier and he commandeered his home territory, the Duchy of Brittany, in 1373 on the orders of Charles V. Once again the peninsula was gravely threatened by English incursion, and again Bertrand du Guesclin thwarted this territorial ambition.

In 1380 the turbulent region of Langueudoc in the south of France was governed harshly by the Duke of Anjou. Inevitably, his subjects revolted and du Guesclin was dispatched to put down the trouble. He began by laying siege to the heavily fortified Chateauneuf-de-Randon. The defenders were on the very point of surrender, when at last the Breton war lord was felled with a fatal wound. He died on 13 or 14 July. His heart, as was the custom, was shrouded in a casket and entombed at Dinan in Saint Sauveur's church. Being such a long way from Brittany, and in an age when there was no refrigeration, the rest of the body of this great warrior was buried piecemeal en route to Bertrand's birthplace.

Just opposite the place du Guesclin is the promenade des Petits Fosses, above the ditch and steep earthworks constructed during the 15th century in the vicinity of the mighty castle keep, the **Porte du Guichet** and the **Coëtquen Tower**. A formidable defensive system, the keep was built in the 14th century and, unusually, is oval-shaped. The Coëtquen Tower is now a **museum** containing some splendid stone monuments and effigies of the Middle Ages. The imposing **Porte du Guichet** (13th century), was walled up for over 300 years, only being re-opened and restored in 1932. The Dinan **ramparts**, over 3 km (2 miles) in length, were constructed during the 13th century and are considered among the best that remain in Brittany. Apart from the demolition of the Porte de Brest in the l9th century, the ramparts walls are still virtually intact, and still broached by the early gateways—Guichet, Jerzual and Porte Saint-Malo—all

*T*he great château castle keep of Dinan. Note the unusual oval shape and the massive machicolations. It was thrown up in 1382 and is now a revealing history museum.

built originally during the 13th century. Porte Saint-Louis is the odd one out, being built in 1620.

Between place du Guesclin and the knight's entombed heart in Saint-Sauveur, is the delightful **rue de l'Horloge**, unmistakable for the distinguished 15th-century **belfry tower** and clock donated to Dinan by the Duchess Anne in appreciation of a fortified town she called "the key to my casket". This is certainly one of Dinan's most scenic streets, narrow and cobbled, where the tourist office is housed in a former 16th-century villa. At the end of the *rue*, some of the best 15th-century half-timbered dwellings in town may be seen in the **place des Cordeliers**, while nearby, off the Grand Rue, is a second impressive church, the 15th-century **Saint-Malo**, containing among other treasures a magnificent *orgue anglais* (English organ), now classified as a historic monument.

Until the great viaduct was constructed in the mid 19th-century, the main entry into Dinan was via the rue

*R*ue de l'Horloge
Dinan, and the Duchess Anne belfry, 15th century. The tourist office, on the right, is housed within a medieval town house.

du Jerzual and the **rue du Petit-Fort**. The latter is a precipitously steep and cobbled street, which is a delight to the eye and still primarily medieval of aspect. There is an ancient governor's house here (now a weaver's workshop), and a 17th-century tannery sandwiched between a number of attractive cafés, restaurants and craft shops. This quarter of old Dinan inspired many artists, notably Corot. Riverside Dinan is every bit as enchanting as the ancient high town, especially around the picturesque Pont Gothique. There is a fine bird's-eye view of this once bustling commercial river port from the viaduct road almost 40 m (130ft) high, and which spans the steep-sided Rance valley; it is now part of the N176 Lamballe–Dol route. Only leisure craft and sightseeing launches now use the little port, the latter being very popular. They ply the Rance river from Dinan to Dinard and Saint-Malo, providing visitors with a most scenic 2½-hour cruise throughout the summer season. For details enquire at Emeraude Lines, quai de la Rance, tel: 96-39-18-04.

There are, of course, some picturesque restaurants hereabouts, and there is also a scenic towpath walk downstream to Taden or upstream to **Lehon.** The latter is another gem which boasts imposing ruins of an ancient castle and abbey ruins on the site of a monastery which was founded in the 9th century and patronized by no less than another Breton hero, Nominoë. There is also an imposing church and the village itself is rich in photogenic 17th-century houses. The **castle** remains on an isolated knoll, and dates from the 13th century.

Downstream, **Taden** also displays some evocative ruins, including those of a once-magnificent Gallo-Roman villa. More practically, there is a large and immaculately manicured touring site here—Camping International Municipal de la Hallerais. There is spacious accommodation for 250 units and every modern convenience is provided, including a supermarket. This four-star site is open from March to October, tel: 96-39-15-93. Adjacent, there is access to a scenic stretch of Rance river towpath below here, and it is a recommended base close to Dinan. There is another nice way-marked circuit walk which begins at Dinan and takes in some particularly pretty stretches of country, like the Bois de Tressaint and Lehon. A free map of this 3-hour walk (12 km, or 7½ miles), is available from the tourist office—ask for the *randonnée à pied.*

Visitor facilities at Dinan are excellent and choice of accommodation is wide. There are 36 hotels (both with and without restaurants) and almost double this number of traditional eating houses and fast-food outlets. There are five camping sites in the vicinity and a first-class youth hostel, the Moulin de Méen, Vallée de la Fontaine des Eaux, tel: 96-39-10-83. The SNCF station is in place du 11 Novembre, tel: 96-39-22-39.

There is an efficient taxi service and cars may be hired from Europcar, 48, rue de Brest, tel: 96-85-07-51. Leisure amenities are comprehensive too, including a swimming pool, a two-screen cinema, municipal and private tennis courts, and horse-riding a short distance from the centre at Quévert. The château museum (which displays some fascinating paintings of old Dinan) is housed in the Donjon de la Duchesse Anne, and is open daily during the summer from 10 a.m. to 6.30 p.m. continuously. Market day is Thursday and guided tours around the old town are organized daily in season. For further details, contact the tourist office, tel: 96-39-01-64.

For those returning to Dinard, the riverside road from Dinan alongside the Rance is a rural treat which should be sampled if time allows. Largely following the D12 minor road, this is a very quiet and scenic alternative for much of its length to the busy and bland direct link, the D766. The Rance valley is exceptionally green and fertile, tree-rich and nicely undulating, with numerous side roads and small tracks running down to secluded riverside communities and half-hidden fishing harbours.

North of Taden, there are lots of interesting pause points, from the **Écluse du Chatelier**, a lock that governs the flow of the Dinan waters, to the suspension bridge of **Pont Saint-Jean**, and the inevitable escalation of small-boat anchorages and marina activity on approach to the estuary mouth and the celebrated Rance dam. La Landriais and La Richardais, once very influential commercial ports and boat-building yards, are being modernized to conform to the standard boat-park concept now prevalent throughout western Europe. There are still lots of pleasing vistas along here though, notably across the river from tiny havens like le Minihac to Saint-Jouan-des-Guerets on the eastern bank. Thankfully, a number of colourful and old-world enclaves still exist for the

back-lane wanderer between Dinan and Dinard.

There are several other attractive objectives within a reasonable distance of Dinard which might be considered, and the first of these is **Jugon-les-Lacs**, inland to the south-west, and about 40 km (25 miles) distant from Dinard. This is an ancient and very picturesque cluster of houses around an original 13th-century church, which manages to retain a genuine atmosphere of a rural Breton settlement, despite heavy restoration and improvement in places. The location is enhanced by surrounding low hills, generously cloaked with trees, and by two rivers which join here to form an impressive lake—almost 80 hectares (200 acres) in extent—much appreciated by locals and visitors alike. There is, of course, a *base nautique* with a sailing school specializing in dinghy handling and windsurfing. Canoes and kayaks may be

*J*ugon-les-Lacs west of Dinan; another beauty spot well worth a detour, especially by those who like to combine watersport with history study.

hired, with tuition being available for beginners, and there are guided canoe trips around the lake. The little town is well geared to tourism, being a recognized beauty spot, with one or two high standard and atmospheric restaurants, hotels in the vicinity and a well-run municipal campground close to the lake. There are one or two impressive buildings in Jugon apart from the church, like the old manor house off the place Centrale, plus some pleasant local walks alongside the lake waters. The tourist office telephone number is 96-31-61-62.

For a glimpse of more ancient Brittany on the return route to Dinard, follow the river course north via country lanes for some 10 km (6 miles) to the secluded location of the **Château de la Hunaudaie**, which lies just off the D28 to the south-west of Pléven. This austere and even grim 12th-century construction is remote even today; how well hidden it must have been in medieval times. Much attacked for all its seclusion—or perhaps even because of it—the forbidding castle was later converted to a Renaissance manor and vestiges of the later grandeur still remain. This is typical of the many fortified redoubts which once dominated the turbulent region and which, despite periodic assault and subsequent pillage through the centuries, still survive to stir the imagination of the onlooker. Hunaudaie, with its moat, gaunt towers and massive ramparts, is solid, emotive evidence of a past both brutal and excitingly romantic.

From here it is but a short distance to Plancoët, the little town on the Arguenon river where the writer Chateaubriand chose to live at one period of his life. It is now one of the stop-overs on the Chateaubriand heritage trail. The coast road back to Dinard, via the bay of Lancieux and Saint-Briac, is rock-girt and undulating, with Saint-Briac providing most of the delights of a plush resort, but for an outlay that is more realistic for many holidaymaking families.

Saint-Briac and **Lancieux** share some extensive sandy beaches, and there is a photogenic fishing harbour and small-boat haven at Saint-Briac which holds a celebrated seagull festival in August, one of the most strongly supported in northern Brittany. There are impressive distant views from the bay foreshore, where, at low tide, you can walk around the Lancieux peninsula. The peninsula is traced by the long-distance GR34 north-east to where Saint-Lunaire has now become almost an integral part of Dinard. There is a much-visited cliff grotto here and the headland tip (Pointe du Decollé), is reached by a narrow cliff ridge, appropriately, called the Saut de Chat (Cat's Leap). There are yet more impressive coast views from this vantage point.

An extended day-trip circuit by car is that which takes in three other high spots of the coastline west of Dinard—notably those of Saint-Jacut, Saint-Cast-le-Guildo, and finally the regal Cap Fréhel. The first is an appealing place for its setting, quite literally straddling its own peninsula which separates the bays of Lancieux and Arguenon. The centre of a huge oyster and mussel farming area, **Saint-Jacut-de-la-Mer** is an established holiday resort, partly attractive for its fishing village atmosphere. Some impressive panoramas can be gained from the nearby Pointe du Chevet and Pointe du Chef.

Across the water to the north-west at nearby **Saint-Cast** is La Digue, the principal landscape feature of this second peninsula resort. It is a 2 km (1-mile) esplanade adjoining yet another fine sand beach that slopes gently and makes Saint-Cast a much-visited place because of its safe bathing. From this headland extremity there are more wide vistas across the oyster and mussel beds of Frênaye bay, and there is also some scenic coastal walking, again along sections of the GR34. Saint-Cast has its historic spots too, as evidenced by the vestigial remains of a 14th-century castle, and a memorial column recording the repulse of numerically superior English forces in 1758, during the Seven Years War. More practically, there is an indoor heated sea-water swimming pool, tennis courts, cycle hire and boat trips around the bay. For active watersport enthusiasts, there is a sailing school with dinghy and windsurfing equipment for hire. There is also a 9-hole golf-course at Pen-Guen, on the coast just south of the town centre. Market day is Friday, and the tourist office telephone number is 96-41-81-52.

Cap Fréhel is one of those dramatic headlands of northern Brittany which almost every first-time visitor feels compelled to see. Certainly, it is one of the great natural jewels of the Côte d'Emeraude between Dinard and Saint-Brieuc, and while it might be said that it lies at the extremity of any Dinard day-trip, many visitors who base themselves at the Rance estuary resort do make this almost obligatory pilgrimage.The approach to the cape is not particularly impressive; indeed, it is for the large part a treeless and almost bleak moorland, especially after the lush Rance valley. There are, though, two distinct and worthwhile rewards for those who take the D16 lane northwards from the tiny Frênaye bay settlement of Port-à-la-Duc. **Fort-la-Latte** at the wild and windswept point of the same name is quite as impressive as tourist office brochures claim; an enduring monument, if nothing else, to the quality of medieval military architecture, and as

spectacular a man-made edifice as the natural grandeur of the surroundings.

The location is an acknowledged beauty spot, romantically enhanced by the massive fortress which hoves into view as the approach footpath rounds a pencil-slim Neolithic menhir, called **Gargantua's Finger**. The fabled medieval giant—whose name was taken as the title of a famed work by Rabelais in the 16th century—is also associated with the Arthurian romances and is thus a popular mythical figure in parts of Brittany. The monster was apparently quite active in this region, for some singular boulders and rocks forming Mont Garot (to the southwest of Saint-Malo) are known as Gargantua's Teeth.

Beyond and below the menhir, and accessible only to pedestrian visitors, stands Fort-la-Latte, facing the open sea defiantly. Originally built in the 14th century and much restored in later centuries, it still retains a forbidding feudal aspect and a proud record for any stronghold created in the Middle Ages. It was never captured during all its long existence, its defensive ramparts never being breached—not even by the English navy, as the local guidebook proclaims!

The drawbridge portal, courtyard, guardroom and garrison lodgings are all evocative of a long-gone era, as are the great keep, the cannon-ball kiln and the huge ramparts towering above the granite cliffs and the sea far below. The fort is open daily from June to September and is approximately 15 minutes' walk from the car-parking area. There are some splendid seascapes for those prepared to tackle the steep stairway to the machicolated keep parapet and capping watch-tower. Blue sky and sunshine may be best for photographing this lonely outpost of a bygone age, but la Latte appears at its most dramatic when clouds scud and storm-whipped waters batter the craggy headland.

The same could be said for **Cap Fréhel** at the nearby peninsula tip, no less impressive in its way for undiluted natural grandeur formed by sheer, multi-hued cliff faces and offshore reefs invariably stirring up white-water and clouds of spume. The panoramic sweep from this place is immense—you can even see as far the Channel Islands on a really clear, bright day. The lighthouse, stoutly constructed but short on elegance, occupies a pinnacle some 70 m (230 ft) high and throws its 3,000 watt beam for a distance of over 100 km (60 miles). It is open daily from Easter to 10 September, when visitors can enjoy an even more elevated view of their surroundings from the gallery.

There is a clearly defined and much used circular footpath of the cape extremity, which takes in all the most impressive features like the sea-bird havens and the rose-tinted granite faces which may be studied from a viewing platform. For nature lovers this is an especially hallowed location, for there are over 300 hectares (740 acres) of wild, cliff-top moorland where sea-birds nest along the mainland cliffs and on the little offshore islands. Shags, kittiwakes and guillemots are all resident hereabouts, while from August onwards the bird-watcher will be

The best of the north Brittany beaches begins with Pléhérel plage just west of Cap Fréhel. A popular spot with touring caravanners.

rewarded with sightings of migratory gannets, terns and shearwaters.

For walkers, the whole peninsula is traced by the GR34, at its most majestic in places but becoming friendlier and more pretty along the western peninsula flank, where it traverses a number of pine plantations before descending down to the contrasting delight of conifer-fringed **Pléhérel Plage**. Here there are king-sized sand-dunes above the beaches and little indented coves seaward of the D34. This is a harbinger of the many silver strands and the clear blue sea to come, for the traveller heading westwards towards the Bay of Saint-Brieuc and the colourful *granit rose* coast.

This is an enclave much-favoured by the caravanning and camping fraternity for there is a wide area of dune and pine terrain immediately above the shoreline. There are also a number of *gîtes ruraux*, just a selection of the 800 or so which exist within a region which really leads the way in Brittany for countryside holidays. There is a youth hostel at Cap Fréhel, just to the south of La Ville Hardrieux hamlet. Open only during July and August, the telephone number is 96-41-48-98. The succession of sweeping bays, backed by dunes and pines, which now appear for those following the coast road, create the definitive Brittany holiday scene for most visitors.Under clear skies at least, the glittering strands extend vastly and invitingly, while the deep blue sea and white-water breakers *are* almost irresistible to children and all those who are young at heart.

Seaside fun facilities proliferate either side of sedate Sables-d'Or-les-Pins. Children and young people use these beach buggies heavily.

This super sand landscape begins at Pléhérel Plage, then continues and grows marginally more spectacular, if that were possible, around Sables-d'Or and Erquy. **Sables-d'Or-les-Pins**, to give it its full title, nestles compact among pine trees. A string of comfortable sea-front hotels engender something of a dignified and sedate atmosphere through the scattering of up-market holiday houses and the 9-hole golf course. This is a popular enclave with holidaymakers seeking the more tranquil Breton seaside.

At the southern end of this smaller, quality resort, lies the original and ancient village of **Plurien**. There is a 12th-century church here which was once a Knights Templar chapter house. This is close to a nicely landscaped three-star municipal touring site which is open from mid-June to mid-September, tel: 96-72-17-40. Along the foreshore of Sables-d'Or there are no less than seven hotels (one- and two-star), within half a kilometre or so, all of them open seasonally only, and most of them providing restaurant service and sea views of the most delightful kind. For a full list of accommodation in the area, contact the tourist office, tel: 96-41-53-81. Except during the high season (mid-July to mid-August), vacancies are usually readily available in this vicinity.

Following the single but impressive beach of Sables-d'Or, the multiple strands of **Erquy** at the eastern extremity of Saint-Brieuc bay still come as something of a scenic surprise, and are compounded on a sunny day by the brightness and exotic colour which seems to pervade this stretch of the Emerald Coast. Erquy is a rapidly growing resort, tourism inexorably taking over from commercial fishing, although the cliff-backed port still does brisk business with its *fruits de mer* harvest. It also competes scenically with an ever-expanding marina.

There are some nice headland walks around nearby Cap d'Erquy from the road-end car-park, which are rewarding with their impressive views across the bay. Other attractions hereabouts are the hilltop quarry waters creating what are known locally as Les Lacs Bleu and a low tide foreshore footpath provides access to the chapel of Saint-Michel, atop its miniscule islet.

South-west of here is the **Château de Bienassis**—one of the last of the medieval châteaux to be constructed in France—a majestic ramparted mansion originating from the 15th century, within a most gracious parkland setting. Much restored during the l7th century, the interior contains some splendid examples of Louis XIV furniture and period porcelain. This elegant pink sandstone mansion is still a family home, yet it is still protected by a moat and other remnants of medieval military defences. It is open to visitors daily from June to mid-September. See it if you can, if only for the impressive jardin anglais and the atmospheric setting.

Le Val-André

While Dinard was being created as a seaside resort for affluent visitors from America and Britain around the turn of the century, other prospective developers were seeking somewhere comparable along the 500-km (300-mile) *département* coastline, something equally attractive for those not *quite* so

financially flush. They found it where another superb expanse of silver sand carpeted the foreshore, seaward of the little market town of Pléneuf.

The brand new resort was named Le Val-André, and so successful did the project prove to be that even the centuries-old Pléneuf had to acknowledge the usurping money-spinner through a new, official tag: Pléneuf-Val-André. A huge increase of summer visitor traffic was assured once the allure of the leisure oasis was broadcast, with the claim that here, in the Bay of Saint-Brieuc, was the biggest and best sand beach along the whole north coast of Brittany. It helped, in 1880, that the resort creator was one Charles Cotard, a colleague of Ferdinand de Lessops (of Suez Canal fame). Architectural remnants of the grand age still remain, as evidenced by elegant old villas, some retaining their bow window façades, hallmarks at that time of the

The headland and pleasure port of Piégu at Le Val-André. A scenic footpath winds around this point at a resort rated highly by visitors.

influential *charme anglais*. Also traditional is the 2½ km (1½ mile) long esplanade above the super-fine beach which links the sailing centres at either end of the bay—Port Dahouet and Port Piégu. The cleanliness standard of the beautiful beach is, if anything, even higher than it was at the end of the last century. It is another golden nugget in the national treasury of tourism, this one more than justifying the official change of *département* name for the 1990s from the mundane Côtes-du-Nord to Côtes d'Armor. This is doubly apt, since it is not only phonetically more attractive, but it also rekindles a link with early Breton history, *armor* being Celtic for sea.

There *are* faint similarities to Dinard since the bay setting is backed by relatively steep cliffs, now dotted with hotels (thankfully only one or two high-rise ones), summer houses and apartments, and while there is nothing that can quite compare with the regal Rance estuary, the blonde sand centrepiece and the surroundings make Le Val-André a very close contender to the recognized top regional resort.

Yet another much-patronized small-boat mecca, this one is a specially designated sailing centre, one of just a dozen or so around the entire coastline of France which is government recommended. The Base de Dahouet is open all year and provides facilities for over 300 visiting craft on pontoon moorings with all mod-cons including water and mains electricity. In the resort centre, close to laid-out formal gardens and tennis courts, is the popular casino, and the tourist office with its Anglophile address in rue Winston Churchill. Among other leisure attractions are two horse-riding centres, pitch-and-putt golf and a fine cliff-top municipal swimming pool (heated and covered), adjacent to a high-standard touring site for campers and caravanners, which is open from April to September.

Apart from all the sailing and sea-fishing potential, sightseeing launches ply to the Ile de Bréhat, just offshore of Paimpol, while local land-based exploration is made easy by a choice of marked pedestrian routes. The **Pointe de la Guette** is one favoured walker objective from Dahouët, or inland alongside the river. Another follows the headland part around the Pointe de Pléneuf, at the northern end of the bay, and then goes along the scenic Plage des Vallées. From the carpark at Le Piegu, there is a vantage point overlooking Le Verdelet island, which is a nature reserve and nesting place for gulls, shags and cormorants. A new sporting project, a fine 18-hole golf-course, has been created just to the east of town (opens summer 1992), complete with a hotel. The course is laid out across a varied landscape including undulating part-woodland, and links terrain behind the Plage de Nantois. There is also a riding stable adjacent.

While there are reasonable shopping facilities in Le Val-André, it is essentially a seasonal precinct and nearby Pléneuf old town is much more practical, especially for visitors who may require a bank or a comprehensive choice of foodstuff. Market day (Tuesday) is particularly fruitful in this respect when the central square is filled with local produce stalls. Conversely, for restaurant or café choice in season, Le Val-André is understandably richer, providing some 25 eating houses varying from the best of traditional restaurants, to the ever-popular Breton *crêperies* and pizzerias. All of these do brisk business during high summer and notably in the evenings, when the long beach gradually empties of sun-worshippers and watersports enthusiasts.

There are so many splendid beaches along the Côtes d'Armor that one can almost experience a surfeit of seaside delight at times. An inland interlude offers a welcome change of scene—less frenetic, less crowded, and more green and fruitful by contrast—for seekers of old-world Bretagne. From a Val-André base, there are three interesting excursion targets, and four if Saint-Brieuc is included. The latter could hardly be described as green and uncrowded, but the *département* prefecture does have its high spots.

Nowadays, **Lamballe**, 14 km (8½ miles) south of the coast via the D791, is perhaps best known for the **Haras National Stud Centre**, in place du Champs-de-Foire beside the pretty river Gouessant. Some 400 horses are kept here, not only thoroughbred racers but diverse breeds too, like the gentle giant Breton draughthorse and, at the other end of the scale, tiny Connemara ponies. Created in 1825, this is one of the largest equine centres in France. You can see the world of the horse here, from tack-room to blacksmith's forge, and from carriage-room to stables. There is also a riding school and the centre is open daily in the afternoons. Entry for visitors is free of charge.

Lamballe is also interesting for its rumbustious past, visual evidence of which remains in the place du Martray, just off the spacious main square of this hill-town, in the shape of the medieval **Executioner's House**. It is now the tourist office, and a two-part museum exhibiting regional historic artefacts and paintings by a talented local artist, Mathurin Meheut. There are one or two other old houses of character nearby.

Lamballe was once capital of the ancient Penthièvre region (12th to 15th centuries), and its most notorious character was a princeling heir to the dynasty, the Duc de Penthièvre, who led such an industrious life of dissipation that he was dead at 20! His widow was dogged by misfortune too, since she was befriended by Marie-Antoinette, and like the queen, the princess eventually lost her head during The Terror which followed the French Revolution, in 1792.

The old centre is mellow and picturesque, still evocative of times past through some of the architecture, and there are nice elevated views over the river valley from the belvedere of the Gothic church of Notre-Dame, perched on its wooded ridge. Much of Lamballe, however, is modern as one might expect from a recognized centre of commerce and there is a degree of peripheral development, though this is not excessive. In the centre there is a good choice of restaurants and cafés, and there are four hotels. The three-star Angleterre has 21 rooms, and is open all through the year, tel: 96-31-00-16. There is also a two-star touring site, the municipal Saint-Sauveur which is open from mid-June to mid-September.

Take the D768 south again, and after a pleasant rural drive of some 18 km (11 miles), another much more dramatic hill-town hoves into view. **Moncontour** is very different from Lamballe, an intriguing remnant of ancient Brittany, unencumbered by any outlying build-up and still essentially a medieval fortified hill-town. Commanding the heights above two wooded valleys, this was a very important military crossroads in olden times, as reflected by the massive rampart remains and defensive towers surrounding the imposing 16th-century **church of Saint-Mathurin**.

The church itself, surrounded by some delightful half-timbered houses, narrow cobbled streets, and stairways and arches, boasts a richly furnished interior, but it is the vestigial remnants of the past which will fascinate the observant stroller. There was a great château here once and some formidable fortifications, as the Mognet and l'Ouest towers indicate. In medieval times the settlement was accessible by only the narrowest of gateways like the surviving postern arch of Saint-Jean.

There is much of interest in the immediate vicinity of Moncontour, including another ancient fortress château, Les Granges, just to the north of the village, which is one of several hereabouts. A settlement since the 9th century and fortified since the 11th century, Moncontour is still delightfully atmospheric, photogenic and friendly. Guided tours are organized during July and August from the *Syndicat d'Initiative*, tel: 96-73-41-05.

Once again, there is a fair choice of restaurants here—try Les Remparts, rue de l'Union, for traditional Breton fare. Moncontour is a recommended lunch stop anyway, as it is an interesting and typically rural Breton community, largely off the beaten track.

Take the D44 west from Moncontour, and after another pleasant cross-country traverse along a road where the traffic is generally light, you will arrive at L'Hermitage-Lorge, in the forest of the same name. The D7 northwards from here is scenic (despite the adjacent railway line) and it leads on to **Quintin**, another charming old market town, venerable but distinctly different from either Lamballe or Moncontour.

Quintin displays the remains of a 16th-century castle, as well as some colourful terraced streets which cascade down the hillside to an imposing lake created from the Gouët river. An historic weaver's town, once one of the principal sources of Brittany linen, some of the nicest remaining old houses will be found in Grand Rue and in place du Martray. Although the castle is only vestigial, there are a dozen monuments to the past (for example, the Fontaine Notre-Dame-de-la-Porte), and where the great castle once stood there is an 18th-century château which is open to visitors. There are footpath walks around the lake and along the Gouët river. The town environs are dotted with old mills, Neolithic megaliths, and half-hidden 18th-century merchants' mansions. In all it is a very nice little feudal town, boasting three hotels, a choice of *chambres d'hôte* and a two-star municipal camping site beside the lake, which is open from Easter to October. There are half a dozen high-standard restaurants here and the town is served by the railway. The *Syndicat d'Initiative* is in place 1830, tel: 96-74-01-51, and market day is on Tuesday. Some 3 km (2 miles) south, is a lovely park surrounding the 18th-century Robien château; there is visitor access to the gardens, but not to the house.

Returning to Le Val-André, one might consider **Saint-Brieuc** *en passant,* despite the dense commercial growth which has spreads outwards from its ancient centre. Almost up to World War II this was a sedate river port and quiet market town, seat of an ancient bishopric, founded by a Welsh monk Brieuc, (or Briocus) in the 5th century.

Saint Brieuc and the river port now much tamed and canalized. This is the elevated view from the N12 viaduct.

It is the capital of the Côtes-d'Armor *département*. Vibrant and very busy today as a direct result of a vastly enlarged industrial area, there has nevertheless been some imaginative modernizing. This includes a striking new pedestrian precinct and a covered market directly opposite the 14th-century cathedral, which does blend surprisingly well with the maze of narrow streets and venerable half-timbered houses of old Saint-Brieuc. Some of the best examples of these old houses can be seen in the rue Fardel and in the rue Gouët where James II of England lodged in 1689.

Unquestionably, though, it is the mighty **cathedral of Saint-Stephen** that is Saint-Brieuc's treasure of the past, for here stands one of the finest fortified churches to be found in the region. Severe of outline, even bleakly austere, it is at once a religious fount and bastion of powerful strength. Sturdy towers, tiny windows—almost arrow slits in places—and huge reinforcing buttresses testify to the imperative double purpose of the original. It was not only the tombs of bishops that the local populace intended to protect in those turbulent Middle Ages! Twice besieged in the 14th century, attacked and pillaged by Spanish forces in the 16th century, and a sanctuary for the desperate during the Reign of Terror following the Revolution, both the cathedral and town were terribly damaged periodically. Nothing remains of the 17th-century defensive ramparts.

The riches within the medieval church were equalled by those of a more practical nature which flowed into and out of the town's busy port, **Le Légué**, which, unlike Saint-Malo, was relatively undefended against incursion from the sea. The town elders tried to offset this by creating a fortress cathedral, but Saint-Brieuc still paid a heavy price for being an affluent bishopric and port, situated in a vulnerable location. The port area of Le Légué is attractive even today, being flanked by lushly wooded valley slopes. The Gouët river has now been severely canalized, however, but the best view is from the viaduct span of the N12, just north-east of the centre. For more about Saint-Brieuc's past, there is an interesting history museum in the rue des Lycéens-Martyrs, open daily except Mondays. There is a printed circuit guide of the old town, freely available from the tourist office (in rue Saint-Grouéno) which is open all year, tel: 96-33-32-50. It can also be obtained from the tourism pavilion beside the N12 at Yffiniac (8 km, or 5 miles, east), which is open from 1 June to 15 September.

Before returning to Le Val-André, nature-lovers might consider turning seaward off the N12 at **Yffiniac**. The coast road is certainly quieter and prettier and it is here you will find the ancient village of Hillion with its 12th-century church and modern, much-appreciated **Maison de la Baie**, in a very attractive setting. This is a national maritime wildlife centre created to enlighten visitors about the world of nature within the protected area of Yffiniac bay. Visitors may enjoy boat trips to sea-bird sanctuaries and nature

study tours, which are organized from here. The centre is open all year, tel: 96-32-27-98.

Any driver venturing westward from Saint-Brieuc via the N12 for the first time, might well feel a few pangs of disappointment. Where is all the Brittany beauty, the Celtic atmosphere, the rustic romance? Certainly, it is nowhere adjacent to the N12 expressway, a world of traffic density and urban clamour. The fast road to the west is essentially for those racing against time, particularly since the landscape is bland to the point of boredom, except in the vicinity of Guingamp and Belle-Isle-en-Terre.

Guingamp occupies a river valley flanked by gentle hill ridges, and this *is* a picturesque old town in the centre at least, a *ville fleurie* watered by the meandering river Trieux. It was once a Roman way-station, and then a fortified redoubt from the 9th century— it still retains rampart and tower remnants from the 15th century when there was a great castle here. The Gothic church of Notre-Dame was built in the 14th century, around the time King Edward III of England attacked and held the town for a year in 1343. It was here, incidentally, that the great army under Bertrand du Guesclin was assembled before the Battle of Auray in 1364 during which Charles de Blois was killed, du Guesclin was captured and Jean de Montfort succeeded to the dukedom of Brittany. Today, Guingamp, like Saint-Brieuc, is much afflicted by peripheral development, but the Trieux river valley is still verdant and pastoral, and the town itself provides good visitor facilities. The tourist office is in place du

Vally, close to the remaining rampart walls, tel: 96-43-76-89.

Westwards, just to the north of the N12, the isolated hill of **Menez-Bré** at 302 m (990 ft) breaks the plateau sky-line quite dramatically, while **Belle-Isle** partially deserves its name for the pretty hill-flanked setting at the con-fluence of the Léguer and Guic rivers. You will find the 15th-century chapel Locmaria here, which is associated with a rags-to-riches legend of a local girl. Further west still, Morlaix *does* deserve high marks for atmosphere, character and historic interest.

Back at Saint-Brieuc, those wishing to discover more of beautiful Brittany should opt for the D786 which veers off the N12 north of Le Légué port, for a traverse of the Côte du Goëlo. This is the seaboard section along the western shore of Saint-Brieuc bay, between Saint-Brieuc and Paimpol. It is still part of the Côte d'Armor.

The first delight which I urge you to see is the little port of **Binic**, situated shyly just off the coast road. After busy Brieuc, it is a double delight upon which to come—an old-world or-thodox fishing village which has not radically been altered by the demands of contemporary tourism. It is a rec-ognized resort nowadays certainly, but the atmosphere is traditional, the pace gentle and unhurried, and the sea-front architecture and port are a camera-clicker's target. It has fine sand beaches which are backed by low, wooded hills and cliffs.

T he pretty little resort and small-boat harbour of Binic. This old-time fishing port is a delightful haven of tranquility after the bustle of Saint Brieuc.

Once a deep-sea fishing port, most of the craft tied up in the harbour today are leisure boats, but there is still enough commercial activity to impart a genuine working port air, which all adds to the charm of the place. There is generous car-parking space right opposite the beach, and except for high days and holidays there is ample room for all. It is a recommended stop-over, with good facilities and one or two nice local attractions, like the village of Lantic a short distance inland, which boasts a lovely little 15th-century chapel, now designated a national historic monument. Near here too is Les Ajoncs d'Or at Kergrain, a much-patronized international 18-hole golf course, tel: 96-71-90-74.

At Binic there is also a scenic 3 km (2-mile) footpath along an old *Sentier des Douaniers*—a section of the long-distance GR34—which is especially attractive south along wooded cliffs to Pointe de Pordic. For watersports, Binic is only beaten by the next, much larger, complex which is Saint-Quay-Portrieux, 6 km (4 miles) further along the coast. The telephone number for Binic tourist office is tel: 96-73-60-12.

The much-heralded scenic feature of **Saint-Quay-Portrieux** is the new harbour and port area created in 1990, which excites some more than others. The massive pincer-shaped breakwater extends, obtrusively or impressively, (depending upon the eye of the beholder) from the natural half-moon harbour. However, since the man-made enfolding arms can now accommodate 1,000 or more pleasure craft and work boats, perhaps it is more an asset than an eyesore. No doubt the patina of time will eventually soften

the stark outline of a complex in concrete which has profoundly changed the physiognomy of an erstwhile haven of nature—the latter having now become, in effect, an inner harbour.

The fine sand beaches remain the same though, and while the peripheral linear development of the town expands steadily to keep pace with the huge public-works project, there are a number of agreeable unspoiled enclaves along and alongside the seafront, which make the resort one of the leading holiday bases in the Saint-Brieuc bay area. Primarily this is a beach-lazing and watersport mecca, for there are no less than five major sand beaches in the neighbourhood. Four of these boast organized children's clubs during the high summer season, and three are patrolled by lifeguards equipped with fast, inflatable rescue craft. Between Châtelet and Casino beaches there is also an outdoor swimming pool. There are two sailing schools, plus lots of summer events—notably the July nautical festival.

Saint-Quay is also a resort which provides lively after-dark entertainment, provided by a casino, night club, discotheque and a whole skein of bars and cafés, some two-dozen in all. There is a quieter, more traditional Saint-Quay too, reflected through the smaller, less patronized beach coves, the footpath walks (again along sections of the GR34) and the well-attended Breton *pardon* held annually on the third Sunday in September. There is a wide choice of visitor accommodation, with nine hotels, numerous *chambres d'hôtes* and a pleasantly located three-star campground, the beachside Bellevue, which is open from

The foreshore at Saint-Quay-Portrieux which here looks as secluded as it was a couple of decades ago. Today it is adjacent to a huge new harbour complex.

Easter to September. There are 12 restaurants and half a dozen fast-food outlets. Saint-Quay is also a fine sea-angling centre. There are sightseeing boat trips to Bréhat Island. The tourist office is in rue Jeanne-d'Arc, tel: 96-70-40-64. If using public transport, the resort is reached by train to Saint-Brieuc followed by the connecting bus service a 20 km (12½ mile) ride.

North of Saint-Quay, along the D786, a gradual scenic and atmospheric change occurs. It is only subtle, but the perceptive traveller will become aware of a slightly grander, less-tamed landscape, pervaded by a faint Celtic ambience, which becomes steadily more marked with westward progress. Many more of the town and village names are distinctly un-French, like Plouha, Goaz-Bihan and Pléhédel. From market towns lying inland, like **Plouha**, it is but a short drive to the sea and more fine beaches and coves. Not surprisingly, Plouha is much favoured as a residential choice of many retired ex-navy personnel. There is a good riding stable here, specializing in *randonnée* excursions across country—Ranch des Ajoncs d'Or is open all year, tel: 96-20-32-54. The beach close to Plouha (Le Palus), is a picture-postcard cove of granite cliffs enclosing a silver-sand sweep, with a verdant valley approach. Fringed with shingle, the sand is revealed extensively at low water. There is a nice cliff-top stroll from here, towards Plouha point.

Back on the D786, at quaintly named La Dernière Sou ("The Last

Farthing"), students of modern history will want to take the short minor road to **Plage Bonaparte**, which is not only very beautiful in its own right, but is celebrated for a small but important World War II triumph. It was here in June 1944, that a large group of allied aircrew who had been rescued from all across northern France, were assembled. An incredible total of 135 airmen were then embarked under the very noses of the coastal patrols, from what was then a remote and secretive beach of German-occupied France. They were all ferried safely back to England, and there is a memorial plaque on the beach to this act of stealthy derring-do. The beach is now extremely popular, not only with the swimmers and sun-worshippers, but also with walkers and horse-riders who can enjoy both sea-level and cliff-top jaunts along what is still an unspoilt stretch of coast. There is a large car park adjacent to the foreshore.

H ere, still well off the beaten track, the half-hidden Bonaparte plage, the scene of a great allied airmen escape during 1944 from German occupied France.

A little further along, **Port-Lazo** (seaward of Plouézec) is located within a 17 km (10½ mile) stretch of *côte sauvage,* where granite cliffs and sandy coves again dominate, edging upland plateau heath. Pointe de Minard is particularly favoured by shoreline anglers, as is the adjacent coastal path by walkers. A picturesque small-boat haven, this is another tranquil backwater, an extension of Plouézec town, which provides good holiday amenities with all services, including two hotels and a camping site.

West of the prominent Pointe de Plouézec, you encounter the Anse de

278

The abbaye de Beauport, ancient monastic ruin adjacent to Kerity village. Another religious cluster of stonework which has endured since the 13th century...

Kérity village, itself much-visited for the ruins of the **Abbaye de Beauport** which was built at the beginning of the 13th century by the Comte de Penthièvre—head of the fiery dynasty that ruled from Lamballe.

Much publicized by regional brochures, the old priory is frankly a bit of a disappointment, and is nowhere near as impressive as many, far less lauded remnants of old France. There is, however, still a faint air of decayed grandeur about the place, emphasized by the gaunt tracery of skeletal stonework. The setting is rustic, with some nice footpaths in the area along the

...And beside the abbey shell a stretch of well-signposted long-distance footpath providing easy access to Paimpol. Pedestrian routes are not always so well signposted!

Paimpol, a vast sheltered bay studded with islands, peninsulas and offshore reefs, culminating with one of France's best-known wildlife sanctuaries, accessible to pedestrians only, the **Ile de Bréhat**. The whole expanse is a very dramatic vista at times, depending equally on the weather and the state of the tide. This is especially true from view-points like the foreshore below

low wooded cliffs bordering the sea. Of the original building, only the principal nave remains, though much of the ornate Gothic chapter house alongside is intact, including an impressive ancient refectory. The abbey is open daily during the summer, from mid-June to mid-September. There is, by the way, a delightful stretch of the GR34 leading from the abbey almost into Paimpol centre via a bayside path. There is also a well-run municipal campsite, Crukin-Kérity, located on the foreshore. Just 2 km (1 mile) from Paimpol, this two-star site is open from Easter to mid-September.

Paimpol

Paimpol is a very agreeable base, still very much a working port and market town. It is practical yet colourful, donning its mantle of tourism easily, yet not chasing fickle finance too overtly— a difficult blend to achieve for a historic fishing port increasingly attractive to holidaymakers. So far, at any rate, Paimpol has managed to stay genuine with a true Breton air which adds to visitor pleasure. From the deep-sea harbours to the fish market, and from the narrow back streets to some elegant squares, it is a place of easy and quiet enjoyment. Lively and yet not frenetic, it is still governed tangibly by the open sea as it has been for centuries.

Not so long ago Paimpol was wholly and solely a fisherman's town, where half the working population would disappear for months on end in search of Icelandic cod in the north Atlantic, in what were often small and vulnerable sailing vessels. The legacy of that hard-life history remains, reflected

Resurrected from the scrapyard, the Mad Atao. A restored Breton sailing boat in Paimpol harbour which becomes a focal point on fête days.

through the **maritime museum** and by the permanently moored *Mad Atao*, an old-time fishing boat rescued from ignominious old-age as a ballast barge. Now resurrected as a historic monument, it looks sturdily out of place somehow, among all the shiny fibreglass leisure craft that crowd the harbour waters. There is more evidence of past prosperity exhibited by some 16th-century ship-owners' town houses, notably around place du Martray. Pierre Loti, an honoured 19th-century novelist who wrote about the lives of Paimpol fishermen lived here, not far from another celebrated local lad, a songster called Theodore-Botrel (1868–1925) who has a square named after him. His well-loved ballad, "La Paimpolaise", is still performed on fête days like the August *Festival du Chant de Marins.* Off the place de Verdun, by a medieval tower once part of the parish church, there is a monument to the Breton bard.

Other picturesque parts of town are the small Latin Quarter, the lively rue de l'Oise and place Gambetta fish market, which displays all the fruits of the sea, together with fine fresh fruit and vegetables and, of course, displays of fat garlic cloves—a speciality of the region. (Market day is Tuesday.) In the

W orld War II memorial to the seamen of Paimpol. Homage is paid by General De Gaulle with a signed inscription on the base.

rue Saint-Vincent is a memorial chapel to fishermen, while at the water's edge, off quai Pierre Loti, is a particularly evocative monument. The distinctive Cross of Lorraine commemorates the 1940 escape to England of 30 Paimpol ships and their crews, and the 470 seamen of the Free French forces subsequently killed. A message of fond remembrance by General de Gaulle is carved into the Breton-granite base. It was he who declared courageously in those ominously dark days, that, "France may have lost a battle, but she has not lost the war". These are just a few interesting features of the town's maritime history. There is much contemporary pleasure to be enjoyed simply by people-watching on a warm summer evening from one of the quayside pavement cafés or restaurants, off the place République. There are a couple of small sandy beaches, one of which (Plage de la Tossen), forms part of the protected sea-bathing area. There is also a health and fitness course, a children's play area and minigolf 1½ km (1 mile) south-east of the centre. All of this helps to make Paimpol a holiday town, though not a recognized holiday resort—a positive virtue for some visitors.

As a touring base, Paimpol is strategically located for a number of interesting excursion targets on the northern end of the Côte de Goëlo. The first and perhaps most popular is the **Ile de Bréhat**, a ten-minute ferry ride off the mainland from Pointe de l'Arcouest, itself just 5 km (3 miles) north of town. There is a car-park here capable of accommodating 1,000 vehicles, and only rarely at holiday peak times does it fill completely.

Take the D15 minor road north-west from Paimpol and in 5 km (3 miles) you will be in **Loguivy** on the tip of the peninsula and at the very mouth of the Trieux estuary. The pretty fishing harbour is tucked away and virtually unspoilt, being sufficiently off the main tourist track to retain almost all the traditional character of a Breton lobster-fishing village. The approach lanes are rural and there are nice views seaward. There is pleasant coastal walking in the vicinity too, again courtesy of the GR34.

Drive westwards from Paimpol for 5 km (3 miles) along the D786, and you come to the viaduct crossing of the Trieux estuary which reveals a bird's-eye view of **Lézardrieux**, an oyster-farming community which boasts a pleasingly traditional main street and square beside the 18th-century church. Turn north from here to see a strange natural feature of the coastline, the **Sillon de Talbert**. This finger-shaped shingle causeway really is an odd geological feature. Less than 100 m (330 ft) wide, it extends for some 2 km (1 mile) seawards, and between tides it gathers prodigious amounts of seaweed. This seaweed is collected and heaped, and after a period of sun drying, it is processed in a nearby plant at Pleubian, where there is also a research station devoted to seaweed study, open to visitors in July and August.

Turn south from Lézardrieux and follow a picturesque river valley route to Pontrieux which has an interesting halfway stop at the **Château de la Roche-Jagu**. This is an impressive 15th-century stronghold approached via a princely tree-lined drive to a location high above the river Trieux.

A Car-free Bird Haven

Bréhat island itself is renowned, not only as a magnificent sea-bird sanctuary, but also for its variety of flowers and pink rock outcrops, so prevalent further along the well-named Côte de Granit Rose. From the landing stage at Port-Clos, it is about ½ km (⅓ mile) to Le Bourg. Around the much-restored medieval church is a cluster of houses and a restaurant snack bar. Inhabited since the 5th century (there was a monastery established here by a monk fleeing from Great Britain), the history of the island is turbulent, and it was much assaulted in the 15th and 16th centuries by both English and Spanish forces. Today, it is very pretty in parts, notably at the south-western corner, and is very peaceful due to the dearth of vehicles (save service tractors). Concrete paths are way-marked to island high spots like the chapel of Saint-Michel, and the lighthouse at the northern isle extremity. Bréhat is approximately 3 km (2 miles) long and 1½ km (1 mile) across at its widest. Ferry enquiries (summer season) are from Embarcadere de l'Arcouest, tel: 96-55-86-99. Bicycles can be carried if room is available on board.

Now state-owned and fully restored, the castle was converted to a residential château at the time of the Renaissance and the interior contains a surfeit of massive fireplaces; an indication of just how cold the place must have been behind those metre-thick, almost windowless rampart walls. Note the tiny, high location windows, still guarded by weighty wrought-iron grills. Note too, the imposing chimneys on the frontal elevation, decorated with carved stone crowns. There are fine views from the castle surround across the richly wooded valley. The castle is open daily, from April to September.

A steep descent to the floor of the valley along the D787 leads you to **Pontrieux**, which in medieval times was the first bridge settlement below the Trieux estuary. This little town is another of those delightful half-hidden gems, with distinctive architectural features and unusual triangular-shaped places. Around the site of the old bridge there are half-timbered and dressed stone houses—the Maison "Tour Eiffel", sports distinctive round windows. It is a very appealing rural base with hotel, *gîte* and camping accommodation, ideal for those who also enjoy river canoeing. The *Syndicat d'Initiative* telephone number is 96-95-14-03. For those based at Paimpol this is a recommended lunch stop. One might consider completing the circuit by returning to Paimpol via Pommerit-Jaudy and La Roche-Derrien, the former being a picturesque hamlet and the latter the ancient linen capital of Trégor region. **La Roche-Derrien** is another ancient town of character basking in a pleasing rural setting on the river Jaudy, again a recognized canoeing and country walking centre, with a riding stable of repute. There is comfortable accommodation here, with a choice of hotels among the half-timbered houses, and a church dating back to the 11th century. La Roche-Derrien, like other settlements of the Trégor region, is known for its bread baked in wood-fired ovens, *pâté de campagne*, cider and apple spirit aged in oak barrels, and—increasingly—organically-grown fruit and vegetables. La Roche *Syndicat d'Initiative* telephone number is 96-91-50-22.

The Pink Granite Coast

West of the Jaudy river the geology of the Brittany seaboard changes yet again, this time to a rugged terrain of massive rock outcrops. These outcrops are often so extensive that they create a moonscape of weird grandeur, devoid of trees or indeed any vegetation worthy of the name in places—there is nothing rosy about the eastern end of the Côte de Granit Rose. The recognized gateway to this area is **Tréguier**, although this well-watered, green valley enclave exhibits scant evidence of the rock-strewn coast to come.

Indeed, the location of this ancient and sprightly harbour is particularly striking at its half-moon confluence of the Jaudy and Guindy rivers, which form something of a natural moat around half the town. The gentle, undulating country rising above the estuary valley adds to the cosy charm of the town. It is the huge **cathedral** and its venerable connection with Saint Yves (or Saint Tugdual), that is one of Treguier's great gems. This is a splendid flamboyant edifice which was started in the 11th century (one Romanesque tower still stands), though principally dating from the 13th century. The hallowed treasure of the interior is the tomb of Saint Yves, who was protector of the poor and—somewhat oddly—also the patron saint of lawyers. A massive *pardon* takes place here annually on the third Sunday in May, attended by many thousands of pilgrims. The cathedral cloister which was created in the 15th century is arguably one of the finest in the Republic, a perfectly proportioned quadrangle enhanced by arches of delicately carved tracery.

There are also a number of notable secular buildings including the old bishop's palace (now the *mairie*), the town house of Duc Jean V, the imposing twin towers which flank the old town gate at the quayside and a sprinkling of 15th- and16th-century houses. One of these houses is the birthplace of Ernest Renan, a nationally revered 19th-century author and philosopher, the house now a museum. There is a yachting marina here, naturally, plus some nice strolling space in the Bois du Poète and along the valley river banks. The sea used to rise a bit higher than nowadays, hence the old corn lofts along the rue Renan, which give a clue

*P*lougrescant and the most photographed building on the channel coast of Brittany; the House in the Chasm.
There is a whole moonscape of boulder-strewn foreshore here.

to the town's maxim that Tréguier is "well seated on its hill, with its feet in salt water". There are comprehensive tourist facilities, with a choice of five hotels and a dozen or so restaurants and cafè-bars. There is no campsite in town, La Roche-Derrien (6 km, or 4 miles, south), being the nearest. Guided tours of this fascinating harbour town are organized during July and August—contact the *Syndicat d'Initiative* at the *mairie*: tel 96-92-30-19. Tréguier is the historic capital of the ancient Trégor district, and was once a bishopric.

The area in the immediate vicinity of the town is known as the Côte des Ajoncs (Gorse Coast), banks of which (a butter-yellow carpet in season) spread prodigiously across the upland heath. It is all typically Breton, but if there is one single picture that epitomizes this northern coastline at its most rugged and intriguing, it is the **Maison du Gouffre** (House in the

Chasm), near Plougrescant. This tiny dwelling, tightly sandwiched between two enormous boulders, tide-washed fore and aft, appears on all the regional Brittany brochures and is a postcard best-seller at souvenir shops. An absorbing spot on this rock-dominated foreshore, some 10 km (6 miles) north of Tréguier, it is reached via narrow lanes which thread their way between high banks, across a tree-poor but gorse-rich plateau which is broken only by isolated homesteads and farming villages in the main. As the shoreline looms, however, it is uniquely Breton. Pors-Hir, close to Pointe du Château, is a cove highlighted by the little house in the rocks, with some very impressive granite formations and cliff fissures in the vicinity. Happily, the authorities have kept the area as natural as possible so far—long may it so remain.

Perros-Guirec

The craggy scene continues westwards past the beauty spot of Buguélès, until a splash of golden sand, backed by an inviting little touring site, heralds Port le Golf beach. Seaward, the scene is still one of broken-toothed reefs and islets, but gradually the coastal country softens, becoming greener and more covered in trees. Trevou-Tréguignec heralds the start of one of Brittany's most popular holiday strips, which extends around the bulging headland for some 25 km (15½ miles) or so of definitive seaside delight. At the heart lies the large, all-purpose resort of Perros-Guirec.

Here the much-vaunted pink granite really is apparent—even the 12th-century church of St James blushes

with a roseate hue. It is not, however, merely the *granit rose* that attracts the visitor, but the beautiful silver-sand beaches, the offshore seascape dotted with outcrops like the Seven Islands, plus all the holiday amenities that the French build so well into their purpose-planned resorts.

Perros-Guirec, now offering every kind of holiday mod-con, has a venerable past, which began in the 6th century when a settlement was created by yet another Welsh migrant monk called Guirec; there is though but little visual evidence in town of this ancient past. There are two distinct halves to the linear and somewhat rambling resort, the eastern part of which extends from the large and original fishing port (now much developed), of Saint-Quay-Perros, to the elevated Pointe du Château belvedere and the up-market western strip which continues from this point to the best of the golden sand beaches—**Trestraou**. The esplanade of this fine plage is lined with a variety of leisure amenities from a casino, restaurants, cafés and watersports centres of every description, to sailing schools and a *thalasso-thérapie* sea-bathing station. From this beach there are also direct boat trips to the Sept-Iles bird sanctuary, where sightseers can get very close to what is claimed to be the largest puffin colony in France.

At the eastern end of town there is more watersport potential, from skin-diving to boat fishing, while the port marina, a vast nautical parking lot with room for some 60 visiting leisure craft. There is more of a working harbour atmosphere at the Saint-Quay part of town, which also sports one or two colourful and intimate night spots, around the lower town district.

Another change of coastal scene occurs just east of Perros where, quite abruptly, the landscape becomes more wooded and attractively undulating. Indeed the resort town centre straddles the crest of a steepish hill. The church apart, there is not a great deal of historic interest, but there is a good variety of shops and some pleasant local walking, again along the *Sentiers des Douaniers* which starts just above Trestraou plage. The scenic coast path may be followed to neighbouring **Ploumanac'h.**

This ancient and once separate port is now almost linked by development to Perros, and is a small resort famed for some of the best of those rose-pink rocks. Indeed, it is called the "Cité de Granit Rose" nowadays, an enclave of holiday apartments, conifer-edged coves and beaches forming a foreshore that reveals some wide vistas, especially

from Tourony plage. Here a veritable chaos of enormous pink- and copper-coloured boulders make the human rock-scrambler feel very insignificant. Seawards lies the tiny island capped by Château Costaeres, and beyond, the Seven Islands.

Trégastel-Plage is no less impressive and many of the giant boulders are individually named here. They certainly stir the imagination of most visitors, particularly at Coz-Porz Plage which is liberally endowed with mighty outcrops. There is even a large and comprehensive aquarium and **wildlife museum** housed within what was once a rock chamber church. Beneath countless tonnes of pink granite, a wide

T he pink rocks of Ploumanac'h plage. This fascinating foreshore of colour is now virtually a suburb of Perros-Guirec.

variety of local and tropical fish now fascinate countless visitors in caves once inhabited by Neolithic man. There is a choice of campsites here, for it is an area popular with the touring fraternity.

There is more good cliff walking hereabouts, plus a number of secluded sun-bathing coves available to those who don't mind picking their way among the rocks. All along the Perros-Guirec stretch of coast there are landmarks of interest, like chapels, lighthouses, belvederes, lifeboat stations and viewing tables. Unquestionably "Queen of the Breton Corniche", Perros and its satellite resorts can become heavily populated in high summer. Since, however, a wide swathe of coastal country is encompassed, there is seldom any feeling of excessive crush; of either traffic or people. There is also a massive choice of visitor accommodation of every description, between Trevou-Tréguignec and Trébeurden.

With good local bus services and coach excursions operated by Tourisme Verney (tel: 96-37-02-40), there are several interesting objectives, not least the neighbouring resort of Trébeurden on the shores of Lannion bay. Again, there are some handsome sand beaches here (Tresmeur and Port Tremen), plus Grand Island (**Ile Grande**), which is accessible by road, and where there is an ornithology centre and a number of megalithic monuments. In total contrast, there is also the telecommunications radome and museum a short distance inland at Pleumeur-Bodou, plus the **Planétarium du Trégor** which lays on astronomic lectures and vivid displays, with some programmes in English (for information, tel: 96-91-83-78).

Back in time again, there is an impressive Gaulois village reconstruction here too, in an area now classified as a science park, just to keep the passing of centuries in perspective. The village is open daily during July and August, proceeds going to the care of children worldwide, through the MEEM association (du Monde des Enfants, aux Enfants du Monde). This is a quieter, smaller resort than Perros,

H elpful information panels are a feature of the coast around Perros-Guirec, for both pedestrians and drivers.

A whole variety of supervised pursuits with strong youngster appeal make Trébeurden a very popular family resort.

though purpose-built and popular with families. There is lots of alternative accommodation, including ten touring sites in the vicinity, and full services and amenities are provided, including a natural world exhibition on Millau Island. Trébeurden, with Pleumeur-Bodou, is a place where pastoral Brittany and contemporary French leisure demands meet and mix amicably. Still essentially a blend of seaside and country, there is no escalating garishness which often intrudes into coastal high spots like this one. It is a good base for holidaymakers with children. The tourist office is in place de Crec'Héry, tel: 96-23-51-64.

Lannion, very different of aspect, nevertheless holds appeal for those who prefer an orthodox town centre from which to make local forays. A market town set deep on the valley floor of the river Loquivy, there is a working honesty which prevails; Lannion is free of frills and quite attractive for it. There are lots of diverse shops where the visitor can go window-shopping or buy quality souvenirs, like paintings produced by local artists, or pottery pieces thrown by resident artisans. Lively on market day (Thursday) the river bank by the bridge is dominated by the great Augustinian **convent of Saint-Anne**, built in the 18th century.

For a town founded in the 11th century, there is not too much historic treasure, but there are some picturesque 15th- and 16th-century half-timbered houses and a 16th-century church, which is accessible via a steep pedestrian street, which lend character to this split-level river port. Place

Leclerc is the old town hub and the rue Geoffroy de Pontblanc is named after a local hero knight of the 13th century who was killed while defending Lannion against the invading English. In the Middle Ages this region was a favoured stronghold of the Knights Templars, and the 12th-century **church of Brélevénez parish** (just to the north of the centre), is visual evidence of this ancient chivalric order. There is an elevated view across Lannion from the top of the steep (and many), access steps.

Now a centre of the electronics industry, there is much development and modernization around the Lannion outskirts, particularly to the north. Traffic flow is heavy at times, perhaps befitting this old "capital of Trégor", which now plays host to the National Telecommunications Research Centre. Attractive to some visitors as a base nonetheless, there are some 15 hotels, a choice of *chambres d'hôtes*, a well-run 70-bed youth hostel, and four campsites in the vicinity. A range of diverse eating houses provides fare from the traditional to the exotic. Lannion is served by the SNCF, there is a local bus service, and both car and cycle hire are available. The tourist office is in quai d'Aiguillon, right on the river and adjacent to the large central car park, tel: 96-37-07-35, or 96-46-41-00. It is a helpful source of freely available pamphlets (in English), about local walks. A popular excursion target from here is **Armoripark leisure park**, at Bégard, some 18 km (11 miles) distant. Every fun factor is here for adult and children, from aqua-centre to ice rink and in between, farm animal enclosures and a fairground, solarium and Jacuzzi.

*S*and-yachting at the base nautique *of Plestin-les-Grèves. There are beaches in Brittany that lend themselves admirably to this sport.*

About 18 km (11 miles) south-west of Lannion, via the D786, is **Saint-Michel-en-Grève**, and another beautiful beach of silver sand which extends for some 7 km (4½ miles) around a sheltered inlet of Lannion bay. This is the start of a scenic corniche road where, halfway along the route, the much-climbed and well signposted Grand Rocher towers above the shoreline to reward climbers with lofty distant views. There is a sand-yachting and sailing centre at *Plestin-les-Grèves* plage, where youngsters can get themselves dramatically and satisfyingly plastered in wet sand at certain states of the tide. The onshore winds can have the fragile sail craft racing at

*T*ourist office and quayside at Locquirec; the most north-easterly of Finistère resorts, and one of the most picturesque.

surprisingly fast speeds across the wet, billiard-table terrain.

Finistère

The pretty corniche road winds above wooded cliffs before descending down into **Locquirec**, the first settlement across the Finistère boundary and a portal of appropriate charm. It is an uncrowded Breton pearl, a small fishing port and township, as yet unmarred by any crowding marina. There are some comfortable hotels hereabouts, where tranquility is still considered an essential asset, as vital as the fine selection of rock-protected sandy coves between here and the bay of Morlaix. Small it may be, but Locquirec lacks none of the vital holiday requirements—it has a first-class sailing school and good fishing potential in unpolluted waters. There is also good local walking across part-wooded

cliff-tops, while the local gastronomic speciality is crab. A helpful tourist office will be found in the place du Port on the quayside, tel: 98-67-40-83.

There are other delightful backwater havens to be explored around the first Finistère headland, like Guimaëc and Plage du Moulin de la Rive, Saint-Jean-du-Doigt and Primel-Trégastel, all reached via a narrow and undulating coast road. At the village church of Saint-Jean, the severed finger of the saint is said to be held—a relic brought back from the Holy Land by returning pilgrims in the early 15th century. **Primel-Trégastel** is located in a green hill setting above the sea. There is a rock-studded inlet here worthy of any *côte sauvage*, the Pointe de Primel, a favoured walker's target for its views and chaos of rose-hued rocks.

Brittany's Land's End

It is often assumed that the nearer one gets to any land mass extremity, the more dramatic and delightful the

*T*he seclusion of *Plougastnou sands, not far from Saint-Jean-du-Doigt. This is an area much favoured by those seeking beach seclusion.*

scenery will become. This is not true of course, and to save any disappointment, don't expect *too* much from the remainder of the Channel coast country west of Morlaix bay. All the really finest sand beaches are behind now and despite odd glowing exceptions, there is nothing like the profusion available to Côte d'Armor visitors. Nonetheless, there are many compensations, not least the marked increase of true pastoral ambience, which seems to descend upon the western tip of the great peninsula and which prevails virtually unbroken, save for the immediate environs of Brest.

Celtic attitudes still rule the life-style and pace of Finistère, where no one hurries unnecessarily, where lunch breaks are long and leisurely, and where folk still chat amiably at street corners and somehow find time to enjoy the simple pleasure of gazing at a distant view. The landscape here is often stern, sometimes harsh and much of it remains stubbornly untameable—notably around the Aber Coast—emphasizing still how puny man is and how futile all the frenetic scurrying of the human race. Moss-encrusted menhirs and ancient burial mounds which mark the sparsely populated uplands stand silent sentinels, as isolated and detached today as they have remained through long centuries. For some visitors, this very austerity of nature is itself an invigorating tonic. Not that one is conscious of wild western Finistère on the approach to **Morlaix**, a lively, friendly and historic town, as bustling and colourful a river port as any in the Brittany region.

Drivers using the N12 expressway will gain a fine bird's-eye view of the sub-prefecture straddling the Morlaix

*T*own plan of Morlaix.

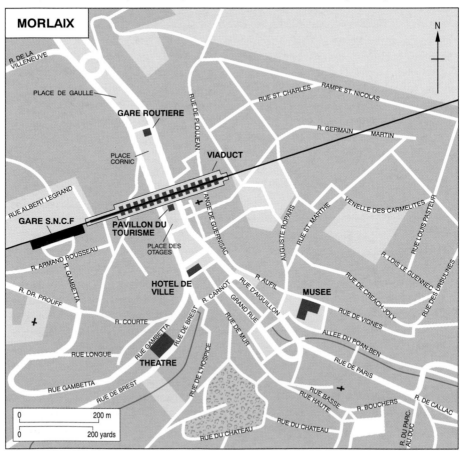

The lively maritime heart of old Morlaix. On the right is the famous tobacco exchange and in the background the massive arches of the 19th-century railway viaduct.

river from the comparatively new viaduct spanning the deep valley. From this high-level vantage point you can see another massive viaduct, a two-tiered, multi-arched viaduct structure which was constructed in 1864 and which carries the Paris—Brest railway line. Stylish despite its essentially practical purpose, it displays a strong, rounded beauty, a feature totally lacking in the contemporary N12 road bridge. Comparing the two and contemplating both form and workmanship, one can see why architecture of the craftsman era is so hungrily admired today. The powerful stone-built

landmark of 19th-century Morlaix, is a glowing monument to the age of steam.

The viaduct though is itself modern compared to the long history of this river-port town. It has been inhabited since the Gallo-Neolithic age, with evidence of the distant past reflected in relics like the Barnenez burial chamber, north of town on the estuary shore, estimated to be more than 6,000 years old.

The importance of the location was quickly recognized by the Romans too—a ravine-like valley, easily defended, and with quick access to the open sea, doubly favoured because it was also a good fording place where the Jarlot and Queffleuth rifts joined (and still join) to form the course of the Morlaix river. By the year 1,000, there was a great castle on the rocky promontory and the town, increasingly peopled by fishermen and merchants, gradually grew below.

With growth came prosperity and the necessity for defensive walls in the 14th century when there was much blood-letting in the region due to the War of Succession. In the 16th century the bay was invaded by a large fleet of English ships in reprisal for a corsair raid on Bristol. The town was ransacked but the raiders paid heavily for the incursion. As a consequence a fortress, the Château de Taureau was erected to command the entrance to Morlaix bay and it stands guard still. A favoured watering-hole of historic figures like Duchess Anne of Brittany (1506) and Mary Queen of Scots (1548), the town's greatest height of affluence and importance was reached in the 17th and 18th centuries when the port boasted a vast tobacco factory and exchange and was elevated to the most important corsair base in France. Tobacco production and dealing (much of which attracted ferocious smuggling and piratical pillage) vastly outstripped an ancient Morlaix textile industry and when the French Revolution broke something like 2,000 to 3,000 tonnes of the leaf were being produced and processed annually.

Today, many of the town houses, churches and municipal buildings still reflect the wealth of that rumbustious wheeler-dealer age. Many of the fine merchant villas survive, including the house occupied by duchess Anne who was, perhaps appropriately, given a miniature golden ship and other sumptuous gifts by the fat-cat city fathers. Typical of many surviving medieval dwellings, the house is fascinatingly lop-sided now, the three-storey wooden

T he house in Morlaix where Anne of Brittany really did stay in 1505 (there are numerous less-authentic claimants). A marvellous example of medieval architecture.

frontage decorated with carved statues of gargoyles and religious figures.

There are a number of intriguing—if fragmentary—remnants of the past around the town centre, while the 15th-century **church of Saint-Melaine** overshadowed by the railway viaduct, may be dwarfed but nothing is lost of its delicate design and elegant proportions. Such pleasurable lightness of architectural touch is not always so apparent in flamboyant Gothic buildings. Morlaix **museum**, within a one-time Jacobin church (also of 15th-century origin), displays some famous paintings by French, Italian and Dutch artists, in addition to some revealing exhibits of a pastoral past.

Morlaix port remains in demand today, much as it always has, and while the quayside is still occupied by a huge tobacco warehouse and market, the tobacco barons are thin on the ground nowadays. In an age of leisure, it is leisure craft that clamour and jostle for space amid a forest of yacht masts and bobbing white hulls. It is a particularly favoured haven for those on voyage around the Brittany coast. In fact, Morlaix is a leading Finistère yacht basin, interminably busy and with much onlooker appeal, being so closely adjacent to the old town centre.

The whole of Morlaix is really quite compact, there being no excess of peripheral development. This fact, combined with its picturesque waterside setting, makes it ideal for pedestrian exploration. There are plenty of quality shops, lots of atmospheric bars and eating houses, and quaint elevated parts reached via steep steps or narrow and sometimes cobbled alleys. The heart and hub is the place des Otages,

almost literally under that towering viaduct. The town has naturally capitalized on its colourful past and while visitors are well served, there is no excess of tourist-trap commercialism. The town retains its genuine character well and is a recommended base for the westernmost tip of the Brittany peninsula, for all those who prefer to make their excursions from urbane and comfortable surroundings.

The North-Western Corner

Strategic for both coastal and hinterland excursions, the Morlaix exit routes westward, lead immediately into rustic if not spectacular country. Keep to the well-surfaced and well-signposted minor roads though, for the most tranquil progress. On the southern loop, take the D712 for 12 km (7½ miles) and you will arrive at one of Brittany's finest parish closes, on the north-eastern fringe of the Armorique nature park **Saint-Thégonnec** is unquestionably one of the most impressive of all the Breton parish closes; a 16th-century cluster of imposing church, triumphal archway, ossuary and Calvary. The latter, apart from its religious significance, also displays clearly medieval pilgrim dress. It is a much-visited shrine, of course, so try to see the village early in the day if possible.

Westwards, following the course of the river Élorn, **Landivisiau** is a typical market town of inland Finistère, the town centre a spacious square fronted by a sturdily built church of austere granite. There are some nice municipal gardens here, graced by tall trees alongside the river, where a health and fitness course is laid out. The leisure

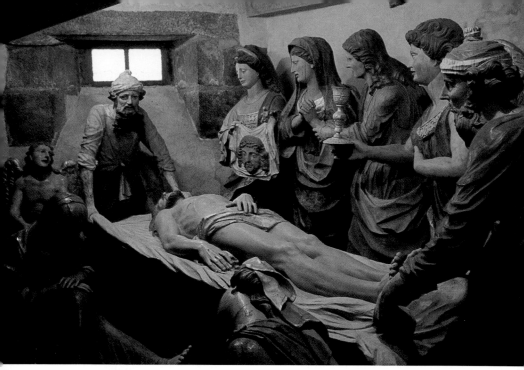

This imaginative crypt tableau of the Passion in the chapel museum of Saint-Thégonnec. The figures are 17th-century wood carvings.

park is called the Vallée des Enfants. There is ample visitor carparking and Landivisiau is a congenial lunch or overnight stopping place. There is a touring site adjacent to the sports centre and swimming pool. One or two vestigial remnants of the old town survive, including a 17th-century chapel and a 15th-century decorated fountain. Don't be deterred by the plethora of storage depots and light industry enterprises on the outskirts of this town, one of the Republic's principal Brittany cattle-markets.

The Elorn valley is at its prettiest west of here, both sides of the D712, with wayside highlights like the waterfall at Pont Christ, deserted riverside mills, and La Roche-Maurice, famous for its parish close, mainly attractive, however, to those who may have had their fill of old churches, for the eyrie setting of the bijou hill-village itself and the brooding 14th-century castle ruin.

Landernau, once the capital of Léon region, is most famous for its early 16th-century bridge, the Pont de Rohan, spanning the Élorn, and its venerable dwelling houses almost adjacent to the tourist office. There is an English connection in this colourful market town—the 16th-century church of Saint-Thomas of Canterbury. There are good tourist facilities, including river-boat trips to Brest. There is some pleasing surrounding countryside too, notably on the right bank of the river, in the forest of Landernau, which extends over some 200 hectares (500 acres) with marked footpaths and a castle ruin. There is an agreeable and secluded farm touring site here, called

Coat Bihan, which is open all year. Landernau is a recommended inland base with half a dozen hotels, a similar number of restaurants and a tranquil atmosphere. The tourist office is at 1, rue du Pont, tel: 98-85-13-09.

From Landernau the direct route to Brest is via the D712, but a prettier detour south and west, takes in **Daoulas** and Plougastel-Daoulas. The former is famed for its regal 12th-century abbey, the cloisters of this Franciscan monastery being particularly striking. This is just one among several treasures of the Middle Ages, however, again in a nice riverside setting complete with a 16th-century parish close. The great railway viaduct, like that of Morlaix, is dominant, yet not overpowering.

For those who enjoy forays off the beaten track, try exploring the peninsula which extends south-west from **Plougastel-Daoulas** across acres of fruit-growing terrain (particularly strawberries) to Pointe de Kerdéniel. There is a nice walk from the road-end car-park, culminating with extensive views across the Brest roads.

The Léon Land's End

Brest is not a city endowed with great visitor appeal. The great naval base was almost totally destroyed in World War II then rebuilt on a grid pattern which may be practical but is not very stimulating. The post-War planners seem to have had difficulty deciding on a city centre, which is ostensibly around the place de la Liberté, yet which somehow stretches extensively (and confusingly to a stranger), particularly along the rue de Siam. This major thoroughfare was named after a

long-ago visit by oriental emissaries, and is blessed with a multiplicity of look-alike side turnings.

The huge port has, of course, a history as illustrious and colourful as any in France, but there are, alas, only a few visual scraps marking the great age of glory. To learn something of old Brest, the naval capital of western France, visit the **Musée de la Marine** in the waterfront château; this is the only section of a once-great fortress open to visitors. It is located off the cours Dajot, itself laid along an ancient rampart line. On the opposite side of the Penfold river is the only major medieval remain, the **Tour Tanguy**, also a museum of pre- and post-Revolution Brest and containing an impressive armoury. There is a third museum in this compact enclave of culture, a permanent fine-art exhibition in the rue Traverse. Here are housed works by world-renowned masters, including those of the Pont-Aven school.

As for the remainder of this modern, busy and crowded working port, there is the huge, super-modern **Oceanopolis pavilion** at Port de Plaisance du Moulin Blanc. It lies alongside the N165, some 6 km (4 miles) east of Brest's château, and you must negotiate the commercial port area, a somewhat grim clutter of railway sidings, loco-sheds and giant oil refinery storage tanks before arriving there. The scene lightens appreciably at the pleasure port though, where there is a vast car park and the Great White Crab, a futuristic mushroom-dome containing a cultural centre and Europe's largest aquarium. Here 500,000 litres (110,000 gallons) of sea-water and an enormous variety of aquatic occupants, await to transport the visitor on a dramatic marine odyssey. There is a popular 18-bed youth hostel near here in the rue de Kerbriant tel: 98-41-90-41. For those opting to stay in the city, there are no less than 24 classified hotels, plus all the facilities and amenities that one would expect to find in a major city and port of France. The tourist office is in place du Général-Leclerc, tel: 98-44-24-96.

Brest was, and still is, a naval dockyard of prime importance; even now only French nationals are allowed within the dock and arsenal, but, this is not a disastrous prohibition to most foreign visitors, especially those on holiday. Exit from the city centre westwards is well signposted and smoothly efficient outside the rush hours. The traverse of the urban build up is surprisingly quick and within 20 km (12½ miles) one is again in a green and pastoral corner of Finistère, exemplified by **Pointe de Saint-Mathieu** and **Le Conquet**.

The first boasts an atmospheric 16th-century ruined abbey, currently being restored, beside a monument to sailors lost at sea, and a handsome 19th-century lighthouse, one of many beacons in the dangerous waters between Brest roads and the island of Ouessant (Ushant). There are some fine seascapes from here across the reef-scattered channel to the Ile Molène, and just a short distance further around the headland lies the film-set harbour of Le Conquet.

Surrounded by cliffs yet with a green, rolling backdrop and seemingly a million miles from Brest, there is good coastal walking here, and an old-world working port which reaps rich shell fish harvests from the surrounding seas. The little town is delightfully traditional and still retains strong Celtic connections with Wales, one street being named rue Llandilo. Ferry boats ply from here to Brest, Molène and Ushant, details being available from the *Syndicat d'Initiative*, tel: 98-89-11-31.

Ile d'Ouessant is now an acknowledged holiday island, with comprehensive services open during summer, including four hotels, *chambres d'hôtes*, furnished apartments and a touring site. There are bus, car-hire and taxi services, and cycles (very popular with island explorers) may also be hired.

Rugged, windswept and virtually treeless, the island is roughly 7 km (4½ miles) long, and boasts the small town and port of Lampaul, located in the shelter of a crab's claw bay. The ferry boats dock at Le Stiff in the bay north-east of the tiny capital. Part of the vast Armorica nature park, this craggy patch of half-tamed wilderness is rich with dramatic cliff formations and sea-bird colonies. It also has modern leisure amenities like tennis, horse-riding, a sailing school, ecomuseum, discotheque and cinema. The telephone number of Lampaul *Syndicat d'Initiative* is 98-48-85-83. Apart from the ferry boats, there is a daily air service from Brest with a company which is called, cutely, Finist'Air.

Back on the mainland and some 5 km (3 miles) north of Le Conquet, is the Republic's Land's End and the most westerly tip of France the **Pointe du Corsen**. It is much visited for this reason, although the setting is not nearly so dramatic as that of Pointe Saint-Mathieu. The sea views, however are sweepingly wide. North of here the traveller enters *Aber* country—a low-lying plateau and heathland broken by occasional tree stands, the coast fissured by estuaries and inlets which create low-banked tidal mud-guts. Some of the water courses are scenic at high water—**Aber-Wrac'h** is the most impressive—but after the princely splendour of the Breton coast to the east, the Côte des Abers is pleasant though not memorable. Much of the pleasure in meandering hereabouts lies in the dearth of cars and crowds, and the rustic tranquility, little changed in many

*A*ber Wrac'h estuary; *the most scenic of north Finistère tidal inlets. Most of the others are somewhat disappointing.*

respects from that of pre-War France—especially in and around the less obvious bays and inlets.

At **Plouguerneau** there is a museum devoted to seaweed gathering and processing (the traditional industry of this estuary-split terrain), while one of the prettiest enclaves lies to the north around **Guisseny**. At the mouth of Quillimadec river this very ancient village, a settlement since the 5th century, boasts a rugged coastline, punctuated by wide sand beaches, and is much favoured by small-boat enthusiasts and horse-riders. At Brignogan-Plages, now an established and growing resort, the tide recedes impressively to leave some 5 km (3 miles) of silver strands. There are also some curious granite rock formations along the foreshore, plus a sprinkling of ancient chapels and even more venerable menhirs as evidence of that misty pagan past.

299

Around 12 km (7½ miles) inland from here lies **Le Folgoët**. Once a self-contained parish village, it is now virtually a suburb of Lesneven, but remains a pilgrimage centre of great renown. One of Brittany's largest *pardon* ceremonies is celebrated here annually in early September, around the massive Gothic **church** erected in the 15th-century. The architecture of the church might be a little too ornate for some, and the years have not treated the stonework kindly. The interior treasures are impressive though, especially the medieval rood screen. The village is suffused with Breton legend, and there is a **folk museum** housed in an adjacent 15th-century manor house complex. **Lesneven**, a venerable cattle-market town, boasts a handsome main square where a bustling and colourful market is held every Monday. There are some elegant 17th-century cloisters around the chapel, and you can visit the Léon museum, which contains prehistoric and Gallo-Roman artefacts, Breton statues and pottery from the Middle Ages, and 19th-century furniture and costume.

Saint-Pol-de-Léon

Those based at Morlaix who are eager to see the best of the nearby Channel coast, should head directly north for Saint-Pol-de-Léon, richer scenically and historically than much of the Côte des Abers. The D73 minor road is the most interesting approach, skirting Morlaix river and estuary *en route,* and revealing the oft-missed little resort of **Carentec**, which is surrounded by some delightful wooded cliffs and marked footpaths to Pointe de Cosmeur and Pointe de Penn al Lann. Offshore, the forbidding **Château du Taureau** built in 1542, and more recently used as a prison, may be visited. Trips are organized through the Carentec *Syndicat d'Initiative*, tel: 98-67-00-43.

Still gratifyingly compact and little more than village-sized, Saint-Pol still epitomizes traditional Finistère. And so it should, with such a long and illustrious history reflected through the huge 13th-century former cathedral, now a national monument, and the nearby Chapelle du Kreisker, with the most splendid soaring belfry. The streets of this small market town radiate invitingly from the main square, which has a large car park adjacent to the tourist office and shopping precinct. The beach roads are well signposted—the Champ de la Rive is a scenic route to the sea revealing a nice view from the landmark Calvary, over the Penze estuary.

Sainte-Anne Plage, by the little port of Pempoul, is the most popular with swimmers and sun-bathers, itself close to a landscaped and tree-shaded park, Kernevez. There are three hotels in Saint-Pol, a dozen bed-and-breakfast houses, and a similar number of restaurants and *crêperies*. There are two touring sites some 2 km (1 mile) distant which are located on the foreshore. A growing sailing and fishing resort, there is also tennis and mini-golf. A good riding stable specializing in *randonnée* excursions lies just south of town and is called the Centre Equestre du Mouster. Cycles can be hired in town—details can be obtained from the tourist office, place de l'Eveché, tel: 98-69-05-69.

The Russian-sounding town of **Roscoff** is another ancient Finistère

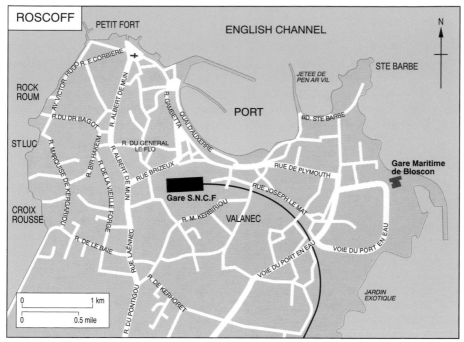

ROSCOFF

PETIT FORT

ENGLISH CHANNEL

N

STE BARBE

JETEE DE
PEN AR VIL

ROCK
ROUM

PORT

BD. STE BARBE

ST LUC

R. DU GENERAL
LE FLO

RUE DE PLYMOUTH

Gare Maritime
de Bloscon

Gare S.N.C.F

CROIX
ROUSSE

RUE JOSEPH LE MAT

VALANEC

VOIE DU PORT EN EAU

VOIE DU PORT EN EAU

JARDIN
EXOTIQUE

0   1 km
0   0.5 mile

T own plan of Roscoff.

port, lying 5 km (3 miles) north of Saint-Pol-de-Léon. First settled by the Romans, it has for centuries been linked to the British Isles through a recognized sea route. Mary Queen of Scots visited it as child in 1548, and Charles Stuart disembarked here after his defeat in the disastrous battle of Culloden in 1745. The bonnie prince would surely recognize the very distinctive Gothic belfry of **Notre-Dame de Kroaz-Baz church**, built in the same century and the town's most eminent landmark.

Other claims to fame by breezy Roscoff are that it is one of the most famous eminent maritime biology centres in Europe, and that it is the birthplace of *thalassothérapie* (sea-water

therapy)—there are two extensive residential health clinics here. Still old-fashioned, relaxed and not excessively commercialized, Roscoff is compact and interesting for the visitor, with a good choice of holiday amenities. It has a large aquarium housing over 300

A Dramatically-located Sailing School Offshore Batz Island is now a recognized young person's sailing centre, and is run in conjunction with a comprehensive youth hostel, which is open from April to October. Sea canoeing and orthodox sailing are enjoyed from this *école de mer*, 15 minutes' ferry journey from Roscoff port. Very Breton of aspect, like Ouessant and many stretches of the far west mainland coast, the cottages are low-built to shrug off the sometimes savage winter gales, and the Finistère folk are proud of their heritage and a seafaring past that until only very recently was hard and dangerous.

Roscoff, a delightful little ferry port which lands the visitor deep in north-western Brittany where the maritime way of Breton life still prevails.

sea species, an oceanographic museum, and an exotic sub-tropical garden created on a huge granite rock outcrop. Town facilities include 18 hotels, a dozen restaurants, a choice of *crêperies* and café-bars and three campgrounds in the near vicinity. Cycle hire is available from the SNCF station, tel: 98- 69-70-20. Other information can be obtained from the Maison du Tourisme, rue Gambetta, tel: 98-61-12-13. Market days in Roscoff are on Wednesdays.

Inland of this "Coast of Legend" as it is known, the low plateaux are sparsely populated. They are no longer densely wooded as they once were, but consist of extensive farm fields of vegetable and root crops, especially artichokes, which thrive hereabouts. Narrow lanes, hedged and banked, lead to occasional villages and farming hamlets. It is pleasant if undramatic terrain, inclined to appear bleak under grey skies, and there are many granite crosses, old manor ruins and numerous chapel and church steeples, unmistakably Breton of outline. One can see why the coast is the major magnet, although there are one or two objectives inland that are worth pursuing.

The evocative ruins of the **Château de Kergornadeach** is one such spot worth visiting. This castle was the last genuine fortress to be built in France (1620–30). It is not easy to find although it is quite well signposted, and lies some 14 km (8½ miles) south-west of Saint-Pol-de-Léon in a secretive and surprisingly lush valley setting. While not open to visitors ,a good close up-view may be had from the lane beside this imposing skeletal sentinel of the past.

Much more visited and far more famous, is **Château de Kerjean**, a few kilometres south, off the D12 road. Built in 1550 by a merchant adventurer, even Louis XIII acknowledged it as "one of the handsomest homes in the Kingdom". Part ruin, part skilfully preserved and restored, the huge state-owned property is at the heart of a majestic 800-hectare (2,000-acre) park

Château de Kergornadeach. Atmospheric ruins of the last purpose-built fortress to be constructed in France (1620) not far from Saint-Pol-de-Léon. The tower machicolations though are just decorative.

rich in Renaissance relics. It is architecturally rich too, protected by both outer and inner ramparts and a moat, the interior being no less impressive for its display of paintings and artefacts of the 17th and 18th centuries. Open daily, the guided tour around this fine monument to the past takes about an hour. In high summer evening festivals are laid on, enabling the visitor to travel back in time some five centuries in the space of an hour or so in the company of actors in medieval garb. This participation in a vivid kaleidoscope of old Finistère, makes a fitting finale to the exploration of far western Brittany.

For the Energetic or Easy-Going, Activity Choice is Wide in Tourist-Conscious Brittany

Mountains apart, Brittany offers the most invigorating climate in France for the sporting enthusiast. While sun-seekers can create windless conditions on the beaches, the near-constant sea-breeze is a blessing to all engaged in enjoying the peninsula through physical pursuits. Walkers, cyclists, small-boat sailors and hang-glider pilots all appreciate the zephyrs which make Brittany summers comfortable. Here you can jog with vigour or amble at your ease with little fear of dehydration from the benign Breton sunshine.

Sport

For the outdoor enthusiast Brittany is not the grandest, nor the most spectacular of French landscapes. For colour and scenic excitement one must concede that the Alps bordering the Mediterranean, the Pyrenees or sun-drenched Provençe come top of the list. What the peninsula *can* offer, however, is a rugged coastline that occasionally verges on the majestic,

*T*he Loire-Atlantique coast—especially the vicinity of La Baule—is a top favourite with wind-surfing enthusiasts.

which is washed by relatively unpolluted waters and which is studded by many fine sand beaches.

Watersport

For sea bathing *au naturel*, during late July or August at least, the region takes some beating. For wet-suit watersport, whether wrestling with a sailboard or paddling a kayak on the rivers, canals, estuaries or sheltered bays like Morbihan, Brittany is distinctly attractive—particularly for cruising canoeists as opposed to white-water addicts. Those prepared to portage around some 75 locks for example, can cruise the 285 km (177 miles) from Saint-Malo to Nantes (via Rennes and Redon), crossing the peninsula at one of its widest points and making a very interesting link between two seas, the route revealing a stimulating wealth of pastoral Brittany. For long one of mainland Europe's favoured small-boat cruising grounds—despite the tricky tides around Ushant—there is also scenic if less hair-raising sailing, not only within Morbihan gulf, but also around Auray, Saint-Malo, Paimpol and in the Bay of Douarnenez, off the Crozon peninsula in far western Finistère.

Canoe-touring is almost as popular as it is in the Dordogne, for the kayak and canoe (particularly those containing all the gear to allow self-contained independence) provide one of the best methods of seeing the variety of river valleys and canal country from a car-free environment. As one of the best sea-encircled regions in western Europe, Brittany can also offer every facility to the orthodox yachtsman, since there is a great variety of tides and coastline configurations. Beginners or expert sailing buffs will find clubs and equipment for sale or hire in all the recognized coastal resorts, especially those that have earned the accolade of "sailing towns", such as Crozon-Morgat, Perros-Guirec and Pléneuf-Val-André.

Inland, there are hundreds of kilometres of navigable routes, able to accept all craft with a draught of less than 1.2 m (4 ft). The river and canal network throughout the region is furnished with purpose-built leisure harbours, moorings, information centres, water pick-up points, toilets and even, occasionally, overnight accommodation ashore. There are many regional companies offering a complete range of craft for hire, from single-seater

*E*xperienced orthodox yachting fans rate Brittany waters as the best cruising grounds in western Europe.

kayaks to fully-furnished family cruisers. For further information and lists of yachting schools, contact Comité Régional de Tourisme, 3, rue d'Espagne, BP4175, 35041 Rennes, tel: 99-50-11-15. For details about water-skiing or power-boating, write to Ligue de Bretagne de Ski Nautique, BP99, 49303 Cholet, Maine-et-Loire.

The majority of coastal resorts have small-craft launching and beaching ramps for visitors who may be towing their own vessels, while minority sports like sand-yachting and scuba diving, may be followed in a number of places throughout Brittany. Sub-aqua diving is also becoming steadily more popular in several peninsula locations. Where the Breton continental shelf exists, for example, there is a wealth of fish and plant life beneath some crystal-clear waters, plus several underwater archeological sites. While not as warm as the Mediterranean (and rather more boisterous owing to tides and currents), the Breton waters offer an invigorating challenge to undersea explorers. For prospects and locations, write to Comité de la Federation Française d'Etude des Sports Sousmarin, 78, rue Ferdinand-Buisson, 44600, Saint-Nazaire.

Lastly, for those who fancy pottering along the most famous of all the Breton canals, the Nantes–Brest navigation, together with long reaches of the Aulne and Blavet rivers, there are some 20 waterside enterprises where day-boats, family cruisers or even luxury barges may be hired. The boating season extends from early spring to late autumn and there are reduced off-season rates. For all details about canal or river cruising, contact the Comité des Canaux Bretons, ABRI, 3, rue des Portes-Mordelaises, 35000 Rennes, tel: 99-31-59-44.

For information about sailing tuition and/or regional club locations in Finistère, write to Ligue Bretagne, 2 cours de la Bôve, Lorient 56100. For information on Morbihan, write to Ligue Bretagne, 26 rue Jeanne-d'Arc, 56000 Vannes. For information on both Ille-et-Vilaine and Côtes-du-Nord, write to 1, rue des Fours-à-Chaux, 35260 Cancale. For details

about inland waterway canoeing, write to Des Canaux Bretons, Navigables de l'Ouest, 3, rue des Portes-Mordelaises, 35000 Rennes. This is also a source of information about river and canal cruising with hire craft, where you may roam along some 600 km (370 miles) of navigable water (tel: 99-79-36-26).

Rambling and Hiking

Leisure walking is the most popular visitor pursuit in Brittany, especially

T op of the popularity lists for visitors who prefer terra-firma is rambling. There are many fine coastal paths, like this one at Ploumanac'h on the Granite Rose coast.

day-walking and backpacking. The region is networked by long-distance trails and a wealth of circuit rambles of short to medium duration, some of which have been touched upon in the main text of the guide. In general, the visitor may expect to find well-used and signposted pedestrian paths in the vicinity of almost every natural beauty spot or location of significant tourist interest. Hiking and rambling certainly enjoys advantages in France since the land mass is relatively dry, and even in parts of Brittany the climate can be semi-Mediterranean.

Heavy walking boots and thick socks will not be necessary here in summer. Trainers are now almost standard footwear for leisure walkers, preferably those designed to give ankle support. These are perfectly adequate for short or medium-distance forays and even for long-distance trekking provided your rucksack is only light. Heavier footwear may be needed, however, to offset the carried weight of camping gear. Similarly, light clothing will generally suffice, since heat and dehydration (rather than cold and wet weather), are the prime hazards in high-summer France—even as far north as Brittany. Shorts and vests are seen far more along footpaths and trails nowadays than anoraks and over-trousers. Carry a wool pullover though, and waterproofs. You should also consider a wide-brimmed floppy hat, either in linen or cotton, to act as a shield against a Brittany sun that can shine surprisingly fiercely at times. Remember too, that distances between watering holes can be appreciable. On long distance trails, road walking can be tiring over unshaded terrain, so be reasonable when setting personal distance targets, and for any pedestrian venture more ambitious than a local stroll, you must take a large-scale map and compass. For details about major hiking trails, contact the Fédération Française de la Randonnée Pédestre, 8, Avenue Marceau, 75008 Paris. The principal Brittany trails are the GR3, 34, 37, 38, 39, 341, 347 and 380. There are approximately 4,500 km (3,000 miles) of way-marked routes in Brittany, most of which are covered specifically by the excellent French language Topo-guide handbooks. The address for these guides is Les Topo-guides, 45, rue de Provençe, 75009 Paris. For *gîte* accommodation lists for walkers, contact ABRI, 3, rue des Portes-Mordelaises, 35000 Rennes, or to 33, rue Felix-le-Dantec, 29200 Brest.

Angling

In France, fishing is the main participant sport of the indigenous population, and along almost every reach of the major Brittany rivers and accessible coastal sections, you will see fishing rods almost as thick as the surrounding reeds. It is worth packing your own rod and tackle, for there are many quieter, less-fished waters to be enjoyed. Take the longest rod you can for the wide-water French rivers, plus a selection of floats to cope with widely differing depths and current flow. Float fishing is the favourite method in France, ledgering and spinning less popular.

In hill country, like that around Huelgoat in the Armorica nature park, the fly fisher can enjoy some fast flowing white-water streams, a fruitful source of the trout and, seasonally, the salmon. Because angling is so popular, you will find tackle and bait shops in nearly every town, while many tourist offices dispense free or very reasonable angling maps. These maps show graded waters from first category trout streams, to second category canals, lakes and barrage reservoirs. The open season for trout in Brittany is from March to mid-September. Coarse fishing competitions are now widespread and popular events, being held on most of the recognized angling waters. The migratory salmon returns to some 37 named rivers on the great peninsula, many of which also carry sea trout. Beach-casting along less-frequented coasts, notably those of Finistère, or the offshore islands, may also result in success for the bass hunter.

In total, there are over 10,000 km (6,000 miles) of fishing waters in Brittany, much of which are healthily stocked with a full variety of aquatic life, from eels to edible crabs through game fish, to carp and pike, some of which reach gigantic proportions. Sea-fishing, especially for flat fish, is good, as one might expect from a region extending to one-third of the entire French coastline.

For detailed information on regional angling prospects, contact the appropriate office of the Fédérations Départementales des Associations de Pêche—the addresses and telephone numbers of these are available from local tourist offices in the respective *départements*. The tourist office themselves are often entitled to issue the necessary visitor permits, and camping site owners are often well informed about angling potential in the locality—especially those at sites located along the banks of lakes and rivers. Many campsites are also authorized to issue day-fishing tickets, advise on the hireing of rowing boats, and provide bait sources. Waterside hotels will offer the same services, where resident guests may also have access to private water.

Equestrian Sport

There are now some 4,000 km (2,500 miles) of bridle-ways in Brittany, and horse-riding centres are found within accessible distance of all the major towns and, of course, in recognized pastoral areas of scenic beauty. The tourist office, once again, will give out local information on the kind of riding you may prefer. Some stables specialize in tuition for the whole family (where hunters and half-pint ponies are kept communally), while others concentrate upon hourly or half-day excursions. Yet more are involved with the fast-growing pursuit of long-distance horseback trekking (*randonnée equestre*).

Some stables cater for experienced riders only, some for novices, and other for both. The *randonnées* are organized from centres which tour scenically stimulating countryside, notably within the Armorica park, around Lake Guerlédan, within the forest of Paimpont, and along many of the more exciting coastal stretches. There are all-inclusive guided treks with meals and *gîte* accommodation which may extend to five, six or seven days (or even longer) of horseback exploration, for parties of up to about ten people. The popularity of this sport increases annually and it is unquestionably one of the nicest and most therapeutic methods of leisurely exploration. There are at least 15 centres within each Brittany *département*, and often more. For regional information, write to Ligue Equestre de Bretagne, 16, rue Georges Collier, 56100 Lorient, tel: 97-21-28-58. Or, write to Comité Régional de Tourisme de Bretagne, 3, rue d'Espagne, BP 4175, 35041 Rennes, tel: 99-50-11-15.

On a similar theme, the traditional gypsy horse-drawn waggon is also enjoying a renaissance in suitable areas of the region. There are now a number of stables which specialize in this delightfully slow-paced pursuit where visitors spend their holiday in company and with a gentle-giant draught horse. The routes are always carefully selected along back lanes and farm tracks, often routed through attractive and unspoiled countryside. Further details are available from Comité Départemental du Tourisme Finistère, 6, rue René-Madec, 29000 Quimper.

Other Sports and Pastimes

If you either enjoy or wish to try the exciting sport of hang-gliding, there are one or two recognized places in Brittany where you can leap off selected heights to enjoy eagle-eye views of the landscape. One favoured take-off site is the summit of Menez-Hom in the Armorica nature park. There are several others, and while the sister sport of para-scending is gaining adherents at some of the major seaside resorts, archery (*tir à l'arc*), is another nationwide enthusiast sport. Almost every sizeable town now boasts an archery club, and many of them are only too willing to welcome visitors. The local tourist office or *Syndicat*

Just Looking

In addition to participant activities, there are many spectator sports which may be followed, from traditional Breton wrestling matches, to motor-cycle scrambles which are keenly followed at summer weekend meetings. There is an extensive summer programme of sailing, canoeing and rowing, held on every kind of water. Rivers, canals, coastal and estuary waters are all much appreciated by an increasingly sports-oriented population, while copious use is made of the great Brittany bays like Morbihan and Douarnenez, where all kinds of competitive watersports are pursued vigorously. At the other end of the scale, you can watch the gentle art of *boules* at just about every village and town throughout the peninsula region.

---

d'Initiative will give details about locations and equipment hire.

In Brittany, as elsewhere in the Republic, visitors and locals alike seem to be inspired to follow at least one active pastime, and there is no shortage of first-class facilities for keen novices who may wish to try their hand at a new pursuit. Olympic-standard heated swimming pools are ubiquitous nowadays in France, as are tennis hard-courts. In fact, every preference is catered for, from rock-scrambling to squash, golf to ten-pin bowling, and windsurfing to pot-holing.

Of late, there has been a significant increase of French interest in the game of golf, and Brittany, like most regions of the Republic, is building or planning more courses for the immediate future. In truth, this has been almost the *only* major participant sport that has so far not enjoyed nationwide promotion over the past few decades. There are, as regular visitors know, high-standard

A hang-gliding club making the most of the thermals on the summit of Menez-Hom; Brittany's most celebrated high spot.

heated swimming pools, superb tennis courts (both indoors and out), and field-sport complexes within easy distance of all French cities and towns. The Brittany peninsula is no exception to this national programme of healthy pursuits, and golf especially is growing in popularity all the time.

Whether watching or participating, there are now 21 golf courses open to visitors in Brittany which are mostly located along the coast. In the Côtes-d'Armor there are courses at Saint-Quay-Portieux (18-hole); Pléhédel (18-hole); Pleumeur-Bodou (18-hole); Sables-d'Or-Fréhel (9-hole); and Saint-Cast-le-Guildo (9-hole). In Finistére courses are at: Clohars-Fouesnant (9- and 18-hole); La Forêt Fouesnant (9-hole); Landernau (18-hole); and Crozon (9-hole). Ille-et-Vilaine courses are at: Dinard Saint-Briac (18-hole); Dol-de-Bretagne (18-hole); Rennes, le Rheu (18-hole); Rennes, Saint-Jacques (9- and 18-hole); and Saint-Malo, Le Tronchet (9- and 18-hole). In the *département* of Morbihan, courses are at: Ploërmel (9- and 18-hole); Belle-Ile-en-Mer (18-hole); Saint-Gildas-du-Rhuys (18-hole); and Baden (18-hole). Finally, in Loire-Atlantique courses are at: Missillac (18-hole); La Baule (18-hole) and Nantes (18-hole).

Brittany for Children

In a land where children share more leisure hours with adults, much emphasis is placed on high-standard family holidays. *Gîtes d'Enfants* operate nationwide within 30 or more *départements*, a fair sprinkling of which exist in Brittany. Groups of a dozen or so youngsters, aged from 5 to 13 can enjoy genuine farm life, all part of the holiday programme shared with farming hosts. The blend of fun activities and caring for farm animals is proving increasingly popular. Just one choice of many, no child should find one of these Brittany breaks boring.

Most smaller children seem to need only sea, sand and sunshine on holiday to keep them totally happy. In Brittany all three are there in abundance (especially the southern coasts for the latter), and even inland there is no shortage of freshwater rivers and barrage lakes where agreeable man-made *plages* may be found. Guerlédan lake is one extensive example, and while its beaches may often be narrow and quite tiny, they will keep countless children contented for much of the day. As for the orthodox seaside beaches, nowhere in the Republic provides cleaner or brighter, golden strands. Admittedly the sun does not shine with quite the same strength as the southern French variety, nor is the ambient water temperature quite so high, however, in July or August, you will not hear complaints on either count from healthy children frolicking in fresh Atlantic waters. One word of caution: all the Brittany water, salt or fresh, can present hazards to the unwary, for example, where the current is fast-flowing—and not always obviously so—or where the depths are deceptive. Release tots only at designated bathing places, preferably where there is official supervision. At most *plages* it is also possible to hire inflatable boats or pedalo craft for use within specifically marked areas. For older children, Brittany offers a goodly variety of the natural world. There are some fine aquariums at Brest, Dinard, Saint-Malo,

Vannes and Roscoff, plus some 60 museums within the regional boundaries, each with its own particular interest, many of which are both entertaining and educational. There are a number of wildlife parks and natural wildlife habitats, like Branféré zoo park near La Roche-Bernard, the Morbihan gulf bird-sanctuary south of Vannes, and the Réserve Ornithologique, which is west of Douarnenez in Finistère.

Visits to some of the more dramatic clusters of Stone Age monuments will usually find favour with younger visitors, particularly those like the spectacular standing stone *alignements* of Carnac, or at Lagatjar just west of Camaret-sur-Mer. They will also be fascinated by the Parc de Préhistoire at Malansac, close to Rochefort-en-Terre. This is a theme park designed to stimulate any receptive young mind, and which will perhaps awaken a lasting interest in the ancient past. Here there are cleverly constructed scenes of Stone Age daily life, where Neanderthal hunters and replica animals, long extinct, pose in tableaux of frozen action.

There is no doubt though, that the top choice of the young is the sea-lapped sandy beach. Within a 1,000 km (600-mile) coastline, there is almost an embarrassing number of silver and golden strands between the resorts of Dinard in the extreme north-east and Saint-Brevin-les-Pins in the south-western regional corner. Added attractions in between, like La Baule and Perros-Guirec, confirm that much of Brittany's coast has been developed almost expressly for the enjoyment of the family, the emphasis being on children's and young person's delights.

Wildlife and Nature

Walking holidays combined with wildlife study have increasing appeal for escapees from urban pressures. Parts of Brittany are tailor-made for this satisfying leisure pursuit. Why not circumnavigate the great lake of Guerlédan on foot, catching glimpses of wild creatures during the day and stopping overnight at waterside *gîtes?* You can follow the same theme in many other contrasting areas, from the nature parks of Armorica or Brière, to the surprisingly spacious Paimpont weald.

For many people, however, the seashore has now been replaced by the hinterland for holidaymaking. The seaboards of western Europe today are often synonymous with concrete, cars and overcrowding—even those of Brittany in parts. As the coasts become more and more crowded, nature-lovers inevitably look inland for their leisure targets. There are still many unspoiled, and indeed almost untrodden, pockets of the Brittany countryside where wild boar, deer and otter thrive, well away from mainstream bustle. Brittany, both inland and along the quieter coasts, is still a haven for many species of European animals and birds. These may be glimpsed in passing, or studied with deliberation, by those who can tread softly and observantly along sea cliffs, river banks or forest trails.

Primarily sub-alpine, with deciduous woodland and tundra prevalent, there are a few areas of coniferous forest

T he Brière nature park, where quiet progress with one of the local chalan *flat-bottomed boats may reveal a wealth of wildlife.*

and also a narrow zone of semi-Mediterranean vegetation in the area of the Loire estuary. Most of the common mammals distributed throughout western Europe can be seen in Brittany. The red fox, weasel, little vole, hedgehog, pygmy shrew, rabbit, brown hare and pipistrelle bat are typical examples. Common also—though quite rare in southern England just across the Channel—is the red squirrel, while the American grey, is virtually non-existent in France.

Considerably rarer on the peninsula is the European beaver, which still exists happily in isolated pockets of *marais*, notably in far-western Brittany. Almost anywhere that is excessively marshy may harbour families of the resilient coypu, introduced from South America. A North American cousin of the coypu (imported originally for the fur trade) is the muskrat, which has established itself quite successfully, again in marshy terrain.

The European polecat is resident in Brittany as is the larger and marginally more handsome beech-marten, which favours deciduous woodland as a habitat, or the rock-studded hillsides of scrubby tundra which abound in certain areas. Some of the best wildlife study spots where you may catch sight of larger mammals, deer or wild boar, are the forest of Quénécan, the borders of Guerlédan lake, the forest of Paimpont, the more secluded wooded swathes of country to the north and east of Fougères, near the Normandy border, or in the wooded hills of the Armorica nature park. Additionally, the Grande Brière nature park near Saint-Nazaire, or the Lac de Grand-Lieu to the south of Nantes, could well

reward the patient watcher with sightings of coypu or muskrat, while the waters off Pointe du Raz or the Crozon peninsula are recognized preserves of grey seal colonies.

Almost anywhere in pastoral Brittany is home to smaller mammals like the voracious shrew species, which are in turn the prey of larger carnivores like the weasel, stoat and western polecat, all of which are widespread. Less obvious, though on the increase, are the delightful otter, the badger and—much more rarely—the red deer. Roe deer by comparison, are common and this, the smallest of Europe's species, may be spotted anywhere in the vicinity of adequate woodland cover.

Forced by circumstances, and the inexorable shrinkage of habitat, most mammals have become almost exclusively nocturnal, so that the chances of wildlife study for the visitor are limited. To observe any species, good local knowledge is essential. You need to find evidence of occupation (usually in an isolated location), and then make regular and frequent dawn or dusk forays in the hope of success. The prize is immense, but the pursuit requires infinite patience, and a degree of expertise. Impromptu sightings of wildlife are probably the best the transient traveller can expect. Fortunately, in Brittany, the chances of lucky glimpses of wild creatures going about their business are good. Throughout the region the farms, in general, are fairly small, the fields often hedged or fringed with woodland, and the land not worked to exhaustion. Fields and paddocks are frequently allowed to rest as meadows for years rather than months, and the result is undisturbed habitat for grazers and nibblers like hares, rabbits, voles and wood mice, which in turn attract the larger hunters. Copiously blessed with water margins, the region attracts and holds many water-loving creatures from grey seals to grass snakes, while all the river valleys and estuaries are rich with shoreline life.

Bird life is prolific around the coast, while inland you will often see common buzzards, sparrowhawks, or common kestrels in areas where there is light pressure of man upon the landscape coupled with abundant food—a congenial combination which still occurs over much of central Brittany. In addition to resident birds of prey (together with summer migrants like the goshawk, harrier and hobby), you will also see the common smaller species of birds, as well as the rarer golden oriole and red-backed shrike. Several species of woodpecker thrive in the woodlands as residents, while the shy cousin, the wryneck, visits in summer. Night hunters, like the tawny, barn and little owl, are quite common and well distributed, most often heard by those who are also camping enthusiasts. Pheasant and partridge are common game-birds in Brittany, both species given to exploding with a raucous clatter at times from beneath the feet of the country walker.

Every stretch of water supports a healthy population of moorhens, coots and water rails in addition to the ubiquitous grey heron, while the rare wading bittern—although not often seen— can be identified by its distinctive booming call which rises above reed beds at dusk or long after dark. This secretive bird likes the wetlands of eastern Brittany. The great crested grebe, little grebe, teal, tufted duck, shoveler, common shelduck and mallard on the other hand are widespread and resident, as are the snipe, woodcock and curlew. All these species are best sought where the waters of rivers have been barraged and then left more or less undisturbed. The many estuaries and coastal marshes are also much-favoured haunts. Along the faster-flowing upper river reaches, the flashing kingfisher is frequently seen and just occasionally, in high summer, that most handsome and colourful of migrants, the hoopoe, with its unmistakable call and exotic, retractable head crest.

Brittany's wetlands are rich with reedbed insects and, as a result, all the familiar reptile species are present. These include the common frog, common toad, natterjack toad and common newt. You may also see lizard species in the south of the region that are more usually associated with hotter parts of France, for example, the common lizard, and sand lizard while the snake-like slow-worm inhabits woodland areas where there is plenty of water. The non-poisonous grass snake likes water too, and enjoys swimming in areas where there is a large frog population. The smooth snake looks rather like an adder, but is also harmless. There *are* two poisonous native snakes, the common adder and the rarer asp-viper. The former may be found almost anywhere in Brittany, while the latter is spotted very occasionally in the extreme southeast, on drier, stonier uplands. The bite of either is painful, though rarely fatal. Any budding naturalist deliberately seeking snake habitats, should carry a snake-bite antidote kit, just in case.

If you want to take nature study seriously, choose dun-coloured clothing, and even a camouflage jacket and bush hat—if the hat has a veil attached this will tone down the potentially alarming flash of the face, and will also keep midges and mosquitoes at bay during any long vigil. Carry a pair of standard naturalist binoculars (approximately 8 x 30 magnification), and perhaps a stout walking-stick, which can be used as a steadying unipod when photographing, to help you negotiate rough ground, and to ward off strange dogs. Don't wear strong aftershave or perfume, and make sure you are down wind, that is the wind is towards you, when approaching any wild creature habitat.

Learn as much as you can about your preferred species before going into the field. What are their favoured habitats? What tell-tale signs are they likely to leave? At what hour and season of the year are they likely to be most active? Dawn and dusk are the feeding times of most wild creatures. Dawn is likely to be best for the watcher, since this is the time of least human activity, although dusk is good of course, if badgers or owls are your quarry.

Bird-watchers should be armed with a good, pocket-sized identification guide, preferably with coloured illustrations of the species to be found in Europe. The butterfly population of Brittany is interesting, particularly in the south-east of the region where many species will be seen from late spring to early autumn. The swallowtail, Camberwell beauty, red admiral and peacock are just a few of the more sizeable and dramatically marked, which can be seen basking where there are banks of wild flowers and plants such as fennel, clover, nettles or thistles, along forest margins and at sheltered higher altitudes.

The trees, shrubs and plants of Brittany, which provide the natural cover and food-source for all this wildlife are really quite variegated. There is a wealth of wild flowers and tree species ranging from the deciduous hornbeam, walnut, sweet chestnut and beech, to the poplar, the plane, the pyramidal cypress, the feathery silver birch, plus conifers of every kind and the majestic oak.

Château Choice

For those who might care to try a super-luxury holiday in traditional yet homely surroundings, there are a number of châteaux in Brittany, as there are throughout France, which offer the best of country life together with the best of cuisine. Below is a regional short-list.

Loire-Atlantique

Château de la Jaillière, La Chapelle Saint-Saveur, 44370 Varades tel: 40-98-62-54. Comtesse d'Anthenaise. A stately home owned by a family with a history dating back to the 10th century. Open May to October, four rooms available, swimming and tennis, Loire valley setting, English spoken.

Côtes d'Armor

Manoir de Kergrec'h, 22820 Plougrescant, tel: 96-92-56-06. Vicomte et

Vicomtesse Stéphane de Foquefeuil. A 17th-century manor house located on the foreshore. There are nice walks in spacious grounds, open all year, three double rooms, one four-person suite available, 15 km (9 miles) from Paimpol.

Manoir de Kerguereon, Ploubezre, 22300 Lannion, tel: 96-38-91-46. Monsieur et Madame G. de Bellefon. An authentic 15th-century manor, 8 km (5 miles) from the coast. Two rooms, open Easter to November, English spoken.

Château de Kermezen, Pommerit-Jaudy, 22450 La Roche-Derrien, tel: 96-91-35-75. Comte et Comtesse de Kermel. Typical 17th-century Breton château which has been owned by the same family for 500 years. Four rooms, one apartment (four persons), located in a quiet valley 7 km (4½ miles) from Perros-Guirec, open all year, English spoken.

Ille-et-Vilaine

Château de Léauville, Landujan, 35360 Montauban-de-Bretagne, tel: 99-61-10-10. Marie-Pierre et Patrick Gicquiaux. A charming old manor, fully restored, near Combourg. Good leisure facilities on property including heated swimming pool, six rooms (for two or four persons), open throughout the year, English spoken.

Château de la Motte-Beaumanoir, 35720 Pleugueneuc, tel: 99-69-46-01. Monsieur et Madame Charles Bernard. A private medieval castle in 25 hectares (60 acres) of attractive woodland near Dinan. Open throughout the year, five rooms, two suites and one apartment for four persons, English spoken.

Finistère

Château de Kerminaouët, 29128 Trégunc, tel: 98-97-62-20. Comte et-Comtesse Geoffroy de Calan. A stately home surrounded by 30 hectares (70 acres) of private parkland, close to Pont-Aven. Open Easter to November, 14 double rooms, two apartments, English spoken.

Language Guide

The list on the following pages contains enough words and phrases to cover most practical travel eventualities. Such a brief lexicon can only contain absolute essentials, especially in view of the language which is one of the richest in the world. The following can claim to be nothing more than a building block of the most rudimentary kind. There is no illustration of grammar, nothing about the all-important masculine and feminine genders, nothing about sentence construction and there is no attempt to accompany the words with phonetic spelling. In short, this is a language guide to stimulate further learning through specialized books, tapes and television programmes—preferably all three—then by practising in the best way possible, within the country of origin!

Words that are closely akin to English are omitted, such as *porc* (pork), together with routine courtesy words and phrases like "thank you" and "good day". Lastly, simplicity plus the brevity of the real world is acknowledged, thus "*plein*" is given for a tankful of petrol, and not a wordy if more grammatical alternative.

On The Road

left	**à gauche**
right	**à droite**
straight on	**tout droit**
bends	**virages**
remember (*speed limit reminder*)	**rappel**
slow down	**ralentir**
slow	**lent**
one-way street	**sens unique** or **voie unique**
forbidden	**interdit**
speed	**vitesse**
pedestrians	**piétons**
toll	**péage**
cul de sac	**voie sans issue**
roadworks	**travaux**
poor surface	**chaussée deformée**
give way (*to traffic from right*)	**priorite à droite**
truck route	**poids lourds**
lorry	**camion**
no parking	**interdit de stationner**
no through road	**route barrée**
repair	**reparation**
windscreen	**pare brise**
punctured	**crevé**
brakes	**les freins**
petrol (*low grade*)	**essence**
petrol (*high grade*)	**super**
full (*tank*)	**plein**
broken	**cassé**
breakdown (*of vehicle*)	**en panne**
slippery road surface	**glissante**
tyres	**pneus**
safe journey	**bonne route**
help	**assistance**
Help me! (*emergency*)	**au secours!**
headlights	**les phares**
traffic lights	**les feux**
pretty route (*usually signposted "Bis"*)	**bison futé**
low bridge	**hauter limitée**
Look out!	**Prendre garde!**
Hurry!	**Presse!**
give way (*at roundabout*)	**vous n'avon pas priorité**
Give way (*at junction*)	**cedez le passage**
starter motor	**demarreur**
gear box	**boit-de-vitesse**
spark plug	**bougie**
tow-rope	**corde**
jack	**cric**
injured	**blessé**
anti-freeze	**antigel**
seat belt (*or fan belt*)	**ceinture**
to boil	**bouiller**
driver	**pilote**
I'm lost!	**Je suis perdu!**
found	**trouvé**
screwdriver	**tournevis**
hammer	**marteau**
my car	**ma voiture**
mechanic	**mechanicien**

Food and Eating

breakfast	**petit déjeuner**
lunch	**déjeuner**
indoors	**dans la maison**
outdoors	**dehors**
dinner	**dîner**
to eat	**manger**
drink	**boisson**
drinking water	**eau potable**
meal	**repas**
food	**aliment**
meat	**viande**
bread	**pain**
bread roll	**petit pain**
cheese	**fromage**
ham	**jambon**
fish	**poisson**
cod	**cabillaud**
haddock	**aiglefin**
lamb	**agneau**
oysters	**huîtres**
lobster	**langouste**
head waiter	**maître d'hotel**
waiter	**garçon**
cake	**gâteau**
seafood	**fruits de mer**
grapefruit	**pamplemousse**
peach	**pêche**
veal	**veau**
sugar	**sucre**
vegetables	**légumes**
yoghurt	**yaourt**
all in price	**tout compris**
mushrooms	**champignons** or **cèpes**

jam	**confiture**
sweets	**bonbons**
clear soup	**consommé**
soup of the day	**potage de jour**
chicken	**poulet**
wholemeal bread	**pain complet**
sausage (already cooked)	**saucisson**
self service (restaurant)	**libre service**
apple tart	**tarte aux pommes**
cold meat selection (also plate)	**assiette**
cup	**tasse**
knife	**couteau**
fork	**fourchette**
spoon	**cuillère**
cook	**cuire**
Bill please	**L'addition s'il vous plaît**
raw mixed salad	**crudité**
milk	**lait**
fat	**graisse**
egg	**oeuf**
bottle	**bouteille**
water or wine bottle	**carafe**
turkey	**dinde**
rye bread	**pain de seigle**
melon	**canteloupe**
tuna-fish	**thon**
nuts	**noix**
water ice	**sorbet**
ice-cream	**glacé**
beer (from the pump)	**bière pression**
glass	**verre**
toasted cheese sandwich	**croque monsieur**

lemon squash	**citron pressé**	*playground*	**terrain de jeux**
lemonade	**limonade**	*stroll*	**promenade**
hunger	**faim**	*hiker*	**randonneur**
thirst	**soif**	*hunter*	**chasseur**
very good	**très bon**	*fisherman*	**pêcheur**
bad	**mauvais**	*traveller*	**voyageur**
vintage (wine)	**cru**	*vineyard*	**vignoble**
bun	**brioche**	*wild*	**sauvage**
garlic	**ail**	*footpath*	**sentier**
pineapple	**ananas**	*rucksack*	**sac à dos**
		sleeping bag	**sac de couchage**

Out of Doors

		return	**retour**
earth	**terre**	*starting point*	**point de départ**
sky	**ciel**	*suntan oil*	**huile solaire**
wind	**vent**	*on foot*	**à pied**
breeze	**brise**	*countryside*	**campagne**
good weather	**beau temps**	*country*	**pay**
bad weather	**mauvais temps**	*leisure*	**loisir**
rain	**pluis**	*tree*	**arbre**
fog	**brouillard**	*star*	**étoile**
changeable	**variable**	*dawn*	**aube**
cloudy	**nuageux**	*shelter*	**abri**
sun	**soleil**	*riverside*	**bord de la rivière**
hot	**chaud**	*spring*	**printemps**
cold	**froid**	*summer*	**été**
chill	**frisson**	*autumn*	**automne**
river	**fleuve**	*winter*	**hiver**
river bank	**rive**	*to bathe*	**baigner**
stream	**courant**	*no entry*	**défense d'entrer**
rivulet	**ruisseau**	*upstream*	**en amont**
fields	**champs**	*downstream*	**en aval**
hill	**colline** or **puy**	*bird*	**oiseau**
woods	**bois**	*rainbow*	**arc-en-ciel**
rock	**roche**	*thunderstorm*	**orage**
games	**jeux**	*thunder*	**tonnerre**

lawn grass	pelouse	second floor	deuxième étage
pond	étang	opposite	en face
forest	forêt	behind	derrière
dark	obscur	bed and breakfast	lit et petit dejeuner
deep	profond	full board	pension complète
study	étude	stairs	escalier
cliff	failaise	dormitory	dortoir
tired	fatigué	welcome (reception)	accueil
farm	ferme	reading room	salle de lecture
leaf	feuille	bell	cloche
search	fouille	to ring	sonner
cool	frais	rest	repos
frost	gel	rent	louer
stone	pierre	roadhouse	auberge
sunstroke	insolation	What is the nightly charge?	Quel est le prix pour la nuit?
flood	inondation		
savage dog	chien méchant	front	face
butterfly	papillon	rear	arrière
bull	taureau	to leave	quitter
marsh	marais	key	clé
snowstorm	tempête de neige	full	complet
		upstairs	en haut
		downstairs	en bas

Accommodation

bed	lit
room	chambre
with bath	avec bain
with shower	avec douche
dining room	salle à manger
twin beds	lits jumeaux
shade	ombrage
quiet	tranquil
clean	prop
home	maison
holiday camp	camp de vacances
first floor	premier étage

Shopping

shops	magasins
chemist	pharmacie
bakery	boulangerie
butcher	boucherie
food store	alimentation
grocery	épicerie
cooked meat shop	charcuterie
cake shop	pâtisserie
bank	banque
clothes	vêtements

jeweller	bijoutier		quick	vite
watch-maker (repairer)	horloger		now	actuel
shoe shop	magasin de chaussures		understand	comprendre
			friend	ami
shopping precinct	centre commercial		much	beaucoup
film	pelicule		little	petit
colour slide	diapositif		need	besoin
newspaper shop	magasin de la presse		well	bien
closing time	heure de fermeture		soon	bientôt
opening time	heure d'ouverture		free	gratuit
wine cellar	cave		ticket	billet
hairdresser	coiffeur		information	renseignements
furniture shop	meubles		each	chaque
fish shop	poissonnerie		to have	avoir
book shop	libraire		notice	avis
How much?	Combien?		before	avant
expensive	cher		other	autre
cheap	pas cher		workshop	atelier
presents (souvenirs)	cadeaux		repair	reparation
traveller's cheques	chèques de voyage		light	allume
cheque book	carnet de chèques		count	compter
cash till	caisse		phone book	annuaire
stamp (postage)	timbre		to discover	decouvrir
manufacturer	fabricant		to ask	demander
closed for holidays	fermeture annuelle		difficult	difficile
charge card	carte de credit		easy	simple
to buy	acheter		available	disponible
to sell	vendre		entertainment	divertissement
money	argent		give	donner
closing-down sale	liquidation totale		listen	écouter
			equal	égal

General

agreed	d'accord		delighted	enchanté
belongings	affaires		at last	en fin
round trip	aller-retour		strange	bizarre
			later	plus tard

at once	**immédiatement**	*pottery*	**faïence**
child	**enfant**	*trust*	**confiance**
wife	**epouse**	*fact*	**fait**
husband	**mari**	*happy*	**heureux**
today	**aujourd'hui**	*history*	**histoire**
yesterday	**hier**	*century*	**siècle**
tomorrow	**demain**	*timetable*	**horaire**
day	**jour**	*town hall*	**hôtel de ville**
week	**semaine**	*here*	**ici**
month	**mois**	*even*	**pair**
year	**année**	*odd*	**impair**
daily	**quotidien**	*hospital*	**hôpital**
weekly	**hebdomadaire**	*perfect*	**parfait**
monthly '	**mensuel**	*waterproof*	**imperméable**
yearly	**annuel**	*incredible*	**incroyable**
next year	**prochain année**	*interesting*	**intéressant**
this year	**cette année**	*head*	**tête**
half	**demi**	*hand*	**main**
approximately	**à peu près**	*foot*	**pied**
illness	**malade**	*never*	**jamais**

Information to Help You Have a Good Trip

La Baule

Tourist office and *Syndicat d'Initiative*
9, place de la Victoire
44500 La Baule
Tel: 40-24-34-44
Annexe in place des Palmiers La-Baule-les-Pins, Tel: 40-60-22-13.

SNCF train information:
Tel: 40-60-50-50 (Escoublac)

Camping and caravan parks:
La Roseraie
avenue Jean-Sohier
La Baule Escoublac
Tel: 40-60-46-66
Four-star park.

Camping Municipal
La Baule-les-Pins
Tel: 40-60-11-48
Three-star park.

Centre de Thalassothérapie (sea-bathing tonic and cure centre):
boulevard de l'Océan
Tel: 40-24-30-97
Open all year.

There are 40 clubs devoted to 36 sporting activities, most of which are open all year round, earning La Baule the title of La Grand Station Sportive d'Europe.

Emergency Services

Police: Tel: 40-24-23-22 (police secours)
Gendarmerie: avenue des Ondines, Tel: 40-24-48-17
Municipal ambulance service:
5, avenue Romano,
Tel: 40-60-24-34 or 40-61-01-92
Garage breakdown service (day and night): M. Dousset, Chemin de la Furguai, Tel: 40-24-28-18 (day), 40-24-36-07 (night)

Cancale

Tourist office
44, rue du Port
F35260 Cancale
Tel: 99-89-63-72
When closed information can be obtained from the town hall, rue du Port, Tel: 99-89-60-15.

Travel information: nearest SNCF station, St Méloir-des-Ondes, 5 km (3 miles).

Camping sites: *there are half a dozen camping and caravanning sites in the vicinity, two of the most popular (and closest to the sea) being the Municipal le Grouin (open April to September) and the Municipal Port-Pican (open briefly from July to the end of August).*

Cancale provides a wide and varied selection of bed-and-breakfast houses, together with furnished, self-catering apartments (70 of the former, over 30 of the latter). A full list of addresses and current pricings is available from the tourist office, or the Syndicat d'Initiative *at the mairie out of season.*

Emergency Services

Gendarmerie: avenue de Scissy,
Tel: 99-89-60-21
Medical emergency service:
SAMU, Tel: 99-59-16-16
Service station and repair garage:
route de Pontorson, La Croix Desille, Tel: 99-81-40-29

Carnac

Tourist office
BP 65
56340 Carnac, Morbihan
Tel: 97-52-13-52
Open all year at 74, avenue des Druides, Carnac-Plage, and during the summer only at place de l'Église, Carnac-Ville.

Travel information: SNCF nearest station is at Auray. Train information is available from Carnac tourist office or Auray station. Tel: 97-24-00-06

Camping and caravan sites:
La Grande Métairie
on route des Alignements de Kermario
Tel: 97-55-71-47
Four-star. Open 24 May to 13 September. Among a wealth of caravan and camping parks, this is the nearest to the Carnac megaliths.

Emergency Services

Gendarmerie: 40, rue Saint-Cornély, Tel: 97-52-06-24
Hospital (Auray) du Pratel:
Tel: 97-56-42-42

Dinard

Tourist Office
2 boulevard Féart
BP140
35802 Dinard
Tel: 99-46-94-12

Travel information: train service, Dinard–Paris via Saint-Malo, SNCF, Tel: 99-56-08-18
Frequent regular bus service to Saint-Malo, Dinan and Rennes.

Youth hostel:
Ker-Charles
8, boulevard l'Hôtelier
Tel: 99-46-10-32
Open April to October.
120 beds.

Touring sites:
Le Prieuré
avenue de la Vicomté
Tel: 99-46-20-04
Four-star, 200 m (220 yd) from
the beach and open from April
until September. There are three
others in the area.

Emergency Services
Police emergency: Tel: 17
Medical emergency:
Tel: 99-82-71-11
Repair garage (all makes):
Garage du Parc, Z.A. de
l'Hermitage, La Richardais
Tel: 99-46-13-38

Morlaix
Tourist Offices:
Syndicat d'Initiative and *Office du*
Tourisme
place des Otages
29203 Morlaix
Tel: 98-62-14-94

Travel information: SNCF, rue
Gambetta, Tel: 99-88-08-88. Paris
is just four hours away via TGV.

Youth hostel:
3, route de Paris
Tel: 98-88-13-63

Camping site:
Baie de Terenez
8 km, or 5 miles, north at Plouezoch, open Easter to September.

There are eight chambres d'hôtes
in Morlaix and 16 in the district,
plus a good selection of furnished
seasonal apartments—ask the
tourist office for the NID Vacances
listing.

Emergency Services
Gendarmerie: rue de Poulfanc,
Tel: 98-88-58-13
General hospital: rue Kersaint
Gilly, Tel: 98-62-61-60
Ambulance: Léon and Trégor, 40
rue des Brebis, Tel: 98-88-06-60
Repair garage: Bourven, route de
Paris, Tel: 98-88-18-02

Nantes
Tourist office
place du Commerce
44000 Nantes
Tel: 40-89-50-77

SNCF train information:
Tel: 40-08-50-50

Airport: Tel: 40-75-30-78

Youth hostel: Auberge de
Jeunesse, Tel: 40-74-61-86

Camping sites: Petit-Port
camping ground, Tel: 40-74-47-94

Emergency Services
Police: place Waldeck-Rousseau
Tel: 40-74-21-21
Hospital accident emergency
service: Tel: 40-48-35-35
Car breakdown service:
Tel: 40-74-68-39

Paimpol
Tourist office
Mairie de Paimpol
rue Pierre Feutren
Tel: 96-20-83-16
If not open go to the town hall.

Travel information: SNCF link
to Guingamp (main-line
Paris–Brest), Tel: 96-20-81-22

Youth hostel:
Parc de Kéraoul
Tel: 96-20-83-60
80 beds, canoeing centre, occupies
a small château.

Camping sites:
Municipal site
Camping de Crukin
Tel: 96-20-78-47
Adjacent to Beauport abbey.

Camping de Beauport
Tel: 96-22-09-87
Two-star.

Emergency Services
Gendarmerie: rue Pellier,
Tel: 96-20-80-17
Hospital (Centre Hospitalier):
Chemin de Malabry,,
Tel: 96-55-60-00
Repair garage: Reparation
Autos, Industrial Zone (Z.I.)
Tel: 96-20-83-94 or 96-20-98-39

Perros-Guirec
Tourist Office
21, place de l'Hôtel de Ville
Perros-Guirec
Tel: 96-23-21-15
Open all year. There is also an
information pavilion at Trestraou
plage, high season only.
Trégastel office: Tel: 96-23-88-67
Trébeurden office:
Tel: 96-23-51-64.

Travel information: nearest
railway station Lannion, 10 km
(6 miles) south. Local bus service
to Lannion, Trégastel and
Trébeurden. Reservations at
tourist office.

Camping sites:
Tréstraou Municipal
avenue du Casino
Tel: 96-23-08-11
Three-star. Open Easter to
September. There are three more
in the vicinity. There are also
some 2,000 furnished houses and
flats in Perros.

Emergency Services
Gendarmerie: rue des Frères le
Montréer, Tel: 96-23-20-17
Hospital (emergency): Lannion,
Tel: 96-05-71-11
Ambulance: Tel: 96-23-37-32

Pontivy
Tourist office
61 rue Général de Gaulle
56300 Pontivy
Tel: 97-25-04-10

When above is closed:
Syndicat d'Initiative
Mairie, place Aristide Briand
Tel: 97-25-00-33

Travel information: railway
station (Saint-Brieuc—Auray
line), SNCF Gare, rue d'Iéna
Tel: 97-25-00-20

Post Office: PTT, rue Friedland,
Tel: 97-25-05-96

Youth hostel (Auberge de
Jeunesse) and *gîte d'étape*:
Ile des Récollets
Tel: 97-25-58-27

Camping site:
Camping municipal du Douric
Tel: 97-27-92-20 (or 97-25-09-51)
Open April to September.

Emergency Services

Police emergency: Tel: 17
Gendarmerie: 2, rue du
Deuxième Chasseur,
Tel: 97-25-00-75
Pontivy hospital: Hôpital Hubert
Jégourel, place Ernest Jan,
Tel: 97-25-46-66
Ambulance: Ambulances Collet,
3, rue des Moulins
Tel: 97-25-54-45

Quiberon

Tourist office
7, rue de Verdun
56170 Quiberon
Tel: 97-50-07-84

Travel information: railway
station, SNCF, place de La Gare,
Tel: 97-50-07-07. The June to
September service runs direct to
Quiberon; other months there is
a coach connection between
Auray and Quiberon.

Youth hostel: 45, rue du Roch-
Priol, Tel: 97-50-15-54

Camping and caravan sites: *there
are eight sites, three of which are
three-star graded.*

Emergency Services

Gendarmerie: 147, rue du Port de
Pêche, Tel: 97-50-07-39 (for
emergency, dial 17)
Ambulance service: France
Ambulances, 10, rue de la Gare,
Tel: 97-50-10-52
Car repair garage (all makes):
Garage Bouju Sodap, avenue du
Général de Gaulle,
Tel: 97-50-07-42

Quimper

Tourist Office
Halles Saint-François
rue Admiral de la Grandière
Tel: 98-95-04-69

Travel information: SNCF
railway station, place de la Gare
(Lorient–Dournenez line),
Tel: 98-90-50-50

Airline information from the
tourist office (the airport is
6 km, or 4 miles, south-west at
Pluguffan).

Youth hostel: Auberge de
Jeunesse, 6, avenue des Oiseaux,
Tel: 98-55-41-67

Camping and caravan sites:
Municipal Site
avenue des Oiseaux
Two-star.

Castel Camping de l'Orangerie de
Lanniron
Tel: 98-90-62-02
*2 km (1 mile) south of the city
centre on route Bénodet; four-star.*

Emergency Services

Gendarmerie: 1, route de Pont-
l'Abbé, Tel: 98-55-09-24
Hospital centre: 14 bis, avenue
Yves-Thépot, Tel: 89-52-60-60

Le Val-André

Tourist Office
rue Winston Churchill
BP 125
22370 Pléneuf-Val-André
Tel: 96-72-20-55

Travel information: nearest
railway station, SNCF, Lamballe
(TGV to Paris in three hours;
approximately 14 km or 8½ miles
south).

Camping sites: Camping des
Monts Colleux, rue Jean-Lebrun,
Tel: 96-72-95-10
*Three-star. Bungalows for hire.
There are four alternative sites in
the vicinity.*

Emergency Services

Gendarmerie: rue de la Mer
Tel: 96-72-22-18
Ambulance service: Robert
Chantal, rue Pasteur (place de
l'Église), Tel: 96-72-25-04

Vannes

Tourist office
1, rue Thiers
56000 Vannes
Tel: 97-47-24-34

SNCF train information:
Tel: 97-42-50-50

Camping and caravan sites:
*There are 12 sites in the vicinity
of Vannes, the nearest being
Camping Conleau (municipal),
Tel: 97-63-13-88, open April to
September.*

Emergency Services

Police: 17, Gendarmerie
Tel: 97-54-22-56
Centre Hospital: Tel: 97-01-41-41
SAMU (hospital emergency):
Tel: 97-54-22-11
Car repair garage (one of
several), Ford, 41 rue du Vincin,
Tel: 97-63-10-35

Vitré

Tourist office and
Syndicat d'Initiative
place Saint-Yves
35500 Vitré
Tel: 99-75-04-46

SNCF train information:
Tel: 99-75-00-47

Post office: place de la
République

Camping sites:
Camping Municipal Saint-
Etienne
Tel: 99-75-25-28
Open all year.

La Guennelais
Tel: 99-75-11-16
Farm site.

Emergency Services

Police: rue des Bénédictins,
Tel: 99-74-65-00
Gendarmerie: place du Champ de
Foire, Tel: 99-02-30
Hospital centre: Route de
Rennes, Tel: 99-74-67-67

The Right Place at the Right Price

Hotels

Whichever town you visit in Brittany there will be a good range of hotels from which to choose, with several dozen in each of the larger towns and cities. The Ministry of Tourism classifies hotels from one- to four-star on the basis of their facilities, but below an indication of price per room has been given. French hotels normally charge per room which gives good value for couples. In the more expensive hotels most rooms will come with an adjoining bathroom.

The hotels have been classified by price as follows:

| | up to 350F;
|| 350–600F;
||| over 600F.

This is the cost per night for a room. Breakfast is usually charged extra. These price ranges should only be viewed as guides as hotels may have some rooms available that fall into the price band above or below the one in which they have been placed, and prices vary from season to season.

Ancenis

Hôtel le Val de Loire |
Tel: 40-96-00-03
40 rooms. Logis de France. Access for the disabled. With restaurant.

La Baule

Hôtel Alexandra ||
boulevard Dr R. Dubois
Tel: 40-60-30-06

Hôtel Les Almadies |
146, avenue de Lattre-de-Tassigny
Tel; 40-60-79-05

Hôtel Bellevue-Plage ||
Tel: 40-60-28-55
34 rooms. Sea views. With restaurant.

Hôtel Castel Marie-Louise |||
Tel: 40-60-20-20
29 rooms. Sea views. With restaurant. Relais Château.

Hôtel Clemenceau |
42, avenue G. Clemenceau
Tel: 40-60-21-33
16 rooms.

Hôtel le Coralli |
Tel: 40-60-29-82
8 rooms. With restaurant.

L'Espadon |||
Residence du Golfe
avenue de la Plage
Tel: 40-60-05-63
Panoramic penthouse setting.

Hôtel l'Hermitage |||
Esplanade François-André
PO Box 173
F-44504
Tel: 40-60-37-00
220 rooms. Sea views. With restaurant.

Hôtel Majestic |||
Tel: 40-60-24-86
72 rooms. Facilities for the disabled. No restaurant.

Hôtel la Palmeraie |
Tel: 40-60-24-41
23 rooms. Logis de France. With restaurant.

Hôtel Saint Bernard |
Tel: 40-60-32-02
7 rooms. Lacks a restaurant.

Hôtel Welcome |
Tel: 40-60-30-25
18 rooms. Sea views. Lacks a restaurant.

Brest

Hôtel les Ajoncs d'Or   I
1, rue Amiral Nicol
Tel: 98-45-12-42
*17 rooms. Access for the disabled.
Brittany Hôtel. Lacks a
restaurant.*

Abalys Hôtel   I
7, avenue Clemenceau
Tel: 98-44-21-86
*23 rooms. Sea views. Lacks a
restaurant.*

Hôtel Balladins   I
Plougastel Daoulas
Tel: 98-40-68-70
*42 rooms. Access for the disabled.
Lacks a restaurant.*

**Hôtel Belvedere
Best Western**   II
Sainte Anne du Portzic
Tel: 98-31-86-00
*30 rooms. Access for the disabled.
Sea views. With restaurant.*

France Hôtel   I
1, avenue Amiral Reveillere
Tel: 98-46-18-88
*40 rooms. Sea views. With
restaurant.*

Hôtel Oceania   IIII
82, rue de Siam
Tel: 98-80-66-66
82 rooms. With restaurant.

Cancale

Hôtel le Chatellier   I
Tel: 99-89-81-84
13 rooms. Lacks a restaurant.

Hôtel Continental   II
quai Thomas
Tel: 99-89-60-16
*19 rooms. Logis de France. With
restaurant.*

Hôtel Emeraude   I
quai Thomas
Tel: 99-89-61-76
16 rooms.

Hôtel la Houle   I
rue Gambetta
Tel: 99-89-62-38
12 rooms.

Hôtel la Pointe du Grouin   II
Tel: 99-89-60-55
*18 rooms. Sea views. Logis de
France. With restaurant.*

Carnac

Hôtel Armoric   I
avenue de la Poste
Tel: 97-52-13-47
25 rooms. With restaurant.

Hôtel le Bâteau Ivre   II
Tel: 97-52-19-55
*20 rooms. Sea views. Swimming
pool. With restaurant.*

Hôtel le Diana   III
21, boulevard de la Plage
Tel: 97-52-05-38
With restaurant.

Hôtel Hoty   I
15, avenue de Kermario
Tel: 97-52-11-12
With restaurant.

Novotel Tal-Ar-Mor   III
Tel: 97-52-16-66
*Close to sea-bathing centre. With
restaurant.*

Hôtel du Tumulus   II
Tel: 97-52-08-21
*28 rooms. Sea views. Swimming
pool. Logis de France.*

Concarneau

Hôtel la Crêpe d'Or   I
Tel: 98-97-08-61
27 rooms. With Restaurant.

Grand Hôtel   I
Tel: 98-97-00-28
*33 rooms. Lacks restaurant. Views
of the sea.*

Hôtel de l'Ocean   II
Tel: 98-50-53-50
*40 rooms. With restaurant. Views
of the sea. Swimming pool.*

Hotel des Sables Blancs   II
Tel: 98-97-01-39
*48 rooms. With restaurant. Views
of the sea.*

Hôtel Ty Chupen Gwenn   II
Tel: 98-97-01-43
*15 rooms. Lacks restaurant. Views
of the sea.*

Dinard

Les Alizé's   I
9, rue des Mimosas
Tel: 99-46-80-80
20 rooms.

Hôtel Améthyste   I
place du Calvaire
Tel: 99-46-61-81
15 rooms.

Hôtel Beauséjour   I
place du Calvaire
Tel: 99-46-13-61
10 rooms.

Le Crystal   II
rue de la Malouine
Tel: 99-46-66-71
30 rooms. Lacks a restaurant.

Le Grand Hôtel   III
46, avenue George Cinq
Tel: 99-46-10-28
93 rooms.

Reine Hortense   III
19, rue de la Malouine
Tel: 99-46-54-31
10 rooms.

Novotel   II
avenue Chateau Hébert
Tel: 99-82-78-10
*Thalassothérapie centre with 106
rooms. With restaurant.*

Hôtel des Sables   I
Tel: 99-46-18-10
Lacks a restaurant. 34 rooms.

Fougéres

Hôtel Mainotel (Beauce)   II
Tel: 99-99-81-55
*50 rooms. With restaurant.
Swimming pool.*

Hôtel Saint Christophe   I
Tel: 99-95-11-07
8 rooms. With restaurant.

Taverne Hôtel du Commerce   I
Tel: 99-94-40-40
25 rooms. With restaurant.

Hôtel les Voyageurs   I
Tel: 99-99-08-20
37 rooms. With restaurant.

Lorient

Hôtel Arcade   I
9, Cours de Chazelles
Tel: 97-21-20-20
50 rooms. With restaurant.

Arcantis Cleria Hôtel   I
27, blvd Franchet d'Esprey
Tel: 97-21-04-59
33 rooms. Lacks restaurant.

Hôtel D'Arvor   I
104, rue Lazare Carnot
Tel: 97-21-07-55
20 rooms. With restaurant.

Hôtel Mercure   II
31, place Jules Ferry
Tel: 97-21-35-73
58 rooms. Lacks restaurant.

Novotel Lorient Caudan   II
Tel: 97-76-02-16
88 rooms. With Restaurant and swimming pool.

Morlaix
Hôtel d'Europe   II
1, rue d'Aiguillon
Tel: 98-62-11-94
65 rooms.

Les Halles   I
23, rue du Mur
Tel: 98-88-03-86
14 rooms. Restaurant.

Hôtel Minimote   I
allée des Peupliers
Saint-Martin-des-Champs
Tel: 98-88-35-30
22 rooms. Lacks restaurant.

Hôtel du Port   I
Tel: 98-88-07-54
25 rooms. Lake/river/canal views. Lacks a restaurant.

Nantes
Hôtel Abbaye de Villeneuve   III
rte des Sables d'Olonne
Les Sorinières
F-44840
Tel: 40-04-40-25

Hôtel Amiral   I
26 bis, R. Scribe
Tel: 40-69-20-21

Hôtel de la Bourse   I
19, uai de la Fosse
Tel: 40-69-51-55

Hôtel de la Duchesse-Anne   II
3, place de la Duchesse Anne
Tel: 40-74-30-29

Hôtel de France   II
24, rue Crébillon
F-44000
Tel: 40-73-57-91

Hôtel Graslin   II
1, rue Piron
Tel: 40- 69-72-91

Hôtel le Longchamp   I
78, route de Vannes
Tel: 40-76-96-88

Sofitel Nantes   III
15, blvd Alexandre Millerand
F-44000
Tel: 40-47-61-03

Paimpol
Hôtel les Chalutiers   I
Tel: 96-20-82-15
21 rooms. Sea views. Lacks a restaurant.

Hôtel Duguay-Trouin   I
uay Duguay-Trouin
Tel: 96-20-80-76
Closed 29 September to 20 October. 16 rooms.

Hôtel de la Marne   I
rue de la Marne
Tel: 96-20-82-16
13 rooms. With restaurant.

Relais des Pins   III
RN 786, Pont de Lézardrieux
Tel: 96-20-11-05
Open all year, a semi-rural setting. 32 rooms.

Repaire de Kerroc'h   II
Tel: 96-20-50-13
Open all year. 25 rooms.

Perros-Guirec
Hôtel au Bon Accueil   I
Tel: 96-23-25-77
21 rooms. Sea views. With restaurant.

Grand Hôtel de Trestraou   II
boulevard Joseph-le-Bihan
Tel: 96-23-24-05
68 rooms. Sea views. With restaurant.

Le Gulf Stream   I
26, rue des Sept-Iles
Tel: 96-23-21-86
12 rooms. Sea views. With restaurant.

Hôtel de la Mairie   I
place de l'Hôtel de Ville
Tel: 96-23-22-41
22 rooms. Lacks a restaurant.

Hôtel le Sphinx   II
Tel: 96-23-25-42
17 rooms. Sea views. Access for the disabled. With restaurant.

Hôtel les Violettes   I
Tel: 96-23-21-33
17 rooms. Access for the disabled. With restaurant.

Pontivy
Hôtel de l'Europe   I
rue de la Mairie
Tel: 97-25-11-14
20 rooms. Access for the disabled. With restaurant.

Hôtel Robic   I
2 rue Jean Jaurès
Tel: 97-25-11-80

Le Rohan Wesseling   II
30, rue Nationale
Tel: 97-25-02-01
19 rooms. France-Accueil. Lacks a restaurant.

Quiberon
Hôtel Beau Rivage   II
11, rue de Port-Maria
Tel: 97-50-08-39

Hôtel la Caravelle   I
9, boulevard René-Cassin
Tel: 97-50-13-64
Sea views.

Hôtel de la Plage   II
Sr Pierre Quiberon
Tel: 97-30-92-10
49 rooms. Sea views. Access for the disabled. Logis de France. With restaurant.

Hôtel Ibis   II
avenue des Marroniers
Tel: 97-30-47-72
Heated swimming pool.

Hôtel de l'Ocean   I
Tel: 97-50-07-58
37 rooms. Sea views. Logis de France. With restaurant.

Hôtel Roch-Priol   I
rue des Sirènes
Tel: 97-50-04-86
Low-calorie menus for guests.

Sofitel Dieteique   III
Pointe de Goulvars
F-56170
Tel: 97-50-20-00

Quimper

Hôtel Arcades   ⫼
21, avenue de la Gare
Tel: 98-90-31-71
Opposite SNCF.

Hôtel le Griffon   ⫼⫼
131, route de Bénodet
Tel: 98-90-03-30

Manoir du Stang   ⫼⫼⫼
La Forêt-Fouesnant
F-29940
Tel: 98-56-97-37

Hôtel la Tour d'Auvergne   ⫼⫼
13, rue des Reguaires
Tel: 98-95-08-70

Rennes

Altea Hôtel   ⫼⫼
1, rue de Cap
Maignan
Tel: 99-29-73-73
140 rooms. With restaurant.

Hotel Lanjuinais   ⫼
11, rue Lanjuinais
Tel: 99-79-02-03
33 rooms. Lacks a restaurant.

Novotel Rennes Alma   ⫼⫼
avenue du Canada
Tel: 99-50-61-32
99 rooms. With restaurant.
Swimmig pool.

Le Val-André

Hôtel le Clemenceau   ⫼
131, rue Georges Clemenceau
Tel: 96-72-23-70
Open all year, 23 rooms. Lacks a restaurant.

Hôtel de France and Logis de France Petit Prince annexe   ⫼
Open April to November; 50 rooms.

Grand Hôtel du Val André   ⫼⫼
80, rue Amiral Charner
Tel: 96-72-20-56
Sea views, open 20 March to 11 November, 39 rooms.

Hôtel de la Mer   ⫼
63, rue Amiral Charner
Tel: 96-72-20-44
Open all year, 16 rooms. Traditional cuisine.

Pasteur   ⫼
rue Pasteur Pléneuf
Tel: 96-72-22-52

Hôtel Printania   ⫼
34, rue Charles-Cotard
Tel: 96-72-20-51
Open mid-March to October, 20 rooms. Lacks a restaurant.

Vannes

Villôtel Anne de Bretagne   ⫼
42, rue Olivier de Clisson
Tel: 97-54-22-19
20 rooms. Lacks a restaurant. Villotel.

Aquarium Hôtel   ⫼⫼
Parc du Golfe
Tel: 97-40-44-52
48 rooms. Sea views. Access for the disabled. With restaurant.

Hôtel la Chaumière   ⫼
12, place de la Libération
Tel: 97-63-28-51
13 rooms. Lacks a restaurant.

Hôtel de France   ⫼
57, avenue Victor Hugo
Tel: 97-47-27-57
25 rooms. Lacks a restaurant.

Hôtel à l'Image Ste Anne   ⫼
8, place de la Libération
Tel: 97-63-27-36
35 rooms. France-Accueil. With restaurant.

Hôtel la Marébaudière   ⫼⫼
4, rue Aristide Briand
Tel: 97-47-34-29
41 rooms. Access for the disabled. With restaurant.

Hôtel La Marée Bleue   ⫼
8, place Bir-Hakim
Tel: 97-47-24-29
16 rooms. With restaurant.

Hôtel le Relais Nantais   ⫼
38, rue Astride Briand
Tel: 97-47-15-85
16 rooms. Lacks a restaurant.

Hôtel le Roof   ⫼⫼
Presqu'Ile de Conleau
Tel: 97-63-47-47
41 rooms. Sea views. Access for the disabled. Best Western. With restaurant.

Vitré

Hotel le Château   ⫼
5, rue Rallon
Tel: 99-74-58-59
15 rooms. Open all year. Villotel. Lacks a restaurant.

Hôtel la Grenouillere   ⫼
Tel: 99-75-34-52
34 rooms. Waterside views. Access for the disabled. With restaurant.

Hôtel le Minotel   ⫼
Tel: 99-75-11-11
17 rooms. With restaurant.

Petit Billot   ⫼
place du Général-Leclerc
22 rooms. The restaurant is closed from December to January.

Restaurants

There are plenty of restaurants to tempt the palette in the region. As restaurants rapidly come and go only a small list of particularly recommended ones has been given here. Each regional tourist board produces its own list of local restaurants which is updated annually. The visitor is advised to obtain this list from the nearest tourist office to where they are staying.

La Baule

Restaurant le Bretagne
18, place Général Leclerc
Tel: 40-60-03-65

Restaurant Le Pekin
16, avenue des Ibis
Tel: 40-60-35-54
Chinese.

le Salisbury
place de la Victoire
Tel: 40-60-09-89

Cancale

Le Bricourt
rue Duguesclin
Four-star Michelin

Le Continental
quai Thomas

Carnac

Crêperie Chez Yannick
8, rue du Tumulus
Tel: 97-52-08-67
Specializes in sea food dishes and regional crêpes.

Dinard

Dragon d'Émeraude
boulevard Féart
Much-frequented Chinese restaurant.

l'Equinoxe
plage de l'Écluse
Salon de thé.

Le Glacier
plage de l'Écluse
Wide choice of ice-creams for those with a sweet tooth.

Mont-Saint-Michel
boulevard l'Hôtelier
Recommended for its duck fillet and grilled salmon.

La Vallée
avenue George Cinq
Specializes in lobster dishes.

Morlaix

La Marée Bleue
rampe Saint-Melaine
Tel: 98-63-24-21
Adjacent to the famous viaduct. Speciality fish dishes.

Paimpol

l'Agapanthe
quai Duguay-Trouin
Regional specialities.

Le Croissant d'Or
quai Duguay-Trouin
Traditional Breton meals.

Le Pub
rue des Islandais
Atmospheric piano bar.

Perros-Guirec

Le Homard Bleu
Tel: 96-23-24-55
Haute cuisine *in* belle époque *surroundings.*

Les Vieux Greements
Perros port
Tel: 96-91-14-99
Galettes *and* crêpes.

Quiberon

La Petite Bretonne
3, quai de l'Océan
Atmospheric seafood terraces.

Roch-Priol Hotel-restaurant
rue des Sirènes
Tel: 97-50-04-86
Low-calorie menus for guests.

La Roseraie
2, quai de Houa
Port-Maria
Tel: 97-30-40-83
Gastronomic speciality house.

Quimper

Restaurant à la Fringale
4 bis, avenue de la Libération
Tel: 98-90-13-12
Speciality is fish dishes.

Le Grande Café de Bretagne
18, rue du Parc
Tel: 98-95-00-13
Speciality is brochette de coquille Saint-Jacques.

Le Jardin d'Été
15, rue du Salle
Tel: 98-95-33-00
Atmospheric with choice grilled dishes and dessert selection.

Le Val-André

The Best of Frites
Port de Dahouët
Fast food.

l'Hostellerie du Centre
rue Georges Clemenceau
Traditional cuisine.

Vannes

Restaurant l'Andaluz
18, rue des Vierges
Tel: 97-47-57-71

La Capitainerie
32, rue du Port
Tel: 97-47-54-50
Speciality fish restaurant.

Piazza d'Italia
30, rue Thiers
Tel: 97-47-09-34

La Petite Alsace
13, rue de Closmadeuc
Tel: 97-54-08-96
Alsatian dishes.

Restaurant Sidi-Boud-Said
30, rue Thiers
Tel: 97-42-65-07
Tunisian.

La Varendre
22, rue de la Fontaine
Tel: 97-47-57-52

Index

Page references in **bold** refer to main entries; those in *italic* refer to illustrations.

Abélard and Héloïse 77, 118, **119**, 160
Aber Wrac'h 299
Abers, Côte des 299
Aiguilles de Port Coton 172
Ancenis Castle *116*, 117
angling 308–9
Anne, Duchess of Brittany 35–6, 126, **136–7**, 221, 294
Anse du Guesclin 242
Apothicairerie Grotto, Belle Isle 172
Araize, Forêt de 113
Argol 201
  Musée de Cidre 194
Armor, Côtes d' 51
Armorican National Park 53, 195–6, **202**
Armoripark leisure Park 289–90
Arthurian legends 38–9, 75–7, 81–3, 230–5, 265
Arrée, Monts de 46, 205–8
Audierne 187–8
Aulne, river 47, 53, 202
Aumone, Châeau de l' 239
Auray *51* 160–2
  Battle of 1364, 258, 274

Bais 109
Bangor 172
Barbetorte, Alain 35
Barenton, Fontaine de 82, *234*
Battle of the Thirty 1351, 221–2
Batz Island 301
Batz–sur-Mer 146
Baule, La 50, 77, **142–5**
  accommodation 144
  sports facilities 145
Beauport, Abbaye de 279–80
Beaumanoir, Jean de 221–2
Becherel 95
Bel-Air-Priziac, Lac du 176
Belle-Ile 51, 53, **170–2**

  Grand Phare Lighthouse 172
  Le Palais 171
Bélon, river 178
Benodet 184–5
Berrien 207, 208
Bienassis, Château de 268
Binic 275–6
Blavet, river and valley 47, 51, 172, 173, 213, *214*, 218
Blois, Charles de 99, 120, 148, 161, 221, 254–5, **256–8**
Bluebeard 133–4
Bluebeard's Castle 134, *135*
Boel, Le 113
Bon Repos Abbey 213–14
Bono, Le *161*
Bramborough, John 221–2
Brasparts 204–5
Bréhat, Ile de 51, 279, **281–2**
Brest 297–8
  museums 297
  Oceanopolis Pavilion 297
Breton language (Brezoneg) 48, 83
Brézé, Marquis de 122
Brière nature park *34*, 50, 148–9, *313*
Brignognan-Plages 299
Brocéliande, ancient forest of *see* Paimport, Forest of

Caesar's Mound 160
Callac 211
calvaries *36*, 42, 53, 186, 201, 204, *205*
Carmaret-sur-Mer 53, *195*, **196–7**
  Notre Dame de Rocamadour *195*, 196–7
camping 9, 20
carnet 9
Cancale 239–42
  Chapelle de Notre-Dame-du-Verger 242
  Chemin de Ronde 241–2
car hire 16
Caradeuc, Château de 95
Carantec 53
Carcraon, Etang de 108
Careil 146

Carentec 300
Carhaix-Plouguer 205, 208–10
  cycle routes 209, 211
  Roman city 208–9
Carnac 51, 53, 77, **164–8**
  alignements 164–7
  beaches 167
  Museum of Prehistory 167
Carnoët forest 175
Carrier, Jean-Baptiste 128–9
Cathelineau, Jacques 129
Champeaux 106
Chandos, Sir John 161, **258–9**
Chapelle-des-Marais 149
Chapelle-Erbrée, La 106
Charles VIII of France 137, 164
château holidays 316–7
Chateaubriand, François René 50, 52, 93–4, **243–5**, 249, 264
Châteaubriant 113–15
  carrière des Fusillés 115
  Château 114
Châteaulin 202–3
Chatelier, Ecluse de 262
Chatillon-de-Vendelais 106
Cherrueix 237–9
Chèvre, Cap de la 195
children's activities 311–12
Chouans **37**, 105–6, 161, 164
climate 7–8, 45–6
Clisson, Château de 117, 120, 121
Clisson, Olivier de 120
Clohars-Fouesnant 185
Cloucarnac 166
coach travel 12
Combourg 49, **93–5**
  Château de 50, 52, 79, **93**
coiffes 41, 42, 186
Commana 40, 204
Comors, Forest of 224
Comper, Château de 232, 233
  Centre de l'Imaginaire Arthurien Musée 233
Concarneau 53, 80, **178–80**
  boat trips from 180

Fête des Filets Bleus 83, 180
Conguel, Pointe du *171*
Conguet, Le 298
Corong Gorges 211
Corret ("La Tour d'Auvergne") 208
Corsen, Pointe du 298–9
Couesnon, river 87
Crevy, Château de 225
Croisic, Le 146
Crozon 194
Crozon Peninsula 194–7, 200–2
cycling **15–16**, 78, 146, 209, 211

Daoulas 297
Daoulas Gorges 213
Dinan 52, *236*, **253–4**, *255*, **260–2**
Fête des Remparts 254
rue de l'Horloge 260, *261*
St Sauveur Church 255
Dinan, Pointe dc 195
Dinard 51, **230–3**
beaches 252
esplanade *151*
Musée de la Mer 252
sports facilities 252–3
disabled visitors 18, 27
Dol, Mont 91
Dol-de-Bretagne *27*, 49, **89–92**
Cathedral 89, *90*
Grande-Rue des Stuarts 91
museum of local history 90
Promenade des Douves 91
Dompierre-du-Chemin 106
Douarnenez 190, *191*, 192
Douarnenez, Bay of 52, **187–94**
Douron, river 52
driving 9, 12–13, 16–18
car hire 16
documents 9
fuel 17
parking 17–18
regulations 12–13, 17
roads 12, 18
Druids 192, **194**, 234, 235
du Bellay, Joachim 117

du Guesclin, Bertrand 87, 99, 107, 112, 115, 120, 160, 161, **254–9**
Duault, Forêt de 211

Eckmuhl lighthouse 186
economic development of region 44–5
electrical appliances 27
Elorn, river 52
Ellé valley 175
Elven, Tour d' 164
enclos paroissiaux see parish closes
Erquy 53, **268**
Esse 109
Etel 172

Falguérec Nature Reserve 156–7
Faou Le, 204
Faouët, Le 53, **175–6**
Fécamp 231
Fedrun, Isle of 53, 148, 149
ferries, cross-channel 13–14
festivals 41–2, 53–4, 83
cornouaille Festival, Quimper 184
Festival du Chant de Marions, Paimpol 281
Fête des Filets Bleus, Concarneau 83
Fête des Ajoncs, Pont-Aven 178
Fête des Remparts, Dinan 254
Finistère 52–4
Floranges, Forest of 224
Foix, Marguerite de 114, 126, 136
Folgoët 53, **300**
folklore 33, 38–9, 75–7, 81–3, 230–3, 265
Folle-Pensée 234
food 22–6
eating out 23–4
shopping 24–6
Forêt-Fouesnant La, 184
Forges des Salles, Les **214**, *215*, 220
Château 214
Fort-la-Latte 51, **265–6**

Gargantua's Finger 265
Fouché, Joseph 128–9
Fouesnant 53, 184, 185
Fougères 96–8
Château de 95–6, 97
Fougères, Forêt de 98
Cellars of Landéan 98
La Ferme de Chênedet 98
Fouquet, Nicholas 105
François II, Duke of Brittany 114, 126, 136, 221
Freau forest 207
Fréhel, Cap 51, **265–7**
French Revolution 37, 92, 93, 105, 112, 128–8, 245–6

Gauguin, Paul 175, 176, **177–8**
Gavrinis Tumulus 159
gîtes 20
Glénan, Isles de 185
Goëlo, Côte 275–82
golf 311
Gourin 211
Gradlon, King 182–3
Grand-Fougeray 115
Grand Lieu, Lac de 130–1
Grand Menhir 160
Grand Traict lagoon 146
Grandes Randonées 14, 78, 192
Groix, Ile de 173
Grouin, Pointe de *24*
Guérande 50, **147–8**
Guerche-de-Bretagne, La 106–9
fair 107
Guerche forest 106
Guerledan, lac de 47, *212*, **213–16**, 312
Guette, Pointe de la 270
Guingamp 52, 53, **274**
Guiseny 299

hang-gliding 310, *311*
health care 9–10, 26
Hennebont 53, **173–4**
history, of region 33–8
horse-riding 271, **309–10**
hotels 18–19
Houle, La 240
Huelgoat 205–7

Huelgoat forest 82, **205–8**
  Camp d'Artus 207
  Chaos de Moulin 207
  Gouffre, Le *198*
  Grotte du Diable 82, 207
  Roche Tremblante 207
  Théâtre de Verdure 207
Hillion 274
Hunaudaie, Château de la 264
Hundred Years War 36, 88,
  98–9, 101, 112, 115, 120,
  159–60

Ile-et-Vilaine 49

Janze 109
Jaudy 283
Josselin 54, 223
  Château de 51, 120, 219,
  221–3
  doll collection 222–3
Jugan, Jeanne **240**, 249
Jugon-les-Lacs 263

Kergornadeach, Château de
  302, *303*
Kerguéhennec, Château de
  223–4
Kerhinet 148
Kerjean, Château de 302–3
Kerlescan alignement 165
Kermario alignement 165
Kernascléden 219
Kerouat, Moulin de 204
Kerzerho, alignement 165

Lacmariaquer 160
Lagaden 159
Lagatjar 196
Lamballe 52, **271**
  Haras National Stud
  Centre 271
Lancieux 264
Landal, Château de 92
Landernau 296–7
Landes, Ile des 242
Landévennec 201
Landivisiau 295–6
Lannion 52, **288–9**
Lantic 276
Lanvaux, Landes de 50, 152,
  224–30

Largoët castle 164
Larmor Baden 159
Larmor Plage 173
Lehon 261
Lesneven 300
Lezardrieux 282
Lire 117
Locmaria-Berrien 207
Locminé 223
Locquirec 290–1
Locronan 54, 186, **192–3**
  Church of St Ronan 192,
  193
Locronan mountain 193
Loctudy 186
Loguivy 282
Loire-Atlantique 49–50
Lorient 50, 54, **173**

Machecoul 133–4
  Château de 134
Machecoul forest 133
Mael-Carhaix 211
Marcille-Robert 109
  Etang de 108
Meilleraye de Bretagne 116
Malensac, Parc de Préhistoire
  227
Malestroit 224–5
Malleville 230
Ménec alignement 165
Menez-Bré 275
Menez-Hom 199, **201–2**, *311*
Menez-Meur, Maison du
  Parc 203
Menhir du Champ Dolent 91
Minard, Pointe 278
Moncontour 54, **271–2**
money 21
Monsieur Hulot's Holiday
  146
Montfort, Jean de 99, 120,
  148, 160, 161, 221, 256–8
Montmuran castle 258
Mont-St-Michel **85–8**
Morbihan 50–1
Morbihan, Golfe de 156–7,
  159–60
Morgat 195
Morlaix 292–5
Motte-Glain, Château de la
  116–17

Moulinet, Pointe de 252
Mur-de-Bretagne 213, **216**
Muscadet 117–18
Musée Automobile de
  Bretagne 112
Musée de Bretagne (Rennes)
  113
Musée de Cidre 194
Musée Départemental Breton
  (Quimper) 183
Musée de l'Imaginaire
  Arthurien (Paimport) 233
Musée de la Paysannerie 92
Museum of World War II
  (St-Marcel) 225

Nantes 50, **121–9**
  accommodation 127–8
  carnival 54
  Cathedral 124
  Château 125–6, 137
  food specialities 127
  history and development
  121, 124–5, 128–9
  Jardin des Plantes 127
  Maillé-Brézé naval
  museum 122–3
  old centre 124, 126–7
  other museums 126–7
  river excursions 129
Nantes, Edict of 128–9
nature reserves 312
  Brière 148–9, 313
  Cap Sizun 190
  Falguérec 156
  Grand Lieu 130–1
  Ile de Bréhat 279, 281–2
  Pionte du Grouin *241*, 242
  Sept Iles 285
  Le Verdelet 270
Nevez 178
Nizon 178
Noé-Bel-Air, Château de la
  119
Noires, Montagnes 46, 199,
  211
Notre-Dame-de-Tronoën 186

Obéliske de Trente 222
Odet, river 52, 182, 184, 185,
  186
Ouessant, Il d' 298

Oust, river 47
oyster production 159, 239–40

Paimpol 51, 54, 55, **280–1**
  Anse de 278–9
Paimport 233, *234*
  Forest of 81, **229–35**
Palais, le 171
Pallet, le *118*, 119
Paramé 248, **250**
pardons 41, 51, 53, *74*, 79
  Le Folgoët 300
  Josselin 223
  Penhors 186–7
  Pleyben 204
  Sainte-Anne d'Auray
    162–3
  Sainte-Anne de Fouesnant
    184
  Saint-Quay 276
  Spezet 211
  Tréguier 283
parish closes (Enclos
  Paroissiaux) 42, 53, 204,
  205, 295
Pas-du-Houx, Etang du 233
Passay 130, 131–2
Pen en Toul 159
Pen-Mur 152
  Moulin de 152–3
Penhir, Pointe de 196
Penhors, Grand Pardon de
  186–7
Penthièvre, fort de *168*, 169
Perrault, Charles 133–4
Perros Guirec 285–6
Pertre 105
  Forêt du 103, 105–6
Piriac-sur-Mer 149
Plage Bonaparte 278
Plancoët 264
Pléhérel Plage 267
Pléneuf, Pointe de 270
Plestin-les-Grèves 289, 290
Pleumeur-Bodon 287
  Gaulois village 287
  Planétarium du Trégor 287
Pleyben 204
Ploërmerl 229–30
Plomodiern 54
Plougrescant, Maison du
  Gouffre *284*, 285

Plouguerneau 54, **299**
Plouha 277
Ploumanac'h *52*, 286, 307
Plozevet 187
Plurien 268
politics 42–4
Pointe-de-St-Gildas 134
Pont-Aven 45, 54, **176–8**
  Fête des Fleurs d'Ajoncs
    178
Pont l'Abbé 185–6
Pontivy, Château *216*,
  217–18, 219
Pontrieux 283
Pornic 134, *135*
Pornichet 142
Port Lazo 278
Port Louis 172–3
Port-Mer 242
Port-Pican 242
postal services 26
Poulains, Pointe des 172
Poulancre Gorges 216
Pouldu, le 175
Pouliguen 142, 145, 146
Préhistoire, Parc de *226*, 227,
  312
prehistoric sites 53, 81, 82,
  107, 157, 215, 312
  Caesar's Mound 160
  Carnac 165–7
  Gargantua's Finger 265
  Gavrinis Tumulus 159
  Grand Menhir 160
  Logatjar 196
  Menhir du Champ Dolent
    91
  La Roche aux Fées 108
Primel-Trégastel 291
public holidays 54

Quélenec 186
Quelven 219
Quénécan forest 213, 214
Quiberon 51, 139, 169–70
Quiberon Peninsula *139*,
  168–70
Quimper 182–4
  cathedral *181*, 182–3
  festival 83, 184
  museums 183–4
  pottery 184

Quimperlé 174–5
Quintin 54, **272**

Rance dam 253
Raz, Pointe du *188*, 189
Red Bonnets, Revolt of
  209–10
Redon 227–9
Rennes 109–13
  forest of 112
  history 112–13
  Jardin du Thabor 113
  medieval buildings 111
  museums 113
  parliament building *109*,
    111
  restaurants 23
Retz, Gilles de 133, 134
Rhuys Peninsula 159–60
Richemont, Duc de 158, 159
Riec-sur-Bélon 178
Roc'h Trévézel 204
Roche aux, Fées, la 82,
  107–8
Roche-Bernard, La 150–2
Roche-Derrien, La 283
Roche-Jagu, Château de la
  282–3
Rochefort-en-Terre **225–7**
  Château de 51, 225
Rochers, Château des 104–5
  chapel *104*
Roches du Diable 175
Rohan 219–20
  Notre-Dame-de-Bonne-
    Encoutre Chapel 220
Rohan, Ducs de 217–18,
  219–20
Roscoff 300–2
Rostrennen 211
Rothéneuf Haven 246
  carved rocks 246, *247*
Rozé 148

Sables-d'Or-les-Pins 51, **268**
sailing 78, 305–7
Saillé 145–6
St-Aignan 215
St-Amboise forest 207
St-Brévin 135
St-Briac 264
St-Brieuc 51, **272–4**

St-Cast 264–5
St-Fiacre chapel, Faouët 176
St-Gildas-de-Rhuys church 160
St-Gilles-Vieux-Marché 215
St-Guénolé, museum of prehistory 186
St-Jacut-de-la-Mer 264
St-Jacut-les-Pins 229
St-Jean-du-Doigt 54, **291**
St-Lunaire 264
St-Malo 49, 80, **246–50**
  Castle 249
  cathedral 250
  Fort National 249
  museums 250
  Solidor Tower *248*, 249
St-Marc 146
St-Marcel 225
St-Mathieu, Pointe de 298
St-Michel-Chef-Chef 135
St-Michel-en-Grève 290
St-Michel Tumulus, Carnac 166
St-Nazaire 50, **139–42**
  ecomuseum 141
  pont de 135, 139, *141*
  sports facilities 142
St-Nicholas-des-Eaux 218
St-Philbert-de-Grand-Lieu 132–3
  Abbey Church *131*, 132
St-Pol-de-Léon 300
  Cathedral *37*, 300
St-Quay-Pontrieux 276–7
St-Servan-sur-Mer 249, 250
St-Thégonnec 36, **295**, *296*
Ste-Anne-d'Auray 42, 51, 54, **162–4**
  Grand Pardon 162–3
  sanctuary 163–4
  war memorial *162*
Ste-Anne-la-Palud 42, 54
Ste-Anne Plage 300
Ste-Barbe forest 175
Ste-Lumine de Contais 133
Salles, Château des 214
salt-pans 145–6
Sarzeau 159
Saut de Roland 106
Saut de Chat, St Lunaire 264

Scaër 176
Scrignac 207–8
  Maison de la Faune Sauvage de la Forêt 208
security 21–2
Sein, Ile de 187
Sept Iles, les 52, **285**
Sévigné, Mme de 104–5, 174
shopping 24–6
Sillon de Talbert 282
Sillon, Pointe de 197
Sizun 204
Sizun, Cap 190
Spezet 211
Stangala, Site du 186
Suscinio, Château de 159–60

Taden 262
Taureau, Château de 300
taxis 16–17
telephones 26–7
Telegruc-sur-Mer 193–4
Timadeuc, Abbaye de 220
tipping 22
Toullaëron, Roc de *210*, 211
train travel 11–12, 17
  France Vancances pass 14
travel concessions 14
travel documents 8–9
Trébeurden 287–8
Tréboul 192
Trécesson, Château de 236
Trégastel 51, **286–7**
Tréguier 41, 283–4
Tréhorentuec, church of 235
Trépassés, Baie des 189–90
Tressignaux 83
Tristan 39, 77, 231
Tristan Island 192
Trestraou 285
Tronchet, Le 95
Turballe, La 149

Val-André 268–70
  Port Dahouet 269, 270
  Port Piégu *269*
  sports facilities 270
Val Sas Retour 82, **235**
Vallet 117–19
Van, Pointe du 190
Vannes *6*, 51, 54, **153–9**

accommodation 157
Aquarium 157
Cathedral 155
Château 155
food specialities 157–8
medieval streets 156
museums 156, 157
wash-houses 154, 155
Vannes, siege of 1342, 258
Vauban, Sebastian 172, 179, **197**, 247, 249
Vauban, Tour de, Cameret *195*, 196, 197
Vendée Wars 128–9
Verdelt, Le 270
Vergraon, Moulin de 204
Verne, Jules 127
Verne Museum, Nantes 127
Vilaine, river 47, 49, 151
vineyard tours 118
Vioreau forest and reservoir 116
Vitré 49, 100–4
  Château 102–3
  Church of Notre-Dame 101, 102
  Faubourg-du-Rachapt 101, 102
  history 101–2
  sports facilities 103
  Les Tertres Noirs 103

walking 14–15, 78–9, 308
War of Brittany Succession 99, 120, 147–8, 160–1, 221–2, 256–9
Wars of Religion 88, 101, 151, 160
watersports 78, **305–7**
wildlife 313–16, *see also* nature reserves
World War I 38, 113, 163
World War II 38, 113, 115, 141–2, 169, 187, 225, 278

Yffiniac Bay 274
Youth Hostels 20
Ys, lost city of 183, 190, 194

zoo, Pen Mur 152